Labor Divided in the Postwar European Welfare State

This book explains how the success of attempts to expand the boundaries of the postwar welfare state in the Netherlands and the United Kingdom depended on organized labor's willingness to support redistribution of risk and income among different groups of workers. By illuminating and explaining differences within and between labor union movements, it traces the historical origins of "inclusive" and "dual" welfare systems. In doing so, the book shows that labor unions either can have a profoundly conservative impact on the welfare state or can act as an impelling force for progressive welfare reform. Based on an extensive range of archive material, this book explores the institutional foundations of social solidarity.

Dennie Oude Nijhuis is assistant professor of history at Leiden University. He has been a visiting lecturer at Bilgi University, Istanbul University, and Chulalongkorn University and a research Fellow at Yale University's Department of Political Science. Oude Nijhuis specializes in the comparative political economy of labor markets and welfare states and the political economy of European integration. His work has been published in *World Politics*, *Labor History*, *Twentieth Century British History*, and the *Journal of Economic and Social Geography*. His thesis was shortlisted for the annual Dutch Political Science Association (NKWP) Dissertation Award. He has received an NWO-Rubicon grant for a research proposal that aimed to uncover the determinants of organized labor support for redistribution. In 2011 he was awarded the best article of the year prize on a non-U.S. or comparative topic by the journal *Labor History*.

Labor Divided in the Postwar European Welfare State

The Netherlands and the United Kingdom

DENNIE OUDE NIJHUIS
Leiden University

CAMBRIDGE
UNIVERSITY PRESS

CAMBRIDGE UNIVERSITY PRESS
Cambridge, New York, Melbourne, Madrid, Cape Town,
Singapore, São Paulo, Delhi, Mexico City

Cambridge University Press
32 Avenue of the Americas, New York, NY 10013-2473, USA

www.cambridge.org
Information on this title: www.cambridge.org/9781107035492

First published 2013

Printed in the United States of America

A catalog record for this publication is available from the British Library.

Library of Congress Cataloging in Publication data
Nijhuis, Dennie Oude, 1979–
    Labor divided in the postwar european welfare state: the Netherlands and the
    United Kingdom / Dennie Oude Nijhuis, Leiden University.
        pages   cm
    Includes bibliographical references and index.
    ISBN 978-1-107-03549-2 (hardback)
    1. Labor unions – Netherlands – History – 20th century.   2. Labor unions – Great Britain –
    History – 20th century.   3. Social security – Netherlands – History – 20th century.   4. Social
    security – Great Britain – History – 20th century.   5. Welfare state – Netherlands – History –
    20th century.   6. Welfare state – Great Britain – History – 20th century.   I. Title.
    HD6727.N517   2013
    361.6'50949209045–dc23   2012049891

ISBN 978-1-107-03549-2 Hardback

Contents

Tables and Figures

FIGURES

Preface

The first decades after World War II undoubtedly presented a crucial epoch in the development of the modern welfare state. Within a time span of only a few decades, all industrialized countries succeeded in creating intricate systems of social protection that raised many of their citizens out of poverty, significantly reduced market-generated income disparities, and greatly diminished the financial consequences of labor market risks such as unemployment, sickness, disability, and old age. In the immediate postwar period, the bulk of the population living in the industrialized world relied on grossly inadequate levels of protection against hardships resulting from labor market risks. Some thirty years later, many industrialized countries had succeeded in creating cradle-to-grave protection against such hardships for them. The consequences of this for the state's role in society and the improvement it brought to citizens' daily lives were truly astounding.

Yet, crucially, these improvements were by no means shared equally in all parts of the industrialized world. While all industrialized countries experienced sharp increases in both public and private social expenditure in the decades following World War II, they differed markedly in the overall level of this increase, the division within what is popularly known as the "public and private mix," and the degree to which national programs came to contain redistributive features. As a result, they came to differ greatly in their ability to protect their members against the risk of economic misfortune. Most important, they came to differ greatly in their ability to provide adequate levels of social protection for *all* their members. This difference, while grounded in the first decades of the postwar period, has persisted in subsequent years. The countries that created the most solidaristic welfare states in the first postwar decades still provide the most inclusive and redistributive insurance programs. Conversely, the countries that created dual systems of private and public insurance, under which the most affluent enjoyed the highest levels of security while the less affluent often lacked proper insurance, have maintained this duality up to the present day.

This book results from the conviction that we cannot improve our understanding of postwar welfare state development in different countries, and their widely diverging trajectories, without a fundamental reappraisal of organized labor's involvement in the creation and expansion of social policies during the crucial first decades of the postwar period. In some ways this reappraisal seems long overdue. For more than a decade now, traditional labor-centered accounts of the welfare state have been subjected to severe criticism from what can be broadly described as employer-oriented writings. The main purpose of this literature has been to show that employer interest groups have often played a more important, and a more cooperative, role in the development of social policies than previously realized. Yet their strong condemnation of the prominent role attributed to class divisions in much of the literature has obvious consequences for our understanding of organized labor's involvement in the coming about of progressive welfare reform as well. Recent work on welfare state retrenchment, by pointing to left divisions, has similarly provided findings that give good cause to reconsider organized labor's role in the creation and expansion of the welfare state.

So far, and as will be explained at length in Chapter 1 of this book, this much-needed reconsideration has failed to materialize, though. In much of the literature on welfare state development, including nearly all recent writings on the role of employers, labor unions continue to be viewed as natural supporters of the welfare state – including its redistributive consequences. Instances of labor union support for progressive welfare state reform are still generally understood as a logical outcome of workers' interest in obtaining security against labor market risks. Instances of union opposition to the creation and expansion of social insurance programs, if recognized at all, continue to be explained through "voluntarist" notions that emphasize union suspicions of state motives and their fear that increased state intervention might affect their future ability to attract workers.

This treatment of organized labor, I have come to believe, does not do justice to the very diverse and often conflicting nature of workers' demands for security against labor market risks. Nor does it sit well with the fact that the welfare state is mainly about redistributing risk and income between different categories of workers rather than between "capital" and "labor" or "rich" and "poor." This book emphasizes that labor unions, depending on their internal organizational blueprint, value these redistributive consequences in strikingly different ways. My central argument is that the internal organizational structure of labor unions has therefore been of major, and neglected, importance for the success of progressive welfare reform in the first decades of the postwar period.

In recent years, much of the most exciting research on welfare state development has come from a scholarship that has sought to emphasize organized employers' contribution to welfare state development. This book instead lends support to traditional labor-oriented writings by emphasizing organized labor's central role in the coming about of progressive welfare reform. This is not to say that employers have not been influential. The book merely emphasizes the proactive role of labor unions in voicing demands for improved protection for workers against labor market risks and converting these demands into concrete welfare initiatives. In addition, and far more important, it shows that organized employers' responses to demands for increases in public protection against labor market risks depended greatly on organized labor's willingness and ability to support redistribution of risk and income among different categories of workers.

To illustrate my claims, I chose to compare the postwar welfare trajectories of the Netherlands and the United Kingdom. These countries not only provided ideally divergent institutional contexts, but their welfare trajectories are also strongly at odds with conventional (class-oriented) explanations of postwar welfare state development. Perhaps partly as a result of this, both countries are also relatively understudied by comparativists. The goal of this book is therefore not only to revisit our view of organized labor's involvement in the development of the postwar welfare state but also to offer a detailed and alternative history of the coming about of progressive welfare reform, or lack thereof, in the Netherlands and the United Kingdom. Some readers may have doubts about the generalizability of my findings to countries other than the Netherlands and the United Kingdom. For them I have included numerous references to and expositions on other European countries as well as the United States.

In a world where political actors go to great lengths to mask internal divisions, and where strategic behavior often conceals true preferences, establishing social causality can be a difficult task. Uncovering these divisions and real preferences required many months of archive research. These archival forays first opened my eyes to the strong degree to which labor unions, and to some extent also employer interest groups, are driven by normative orientations that emphasize fairness and/or solidarity with weaker group members. By neglecting this and focusing almost completely on rational self-interests, the existing literature has failed to capture a major force behind the success – or failure – of redistributive welfare state development. Partly as a result of this, such terms as "solidarity" and "egalitarianism" are used with frustrating inadequacy. I can only hope that my treatment of these terms is sufficiently precise to offer a conceptual improvement.

Acknowledgments

Writing this book has been a difficult, protracted, and at times daunting task. I am therefore fortunate to have been able to benefit from the support of many friends, colleagues, and institutions. Generous funding from Leiden University's History Department and the Leiden University Fund have enabled me to do research for and write this book. A generous grant from the Netherlands Organization for Scientific Research helped me to revise it. I had the opportunity to do most of the revisions to this book while working as a guest researcher at Yale University's Department of Political Science, which provided an extraordinarily stimulating environment for this endeavor.

During my numerous archival ventures, I received generous and patient assistance from archivists at the National Archives in London, the Modern Records Centre in Coventry, the International Institute of Social History, the National Archives of the Netherlands (Nationaal Archief), the Confederation of Netherlands Industry and Employers (VNO-NCW), the Radboud University Nijmegen's Catholic Documentation Center (Katholiek Documentatiecentrum), the VU University Amsterdam's Historic Documentation Center of Dutch Protestantism (Historisch Documentatiecentrum voor het Nederlands protestantisme), and the Dutch Social Security Agency (Uitvoeringsinstituut Werknemersverzekeringen). The archivists include Frank Kanhai, Lodewijk Winkeler, Piet Hazenbosch, Hans Seijlhouwer, Teun van Lier, and Caroll Lewis.

Academically, I am foremost indebted to Richard Griffiths, who has been my mentor from the first day I walked into his undergraduate lecture up to the present day. I am also grateful to Jeroen Touwen, who not only encouraged me to venture into academics but also proved to be a great source of support and friendly advice in subsequent years. Sharing an interest in economics and labor-related matters, our many discussions broadened my horizon. My greatest thanks go to Peter Swenson, whose work on labor markets and welfare states has reoriented comparative political economy research during the past decade. I am extremely grateful for his enthusiastic support for this book and many comments. Moreover, his commitment to critical research and nonconformism continue to inspire me.

At every stage of the writing process, friends and colleagues have offered countless suggestions, comments, and advice. For their assistance and comments, I gratefully thank Ben Gales, Peer Vries, Thomas Lindblad, Matthieu Leimgruber, Peter Scholliers, Lex Heerma van Voss, Kees van Kersbergen, Jelle Visser, Karen Anderson, Ruud Koole, Leo Lucassen, Doreen Arnoldus, Noel Whiteside, Jacques van Gerwen, Daan Marks, Martijn van der Burg, Hannah Sarvasy, Tom van der Meer, Cátia Antunes, Martijn van der Burg, and Ismail Hakkı Kaddı. At Cambridge University Press, I am grateful to Lew Bateman and Shaun Vigil for their expert guidance.

Last but not least, I want to thank my wife, Ayben. I am grateful to Ayben for continuing to believe in this project and for supporting me even when I left everything else aside to work on this book. It is to her that I dedicate this book.

Abbreviations

TSSA   Transport Salaried Staffs' Association
TUC   Trades Union Congress

THE NETHERLANDS

AAW   Algemene Arbeidsongeschiktheidswet (General Disability Act)
AKWV   Algemene Katholieke Werkgeversvereniging (General Catholic
              Employers' Federation)
AOW   Algemene Ouderdomswet (General Old Age Act)
CNV   Christelijk Nationaal Vakverbond (Christian Union Federation)
CSWV   Centraal Sociaal Werkgevers Verbond (Central Social
              Employers' Federation)
FCWV   Federatie van Katholieke en Protestants-Christelijke
              Werkgeversverbonden (Federation of Catholic and
              Protestant-Christian Employers' Unions)
FNV   Federatie Nederlandse Vakbeweging (Federation Dutch Labor
              Movement)
FvB   Federatie van Bedrijfsverenigingen (Federation of Industrial
              Councils)
GMD   Gemeenschappelijke Medische Dienst (Common Medical
              Service)
KAB   Katholieke Arbeidersbeweging (Catholic Workers Movement)
KVP   Katholieke Volkspartij (Catholic People's Party)
KVW   Katholiek Verbond van Werkgeversvakverenigingen (Catholic
              Federation of Employers' Unions)
MHP   Vakcentrale voor Middelbaar en Hoger Personeel (Federation
              for Middle and Higher Level Personnel)
NCW   Nederlands Christelijk Werkgeversverbond (Christian
              Employers' Federation)
NKV   Nederlands Katholiek Vakverbond (Netherlands Catholic Trade
              Union Federation)
NVV   Nederlands Verbond van Vakverenigingen (Dutch Association of
              Trade Unions)
PvdA   Partij van de Arbeid (Labor Party)
RKWV   Rooms-Katholiek Werkliedenverbond (Roman Catholic
              Workers' Federation)
RvBA   Raad van Bestuur in Arbeidszaken (Council of Directors in
              Labor Affairs)
RVV   Raad van Vakcentralen (Council of Trade Union Federations)
SER   Sociaal-Economische Raad (Social-Economic Council)
SVR   Sociale Verzekeringsraad (Social Insurance Council)
VNO   Verbond van Nederlandse Ondernemingen (Federation of Dutch
              Industries)

VPCW	Verbond van Protestantsch-Christelijke Werkgevers in Nederland (Federation of Protestant-Christian Employers)
VUT	Vervroegde Uittreding (Early Retirement)
WAO	Wet op Arbeidsongeschiktheidsverzekering (Act on Disability Insurance)
WW	Werkloosheidswet (Unemployment Act)
WWV	Wet Werkloosheidsvoorziening (Unemployment Provision Act)

THE UNITED STATES

AFL	American Federation of Labor
CIO	Congress of Industrial Organizations

SWEDEN

ATP	Allmän Tilläggspension
LO	Landsorganisationen i Sverige
SAF	Svenska Arbetsgivareföreningen

A Note on Sources

The comparison of the Netherlands and the United Kingdom in this book draws on a variety of secondary and primary sources. The use of the latter demands some clarification. The search for primary sources to support my argument sent me to both sides of the North Sea. Most valuable for this research were the minutes of various committees of the major union (con)federations in the two countries. In the United Kingdom, these minutes came from the Trades Union Congress (TUC). In the Netherlands, these union federations were (in order of influence) the socialist Dutch Association of Trade Unions[1] (Nederlands Verbond van Vakverenigingen, henceforth NVV); the Catholic Workers Movement (Katholieke Arbeidersbeweging, henceforth KAB); its successor, the Netherlands Catholic Trade Union Federation (Nederlands Katholiek Vakverbond, henceforth NKV); and the protestant Christian Union Federation (Christelijk Nationaal Vakverbond, henceforth CNV). When important decisions in the field of welfare were to be made, the social security experts and leadership of these federations often met in the Council of Trade Union Federations (Raad van Vakcentralen, henceforth RVV).

Both because one of the purposes of this work is to show how union structure matters to the involvement of employer interest groups in welfare state

[1] The English translations of these Dutch organizations are mostly taken from William van Voorden, "Employers Associations in the Netherlands." In John P. Windmuller and Alan Gladstone, *Employers Associations and Industrial Relations: A Comparative Study* (Oxford: Clarendon Press, 1985); and Joris van Ruysseveldt and Jelle Visser, *Industrial Relations in Europe: Traditions and Transitions* (London: Sage, 1996). On some occasions these authors used different translations. While Van Voorden, for example, writes of the Federation of Dutch Industries to describe the VNO, Van Ruysseveldt and Visser use the name Federation of Dutch Enterprises. On such occasions I have allowed myself some academic freedom in choosing one or the other. Similarly, the Sociaal-Economische Raad (SER) is sometimes translated as Socio-Economic Council, Social and Economic Council, and Social-Economic Council. In this case, I have opted for the last. Finally, the Vakcentrale voor Middelbaar en Hoger Personeel has been previously translated as Federation of White-Collar Staff Organizations, the Dutch Trade Union Confederation for Middle and Higher Employees, the Federation of Managerial and Professional Staff Unions, and in many other ways. In this case, I have chosen to use the name Federation for Middle and Higher Level Personnel because this seemed closest to its original meaning.

development and because the records of such groups also provided valuable information on the actions of unions, this work also draws heavily on the minutes of various committee and board meetings of important employer federations. In the United Kingdom, these federations were the Federation of British Industries (FBI), the British Employers' Confederation (BEC), and their predecessor, the Confederation of British Industry (CBI). In the Netherlands, there were so many employer federations that it would take too much space here to list them exhaustively. Of most importance for this research were the minutes of the liberal Central Social Employers' Federation (Centraal Sociaal Werkgevers Verbond, henceforth CSWV) and those of its successor, the Federation of Dutch Industries (Verbond van Nederlandse Ondernemingen, henceforth VNO). Of slightly less importance were the minutes of the Catholic Federation of Employers' Unions (Katholiek Verbond van Werkgeversvakverenigingen, henceforth KVW) and the General Catholic Employers' Federation (Algemene Katholieke Werkgeversvereniging, henceforth AKWV), the Federation of Protestant-Christian Employers in the Netherlands (Verbond van Protestantsch-Christelijke Werkgevers in Nederland, henceforth VPCW), and the general-confessional Federation of Catholic and Protestant-Christian Employers' Unions (Federatie van Katholieke en Protestants-Christelijke Werkgeversverbonden, henceforth FCWV) and Christian Employers' Federation (Nederlands Christelijk Werkgeversverbond, henceforth NCW). As was the case with their union counterparts, the social security experts and leadership of these various employer federations often held meetings in a common platform, called the Council of Directors in Labor Affairs (Raad van Bestuur in Arbeidszaken, or RvBA).

Other primary sources also proved useful. The research on the United Kingdom relies on various government records found in the Public Record Office. Of particular importance were minutes of meetings and correspondence from officials of the Ministry of Pensions and National Insurance, the Department of Health and Social Security, and departments that were responsible for labor and unemployment matters. For the discussion on superannuation in the United Kingdom, I also used records from the Life Offices' Associations (LOA), the main representative of the British insurance industry. Finally, I used several publications issued by various Labour governments, employer federations, and individual unions. For the research on the Netherlands, I interviewed several social security experts and leaders from important unions and used records from the Ministry of Social Affairs. For the discussion on the use of social security programs for early retirement purposes in the Netherlands in Chapter 7, I made extensive use of archives from organizations responsible for the implementation of these programs, including the Common Medical Service (Gemeenschappelijke Medische Dienst, or GMD), the Federation of Industrial Councils (Federatie van Bedrijfsverenigingen, or FvB), and the Social Insurance Council (Sociale Verzekeringsraad, or SVR). When I did my research, these were located at the headquarters of the Dutch Social Security Agency (Uitvoeringsinstituut Werknemersverzekering). Recently, they have been moved to the National Archives of the Netherlands.

Labor and the Development of the Postwar Welfare State

During the late 1960s, the relationship between the British Labour Party and its long-time political ally, the Trades Union Congress (TUC), sharply deteriorated after the former introduced a series of legislative proposals that were strongly rejected by Britain's largest labor union federation. Among these proposals were several ambitious public welfare initiatives.[1] These included the introduction of a statutory national minimum wage, a public pension reform that was popularly known as "superannuation," the introduction of statutory severance payments for all workers, and a promise to achieve nothing less than a "new deal" for the disabled. Despite Labour's broad parliamentary majority, none of these initiatives were to be enacted in their original – redistributive – form. The government's inability to do so was widely celebrated by prominent members of the TUC's main governing body, the General Council, and many of the TUC's most powerful affiliates. Other TUC affiliates, by contrast, expressed their strong disappointment.

The TUC's strong resistance to progressive welfare reform in this period may be viewed as remarkable given the conventional treatment of organized labor in the welfare state literature. Yet its behavior was by no means exceptional. Throughout the postwar period, and as demonstrated in this book, the TUC has actively opposed many welfare initiatives that aimed to deliver adequate levels of social protection to *all* workers. Many of its counterparts abroad have done the same. For instance, at roughly the time when superannuation became an issue in the United Kingdom, the Danish Confederation of Trade Unions (Landsorganisationen i Danmark, or LO) voiced its opposition to a similar

---

[1] They also included an attempt to reform the existing system of industrial relations in the United Kingdom. For an excellent recent discussion of this initiative, see Richard Tyler, "Victims of Our History? Barbara Castle and *In Place of Strife*," *Contemporary British History* 20:3 (2006), 461–76.

proposal in Denmark.[2] In Switzerland too, powerful labor associations have at times resisted attempts to create or extend public sickness and old age insurance programs.[3] And in the United States, the American Federation of Labor (AFL) and Congress of Industrial Organizations (CIO) had before their mid-1950s' merger acquired a reputation for, respectively, their weak support for social insurance development and enthusiastic pursuit of private welfare benefits.[4]

In other countries, such instances of outright union opposition to or weak support for the postwar expansion of the welfare state are far more difficult to find. The TUC's dismissive stance of so many of Labour's welfare proposals during the first decades of the postwar period, for instance, stands in sharp contrast to the strong support given to redistributive welfare initiatives by the main union federations in the Netherlands at the time. In fact, and as we will see, most public welfare initiatives there originated from the labor union movement.[5] Contrary to what occurred in the United Kingdom, the process of postwar welfare state expansion in the Netherlands was also characterized by a remarkable absence of intralabor conflict over the redistributive consequences of these initiatives. In an effort to explain the importance of national labor movements' differing organizational blueprints for the development of welfare states, this book demonstrates why this was the case.

The finding that some labor associations have consistently frustrated attempts to expand the boundaries of the postwar welfare state poses a major challenge to the existing literature on postwar welfare state development. Much of this literature is based on the premise that organized labor supported the postwar expansion of the welfare state and its redistributive consequences. The most influential analytical perspective of the last decades views welfare state formation as a consensual strategy of national labor movements empowered by

[2] On this, see, for instance, Peter Baldwin, *The Politics of Social Solidarity. Class Bases of the European Welfare State, 1875–1975* (Cambridge University Press, 1990), 223–6; Asbørn Sonne Nørgaard, *The Politics of Institutional Control: Corporatism in Danish Occupational Safety and Health Regulation and Unemployment Insurance, 1870–1995* (Aarhus: Politica, 1997), 189–90.

[3] For an excellent recent account on the development of the Swiss welfare state that also mentions this opposition, see Matthieu Leimgruber, *Solidarity without the State? Business and the Shaping of the Swiss Welfare State, 1890–2000* (Cambridge University Press, 2008).

[4] On this, see, for instance, Gaston V. Rimlinger, *Welfare Policy and Industrialization in Europe, America, and Russia* (New York: Wiley, 1971), 81–6; Colin Gordon, *Dead on Arrival: The Politics of Health Care in Twentieth-Century America* (Princeton, NJ: Princeton University Press, 2003), 274–81.

[5] Most existing explanations of the Dutch welfare state's postwar expansion have failed to realize this and have focused mainly on the role of political parties. See, for instance, Robert Henry Cox, *The Development of the Dutch Welfare State: From Workers' Insurance to Universal Entitlement* (University of Pittsburg Press, 1993); Mirjam Hertogh, "*Geene wet, maar de Heer.*" *De confessionele ordening van het Nederlandse sociale zekerheidsstelsel, 1870–1975* (Den Haag: VUGA, 1998); Willem Trommel and Romke van der Veen (eds), *De herverdeelde samenleving. De ontwikkeling en herziening van de Nederlandse verzorgingsstaat* (Amsterdam University Press, 1999); Marcel Hoogenboom, *Standenstrijd en zekerheid. Een geschiedenis van oude orde en sociale zorg in Nederland* (Amsterdam: Boom, 2004).

wartime and postwar political processes. According to this view, labor unions are natural proponents of the welfare state, and welfare state development depends on labor's relative "power resources" against capital.[6] This class-based approach of the welfare state leaves little room for the possibility of consistent labor union opposition to its postwar expansion – unless motivated by union fears over allowing a potentially hostile government to undermine key union functions. This book aims to show that such opposition instead often was grounded in the resistance of labor unions to the redistributive consequences of the welfare state's postwar expansion.

The book argues that our understanding of cross-national differences cannot be advanced without a fundamental reappraisal of the role of organized labor in welfare state development. It argues in particular against the convention of viewing labor union support for welfare state development as the natural outcome of workers' interests in acquiring protection against labor market risks. This study argues against this view by emphasizing that the progress of the welfare state is mainly about redistribution of income and risk among different categories of employers, the self-employed, and most of all, different categories of *workers*. Its main aim is to show how the success of progressive welfare state reform during the first decades of the postwar period depended on the willingness and ability of labor associations to redistribute income and risk within the labor category – or in other words, display broad worker solidarity.

To advance its views, this book emphasizes the importance of national labor movements' differing organizational blueprints for the development of welfare states. It aims to show how unions structure workers' interests and how these in turn affect other groups' interests and political behavior. To demonstrate this, it illustrates how the organizational blueprint of the British and Dutch labor union movements shaped their involvement in the development of the British and Dutch welfare states during the crucial formative first three decades of the postwar period. Throughout this period, the British and Dutch labor union movements were key players in the creation and expansion of public provision for the elderly, unemployed, sick, and disabled. Yet, because of differences in their organizational blueprints, their involvement in the development of these programs differed in important ways. This book shows how these differences led to very different welfare outcomes in the two nations.

REVISITING THE ROLE OF LABOR IN WELFARE STATE DEVELOPMENT

In the comparative literature on welfare state development, labor associations have always played a prominent role. Because the main purpose of the welfare state is to protect workers from labor market risks, the importance attached

---

[6] For a recent example, see Walter Korpi, "Power Resources and Employer-Centered Approaches in Explanations of Welfare States and Varieties of Capitalism," *World Politics* 58:2 (2006), 167–206.

to organized labor's involvement in the development of welfare states is unsurprising. What is quite surprising, however, is that all this attention has not resulted in a strong awareness of the very diverse and often conflicting nature of different groups of workers' demands for security against labor market risks. In much of the literature on welfare state development, workers are treated as a homogeneous group with united interests in the introduction and expansion of public welfare programs. This has resulted in a rather one-sided treatment of the involvement of organized labor in welfare state development. Uniform labor union support for this development is often assumed but rarely verified with systematic evidence.[7] Instances of such support are generally understood as a logical outcome of workers' interests in obtaining security against labor market risks and seldom as an outcome of the willingness of labor associations to redistribute income and risk within the labor category.[8] And finally, cross-national differences in welfare state programs are generally explained by looking at the degree to which workers organize into labor unions as opposed to the *way* in which they do so.[9]

This view of the involvement of organized labor in welfare state development has been put forward most forcefully, although by no means exclusively,

[7] For some references on this assumption from prominent scholars over the years, see Rimlinger, *Welfare Policy and Industrialization*, 9; Alex Hicks and Duane Swank, "The Political Economy of Government Domestic Expenditure in the Affluent Democracies, 1960–1980," *American Journal of Political Science* 32:4 (1988), 1125; Gøsta Esping-Andersen, *The Three Worlds of Welfare Capitalism* (Princeton, NJ: Princeton University Press, 1990), 22–6; Bo Rothstein, *Just Institutions Matter: The Moral and Political Logic of the Universal Welfare State* (New York: Cambridge University Press, 1998), 151; Alex Hicks, *Social Democracy and Welfare Capitalism* (Ithaca, NY: Cornell University Press, 1999), 82; David Bradley, Evelyne Huber, Stephanie Moller, Francois Nielsen, and John D. Stephens, "Distribution and Redistribution in Postindustrial Economies," *World Politics* 55:2 (2003), 193–228; Isabela Mares, *Taxation, Wage Bargaining and Unemployment* (Cambridge University Press, 2006), 2–3; Torben Iversen and David Soskice, "Distribution and Redistribution: The Shadow of the Nineteenth Century," *World Politics* 61:3 (2009), 448; and Hyeok Yong Kwon and Jonas Pontusson, "Globalization, Labour Power and Partisan Politics Revisited," *Socio-Economic Review* 8:2 (2010), 251–81.

[8] See, for instance, Michael Shalev, "The Social Democratic Model and Beyond: Two Generations of Comparative Research on the Welfare State," *Comparative Social Research* 6 (1983), 320; Peter Baldwin, *The Politics of Social Solidarity*, 7; Esping-Andersen, *The Three Worlds*, 22; Silja Häusermann, "Solidarity with Whom? Why Organized Labour Is Losing Ground in Continental Pension Politics," *European Journal of Political Research* 49:2 (2010), 227.

[9] For some prominent studies that emphasize the importance of union strength, see Gøsta Esping-Andersen and Kees Van Kersbergen, "Contemporary Research on Social Democracy," *Annual Review of Sociology* 23 (1992), 191; Rothstein, *Just Institutions Matter*, 151; Evelyne Huber and John D. Stephens, *Development and Crisis of the Welfare State: Parties and Policies in Global Markets* (The University of Chicago Press, 2001), 44; Duane Swank, *Global Capital, Political Institutions and Policy Change in Developed Welfare States* (Cambridge University Press, 2002), 42–3; Iversen and Soskice, "Distribution," 448; Jonas Pontusson, *Inequality and Prosperity: Social Europe vs. Liberal America* (Ithaca, NY: Cornell University Press, 2005), 25–8; and Jonas Pontusson and David Rueda, "The Politics of Inequality: Voter Mobilization and Left Parties in Advanced Industrial States," *Comparative Political Studies* 43:6 (2010), 675–705.

by the adherents of the so-called power resources perspective of welfare state development. This perspective rose to prominence in the welfare state literature in the 1980s and remains influential today. As a derivative of class analysis, the power resources perspective views welfare state development as primarily involving distributive conflict between workers and employers. One consequence of this emphasis on class as an explanatory concept for welfare state development is a strong tendency to view workers – but also employers and the self-employed – as homogeneous groups in which group members share similar risks and resources and thus similar interests.[10] Another consequence is a strong tendency to define labor as a "subordinated" or "disadvantaged" group that needs to be "compensated" or "emancipated" by the welfare state.[11] In this perspective, the outcome of welfare state development depends principally on labor's relative "power resources" compared with those of "bourgeois" or "capitalist" forces.[12]

The latter claim has long received much criticism from those who identify institutional disparities to explain welfare state variation. As noted by a host of scholars over the years, labor's relative "power resources" alone – whether defined in terms of union density levels, social democratic parties' electoral strength and participation in government, or the weakness of bourgeois or capitalist forces – cannot explain welfare state outcomes in many nations.[13] These critical views have not prompted a major reconsideration of organized labor's role in the development of the postwar welfare state, though. Initially, scholars mainly responded by arguing for the importance of Christian democracy

[10] According to Walter Korpi, for example, "[A]t the most general level we can distinguish three socio-economic classes: employers, employees, and the self-employed. Although internally quite heterogeneous, these broad categories define similarities in actors' opportunities and constraints, resources, and risks." Korpi, "Power Resources," 174. According to Gøsta Esping-Andersen and Roger Friedland, in Sweden, "[M]ore than in any other European nation ... the working class has been capable of initiating and imposing its policy preferences." Gøsta Esping-Andersen and Roger Friedland, "Class Coalitions in the Making of Western European Economics." In Esping-Andersen and Friedland, *Political Power and Social Theory*, Vol. III (Greenwich: Jai Press, 1982), 18–19.

[11] According to Walter Korpi, the main aim of the welfare state is to "compensate labor for its disadvantaged position on the labor market." According to Gøsta Esping-Andersen, it is to "emancipate workers from market-dependence." Walter Korpi, *The Democratic Class Struggle* (London: Routledge and Kegan Paul, 1983), 83; Esping-Andersen, *The Three Worlds*, 22.

[12] According to Gøsta Esping-Andersen, "[L]abor's power advantage lies in its numbers." According to Walter Korpi, "[T]hrough its political and union organizations, the working class can decrease its disadvantage in power resources in relation to capital." Korpi, *The Democratic*, 83; Esping-Andersen, *The Three Worlds*, 22–6. See also Huber and Stephens, *Development and Crisis*, 44; and Hicks, *Social Democracy*, 11–12, 82.

[13] For these definitions of labor's relative power resources, see, among others, John D. Stephens, *The Transition from Capitalism to Socialism* (London: Macmillan, 1979); Francis Castles, "The Impact of Parties on Public Expenditures." In Francis Castles, *The Impact of Parties: Politics and Policies in Democratic Capitalist States* (Beverly Hills, CA: Sage, 1982); Huber and Stephens, *Development and Crisis*; and Hicks, *Social Democracy*.

or smaller societal groups such as farmers and the self-employed in shaping welfare state outcomes.[14] More recently, a group of scholars has come to argue that (some) employers may also have had an interest in the postwar expansion of the welfare state. In demonstrating its claims, this new scholarship has successfully argued against the view that labor and capital consistently held opposing interests regarding the welfare state in the first decades of the postwar period.[15]

At the same time, these writings all largely continue to proceed from the assumption of organized labor support for the process of postwar welfare state expansion. An early but influential example of this is Peter Baldwin's comparative analysis of the role of the "middle classes" in bringing about this expansion. Baldwin successfully demonstrates that middle-class groups also have an interest in obtaining security against labor market risks because "the proletariat has no monopoly over uncertainty." Yet he fails to emphasize that support for public, let alone *redistributive*, welfare initiatives does not automatically follow from this. As a result, he does not fully appreciate that the TUC's "skeptical" stance toward superannuation in the United Kingdom was largely the result of the strong resistance against superannuation's redistributive consequences by what may have already been Britain's largest middle-class group at the time, the white-collar salariat.[16]

This mistake has recently been repeated, and arguably in a much more serious manner, by Isabela Mares. In full coherence with her goal to challenge "class-based perspectives" that regard "capital and labor as unified actors," Mares does mention the jealous defense of occupationally organized white-collar unions of their own sickness and old age insurance schemes in the prewar period. Yet she then proceeds as though such unions no longer existed in the postwar period.[17] In fact, and relying on an inadequate supply and interpretation of evidence, she assumes undivided labor union support for redistributive welfare state development in the United Kingdom. She even goes so far as to conclude that "the social policy preferences of the British labor union movement in the

[14] On the role of Christian Democracy, see Kees van Kersbergen, *Social Capitalism: A Study of Christian Democracy and the Welfare State* (London: Routledge, 1995); Kees van Kersbergen and Philip Manow (eds.), *Religion, Class Coalitions, and Welfare States* (Cambridge University Press, 2009). For some excellent accounts that emphasize the role of "middle class" groups such as farmers, the petty bourgeoisie, and white-collar workers in the expansion of the welfare state, see Peter Baldwin, *The Politics of Social Solidarity*; and Stefano Bartolini, *The Political Mobilization of the European Left: The Class Cleavage* (Cambridge University Press, 2000).

[15] For some excellent examples that emphasize employer divisions, see Peter Swenson, *Capitalists Against Markets: The Making of Labor Markets and Welfare States in the United States and Sweden* (Oxford University Press, 2002); Isabela Mares, *The Politics of Social Risk: Business and Welfare State Development* (Cambridge University Press, 2003).

[16] See Baldwin, *The Politics*, 12, 242–3, for, respectively, the earlier reference and his treatment of the interests of white-collar workers and the consequences of this for the TUC's response to Labour's superannuation proposal.

[17] Mares, *The Politics of Social Risk*, 3, 47.

first decades after the Second World War were in no way different from the preferences of unions in Germany and Sweden."[18] This is a conclusion that will be challenged with systematic primary findings in this work.

Most of the recent scholarship on employers treats labor unions in a similar way. Despite their emphasis on skills as an explanatory force for welfare state development, which makes them well aware of the large heterogeneity of the workforce, Torben Iversen and David Soskice, for instance, pay little attention to the possibility that different groups of workers may consequently have appreciated the redistributive consequences of the welfare state's postwar expansion in quite different ways. Insofar as they pay attention to labor unions, they consistently do so under the assumption that these "promote long-term social spending."[19] In his otherwise seminal *Capitalists Against Markets*, Peter Swenson also largely overlooks the widely divergent attitudes of different sections of organized labor toward redistributive welfare state development.[20] None of the recent writings on employers, then, considers union variation as a major factor in explaining the very different response of national employer interest groups toward demands for increases in public protection against labor market risks – an issue to which I will return at length in Chapter 2.

In sum, even the most sophisticated contributions to the literature pay insufficient attention to the wide variety in worker attitudes toward redistributive welfare state development. There has been particularly little attention in the literature for the possibility of strong and consistent labor union opposition to the redistributive consequences of welfare state expansion. Many empirical analyses simply proceed from the assumption that labor union support for the postwar expansion of the welfare state naturally followed from workers' interests in securing protection against labor market risks. This includes those who, like Silja Häusermann, emphasize intralabor conflict over recent welfare state reforms but at the same time presume that the postwar expansion of the welfare state could count on the support of a "unified left ... because the overall direction was expansive."[21] Such views neglect the fact that the postwar expansion of the welfare state did much more than merely provide workers with security against labor market risks. Through risk reapportioning and the

---

[18] Mares, *Taxation, Wage Bargaining and Unemployment*, 218. See also Mares, "Distributional Conflict in Mature Welfare States." In Ian Shapiro, Peter Swenson, and Daniela Donno, *Divide and Deal: The Politics of Distribution in Democracies* (New York University Press, 2008), 43–71.

[19] Iversen and Soskice, "Distribution and Redistribution," 448. See also Torben Iversen, *Capitalism, Democracy, and Welfare* (Cambridge University Press, 2005), 154.

[20] See Swenson, *Capitalists Against Markets*.

[21] Silja Häusermann, "Solidarity with Whom? Why Trade Unions Are Losing Ground in Continental Pension Politics," *European Journal of Political Research*, 227. For an excellent account on the politics of postwar welfare state reform that pays ample attention to intralabor conflict, see Häusermann, *The Politics of Welfare State Reform in Continental Europe: Modernization in Hard Times* (Cambridge University Press, 2010).

introduction of systems of contributions and benefits that increasingly worked to the advantage of the lowest paid, it also massively redistributed risk and income among different groups of workers. And these redistributive consequences were by no means automatically accepted by all workers.

Perhaps more than any other societal group, workers hold multiple and partly contradictory interests when it comes to welfare state development. Different occupational categories of workers differ greatly in terms of income and their exposure to labor market risks. As a result, they also differ greatly in their demands and ability to pay for protection against these risks. Workers with less advantageous risk and income profiles (these two often go together because they, in turn, depend to a great extent on a worker's skill level) are often highly dependent on public intervention to achieve adequate insurance against labor market risks such as unemployment, sickness, and old age. Yet, for workers whose position in the labor market is quite comfortable and who consequently earn generous incomes and have a low-risk profile, the situation is much less clear-cut. On the one hand, such workers may, for instance, appreciate the ability of public insurance programs to provide pay-as-you-go financing – which is something that private insurance schemes often find much harder to do.[22] On the other hand, they will be much less appreciative of public insurance programs' greater ability to reapportion risk in a broad way. After all, they are the ones who will primarily stand to lose from the redistributive consequences of this.

The main purpose of the welfare state, then, is not to "compensate labor for its disadvantaged position on the labor market" – as traditional labor-centered accounts of this development have argued. Nor is it to "emancipate workers from market-dependence."[23] Instead, it is simply to provide adequate levels of social protection for all members of society, a purpose that it primarily aims to achieve by redistributing risk and resources among wage and salary dependents. In this regard, a crucial distinction has to be made between private and public insurance solutions. Compared with their private counterparts, public insurance schemes often tend to be substantially more risk and income redistributive. Public pooling of labor market risks reapportions such risks in the broadest possible way, granting society's more risk-prone members the same level of protection as its less risk-prone members. Most of the time, the redistributive nature of social security programs does not end here because all members seldom share in the common risk pool on completely equal terms. The systems of contributions and benefits of most social insurance programs work to the advantage of their poorer members – who tend to be society's

---

[22] Private pension plans often cannot offer pay-as-you-go financing and are generally based on funded contributions. The appeal of pay-as-you-go financing for privileged workers is that it does not require saving because current benefits are paid for by current contributions. For poorer workers, the added appeal is that systems that are based on pay-as-you-go financing lend themselves better to redistribute income and risk among different categories of workers.

[23] See, respectively, Korpi, *The Democratic*, 83; and Esping-Andersen, *The Three Worlds*, 22.

more risk-prone members as well. Crucially, both the winners and losers of this redistributive process belong primarily to the worker category.

There are at least two reasons why the redistributive consequences of redistributive welfare state development mainly affect the distribution of income among different categories of workers. First, in modern capitalist societies, nearly all breadwinners are workers, and most of national income is divided among workers. This means that workers inevitably also end up paying for the brunt of welfare state expenditure.[24] Second, and as mentioned before, workers differ to a vast degree in income and exposure to economic risk. Skilled manual workers typically enjoy significantly higher wages and greater job security than do semi- or unskilled workers. Some categories of white-collar workers, in turn, enjoy much higher wages than skilled manual workers and are even less exposed to labor market risks. Finally, other categories of white-collar workers earn wages and have a degree of job security that more closely reflect those of skilled manual workers or even of semi- and unskilled manual workers.[25] When these different categories or groups of workers join the same risk pool or come to belong to an insurance scheme with a system of contributions and benefits that works to the advantage of its poorer members, the result is a massive degree of redistribution among them.

Based on the preceding, I put forward a view of organized labor's involvement in welfare state development that differs markedly from conventional views – especially from those put forward by class-oriented lines of analysis. This view starts with the claim that labor union support for redistributive welfare state development cannot be taken for granted. Whether labor unions support redistributive welfare state development, I argue, depends on the kinds of workers they organize. Do they mainly organize skilled workers with a strong position in the labor market? Or do they also organize many workers who can only achieve adequate security against labor market risk through risk redistribution and a redistributive contributory system? Depending on the risk and income profile of their members, unions will value public welfare solutions, and especially their redistributive consequences, in quite different ways. It is for this reason that I argue against the longstanding "consensus in the literature that the policy efficacy of left parties depends on the extent to which they can count on *strong* trade unionism."[26] More important than the organizational strength of labor unions is whether they are willing to redistribute income and

---

[24] They may do so either as contributors or as taxpayers depending on whether benefits are financed from contributions or through general taxation. For different types of financing in different countries, see, for instance, Margaret S. Gordon, *Social Security Policies in Industrial Countries: A Comparative Analysis* (Cambridge University Press, 1988), 20–36.

[25] On the diversity of the white-collar category, see, for example, Michael P. Kelly, *White-Collar Proletariat: The Industrial Behaviour of British Civil Servants* (London: Routledge and Kegan, 1980).

[26] Esping-Andersen and Van Kersbergen, "Contemporary Research on Social Democracy," 191 (emphasis added).

risk within the labor category. This ability to display broad worker solidarity, I argue here, depends on the *way* in which they are organized.

UNION STRUCTURE AND THE EMERGENCE OF THE PUBLIC AND PRIVATE WELFARE STATE

In recent years, scholars have paid much attention to the emergence of so-called dual welfare systems or divided welfare states in nations where private benefits play an important role in providing workers with security against labor market risk.[27] These studies have contributed to our understanding of welfare state development in important ways. First, they have pointed out that nations with relatively low levels of public provision generally offer very generous levels of private (i.e., occupational or, in American parlance, employment-based) provision that enable them to provide overall levels of social spending that are comparable with those of other nations. This means that these nations are not so much "welfare laggards" as "dual" welfare states that rely on a mixture of public and private provision. Second, these studies have pointed out that nations with high levels of private provision are also "divided" welfare states in the sense that they grant very generous levels of security to high-paid, low-risk workers, whereas less privileged workers often lack proper insurance.

These accounts of the growing reliance on private provision in nations often described as "welfare laggards" have provided us with some original insights into the welfare state. Yet, in one crucial respect, the approach of these recent studies has been quite conventional. Although recognizing that this development was in the interest of higher-paid workers, all of them have pointed to employers as the main architects of these divided welfare states. They have consequently gone to great lengths to explain how employers managed to tilt welfare systems toward greater reliance on private provision because labor unions lacked the political clout to push for an extension of universal public benefits for all workers. In this view, the emergence of divided welfare states thus initially presented a political victory of business over labor. The emphasis here lies on "initially," because this recent scholarship has also argued that the emergence of large private programs eventually worked to "reorient labor's interests ... leading many unions to prefer private-sector solutions over public-sector ones."[28]

---

[27] For some excellent accounts that emphasize the importance of the distinction between public and private provision, see Marie Gottschalk, *The Shadow Welfare State: Labor, Business, and the Politics of Health Care in the United States* (Ithaca, NY: Cornell University Press, 2000); Jacob S. Hacker, *The Divided Welfare State: The Battle over Public and Private Social Benefits in the United States* (Cambridge University Press, 2002); Colin Gordon, *Dead on Arrival: The Politics of Health Care in Twentieth-Century America* (Princeton, NJ: Princeton University Press, 2003); and Leimgruber, *Solidarity Without the State?*

[28] Gottschalk, *The Shadow Welfare State*, 2. See also Gordon, *Dead on Arrival*, 281; Hacker, *The Divided Welfare State*, 130–4; and Leimgruber, *Solidarity Without the State?*, 209–12.

This view of welfare state development is quite similar to those of traditional class-oriented writings that have struggled to explain the persistence of low levels of public provision combined with high levels of private provision in countries with strong labor unions, such as the United Kingdom. These writings also explained the emergence of dual welfare systems through the activities of employers and their political allies, arguing that such systems were deliberately created to "divide wage-earners." Scholars such as Gøsta Esping-Andersen and Walter Korpi therefore warned that "private market alternatives to public schemes ... may severely undercut popular loyalty to the public welfare system and introduce new invidious cleavages that are difficult to bridge."[29] The crux of this argument is that the structure of welfare provision, depending on whether it is, respectively, completely public and encompassing or tilted toward higher earners through a mixture of public and private benefits, creates either solidarity or dualities and conflict among workers.

This book presents a different view of such dual welfare systems. Rather than arguing that such systems divide workers by creating dualities among them, it shows that they are themselves an outcome of existing divisions within the labor movement. In doing so, it does not have to argue that labor unions at first pushed for an extension of universal public benefits for all workers, after which the interests of some unions were then "reoriented" in favor of private alternatives. Instead, it proceeds from the recognition that for some unions, the interests of their members are simply better served by pushing for private schemes – or combinations of public and private schemes – that do not redistribute risk and income in a broad way. Of course, this will only be the case if these unions only represent low-risk, high-income workers with a strong position in the labor market. Such unions do exist. Yet, crucially, they are much more common in some nations than in others. A major argument of this book is that the origins of dual or divided welfare systems cannot be explained as resulting from labor's relative weakness against capital. Instead, it is an outcome of occupational unionism – or the division of workers along skill and occupational lines.

The distinctive feature of occupational unions is that they limit their membership to certain, generally privileged, skills and occupations. In nations where occupational unionism is strong, lower-skilled workers without a strong occupational profile (these two features often go together) consequently organize separately from higher-skilled workers. The result is a labor movement that is neatly divided into unions that represent workers who do and those that represent workers who do not depend on redistributive, and thus public, solutions to

[29] Gøsta Esping-Andersen and Walter Korpi, "Social Policy as Class Politics in Post-War Capitalism: Scandinavia, Austria, and Germany." In John H. Goldthorpe, *Order and Conflict in Contemporary Capitalism* (Oxford: Clarendon Press, 1984), 184. See also Walter Korpi and Joakim Palme, "The Paradox of Redistribution and Strategies of Equality: Welfare State Institutions, Inequality and Poverty in Western Countries," *American Sociological Review* 63:5 (1998), 661–87.

achieve adequate insurance against labor market risk. Such unions will inevitably appreciate redistributive welfare state development in very different ways. This difference results from the greater ability of, for instance, craft unions that exclusively represent skilled manual workers to negotiate generous private provisions through collective bargaining.[30] Representing workers with an even more favorable skill profile, occupationally organized white-collar unions can often do the same. Such unions may nevertheless support public welfare initiatives for a variety of reasons.[31] Yet they will have little reason to support any initiative that redistributes risks and resources in a broad way because this goes against the interests of their entire membership. In this, they will differ strongly from unions that organize large numbers of lower-skilled and thus lower-paid and more risk-prone workers.

Crucially, no other type of union organization leads to such a clear division between more and less privileged workers. Even where regional, religious, or sectoral divisions are strong – and the latter is typically the case in nations where occupational unionism is weak – the labor union movement will be characterized by unions with quite diverse membership profiles in terms of income and risk. A central argument of this study is that such unions differ markedly in their stance on redistributive welfare state development from occupationally organized unions that limit their membership to privileged workers. The crucial distinctive feature here is that unions that seek to organize workers regardless of skill and occupation emphasize broad worker solidarity as opposed to occupational identity. When seeking to improve the protection of their members against labor market risk, such unions will therefore be far more likely to consider redistributive welfare solutions. This means that in nations in which the union movement is organized along sectoral as opposed to occupational lines, it will be far easier to achieve adequate levels of social protection for all workers.

Despite their tendency to focus on labor's struggle with capital, some scholars have recognized the importance of the distinction between union organization along occupational versus sectoral lines. Ironically, the importance of union structure seems to have been recognized most fully in the early works of some power resources scholars. In *The Democratic Class Struggle*, for example,

---

[30] Evidence for this can be found in, for instance, the strong attachment of British and American craft unions representing skilled manual workers to "voluntarism" or free collective bargaining. See, for example, Hugh Clegg, *The Changing System of Industrial Relations in Britain* (Oxford: Blackwell, 1979), 436–7; Alan Campbell, Nina Fishman, and John McIlroy, "The Post-War Compromise: Mapping Industrial Politics, 1945–64." In Campbell, Fishman, and McIlroy, *British Trade Unions and Industrial Politics*, Vol. I: *The Post-War Compromise, 1945–1964* (Aldershot: Ashgate, 1999), 77–8; Gary Marks, "Variations in Union Political Activity in the United States, Britain and Germany from the Nineteenth Century," *Comparative Politics* 22:1 (1989), 84.

[31] Most important among these, and as mentioned earlier, is that public schemes are often better able to offer pay-as-you-go financing than private insurance programs.

Walter Korpi mentioned that "it is of significance whether workers are organized on the basis of craft or industry."[32] In *The Transition from Capitalism
to Socialism*, John D. Stephens noted that "the character of labor organization once it develops in a country ... also has an important effect on class
formation and class consciousness."[33] Finally, in his *Politics Against Markets*,
Gøsta Esping-Andersen emphasized the importance of "vertically organized
and nationally centralized trade unionism" for the social democratic road to
victory in Norway and Sweden because "class unity is more difficult to achieve
under conditions of competition between craft workers, unskilled industrial
laborers, and the rural proletariat."[34]

Yet, in the view of these scholars, the importance of union structure lay foremost in the degree to which it extended labor's organizational power against
capital.[35] As a result, they either ranked it secondary in importance to union
strength in their attempts to explain cross-national variation in welfare outcomes or neglected it completely in their analyses. Esping-Andersen, it must be
acknowledged, did cite the relative importance of craft unionism in Denmark
and the lack thereof in Norway and Sweden to show that the industrial proletariat in the latter two nations was "better situated to invoke broad class
solidarity."[36] Yet Korpi, in his chapter on social policy, examined only union
density and the governmental inclusion of left parties in his attempts to account
for welfare variation among nations. Stephens, in turn, explained the absence
of a generous welfare state in the United States only through the "very low
level of labor organization and the absence of a major reformist labor party."
And despite the fact that the division of labor's share of the national income
clearly involves a conflict of interests among different categories of workers,
he directly linked cross-national differences in wage equality to cross-national
differences in union strength.[37]

More recent writings have arguably paid even less attention to the formative
role of labor union structure in shaping workers' interests and political behavior. In fact, much of the recent literature on welfare state development does
not even mention the nature of union organization in the country or countries
under investigation. Earlier, I mentioned the neglect of union structure in historical institutionalists' attempts to explain the emergence of divided welfare
states as well as in the recent scholarship on the involvement of employers.[38]

---

[32] Korpi, *The Democratic*, 39.
[33] Stephens, *The Transition*, 45.
[34] Gøsta Esping-Andersen, *Politics Against Markets: The Social-Democratic Road to Power*
(Princeton, NJ: Princeton University Press, 1985), 88.
[35] According to Korpi, for example, "Working-class power resources can be expected to be greatest where the labour movement is well integrated and has strong support from wage-earners."
Korpi, *The Democratic*, 39.
[36] Esping-Andersen, *Politics Against Markets*, 88.
[37] John D. Stephens, *The Transition from Capitalism to Socialism* (London: Macmillan, 1979), 149.
[38] Recent attempts to explain the success and failure of welfare state retrenchment have paid far
more attention to left divisions. Yet they too often pay little attention to the importance of

While often quite critical of traditional labor-centered approaches to the welfare state, these new writings all largely continue to explain labor union behavior from unexamined assumptions based on class interests. As a result, most of them continue to view organized labor as the natural proponent of the welfare state.

This neglect of the crucial importance of union structure has led to an inadequate understanding of the process of postwar welfare state development – especially in countries such as the United Kingdom, in which the labor union movement is largely organized along occupational lines. In such nations, as we will see, redistributive welfare state initiatives can be expected to have encountered powerful labor union opposition. Yet welfare state scholars nevertheless tend to assume undivided labor union support for redistributive welfare state development there. When confronted with cases in which labor unions displayed little interest in welfare state development or even outright opposition to welfare initiatives, they consequently tend to invoke explanations that fail to take the redistributive consequences of such initiatives into account.[39] The most popular way to explain such instances is by referring to an ideological commitment of the labor union movement to "voluntarism" – the idea that the state has to abstain from direct intervention in the labor market. This commitment is then, in turn, explained as the outcome of union anxiety over the consequences of allowing a potentially hostile "bourgeois" state to undermine union functions.[40]

union structure. This is even the case for those who, like Christine Trampusch, emphasize the importance of collectively negotiated benefits as alternatives to public benefits. See Trampusch, "Industrial Relations as a Source of Social Policy: A Typology of the Institutional Conditions for Industrial Agreements on Social Benefits," *Social Policy & Administration* 41:3 (2007), 251–70.

[39] For such explanations of cases of British labor union opposition to redistributive government intervention in the labor market, see Chapter 2. On the use of union anxiety over the consequences of allowing a potentially hostile state to undermine union functions as an argument for union opposition to (redistributive) state intervention in the labor market in the United Kingdom, see Chapter 2. On similar arguments for the United States, see, for example, Martha Derthick, *Policymaking for Social Security* (Washington, DC: Brookings Institution, 1979), 113; Victoria Hattam, *Labor Visions and State Power: The Origins of Business Unionism in the United States* (Princeton, NJ: Princeton University Press, 1993), 5; Michael K. Brown, "Bargaining for Social Rights: Unions and the Re-Emergence of Welfare Capitalism, 1945–1952," *Political Science Quarterly* 112:4 (1997–1998), 663; Marie Gottschalk, *The Shadow Welfare State*, 43; Stephens, *The Transition*, 89; and Gordon, *Dead on Arrival*, 275. In his otherwise excellent account of the development of the Swiss "three-pillar" pension system, Matthieu Leimgruber explains instances of Swiss union opposition to public schemes through their fear that this would have the effect of "undermining trade union control of industrial relations" because "union-based schemes ... played a key role in unionizing efforts." He also speaks of a legacy of "labor distrust of state-based provision." Leimgruber, *Solidarity Without the State?* 19, 207. I will return at length to these two cases in Chapter 7.

[40] Some, such as Wolfgang Streeck, have noted that craft unions are more likely to display voluntarist behavior than industrial unions but explain this by arguing that "lasting suspicion of a liberal state unlikely to offer unions more than reluctant tolerations makes state-free voluntary

In this work I take a different view on such cases of union disinterest in or opposition to welfare state development. This view begins with the recognition that unions displaying little interest in welfare state initiatives often represent skilled and thus privileged workers who strongly oppose any measures that result in a redistribution of risk or income among different categories of workers. Most welfare legislation, and many other instances of government intervention in the labor market, do exactly this. This means that the voluntarist inclinations of unions are often rooted as much in union anxiety over the consequences of government intervention on wage differentials as in worries about allowing a potentially hostile state to undermine union functions. I will explain this at length in Chapter 2 – which among others deals with the strong voluntarist inclinations of the British labor union movement. The chapter argues that the strength of voluntarism in the United Kingdom cannot be explained without a thorough appreciation of the strong resistance of British craft and occupationally organized white-collar unions to any attempt to redistribute income and risk in favor of lower-paid and more risk-prone workers.

THE ORGANIZATION OF THIS BOOK

In examining the importance of variations within and across labor movements, this book describes how the organizational blueprint of the British and Dutch labor union movements shaped their involvement in the postwar development of the British and Dutch welfare states. It also explains how this, in turn, affected the interests and behavior of major employer interest groups in the two countries. Differences in both the strength and structure of the labor union movements in the Netherlands and the United Kingdom make them ideally suited to illustrate the importance of the latter. The two countries also lend themselves well to a comparison because they embarked on such widely divergent welfare trajectories during the crucial formative first three decades of the postwar period. Neither of these trajectories fits well with conventional views of the welfare state – let alone with those that emphasize the importance of labor's relative power resources against capital.

Over the years, many scholars have, although mostly fleetingly, noted the deviant nature of postwar welfare state development in the Netherlands and the United Kingdom.[41] Despite having the oldest and one of the strongest labor

organization backed by sectional market power appear the most reliable for effective representation of workers." Streeck does not note that this strong "sectional market power" may also give such unions a reason to oppose the redistributive consequences of government intervention. See Wolfgang Streeck, "The Sociology of Labor Markets and Trade Unions." In N. J. Smelser and R. Swedberg, *The Handbook of Economic Sociology* (Princeton, NJ: Princeton University Press, 2005), 269.

[41] On the mismatch between British and Dutch welfare state outcomes and the claims of power resources theorists, see, for example, Göran Therborn, "'Pillarization' and 'Popular Movements'. Two Variants of Welfare Capitalism: The Netherlands and Sweden." In Francis Castles,

union movements in the world, the British welfare state developed into a prime example of a "divided" welfare state. Indeed, the British welfare state quite early in the postwar period acquired a reputation for its inability to provide adequate protection against labor market risk to all workers.[42] Those workers who did obtain adequate (i.e., above subsistence-carrying) levels of protection have always relied on substantial private provision. As we will see, these were always workers with a strong position in the labor market. The following chapters describe this development as the inevitable outcome of the strong opposition of Britain's occupationally organized labor unions to government initiatives that redistributed income and risk between their members and lower-paid, more risk-prone workers. In doing so, it illustrates the folly of assuming labor union support for the development of public insurance programs in the United Kingdom.[43]

In the Netherlands, by contrast, labor's relative "power resources" have always been quite weak.[44] Yet this clearly did not impede the postwar development of the Dutch welfare state in a major way. On the contrary, by the end of the period under investigation here, the Dutch boasted the most generous and redistributive welfare state of its day.[45] Another striking feature of the postwar trajectory of the Dutch welfare state, and one that scholars have struggled to explain, is that the most generous improvements to the system came about under confessional-liberal – instead of labor-dominated – governments. There now exists a large literature that tries to explain this by arguing that confessional parties may introduce generous welfare programs when they are in

---

Comparative History of Public Policy (Cambridge: Polity, 1989), 208; and Michael Hill, *Social Policy: A Comparative Analysis* (London: Prentice-Hall, 1996), 42.

[42] On this, see, for example, Derek Fraser, *The Evolution of the British Welfare State: A History of Social Policy Since the Industrial Revolution* (London: Macmillan, 2003), 252.

[43] The existing literature on the development of the British welfare state is nevertheless in complete agreement that the labor union movement supported its postwar expansion. For some examples, see Robert Taylor, *The Fifth Estate: British Unions in the 1970s* (London: Routledge, 1978), 172; Baldwin, *The Politics of Social Solidarity*, 211; Michael Hill, *The Welfare State in Britain. A Political History Since 1945* (Brookfield: Edward Elgar, 1993), 50; Noel Whiteside, "Industrial Relations and Social Welfare, 1945–1979." In C. J. Wrigley, *A History of British Industrial Relations, 1939–1979: Industrial Relations in a Declining Economy* (Cheltenham: Edward Elgar, 1996), 111; Rodney Lowe, *The Welfare State in Britain Since 1945* (London: Macmillan, 1998), 2; Helen Fawcett, "Jack Jones, the Social Contract and Social Policy 1970–1974." In Helen Fawcett and Rob Lowe, *Welfare Policy in Britain. The Road from 1945* (London: Macmillan, 1999), 158; Isabela Mares, *Taxation*, 178–9.

[44] In the early postwar period, some 40 percent of Dutch workers were organized in labor unions. From the late 1970s on, this percentage fell steadily, to under 25 percent today. In the United Kingdom, union membership stood just over 40 percent in the immediate postwar period. Thirty years later, it had increased to over 50 percent, after which it decreased to about 30 percent today. See Jelle Visser, *European Trade Unions in Figures* (Deventer: Kluwer, 1989), 151–2, 240–1; idem, "Union Membership Statistics in 24 Countries," *Monthly Labour Review* (January 2006), 45.

[45] See Therborn, "'Pillarization'," 208–10.

electoral competition with left parties.[46] Although there may be some truth to this argument, this book instead emphasizes organized labor's crucial role in the introduction of these programs. A major purpose of the book is to describe the striking degree to which parliament followed organized labor's, and to a lesser extent employer interest groups', preferences on welfare state reform in this period. It attributes this to the remarkable willingness and ability of Dutch labor unions to push for welfare state initiatives that redistributed risk and income among their own members and the accommodative stance of employer interest groups on many of these initiatives.[47]

To explain the wide variation in behavior among labor unions in the Netherlands and the United Kingdom, and the consequences of this for the process of postwar welfare state development in the two countries, Chapter 2 begins with an analysis of their organizational differences and puts these differences in historical perspective. It then explores how these differences lead to the development of very different labor markets in the two countries. The chapter illustrates how the stance of unions toward redistribution of income among workers shaped their attitude toward state intervention in the labor market – which often has a redistributive aim and nearly always has redistributive consequences. The chapter then explains how this, in turn, affected the stance of employer interest groups toward demands for improvements in public provision against labor market risk. In doing so, it builds on recent writings on the involvement of employer interest groups in welfare state development and, in particular, on those emphasizing the importance of and scope for cross-class alliances among labor unions and powerful sectors of the business community.[48]

---

[46] See, for example, Van Kersbergen, *Social Capitalism*, 175; Cox, *The Development of the Dutch Welfare State*, 212–13, 135; Peter Hupe, "Beyond Pillarization: The (Post) Welfare State in the Netherlands," *European Journal of Political Research* 23 (1993), 359–86; Robert Goodin, Bruce Heady, Ruud Muffels, and Henk-Jan Dirven, *The Real Worlds of Welfare Capitalism* (Cambridge University Press, 1999), 67; Robert Goodin, "Work and Welfare: Towards a Post-Productivist Welfare Regime," *British Journal of Political Science* 31:1 (2001), 19; Huber and Stephens, *Development and Crisis of the Welfare State*, 165; Kees van Kersbergen, "Religion and the Welfare State in the Netherlands." In Van Kersbergen and Manow, *Religion*, 140–1.

[47] That the Dutch employer community has, on the whole, been quite supportive of the postwar expansion of the Dutch welfare state has often been noted by scholars. See, for example, Göran Therborn, who noted: "While on and off expressing worries about increasing costs, the Dutch employers' representatives in the Social-Economic Council, on the whole, supported the rest of the welfare state expansion in the 1960s. Occasionally, they even came to declare their principled support of extensive social insurance, for social reasons and for reasons of countercyclical economic policy." Therborn, "'Pillarization,'" 215.

[48] See, for example, Peter Swenson, "Bringing Capital Back in, or Social Democracy Reconsidered: Employer Power, Cross-Class Alliances, and Centralization of Industrial Relations in Denmark and Sweden," *World Politics* 43:4 (1991), 513–44; idem, "Arranged Alliance: Business Interests in the New Deal," *Politics & Society* 25:1 (1997), 66–116; idem, *Capitalists Against Markets*; Mares, *The Politics of Social Risk*; Gordon, *New Deals*; idem, *Dead on Arrival*.

Chapters 3 through 6 analyze the introduction and expansion of the major postwar social security programs in the Netherlands and the United Kingdom. These chapters form the empirical "core" of this book. Chapters 3, 4, and 5 show how the internal organizational structure of the British and Dutch labor union movements shaped their involvement in the development of public and private provision for, respectively, the elderly, the unemployed, and the sick and disabled in these countries. These chapters cover a period ranging from roughly the early 1940s to the late 1960s. Chapter 6 explains how some of these programs – such as the Dutch disability insurance scheme – came to be used for early retirement purposes during the 1970s. Because this development took place to a much greater degree in the Netherlands than in the United Kingdom, this chapter focuses mainly on the Dutch case. Along the way, the book makes numerous comparisons to welfare state development in other countries. Chapter 7 discusses the implications of the book's main findings.

2

Labor Divided

In 1951, in an article on the growing importance of white-collar unionism in the United Kingdom, the British economist Guy Routh published a survey of the "distribution of the gainfully occupied population of Great Britain."[1] In this survey, 95 percent of all economically active persons were characterized as "workers." These were divided into nine occupational categories. First on Routh's list were unskilled manual workers, who, according to the survey, represented 12 percent of the economically active population. Second on the list stood the largest occupational group, semiskilled manual workers, who represented some 28 percent of the gainfully occupied population. These were followed by skilled manual workers, who represented an additional 25 percent of the economically active. All other worker-occupations mentioned in the survey belonged to the white-collar category. Although representing only about 30 percent of the economically active at the time, this category was by then already so diverse that the survey subdivided it into six different occupational groups, ranging from shop assistants, to foremen, to clerical workers, to managers, to higher professionals, and to lower professionals. In the years after Routh presented his survey results, the white-collar category would grow rapidly. In 1951, it accounted for roughly 32 percent of all workers. By 1971, this had increased to 43 percent.[2]

Routh's survey is mentioned here because it so neatly demonstrates the relative size and diversity of the British worker category at around the time

---

[1] For the survey, see Guy Routh, "White-Collar Unions in the United Kingdom." In Adolf Sturmthal, *White-Collar Trade Unions: Contemporary Developments in Industrialized Societies* (Champaign: University of Illinois Press, 1996), 166.
[2] See Robert Price and George Sayers Bain, "Union Growth Revisited: 1948–1974 in Perspective," *British Journal of Industrial Relations* 4 (1966), 339–55.

of Britain's first postwar social security reforms.[3] Among those 95 percent
of all economically active persons classified as "workers" were unskilled and
semiskilled manual workers, who held, respectively, very weak and fairly
weak positions in the labor market. But the broad category of "workers" also
included skilled manual workers, whose qualifications enabled them to earn
much higher wages and made them much less prone to labor market risks
such as unemployment. Other workers belonged to the "high end" white-collar
category of "higher professionals," who earned even higher incomes. Finally,
many others belonged to the growing "low end" white-collar legion of nurses,
typists, waiters, telephone operators, and messengers, whose income and risk
profiles were more comparable with those of semiskilled or perhaps even
unskilled manual workers than with those of their more privileged white-collar
counterparts.[4] The interests of these different occupational categories regarding redistributive welfare state development were by no means similar. So, for
example, were most unskilled and semiskilled manual workers, as well as many
low-end white-collar groups of workers, only able to achieve adequate levels of unemployment insurance through risk redistribution with other occupational categories. In this they differed from skilled manual workers and
other white-collar categories, who, as we will see in Chapter 4, were generally
quite capable of achieving adequate provision through collective bargaining.
Finally, some white-collar workers occupied such secure occupations that even
the need to pursue occupational provision against unemployment may have
seemed redundant for them.

In the literature on welfare state development and industrial relations, the
divergence in interests among these different categories of workers is seldom
fully acknowledged. Scholars often fail to examine this divergence even when
explicitly focusing on occupational differences among workers. A good example of this is an investigation of the growth of white-collar unionism in the
United Kingdom undertaken by the industrial relations expert George Sayers
Bain during the mid-1960s. Following the convention of placing the distinction between labor and capital at the center of the analysis, Bain argued that
the British labor union movement had to develop its membership among
white-collar workers in order to avoid becoming "the increasingly outdated
representatives of a declining industrial minority." If the labor union movement

---

[3] The 1946 National Insurance Act had become effective in 1948, three years before the survey
was undertaken.

[4] Some scholars exclusively use the term "white-collar worker" to describe a salaried professional or educated worker who performs clerical, administrative, or management tasks. Such
a limitation of the term makes it necessary to devise a separate way to describe the "low end"
white-collar category described earlier, however, which is why I use the broader definition of the
term. For a long but probably still not exhaustive list of workers who qualify as white-collar
workers, see Bernhard Ebbinghaus and Jeremy Waddington, "United Kingdom/Great Britain." In
Bernhard Ebbinghaus and Jelle Visser, *The Societies of Europe: Trade Unions in Western Europe
Since 1945* (London: Macmillan, 2005), 722.

failed to do so, Bain continued, "its ability even to advance the interests of its manual membership ... [would] be seriously impaired."[5] In coming years, the labor union movement did indeed absorb more and more white-collar workers. Especially from the mid-1960s on, an increasing proportion of white-collar workers unionized. Because white-collar employment numbers were also increasing rapidly, by the mid-1970s, two of every five unionists belonged to the white-collar category compared with one of every five only three decades earlier.[6]

One might wonder, however, how this was to increase the interests of the "manual membership" of the British labor union movement exactly. Of those white-collar workers who organized, nearly all did so within their own white-collar unions, of which membership was generally limited to certain privileged occupations. (Higher-educated white-collar workers were far more likely to be unionized than their lower-educated counterparts.[7]) These unions bargained separately from other unions, guarded wage differentials as jealously as did craft unions representing skilled manual workers, and, mainly because of these differentials, took a stance toward government interference that was quite different from unions that also represented many lower-skilled workers. In fact, and as we will see later in this chapter and in the following chapters, in their resistance to redistributive government intervention, they often sided with employer interest groups. In short, there is good reason to argue against the view that in the United Kingdom strong union organization among one occupational group of workers helps to advance the interests of other groups of workers as well.

Bain's belief that unionization of white-collar workers would help to advance the interests of their manual worker counterparts can be attributed to one of two mistakes that are still often made by industrial relations and welfare state

---

[5] George Sayers Bain, "The Growth of White-Collar Unionism in Great Britain," *British Journal of Industrial Relations* 4 (1966), 304, 331.

[6] See Arthur Marsh and Victoria Ryan, *History Directory of Trade Unions*, Vol. I: *Non-Manual Unions* (Westmead: Gower, 1980), xi.

[7] It has often been noted that unionization in the old manufacturing industries or among manual workers is higher than in the white-collar professions. But here also there are very large and perhaps even larger differences within both categories. Unionization levels among unskilled and semiskilled workers are generally far lower than among skilled manual workers. Similarly, more-educated white-collar workers (but not university graduates), especially when operating in the public sector, are generally more frequently union members than are "low end" white-collar categories, especially when these operate in the service sector. This trend is typical for most countries. It is also a trend that has been noticed throughout the postwar period. In fact, it is for this reason that economists and labor market scholars initially often held that the effect of unionization was to increase wage inequality. See, for example, Milton Friedman, "Some Comments on the Significance for Labor Unions on Economic Policy." In David Wright, *The Impact of the Union* (New York: Kelley and Millman, 1956) 124; and Albert Rees, *The Economics of Trade Unions* (The University of Chicago Press, 1962); John S. Pettengill, *Labor Unions and the Inequality of Earned Income* (Amsterdam: North-Holland, 1980) 3.

scholars: he was either not aware of the vast differences in interests among different occupational categories of workers, or he assumed that worker movements by necessity display some degree of worker solidarity. Yet different categories of workers have many competing interests, and worker solidarity cannot be assumed – at least not in nations in which occupational divisions within the union movement lay these competing interests so clearly bare. Such occupational divisions matter a great deal here. Had Britain's white-collar workers organized themselves predominantly in unions that catered to multiple occupational groups, then Bain's argument would have been valid. Yet, because of a series of coincidental circumstances grounded in Britain's industrialization process, they did not.

A crucial feature of the British labor union movement at the time of Bain's analysis was that it almost completely lacked unions that catered to a wide range of different occupational groups or skills. Despite a strong tendency toward amalgamation in recent years, this is still largely the case today. There are only a few unions in the United Kingdom that could qualify as industrial unions, and even those organize fewer grades of workers than do their counterparts in northwest continental Europe. The most complete industrial union in the United Kingdom is the National Union of Mineworkers (NUM). Even in this industry, however, "privileged" white-collar professions such as managers and undermanagers, foremen, overmen, deputies, shotfirers, and colliery clerks all organize in separate organizations.[8] The same holds for the only other unions that could qualify as industrial unions in the United Kingdom, the National Union of Rail, Maritime and Transport Workers (RMT) and its most prominent predecessors, the National Union of Railwaymen (NUR) and National Union of Seamen (NUS). In other industries, skilled manual workers often also rally in their own unions, leaving unskilled and semi-skilled manual workers to organize in separate general unions. While most of these unions are members of the Trades Union Congress (TUC), this union confederation has done little to diminish the occupational divisions that exist within the British labor union movement. In fact, and as we will also see later in this chapter and in the following chapters, it is mainly because of these occupational divisions that the TUC's authority over its members is notoriously weak and that its function is mostly limited to lobbying government.[9]

---

[8] See J. D. M. Bell, "Trade Unions." In Allan Flanders and Hugh Clegg, *The Changing System of Industrial Relations in Great Britain: Its History, Law and Institutions* (Oxford: Blackwell, 1954) 138; Van Ruysseveldt and Visser, *Industrial Relations in Europe*, 58.

[9] For craft opposition to the creation of a more powerful union federation, see James Fulcher, "On the Explanation of Industrial Relations Diversity: Labour Movements, Employers and the State in Britain and Sweden," *British Journal of Industrial Relations* 26:2 (1988), 246–74. For a more general discussion of this, see also Richard Scase, *Social Democracy in Capitalist Society: Working-Class Politics in Britain and Sweden* (London: Croom Helm, 1977), 35.

In the sharp differentiation of its unions along occupational lines, the United Kingdom closely resembles countries that were once part of its economic and political sphere of influence, such as the United States, Canada, Australia, New Zealand, and Ireland – all countries that through no coincidence are known for their "liberal" labor market and welfare features.[10] At the same time, it differs starkly in this from its continental European counterparts. To be sure, occupational unionism also exists among the countries of continental Europe – and to a greater extent in some of those countries than in others. Yet, crucially, its importance is nowhere as great on the European continent as in the Anglo-Saxon world. In most continental European countries, a certain proportion of organized white-collar workers rallies in separate white-collar unions. Yet, contrary to in the United Kingdom, many of these white-collar unions are organized predominantly along "vertical" lines.[11] Perhaps even more important, in only one continental European country, Denmark, did a strong craft tradition remain in existence during the postwar period.[12] Finally, all continental European countries have strong industrial unions that aim to organize workers regardless of skill or profession.

[10] In Hall and Soskice's typology of "liberal" and "coordinated" market economies, all countries mentioned here belong to the liberal market model. Similarly, all northwest continental European countries, with their industrially organized labor union movements, belong to the "coordinated" categories. These differences between the "liberal" Anglo-Saxon world and "social Europe" have been noted in the welfare state literature as well. Yet, because of the tendency of scholars to focus on class divisions, they have seldom been linked to differences in union structure. For Hall and Soskice's typology, see Peter A. Hall and David Soskice, *Varieties of Capitalism: The Institutional Foundations of Comparative Advantage* (Oxford University Press, 2001), 20. Note also the strong "liberal" features of most Anglo-Saxon welfare states in, for example, Esping-Andersen, *The Three Worlds*, 74.

[11] A partial exception to this is Switzerland, where occupationally organized white-collar unions have always been quite strong. In most other continental countries, white-collar unionism follows either the Belgian or Swedish model. In Sweden, all manual workers organize on an industrial basis within the Landsorganisationen i Sverige (LO, the Swedish Trade Union Confederation). Most white-collar workers organize in separate white-collar unions that are represented by their own white-collar federations. A majority of the members of the largest white-collar federation, named Tjänstemännens Centralorganisation (TCO), are organized along sectoral lines, though. The smaller Sveriges Akademikers Centralorganisationen (SCO, the Swedish Confederation of Professional Associations) is mainly organized along occupational lines. In Belgium, many white-collar workers also organize in separate white-collar unions. Most of these unions are, in turn, represented by the same union federations as are blue-collar unions – but this is not the point here. What is the point here is that these white-collar unions, like their Swedish counterparts, are predominantly organized along sectoral or "vertical" lines. See, for example, Sturmthal, *White-Collar Trade Unions*; Jelle Visser, *In Search of Inclusive Unionism. A Comparative Analysis* (Deventer: Kluwer, 1990).

[12] Vertically organized unions in Denmark are strongest in the food-processing and wood sectors, in the finance sector, and in traditional occupations of the public sector. All three main union confederations in Denmark organize a mixture of occupational and industrial or sectoral unions. See, for example, Anthony Ferner and Richard Hyman (eds), *Changing Industrial Relations in Europe* (Oxford: Basil Blackwell, 1998), 152–3; Jelle Visser, *In Search*, 130, 141; Bernhard Ebbinghaus, "Denmark." In Ebbinghaus and Visser, *The Societies of Europe*, 164–7.

It could be argued that of all continental European countries, the Netherlands has historically differed most from the United Kingdom in terms of the occupational-industrial divide. As a result of its much later industrialization, the subsequent power of socialist ideals during the formative period of the labor union movement, and the impact of religious cleavages, occupational unionism never managed to establish a firm footing in the Netherlands. In contrast to their much longer established counterparts in the United Kingdom, nearly all Dutch craft unions that came into being in the late nineteenth century came to expand their membership by integrating unskilled and semiskilled manual workers at the turn of the century.[13] Many white-collar unions were initially more hesitant to merge with industrial unions representing mainly manual workers or to open their membership to lower-skilled white-collar workers but were eventually forced to do so under strong pressure from the three main union federations, the socialist Nederlands Verbond van Vakverenigingen (NVV; Dutch Association of Trade Unions), the protestant Christelijk Nationaal Vakverbond (CNV, Christian Union Federation), and the Rooms-Katholiek Werkliedenverbond (RKWV, Roman Catholic Workers' Federation) – and the RKWV's successors, the Katholieke Arbeidersbeweging (KAB, Catholic Workers Movement) and the Nederlands Katholiek Vakverbond (NKV, Netherlands Catholic Trade Union Federation).[14] Throughout the twentieth century, these three industrially organized union federations have represented some 80 percent of all organized workers.[15] Although they continued to represent separate white-collar unions, these were also organized exclusively along sectoral lines.

---

[13] For some excellent descriptions of this development, see, for example, Ernest Hueting, Frits de Jong, and Rob Neij, *Naar groter eenheid: de geschiedenis van het Nederlands Verbond van Vakverenigingen 1906–1981* (Amsterdam: Van Gennep, 1982); and Jelle Visser, "The Netherlands." In Ebbinghaus and Visser, *The Societies of Europe*, 446.

[14] The pursuit of industrial unionism by the three main union federations in the Netherlands is well described by Hueting, De Jong, and Neij, *Naar groter eenheid*; Ger Harmsen, Jos Perry, and Floor van Gelder, *Mensenwerk. Industriële vakbonden op weg naar eenheid* (Ambo: Baarn, 1980); and Hugo Klooster, Jeroen Sprenger, and Vincent Vrooland, *Het blauwzwarte boekje: van beroepsorganisatie naar bedrijfsorganisatie* (Amsterdam: Vakbondshistorische Vereniging, 1986). For the opposition of white-collar workers against admission – and thus division – into industrial unions, see, for example, Bob Reinalda, *Bedienden georganiseerd. Ontstaan en ontwikkeling van handels- en kantoorbedienden in Nederland van het eerste begin tot in de Tweede Wereldoorlog* (Nijmegen: Socialistiese Uitgeverij Nijmegen, 1981), 22; Hueting, Harmsen, Perry, and Van Gelder, *Mensenwerk*, 157; John P. Windmuller, *Labor Relations in the Netherlands* (Ithaca, NY: Cornell University Press, 1969), 170.

[15] In 1976, the NVV and NKV merged to form the Federatie Nederlandse Vakbeweging (FNV, Federation Dutch Labor Movement). For an overview of the percentage of unionized workers who were organized by the "big three" over the years, see Centraal Bureau voor de Statistiek, *Overzicht van den omvang der vakbeweging op 1 januari 1920. Bijdragen tot de Statistiek van Nederland* (Den Haag: CBS, 1921), 8–9; Windmuller, *Labor Relations*, 186; Van Ruysseveldt and Visser, *Industrial Relations*, 228; and Jelle Visser, "The Netherlands," 481.

Of course, occupational-based worker organization never completely disappeared from the Netherlands. But because it remained present only in unions that did not belong to the "big three," its role has historically been quite small. Up to the late 1970s, when a new union federation called the Vakcentrale voor Middelbaar en Hoger Personeel (MHP, Federation for Middle and Higher Level Personnel) was awarded a single seat on the Sociaal-Economische Raad (SER, Social-Economic Council), these three federations had a complete monopoly on labor's side of the bargaining table in the country's many corporatist bodies. Today they still hold nine of ten seats in the SER because the MHP has never organized more than 8 percent of all workers.[16] This means that throughout the period under investigation here, the industrially organized big three have served as the exclusive voice of labor in all matters concerning the development of protection against labor market risks for workers – and for other members of society.

The distinction between the strong occupational nature of unionism in the United Kingdom and the overall industrial nature of unionism in the Netherlands just analyzed is well described in the industrial relations literature. The origins of this distinction are equally well documented and understood by labor historians.[17] Even many of its consequences are well described. Over the years, many scholars have, for instance, described the different ideological affiliations of British craft and general unions, with the former sometimes leaning toward the liberal end of the political spectrum and the latter displaying a strong socialist orientation.[18] Moreover, the opposition of British craft and occupationally organized white-collar unions to attempts to decrease wage differentials has so often been noted by scholars that it is now textbook knowledge.[19] A similar opposition has been noted by scholars working on

---

[16] See Jelle Visser, "The Netherlands," 481.

[17] For the origins and growth of industrial unionism in the Netherlands, see above. For some excellent works on the origins of "craft unionism" in the United Kingdom, see, for example, Martin Ross, *TUC: The Growth of a Pressure Group, 1886–1976* (Oxford: Clarendon Press); Wolfgang J. Mommsen and Hand-Gerhard Husung, *The Development of Trade Unionism in Great Britain and Germany, 1880–1914* (London: Allen & Unwin, 1985); Fulcher, "On the Explanation"; Robert Taylor, *The TUC: From the General Strike to New Unionism* (Basingstoke: Palgrave, 2000).

[18] Occupationally organized white-collar unions, of course, also do not have a "socialist" identity. On the distinction between "right" and "left" wing unions within the TUC, see, for example, Lewis Minkin, *The Contentious Alliance. Trade Unions and the Labour Party* (Edinburgh University Press, 1991), 429; Routh, "White-Collar Unions," 201–3.

[19] However, this opposition is often written down in such euphemistic terms that one can hardly discern the strength of this opposition. According to Hans Slomp, for example, "[W]age equality has been *of more concern* to the industrial unions, which organize skilled as well as unskilled workers, than to the British craft unions." Compare this with Scase, who argued, "One of the major features of wage bargaining in Britain has been the efforts of specific unions to preserve, if not increase, differentials as they exist between themselves and others." See Hans Slomp, *Between Bargaining and Politics: An Introduction to European Labor* (Westport: Praeger, 1996), 104 (emphasis added); Richard Scase, "Inequality in Two Industrial Societies: Class, Status and

labor relations in the Netherlands, who explained both the low organizational level of white-collar workers and the rise of the MHP there by the aversion of affluent white-collar workers to the wage-leveling tendencies of industrial unions.[20] Finally, several historians working on different countries have noted instances in which unions representing privileged workers resisted attempts to merge their occupationally organized insurance schemes into broader public schemes.[21]

Yet, and possibly because of the strong scholarly tendency to focus on class divisions, these consequences have not made their way into the broader literature on welfare and labor market development. In Chapter 1, I have already described how the dominant research tradition on the development of welfare states views the involvement in this process of labor unions. In other scholarly fields, a similar view can be discerned. Despite the above-mentioned efforts of many British unions to preserve, if not increase, wage differentials between their members and other workers, in much of the literature on industrial relations, labor unions are simply assumed to bring an egalitarian agenda to the bargaining table that includes wage compression among different categories of workers.[22] It is for this reason that differences in wage equality among nations are commonly explained as an outcome of cross-national differences in union

Power in Britain and Sweden." In Richard Scase, *Readings in the Swedish Class Structure* (New York: Pergamon, 1976), 28. For other references that do clearly show the opposition of craft and occupationally organized white-collar unions to attempts to decrease wage differentials, see, for example, Henry Pelling, *A History of British Trade Unionism* (London: Macmillan, 1971), 226; Colin Duncan, *Low Pay: Its Causes, and the Post-war Trade Union Response* (Chichester: Research Studies Press, 1981), 80; Fulcher, "On the Explanation," 252; Minkin, *The Contentious Alliance*, 429; Lowe, *The Welfare State in Britain*, 292; and W. Hamish Fraser, *A History of British Trade Unionism 1700–1998* (Basingstoke: Macmillan, 1999), 196.

[20] See Windmuller, *Labor Relations*, 170; Ger Harmsen and Bob Reinalda, *Voor de bevrijding van de arbeid: beknopte geschiedenis van de Nederlandse vakbeweging* (Nijmegen: SUN, 1975), 404–5; Reinalda, *Bedienden georganiseerd*, 22.

[21] See, for example, Erich Ritter, *Die Stellungnahme der Gewerkschaften zu den Problemen der Sozialversicherung in Deutschland* (Frankfurt: Wertheim, 1933), 51; Hans Günter Hockerts, *Sozialpolitische Entscheidungen im Nachkriegsdeutschland. Allierte und Deutsche Sozialversicherungspolitik* (Stuttgart: Klett-Cotta, 1980), 97; Gottschalk, *The Shadow Welfare State*, 37.

[22] For some references to prominent contributions over the years, see, for example, Peter Swenson, *Fair Shares: Unions, Pay, and Politics in Sweden and West Germany* (Ithaca, NY: Cornell University Press, 1989), 26; John McIlroy, *Trade Unions in Britain Today* (Manchester University Press, 1995), 61; Richard Hyman, *Understanding European Trade Unionism: Between Market, Class and Society* (London: Sage, 2001), 171; David Card, "The Effect of Unions on Wage Inequality in the U.S. Labor Market," *Industrial and Labor Relations Review* 54 (2001), 297; David Metcalf, Kirstine Hansen, and Andy Charlwood, "Unions and the Sword of Justice: Unions and Pay Systems, Pay Inequality, Pay Discrimination and Low Pay," *National Institute Economic Review* 176 (2001), 61; Samuel Bowles, "Egalitarian Redistribution in Globally Integrated Economies." In Pranab Bardhan, Samuel Bowles, and Michael Wallerstein, *Globalization and Egalitarian Redistribution* (New York: Sage, 2006), 147; Pontusson, *Inequality and Prosperity*, 63.

density levels – and rarely as the result of cross-national differences in union structure.[23]

Apparently, the portrayal of labor unions as the natural defenders of the disadvantaged has become so ingrained in the scholarly imagination that scholars often fail to spot obvious signs or flat-out facts that point to the contrary. A very obvious, and important, example of this lies in the ideological commitment of the British labor union movement to voluntarism. Existing studies have explained this commitment in many ways. None of them, however, have done so by pointing to the British labor union movement's particular organizational features and the resulting resistance of a large part of its membership to any attempt to redistribute income among different categories of workers. This resistance naturally has also had important consequences for attempts to provide adequate provision against labor market risks. For this reason, and because traditional voluntarist explanations such as union suspicions of the "bourgeois" state are often used to explain instances of labor union opposition to welfare state development (see also Chapter 7 on this), the next section of this chapter takes a look at the voluntarist inclinations of the British labor union movement. In so doing, it argues that these inclinations cannot be understood without taking into account the opposition of craft and occupationally organized white-collar unions to any attempt to redistribute income between their members and lower-skilled workers. In the following sections I discuss the consequences of this for our understanding of welfare state development.

REVISITING BRITISH VOLUNTARISM

It is a well-known fact that the British labor union movement has historically been quite reluctant to accept government intervention in the labor market.[24] In the literature on industrial relations, the British labor union movement's aversion

---

[23] See, for example, David Rueda and Jonas Pontusson, "Wage Inequality and Varieties of Capitalism," *World Politics* 52:3 (2000), 35; David Card, Thomas Lemieux, and Craig Riddell, "Unions and the Wage Structure." In John T. Addison and C. Schnabel, *International Handbook of Trade Unions* (Cheltenham: Edward Elgard, 2003), 248–92; André Sapir, "Globalization and the Reform of European Social Models," *Journal of Common Market Studies* 44:2 (2006), 375. It is for this reason also that the rising levels of wage inequality that we have seen in most countries since the 1980s are often explained as an outcome of declining union membership. See, for example, David Card, "Falling Union Membership and Rising Wage Inequality: What's the Connection?" *NBER Working Paper No. 6520* (1998); Richard B. Freeman, "How Much Has De-Unionization Contributed to the Rise in Male Earnings Inequality?" In S. Danziger and P. Gottschalk, *Uneven Tides: Rising Inequality in America* (New York: Sage, 1993); John Dinardo, Nicole Fortin, and Thomas Lemieux, "Labor Market Institutions and the Distribution of Wages, 1973–1992: A Semi-Parametric Approach," *Econometrica* 64 (1996), 1001–44; James S. Mosher, "U.S. Wage Inequality, Technological Change, and Decline in Union Power," *Politics and Society* 35:2 (2007), 225–63.

[24] For a much more extensive treatment of this topic, see Dennie Oude Nijhuis, "Explaining British Voluntarism," *Labor History* 52:4 (2011), 373–89.

to government interference in the labor market is known as "its commitment to voluntarism" or "*free* collective bargaining." This commitment has been particularly visible in the area of wage bargaining. The TUC, for example, never lobbied for a statutory extension of collective-bargaining outcomes. For an extremely long time, it resisted the introduction of a statutory national minimum wage. It has always strongly opposed the introduction of a long-term incomes policy and has seldom proven willing to moderate wage demands in exchange for social security expansion. Finally, and as acknowledged by only a few scholars, in comparison with many of its foreign counterparts, it has taken a quite reluctant stance toward major welfare state initiatives.[25] Such remarkably strong opposition to nearly any form of statutory interference with the wage-bargaining process is hard to find in the industrial unions–dominated countries of northwest continental Europe.[26] It can, by contrast, be found in many other countries where occupational divisions are strong. An excellent example of this is the behavior of the largely occupationally organized American Federation of Labor (AFL) during the first half of the twentieth century.[27]

[25] After comparing the TUC's stance on welfare state development during the first decades of the postwar period with that of the Landsorganisationen i Sverige (LO), Hugh Heclo noted that the TUC never pressed for an expansion of earnings-related benefits or played a constructive role in advancing a coherent labor market policy. See Hugh Heclo, *Modern Social Politics in Britain and Sweden: From Relief to Income Maintenance* (New Haven, CT: Yale University Press, 1974), 152. See also Peter Baldwin's earlier mentioned comparison of the involvement of Swedish, Danish, and British unions regarding the introduction of superannuation in his *The Politics of Social Solidarity*.

[26] Among continental European labor union movements, the Swedish LO is probably best known for its voluntarist inclinations. Yet, crucially, and unlike the TUC, the LO never opposed major welfare state initiatives. From the 1970s on, the LO also pushed for several legislative initiatives that were designed to support its solidaristic wage-bargaining aims. Contrary to its British TUC counterpart, the industrially organized LO thus had few difficulties with accepting and defending the redistributive consequences of government intervention in the labor market. On the distinction between the TUC and LO in the area of welfare state development, see Heclo, *Modern Social Politics*, 152; Baldwin, *The Politics of Social Solidarity*, 243, fn. 137; and Scase, *Social Democracy*, 27–38. For LO views on statutory intervention in the 1970s, see, for example, Gøsta Esping-Andersen and Walter Korpi, "Social Policy as Class Politics in Post-War Capitalism: Scandinavia, Austria, and Germany." In John H. Goldthorpe, *Order and Conflict in Contemporary Capitalism* (Oxford: Clarendon Press, 1984), 184; Rudolf Meidner, "Collective Asset Formation Through Wage Earner Funds," *International Labour Review* 120:3 (1981), 303–18; Derek Robinson, *Solidaristic Wage Policy in Sweden* (Paris: OECD, 1974); Walter Korpi, *The Working Class in Welfare Capitalism: Work, Unions and Politics in Sweden* (London: Routledge & Kegan Paul, 1978); Peter Swenson, *Fair Shares*.

[27] According to Alan Flanders, the AFL before the war, as a result of "the ideology of a self-centred craft unionism," displayed voluntarism "at its most extreme." See Allan Flanders, "The Tradition of Voluntarism," *British Journal of Industrial Relations* 12 (1974), 353. Tellingly, its largely industrially organized counterpart, the Congress of Industrial Organizations (CIO), was not known for having such strong voluntarist inclinations. I will return to this distinction in Chapter 7. Other countries with a strong tradition of craft or occupational unionism are also known for their voluntarist systems of industrial relations. In Ireland and Canada, for example, the largely occupationally organized union movements are known for their voluntarist

In the literature on labor markets and welfare state development, the voluntarist inclinations of the TUC, like those of the AFL, are generally explained as a natural outcome of union suspicions toward allowing a potentially hostile government to undermine union functions. Ever since the eminent British law expert Otto Kahn-Freund popularized the term "voluntarism" in the United Kingdom, it has become orthodoxy to believe that any instance of labor union opposition to government interference with the labor market reflected the belief of unions that "what the state has not given the state cannot take away."[28] In another classic work on the "tradition of voluntarism" in the United Kingdom, Allan Flanders noted the popularity of attributing the voluntarist tendencies of the British labor union movement to "the notion that unions have, as it were, lifted themselves into their present position of power and influence by their own unaided efforts in overcoming employer resistance and hostile social forces."[29] More recently, Geoffrey Finlayson explained the voluntarist inclinations of the TUC by arguing, "In working-class memory, the state could well be equated with sinister rather than friendly forces.... There remained a suspicion that the ulterior motive was to hold the working classes in a subordinate position of tutelage."[30] In full accordance with this line of thinking, Chris Howell recently argued that unions come to rely more on the state when they become weaker in terms of organizational strength.[31]

These interpretations of the voluntarist inclinations of the British labor union movement fit neatly into the prevailing class-based view of industrial

---

inclinations as well. It has often been argued that these inclinations are weaker in Australia and New Zealand (where occupational unionism is also strong), but crucially, this is mainly because the union movements there have been more willing to accept arbitration by the courts. Whether the unions representing privileged workers there have also been willing to accept a massive degree of state interference in the labor market with the aim to redistribute income among workers is an entirely different matter. For some references, see, for example, Fred Power and Donal Guerin, *Civil Society and Social Policy: Voluntarism in Ireland* (Dublin: A&A Farmar, 1997); Bob Russell, *Back to Work? Labour, State and Industrial Relations in Canada* (Toronto: Nelson, 1990); Arthur McIvor and Christopher Wright, "Managing Labour: UK and Australian Employers in Comparative Perspective, 1900–50," *Labour History* 88 (May 2005); Muneto Ozaki, *Negotiating Flexibility: The Role of the Social Partners and the State* (Geneva: International Labor Organization, 1999), 68.

[28] Otto Kahn-Freund, "Labour Law." In Morris Ginsburg, *Law and Opinion in England in the Twentieth Century* (London: Steven and Sons), 244.

[29] Flanders, "The Tradition," 355.

[30] Geoffrey Finlayson, *Citizen, State, and Social Welfare in Britain, 1830–1990* (Oxford: Clarendon Press, 1994), 123. See also Paul Edwards et al, "Great Britain: From Partial Collectivism to Neo-Liberalism to Where?" In Ferner and Hyman, *Changing Industrial Relations in Europe*, 4; Chris Howell, "Trade Unions and the State: A Critique of British Industrial Relations," *Politics and Society* 23 (1995), 157; Campbell et al., "The Post-War Compromise," 76–6; Minkin, *The Contentious Alliance*, 429.

[31] See Chris Howell, *Trade Unions and the State: The Construction of Industrial Relations in Britain, 1890–2000* (Princeton, NJ: Princeton University Press, 2005), 17. See also Peter Ackers and Adrian Wilkinson, "British Industrial Relations Paradigm: A Critical Outline History and Prognosis," *Journal of Industrial Relations* 47 (2005), 450.

relations. In this view, the voluntarist inclinations of the British labor union movement were nothing more than the outcome of a natural distrust of a state that had so often proven to side with labor's capitalist enemies. Instead of handing over key union functions to this state, unions were therefore better off relying on their own voluntary associations. At the same time, scholars often present voluntarism as a key survival strategy of the British union movement. They do so by arguing that once unions allow the government to take over key union functions, they might very well find it more difficult to attract workers – an argument that, as we will see, British unions often espouse themselves.[32] Both arguments are, as will be demonstrated in Chapter 7, commonly used to explain the voluntarist tendencies of other labor union movements that are known for their occupational divisions as well.

What are we to make of these explanations? There is certainly some truth in the view that labor unions will, where possible, prefer to "go at it alone" than to turn to the state for help to achieve their goals. It also makes sense that this propensity is at least partly grounded in union anxiety over allowing a potentially hostile state to undermine key union functions – although the emphasis may then very well lie more on their concerns over their ability to attract new workers than on their suspicions of government motives.[33] Yet the issue here is not whether unions have a general propensity to prefer to "go at it alone." Instead, we must strive to explain the British labor union movement's extraordinarily strong opposition to government intervention in the labor market. There are several good reasons to doubt that the explanations put forward earlier can convincingly account for this. Two of these reasons can be established immediately.

One obvious problem is that traditional voluntarist arguments cannot explain why the industrially organized labor union movements of continental Europe have generally been much more willing to accept government intervention in the labor market. This greater willingness cannot be explained, it should be noted, by the argument that unions become more willing to accept government intervention in the labor market when they become weaker in terms of organizational strength. After all, in countries such as Belgium and Sweden, for example, a much higher degree of unionization has coexisted with a much

---

[32] See, for example, Flanders, "The Tradition," 355.

[33] The unsatisfactory nature of the argument that unions will oppose statutory initiatives with which they would otherwise sympathize because of their suspicions of government motives is aptly expressed by the "Trotskyist" union activist Tony Cliff in his response to the unwillingness of John Boyd, leader of the Amalgamated Union of Engineering Workers (AUEW), to support a resolution calling for the introduction of a statutory national minimum wage at the 1973 Labour Party Conference. Cliff condemned Boyd's voluntarist arguments for this, stating, "John Boyd's excuse used at the 1973 Labour Party Conference, that the trade unions opposed on principle government interference with collective bargaining, won't wash – one can oppose anti-working-class laws and still demand the eight-hour day." See Tony Cliff, *The Crisis: Social Contract or Socialism* (London: Pluto Press, 1975), 58–9.

greater willingness to accept government intervention in the labor market.[34] Nor can it be explained by arguing that the continental European labor union movements simply became less suspicious of their governments because the existence of so-called neocorporatist policy-making institutions resulted in a more harmonious state of affairs there.[35] The problem with this line of reasoning is that it might turn the chain of cause and effect upside down. After all, one could argue equally well and arguably much more forcefully that the fragmented nature of the British labor union movement and its commitment to voluntarism stood in the way of the successful development of such institutions in the first place.[36]

[34] In the immediate postwar period, Belgian unions organized some 35 percent of all workers, which was somewhat lower than in the Netherlands at the time. By the late 1970s, however, this percentage had increased to nearly 60 percent. This increase in union density rates has not led to a lesser willingness to accept government interference in the labor market. On the contrary, judging from the flurry of (redistributive) legislation that was passed during the 1960s and 1970s, this willingness only became greater as union density levels increased. See, for example, Hans Slomp, *Arbeidsverhouding-en in België* (Utrecht: Het Spectrum, 1984). On the "neocorporatist" nature of decision making in Belgium, see, for example, Harold L. Wilensky, *Rich Democracies. Political Economy, Public Policy, and Performance* (Berkeley: University of California Press, 2002), 118; Gerhard Lehmbruch, "Concertation and the Structure of Corporatist Networks." In John H. Goldthorpe, *Order and Conflict in Contemporary Capitalism. Studies in the Political Economy of Western European Nations* (Oxford: Clarendon Press, 1984), 66. See this chapter's footnote 26 on Sweden.

[35] Over the years, many scholars have argued that "neocorporatist" policy-making institutions result in a more harmonious state of affairs by stimulating consensus and inclusiveness. See, for example, Philippe Schmitter, "Reflections on Where the Theory of Neo-Corporatism Has Gone and Where the Praxis of Neo-Corporatism May Be Going." In Philippe Schmitter and Gerard Lehmbruch *Patterns of Corporatist Policy Making* (London: Sage, 1982); Lehmbruch, "Concertation," 74; Graham Wilson, *Business and Politics* (Chatham House, 1990); Colin Crouch, *Industrial Relations and European State Traditions* (Oxford University Press, 1993); Robert Putnam, *Making Democracy Work: Civic Traditions in Modern Italy* (Princeton, NJ: Princeton University Press, 1993); Jelle Visser and Anton Hemerijck, *A 'Dutch Miracle': Job Growth, Welfare Reform and Corporatism in the Netherlands* (Amsterdam University Press, 1997), 68. Others have, in contrast, noted the more likely course of events by arguing that the emergence of corporatist modes of decision making, in turn, depended on "responsible" unions and employer interest groups. For this, see, for example, Kenneth D. McRae, "Comment: Federation, Consociation, Corporatism – An Addendum to Arend Lijphart," *Canadian Journal of Political Science*, 12 (1979), 520; Frans van Waarden, "Dutch Consociationalism and Corporatism: A Case of Institutional Persistence," *Acta Politica*, 37 (2002), 53. One comment can be added to this. Earlier I have mentioned that scholars working on "voluntarism" often explain the voluntarist features of the British labor union movement by arguing that the organizational strength of the British unions allowed them to rely on their own voluntary associations. Interestingly, scholars of neocorporatism often explain the "neocorporatist" features of many continental European countries by arguing that this resulted from strong unionism there. See, for example, Hicks, *Social Democracy*; John Goldthorpe, *Order and Conflict in Contemporary Capitalism* (Oxford: Clarendon Press).

[36] For this, see, for example, Peter Dorey, *Wage Politics in Britain: The Rise and Fall of Incomes Policies Since 1945* (Brighton: Sussex Academic Press, 2001), 5; Scase, "Inequality," 28.

Another problem is that the British labor union movement has itself neither been consistent nor united in its opposition to statutory intervention. For starters, and according to Flanders, the TUC has "at times or in areas of industrial weakness [displayed] ... the greatest readiness to resort to the method of legal enactment, either because collective bargaining was unavailable or because its results were unacceptable."[37] Yet, crucially, it hardly ever displayed such readiness to accept government initiatives that related to the important era of wage bargaining, let alone when these had strong redistributive consequences.[38] Moreover, not all British labor unions have always been equally committed to the ideology of voluntarism. Over the years, many scholars have, for example, noted instances in which craft unions representing skilled manual workers were far more resistant to government interference with the wage-bargaining process than were general unions representing unskilled and semiskilled manual workers.[39] Not coincidentally, skilled manual workers have a much stronger position on the labor market than do their unskilled and semiskilled counterparts. Whereas the former are typically quite able to achieve adequate wages and insurance against labor market risks through voluntary bargaining, the latter often can do so only after a redistributive effort from other worker occupations. Crucially, this gives these different groups of workers a decisively different interest in government intervention in the wage-bargaining process.

The differences just described suggest that there may be another explanation for the voluntarist inclinations of the British labor union movement besides the ones we have seen thus far. This explanation begins with the recognition that government intervention in the labor market often has a distinct redistributive aim and nearly always has redistributive consequences. Most important, these redistributive consequences often primarily affect the distribution of income among different categories of workers. This is, as we saw in Chapter 1, obviously the case with public welfare development. It is equally obviously the case with the introduction of a national minimum wage. After all, the introduction of a national minimum wage can only result in net gains to lower-paid workers if at least some of the higher-paid workers are willing to accept a lesser share of the national income or, in other words, are willing to accept some degree of

---

[37] As a result, the TUC has in the past supported legislation aimed at matters such as labor union recognition, the regulation of working hours, and physical conditions of work. Flanders, "The Tradition," 358.

[38] In this respect, it is crucial to note here that when scholars first used the notion of voluntarism to describe the peculiar features of the British industrial relations system, they referred mainly to the area of trade union recognition and to union distrust of courts of law. See, for example, Clegg, *The Changing System*, 3–6. Over the years, however, the notion has come to be used to explain almost any instance of union opposition to government interference in the labor market. Most significantly, the notion is now commonly used to explain union opposition to direct government interference with the wage-bargaining process.

[39] See, for example, Campbell et al., "The Post-War Compromise," 77–8; Clegg, *The Changing System*, 436–7; Fraser, *A History*, 211; Pelling, *A History*, 236.

wage compression. Other examples can be added to this. For instance, even the introduction of a long-term incomes policy aimed at achieving wage moderation often has consequences that affect the distribution of income among different categories of workers. After all, attempts to introduce such incomes policies are often accompanied by low-pay provisions that allow the wages of lower-paid workers to rise somewhat faster than those of higher-paid workers.[40]

Once we realize these consequences for the distribution of income among different groups of workers and acknowledge that labor unions do not necessarily favor redistributive efforts between workers, then the historic commitment of the British labor union movement to voluntarism can be understood as the outcome of its organizational features as well. An excellent way to illustrate this is by looking at the TUC's long-standing opposition to the introduction of a statutory national minimum wage. From the last decades of the prewar period all the way up to the mid-1980s, the TUC consistently opposed statutory attempts to introduce a general wage floor in the United Kingdom. In the two decades following the late 1960s, the TUC strongly disagreed with its main political ally, the Labour Party, over this. It was not until Labour dropped its already loose commitment to the introduction of a statutory national minimum wage from its campaign documents in the mid-1980s that the TUC General Council first carefully signaled its willingness to accept statutory intervention. In addition, and contrary to most of its European counterparts, the TUC also never lobbied for a statutory extension of collective-bargaining outcomes – which in many European countries came to be seen as a functional equivalent to the introduction of a statutory national minimum wage.[41]

The TUC's strong and long-standing opposition to statutory intervention in these areas goes a long way toward explaining why the United Kingdom was the only European country that up to the introduction of the 1998 National Minimum Wage Act did not have a common floor for wage levels. It did have so-called wages councils that aimed to set minimum wages in a limited number

---

[40] In the debate on Britain's failure to achieve continental-style incomes policies, the opposition of unions representing privileged workers against any attempt to decrease wage differentials has not received the attention it deserves. On the contrary, rather than viewing its potentially leveling effect on wage differentials as a matter that could complicate attempts to achieve union support for wage moderation, scholars have argued that "the injection of notions of equity and fairness and of low pay provisions into recent incomes policies was part of some deceitful ploy instituted by governments with the sole aim of achieving wage restraint." They have argued this despite abundant evidence that the opposition of craft unions to ongoing attempts to achieve wage restraint during the late 1940s was at least partly motivated by their aversion to its declining effect on wage differentials with unskilled workers. For the quote, see Colin Duncan, *Low Pay*, 89. For the latter, see Dorey, *Wage Politics*, 31; Pelling, *A History*, 226.

[41] On this, see, for instance, Rodger Charles, S. J., The *Development of Industrial Relations in Britain 1911–1939: Studies in the Evolution of Collective Bargaining at National and Industry Level* (London: Hutchinson, 1973), 67–69, 106, 204–6; Frank Tillyard and William A. Robson, "The Enforcement of the Collective Bargain in the United Kingdom," *The Economic Journal* 48:189 (1938), 15–25.

of industries. Yet, on the whole, these councils were quite ineffective.[42] All other European countries introduced either statutory minimum wages during the first decades of the postwar period or functional equivalents made possibly by very high collective-bargaining levels. Whereas Finland, Denmark, Switzerland, Germany, and Austria managed to set up effective equivalents by extending collective-bargaining agreements through statutory means, Norway and Sweden have relied exclusively on their very high union (and employer) membership levels to achieve this.[43] Either way, all these countries have been far more successful in addressing the problem of poverty in employment than the United Kingdom has been.[44]

---

[42] For starters, these wages councils were limited to only a number of industries. In the industries in which they were active, they typically set compulsory minimum wage levels that ranged from a mere 30 to 45 percent of the average wage. Often this dismally low level could only be achieved after working overtime. The reason for this was that employers were only liable to pay a minimum remuneration rate, which meant that they could pay a lower hourly rate if bonuses, piece rates, or other emoluments brought it up to required minimum remuneration. Also, many employers were illegally underpaying even these very low minimum remuneration rates. See Chris Pond and Steve Winyard, *The Case for a National Minimum Wage* (London: Low Pay Unit, 1984), 20–9. According to the TUC, employers found it so easy to undercut the minimum wage levels set by the wages councils because fewer than 10 percent of premises were inspected each year, and an overwhelming majority of inspections examined only major companies, whereas it was smaller firms who most often paid less than the wages councils' minima. MRC, MSS.292B/116/1: LPWP 6/2, Collective bargaining, January 27, 1970. Finally, it should be noted that most industries were not covered by wages councils and thus lacked minimum pay rates altogether. Most workers who were classified as "low paid" were therefore not covered by wages councils. See Juan Dolado et al., "Minimum Wages in Europe," *Economic Policy* (October 1996), 353.

[43] For an overview of statutory national minimum wages in Europe, see Lothar Funk and Hagen Lesch, "Minimum Wage Regulations in Selected European Countries," *Intereconomics* 41:2 (2006), 78–92. For an overview of collective-bargaining rates, see Roger Blanpain, *Collective Bargaining and Wages in Comparative Perspective: Germany, France, the Netherlands, Sweden and the United Kingdom* (The Hague: Kluwer, 2005).

[44] To a great extent this can be explained by the much higher levels of wage inequality in the United Kingdom compared with these countries. For some excellent comparisons of the ability of European countries to address the problem of poverty in employment, see Stephen Bazen, Mary Gregory, and Wiemer Salverda, *Low-Wage Employment in Europe* (Cheltenham: Elgar, 1998); Eurostat, *Poverty in Figures: Europe in the Early 1980s* (Luxembourg, Eurostat, 1990). For an overview of comparative levels of wage inequality over the years, see, for example, Jonas Pontusson, "Labor Market Institutions and Wage Distribution." In Torben Iversen, Jonas Pontusson, and David W. Soskice, *Unions, Employers, and Central Banks. Macroeconomic Coordination and Institutional Change in Social Market Economies* (Cambridge University Press, 2000); Michael Wallerstein, "Wage-Setting Institutions and Pay Inequality in Advanced Industrial Societies," *American Journal of Political Science* 43:3 (1999), 649–80. As in the United Kingdom, but to a much lesser extent, both wage inequality and poverty levels have been on the rise in many of the above-mentioned countries. This has resulted in a debate over the need to introduce a statutory minimum wage in many of these countries. In Germany, most unions now support this. See, for example, Gerhard Bosch, *Low-Wage Work in Germany* (New York: Sage, 2008).

It is this latter feature that makes the TUC's long-standing opposition to the introduction of a statutory national minimum wage so puzzling at first sight. By at least the 1960s, and probably long before, the TUC General Council realized quite well that voluntary bargaining was doing little to improve matters for Britain's lowest-paid workers. It also realized that the problem of poverty in employment was not merely the result of low levels of worker organization in certain industries but instead had much to do with the highly unequal wage structure that persisted in the United Kingdom – especially in the lower half of the wage distribution.[45] This meant that the existing wages councils system was, by definition, inadequate to deal with the problem of poverty in employment. After all, it was merely designed to prevent "sweating" in sectors where worker organization was weak or absent. Yet, and although the General Council realized all this very well, it nevertheless continued to oppose the introduction of a statutory national minimum wage for another two decades.

Over the years, many scholars have attempted to explain the TUC's long-standing opposition to the introduction of a statutory national minimum wage. Nearly all of them have attempted to do so by focusing on traditional voluntarist explanations. The explanation set forth most frequently is that Britain's unions feared that its introduction would undermine their function and interfere with their ability to attract new workers.[46] Another common explanation cites union suspicions of government motives or, when Labour was in power, bad relations with the government. According to low-pay experts Chris Pond and Steve Winyard, for example, it was "not difficult to see why the TUC came out so strongly against a statutory NMW [national minimum wage].... Its relationship with the Labour Government deteriorated sharply towards the end of the 1960s.... This, together with a long tradition of 'voluntarism', made it extremely unlikely that any increase in government involvement in the wage determination would be accepted."[47] Other explanations for the TUC's

---

[45] For the TUC's realization of this, see MRC, MSS.292B/116/1: LPWP 6/1: Extent of and reasons for low pay, January 27, 1970.

[46] According to Lewis Minkin, for example, "For years the tradition of free collective bargaining and anxiety over a possible undermining of union functions had been major obstacles to the Movement's support for a statutory minimum wage." See Minkin, *The Contentious Alliance*, 429. In alignment with this view, Chris Howell noted that statutory national minimum wage "may possibly weaken unions because workers can make gains through legislation rather than collective action." See Howell, *Trade Unions and the State*, 181. See also Howard Gospel and Gill Palmer, *British Industrial Relations* (London: Routledge, 1994), 208; David Metcalf, "The British National Minimum Wage," *British Journal of Industrial Relations* 37:2 (1999), 172; George Sayers Bain, "The Minimum Wage: Further Reflections," *Employee Relations* 21:1 (1999), 15–28; Michael Terry, *Redefining Public Sector Unionism: UNISON and the Future of Trade Unions* (London: Routledge, 2000), 157; and Jerold L. Waltman, *Minimum Wage Policy in Great Britain and the United States* (New York: Algora, 2008), 71–7.

[47] Pond and Winyard, *The Case*, 36; Jill Rubery and Paul Edwards, "Low Pay and the National Minimum Wage." In Paul K. Edwards, *Industrial Relations: Theory and Practice* (Oxford: Blackwell, 2003), 460.

opposition to the statutory national minimum wage have focused on union fears that such an introduction would put a ceiling on wage increases or would be meaningless because "the trade union movement had no guarantee that governments would either introduce or establish a minimum at a level acceptable to the unions."[48]

These explanations all overlook another, and arguably much more important, reason for the TUC's long-standing opposition to the introduction of a statutory minimum wage. This reason was the strong antiredistributive stance of its powerful occupationally organized union affiliates. The introduction of a statutory national minimum wage – like any attempt to improve the relative wages for the lowest paid – potentially has severe consequences for the distribution of income among different groups of workers, especially for those within the manual worker category. These consequences are likely to be far more important in motivating occupationally organized unions to oppose statutory intervention than suspicions of government motives or fears that this would undermine their ability to attract new workers – especially because they do not organize large groups of low-paid workers in the first place.[49] After all, these consequences are in direct conflict with their main organizational purpose, which is to preserve and, if possible, to increase the occupational wage differential of their members with lower-skilled and thus lower-paid workers.

This alternative view is certainly reinforced by the long period of TUC apathy toward the problem of poverty in employment. During the first two decades of the postwar period, the General Council devoted little attention to this problem. In fact, and although quite aware of its seriousness, it did not even institute a separate work group to address the problem of low pay in this period.[50] On several occasions during the postwar period, individual unions brought forward motions urging the General Council to express its support for the introduction of a statutory national minimum wage. The first of these was submitted in 1946 by the National Union of Vehicle Builders (NUVB), a union that organized many low-paid workers who were not covered by wages councils. The motion carried substantial support but was not endorsed by the General Council. In the end, it was rejected by a majority of 3,522,000 to

---

[48] Sheila Blackburn, "The Problem of Riches: From Trade Boards to a National Minimum Wage," *Industrial Relations Journal* 51:2 (1988), 131. See also Stephen Keevash, "Wages Councils: An Examination of Trade Union and Conservative Misconceptions About the Effect of Statutory Wage Fixing," *Industrial Law Journal* 14:1 (1985), 217–32; Sheila Blackburn, *A Fair for a Fair Day's Work? Sweated Labour and the Origins of Minimum Wage Legislation in Britain* (Aldershot: Ashgate, 2007), 189.

[49] Because craft unions exclusively organize skilled manual workers, they tend not to represent workers in the lowest deciles of the wage distribution – unless they are active in low-paid industries. An excellent example of such a union was the National Union of Tailor and Garment Workers (NUTGW), which was one of the few craft unions to support the introduction of a statutory national minimum wage in the 1980s.

[50] Duncan, *Low Pay*, 25.

2,657,000 votes. Despite strong General Council opposition to each of them, similar resolutions brought forward in subsequent years generally could count on a fairly stable minority of over a third and just below half of all union representatives. During each of these votes, skill and collar cleavages played an important role.[51]

From the start, then, British labor union views on the introduction of a statutory national minimum wage were highly divided. To some extent, this division may have reflected different views on the consequences of statutory intervention for union organization or the preferred role of government in collective bargaining. Yet, to a great degree, it also reflected the very different attitudes of various unions toward the redistributive consequences of its introduction. This became abundantly clear in the late 1940s when the most consistent opponents of statutory intervention, the craft unions, rallied against Labour's postwar incomes policy. According to the General Council, these unions did so primarily because they were discontent with the reduction in the manual wage differential that had taken place during the war. As a result, it realized the political impossibility of doing something "extra" for the low paid and supported the TUC Congress's recommendation to "recognize the need to safeguard those wage differentials which are an essential element in the wages structure of many important industries, and are required to sustain those standards of craftsmanship, training and experience that contribute directly to industrial efficiency and higher productivity."[52] In subsequent years, Britain's craft unions eagerly set out to restore lost differentials. These efforts were to be quite successful.[53]

Given the strong defense of the occupational wage differential by Britain's craft unions, it is not hard to see why the first serious thinking on the introduction of a statutory national minimum wage came from the Labour Party – and not from the TUC General Council. When Labour came to power in 1964, it immediately considered the introduction of a statutory national minimum wage as a solution for Britain's low-pay problem. Yet it also realized that its introduction could only improve matters for lower-paid workers if wage differentials could be compressed. After all, and as pointed out by a Labour working party on the issue, "profit margins of employers can only be squeezed so far" before they had to "pass costs on to consumers."[54] Thus, unless wages could be compressed in the long term, the minimum wage would only "cause inflation

[51] Campbell, Fishman, and McIlroy, "The Postwar Compromise," 77–8.

[52] MRC, MSS.292/110.44/2b: Special Committee on the economic situation, report of a meeting with the Chancellor of the Exchequer, the Foreign Secretary, and the Minister of Health, 14 November 1949, 6. See also ibidem, 22 November 1949, 2. TUC, *Report of the Proceedings of the 80th Annual Trades Union Congress* (London: September 1948), 290.

[53] See Pond, "Low Pay," 1–10.

[54] PRO, Lab 10/2149: Working party on a national minimum wage, draft report, 31 December 1964.

by starting a wage round that would raise the whole earnings structure."[55] Given their experience with past craft union behavior, Labour's wage experts were quite skeptical as to whether such compression was possible.[56] As a result, the new Labour government first attempted to obtain TUC support for a voluntary incomes policy that only allowed wage increases for the lowest paid. In addition, it aimed to improve matters for lower-paid workers by increasing family allowances, improving housing, and introducing school meals.

It was only when Labour realized the limits of a voluntary approach that it approached the TUC on its intention to introduce a statutory national minimum wage. When TUC officials consequently consulted their main affiliates on the issue, they soon noticed how divided these groups were. As had been the case in the late 1940s, this division strongly correlated with skill cleavages. Whereas the General and Municipal Workers' Union (GMWU), for example, expressed strong support for a statutory minimum, craft unions such as the Iron and Steel Trades Confederation (ISTC) stated their fear that this would "retard progress in improving the wages of those workers whose earnings were above the statutory minimum." White-collar unions such as the National Association of Local Government Officers (NALGO), whose members were generally also well off, added to this that "wage negotiation was a field in which statutory interference could not be tolerated."[57]

Why did unions such as the ISTC and NALGO oppose the introduction of a statutory national minimum wage so strongly? Because these unions often did not even allow low-paid (officially, "unskilled") workers as members, one could hardly argue that their opposition stemmed from fears that a statutory minimum would undermine a key union function and with that their ability to attract new workers. The real reason, then, lay in their opposition to the potential consequences of its introduction for wage differentials between their members and lower-paid workers. The ISTC made this abundantly clear when it justified its opposition by citing the strong opposition of its membership to a suggestion made by employers "some years ago" to concentrate wage increases on the low paid. To introduce a statutory national minimum wage, ISTC officials argued, would have the same effect, because this would "retard progress in improving the wages of those workers whose earnings were above the statutory national minimum." The Civil and Public Services Association (CPSA) justified its opposition even more clearly by arguing that its "membership was unwilling to sacrifice the maximum rate in any contraction of increment scales in order to help those at the lower levels, essentially because many of those at the top felt low paid themselves."[58]

[55] PRO, Lab 10/2228: Draft report working party on a national minimum wage, 22 February 1965.
[56] PRO, Lab 10/2162: Working party on national minimum wage, minutes of the first meeting, 26 May 1964; MRC, MSS.292B/110.44/1: Incomes, costs and prices, 11 December 1963.
[57] MRC, MSS.292B/115.4/3: Low pay: Further appraisal in the light of union comments, annex: summary of union comments, 10 June 1970.
[58] Ibidem.

In the face of such strong opposition from a large and powerful part of its membership, the TUC General Council had no choice but to oppose Labour's plans for the introduction of a statutory national minimum wage. One reason for this was surely that it did not want to alienate its more privileged membership. But another consideration has to be mentioned as well. Since unions representing relatively affluent workers opposed the introduction of a statutory national minimum wage mainly because of its redistributive consequences, they would surely attempt to undo any decrease in wage differentials resulting from its introduction by demanding higher wage increases during future negotiations. The General Council was well aware of this, and an internal note on the subject summed up its consequences quite neatly: "The problem is that simply raising basic rates may raise the wages of all workers by a proportionate amount; this general effect will limit the amount that can be allocated to the lower-paid in the sense that there is an overall limit on what firms can afford to pay without raising prices. If they do raise prices, this will have a disproportionately adverse affect on the real incomes of the lowest paid workers in the economy in general."[59] Under these circumstances, the introduction of a statutory minimum wage would not only be "costly," but it would also have little effect because "differentials would be rigidly maintained and ... prices increased to an extent that would wipe out the effects of the initial increase in low payment incomes."[60]

To be sure, TUC officials also noted the possibility that statutory intervention might have an adverse effect on labor union organization. Yet they did not consider this to be a major problem for two reasons. First, they realized very well that several decades of voluntary bargaining had done little to improve matters for this group. As noted in an internal report by the newly founded low-pay working group, low organization levels alone could hardly explain the persistence of low pay, especially since roughly half of the lowest paid occupations could be found in highly unionized sectors.[61] Second, TUC officials were by no means convinced that the introduction of a statutory national minimum wage would make it more difficult to recruit low-paid workers in the first place. On the contrary, if its introduction could take place in steps, the Low Pay Committee argued in its final report on the issue, it would most likely be seen as an outcome of union efforts.[62] The committee did agree with the General Council that the introduction of a statutory national minimum wage could not work when differentials were to be rigidly maintained. It consequently also had grave doubts about the council's suggestion to set unilateral declarations on what it deemed to be adequate minimum wage levels in various industries.

[59] MRC, MSS.292B/116/1: LPWP 6/2, Collective bargaining, 27 January 1970.
[60] MRC, MSS.292B/116/1: LPWP 4/3, 2 December 1969; MRC, MSS.292B/115.4/3: Low pay, further appraisal in the light of union comments, 8 July 1970.
[61] MRC, MSS.292B/116/1: LPWP 6/1, Extent of and reasons for low pay, 27 January 1970.
[62] MRC, MSS.292B/115.4/3: Low pay: Report, 11 February 1970.

After all, even if such wage targets would result in "some employers paying more, it would hardly result in any trade unions asking for less."[63]

Once the TUC spoke out firmly against the introduction of a statutory national minimum wage, the Labour government decided to drop it. Its awareness of the rigid attachment to preserving wage differentials played a major role in this. In 1969, a government working group published a green paper in which it advised against the introduction of a national minimum wage "through statutory means." According to the working group, the costs of a statutory national minimum wage would depend on the repercussions on the earnings of those who were not lower paid. While the green paper did not contain an exact estimate of these costs, it did point out that "manual workers' differentials have been remarkably stable over the last eighty years."[64] Table 2.1 shows that this statement was no exaggeration: while having made small gains in the first decade following on the onset of World War II (during the 1940s, "flat rate" or equal absolute increases for all workers, which had the effect of narrowing pay differentials, were quite prevalent; during the 1950s, percentage increases again became the norm), the lowest-paid workers were actually worse off in 1982 than they had been in 1886 in terms of their share of the pretax income distribution among manual workers.[65] It should be noted that there is little reason to assume that pay differentials between different categories of white-collar workers followed a different pattern in this period.[66]

In following years, the introduction of a statutory national minimum wage remained an official policy stance of the Labour Party. But this did not result in concrete actions when it returned to power in 1974. The unremitting opposition of the TUC and Labour's awareness of the implications of the insistence of a large part of the labor union movement on maintaining wage differentials played a crucial role in this. Even though internal reports such as those of

---

[63] MRC, MSS.292B/115.4/3: Low pay: Report, 11 February 1970.

[64] Department of Employment and Productivity, *A National Minimum Wage: An Inquiry* (London: HMSO, 1969), 5.

[65] Although corresponding figures for the Netherlands are scarce, it is clear that the variation in manual wages in the Netherlands has decreased substantially during the postwar period. See footnote 88 of this chapter on this. As a result of the statistical efforts of the LO, corresponding figures do exist for Sweden. There the industrially organized LO managed to reduce the total variance in manual relative wages between 1960 and 1980 by a whopping 75 percent. By 1983, the manual wage distribution had become so compressed in Sweden that a relative wage increase of only around 30 percent was enough to carry a worker from the lowest decile of the manual wage distribution all the way to the highest. In comparison, a similar move in the United Kingdom would have required a relative increase of over 200 percent. See Douglas A. Hibbs and Hakan Locking, "Wage Dispersion and Productive Efficiency: Evidence for Sweden," *Journal of Labor Economics* 18:4 (2000), 756.

[66] For an overview of wage differentials among different occupational categories in Britain, see, for example, David Marsden, "Have Pay Systems Become More Flexible in Europe in the 1980s?" In Alan Gladstone and Hyot N. Wheeler, *Labour Relations in a Changing Environment* (Berlin: Walter de Gruyter, 1992), 60.

TABLE 2.1. *Dispersion of Weekly Earnings of Full-Time Male Manual Workers in the United Kingdom, 1886–1982*

Year	Percent Median Lowest Decile	Percent Median Lowest Quartile	Percent Median Upper Quartile	Percent Median Highest Decile
1886	68.6	82.8	121.7	143.1
1906	66.5	79.5	126.7	156.8
1938	67.7	82.1	121.7	145.2
1960	70.6	82.6	121.7	145.2
1970	67.3	81.1	122.3	147.5
1982	68.3	81.8	123.5	152.6

Sources: Chris Pond (1981) "Low Pay – 1980s Style," *Low Pay Review* 4 (1981), 1–10; Chris Pond and Steve Winyard, *The Case for a National Minimum Wage* (London: LPU, 1984).

the Low Pay Committee had been quite clear about the limitations of voluntary action in solving the problem of low pay, the TUC General Council merely starting setting minimum wage targets. Some TUC affiliates – in particular, the general unions – continued to lobby for the introduction of a statutory national minimum wage at the yearly meetings of the TUC Congress. Yet this also merely resulted in calls for the introduction of a national minimum through voluntary means.[67]

Given their own skepticism over the claim that statutory intervention might have an adverse effect on labor union organization, it is interesting to note that TUC officials often resorted to traditional voluntarist arguments to defend their opposition to statutory intervention. One wonders whether many of these arguments were not simply offered out of convenience. Some Labour government representatives certainly seemed to have thought so. When TUC officials argued, for instance, that the introduction of a statutory national minimum wage would be disastrous for collective bargaining for low-paid workers, Labour representatives knew this argument to be invalid because collective bargaining had done nothing to improve the position of lower-paid workers in the last thirty years.[68] When TUC officials much later argued that a statutory national minimum wage might make it more difficult to recruit lower-paid workers, Labour representatives were equally unimpressed. To them, the experience with the wages councils had already shown that this did not have to be the case.[69]

The TUC did eventually come to support the introduction of a statutory national minimum wage. In 1986, a TUC Congress successfully passed a vote

[67] MRC, MSS.292D/160.11/3: Joint Policy Committee, 22 July 1985
[68] MRC, MSS292D/160.31/2: Social Policy Sub-Committee, 7 October 1976.
[69] MRC, MSS.292D/160.11/3: Joint Policy Committee on Poverty, Social Security and Taxation, 22 July 1985.

on this for the first time since 1924.[70] It is hard to say why a majority of labor union members now proved willing to consider its introduction. Existing explanations for this have focused on various factors, ranging from leadership changes in key unions to the continual erosion of the wages councils.[71] The latter explanation certainly seems to have some merit. Yet organized labor's dissatisfaction with the wages council system goes all the way back to the immediate postwar period, and Conservative governments have acted to curb their functioning since at least the early 1970s.[72] This makes it unlikely that union dissatisfaction with the wages council system alone explains the TUC's change of heart on the minimum wage issue. It is likely that other developments also played a role in this. One such development could have been the strong organizational decline of the major opponents of the introduction of a statutory national minimum wage, the TUC's craft union affiliates.[73]

Whatever the reasons, it should be noted that it still required "some adroit work by the TUC staff to create a majority at the Congress" because many unions remained staunchly opposed to the introduction of a statutory national minimum wage. Tensions within the labor union movement over the issue apparently ran so high that when the General Council finally did manage to agree on it in the context of an incomes policy, the Labour Party turned it down as undeliverable.[74] Among the unions that were still opposed to the introduction of a statutory national minimum wage were the usual craft suspects, such as the Electrical, Electronic, Telecommunications and Plumbing Union (EETPU), which complained of having been "bounced towards acquiescence" on the issue.[75] Many white-collar unions such as NALGO also continued to oppose the introduction of a statutory national minimum wage. By contrast, most general and industrial unions supported statutory intervention.[76]

The only major general union that initially had its doubts was the Transport and General Workers' Union (TGWU). The hesitation on the part of the TGWU leadership seems to have been the result of a genuine concern that statutory interference might undermine its ability to attract new workers.[77] Yet, crucially, this did not stop it from supporting the introduction of a statutory national minimum wage in the end – just as it had supported its introduction in previous

[70] See Roger Bowlby, "Union Policy Toward Minimum Wage Legislation in Postwar Britain," *Industrial and labor Relations Review* 11:1 (1957), 72.
[71] See, respectively, Minkin, *The Contentious*, 429; and Metcalf, "The British," 172.
[72] On this, see, for instance, Waltman, *Minimum Wage*, 73–5.
[73] For the declining share of the total union membership held by Britain's craft unions, see See Ebbinghaus and Waddington, "United Kingdom/Great Britain," 739.
[74] See Minkin, *The Contentious Alliance*, 430–1.
[75] Ibidem, 411.
[76] For a list of union supporters and opponents, see MRC, MSS.292D/116/6: Public Services Committee, Low pay in the public services, 5 July 1983; Ibidem, TUC Economic Committee, Low pay, 11 May 1983.
[77] See, for example, Terry, *Redefining Public Sector Unionism*, 158.

years. Other general and industrial unions such as the NUR and National Union of Public Employees (NUPE), which both organized many low-paid workers, specifically argued against the view that a statutory national minimum wage would undermine their ability to attract workers. During discussions in the General Council, NUPE representative Rodney Bickerstaffe "could not believe that powerful unions were going to be undermined by a minimum of the kind envisaged." He also pointed out that "traditional union methods had not prevented the lower paid from suffering."[78]

Craft unions such as the EETPU, by contrast, motivated their opposition by arguing that "no amount of playing with words should disguise" that "proposals for a national minimum wage are ... one of a redistributionist trend."[79] It went on to warn that this would "discourage the taking on of skills which was so necessary for a prosperous economy."[80] Other craft unions resorted to similar arguments to voice their opposition.[81] They also warned that they would seek to reverse any resulting reductions in wage differentials that their members might experience. During the 1990s, the EETPU's successor, the Amalgamated Engineering and Electrical Union (AEEU), repeated this threat.[82] The events surrounding the introduction of a minimum wage illustrate that this was still a very powerful tool to influence events.

When the introduction of a statutory national minimum wage finally became possible after the election of New Labour in 1997, many commentators noted that its hourly rate was set well below both the level demanded by some unions and the level promised by Labour when it was still in opposition. During the early 1990s, the Labour Party had committed itself to a minimum wage that equaled half of average male earnings, a percentage that was to increase to two-thirds over the years. When the statutory national minimum wage finally came into effect in April 1998, its level was between 43 and 46 percent of average male earnings.[83] This lower level, and Labour's refusal to allow for an automatic yearly increase of the hourly rate, drew protests from several unions.[84] Yet, given the rigid attachment of unions such as the AEEU to existing wage differentials, it is hard to see how a much higher rate could have been feasible. It seems hard to disagree with David Metcalf's assessment that this change in policy resulted from Labour's concern that a level equaling half of male earnings would "have serious adverse economic effects" and its

---

[78] MRC, MSS.292D/116/8: General council minutes, 23 July 1986.
[79] MRC, MSS.292D/116/8: Fair wages strategy, 21 May, 1986.
[80] MRC, MSS.292D/116/8: General council minutes, 23 July 1986; MRC, MSS.292D/116/6: TUC Economic Committee, Low pay, 11 May 1983; Ibidem: Public Services Committee, Low pay in the public services, 5 July 1983.
[81] MRC, MSS.292D/116/8: Letter from the engineers' and managers' association, 9 June 1986.
[82] See Dorey, *Wage Politics*, 222.
[83] See Metcalf, "The British National Minimum Wage," 179.
[84] On this, see Dorey, *Wage Politics*, 221; Metcalf, "The British National Minimum Wage," 173; and Fraser, *A History*, 253.

belief that it "would be a political and economic mistake to allow the level of the minimum wage to be determined in a way that took no account of wider economic and social circumstances, such as employment levels and *income distribution*."[85]

SHAPING SOLIDARITY: UNION STRUCTURE AND THE REPRESENTATION OF WORKERS' INTERESTS

The preceding account of the TUC's long-standing opposition to the intro-duction of a statutory national minimum wage served mainly to illustrate how the insistence of a powerful section of the British labor union movement on maintaining wage differentials complicated attempts to improve the earn-ings of lower-paid workers in the United Kingdom. Since labor's share of the national income is to a very large extent fixed by economic conditions that are beyond its exclusive control, efforts to improve matters for lower-paid workers must involve a redistributive effort between different grades of workers. The most obvious way to do so is by reducing wage differentials. Yet, in the United Kingdom, powerful craft and other occupationally organized unions opposed any attempt to compress wages between their members and lower-skilled or otherwise lower-graded workers.

By complicating attempts to improve the relative wages of lower-paid work-ers, the resistance of these unions to wage compression also indirectly made it more difficult to provide adequate social protection from labor market risks for less-affluent workers. This difficulty arose in many ways. Resistance to wage compression, for instance, made it more difficult for lower-paid workers to finance adequate social protection against risks such as unemployment and sickness or to save for old age. It also made it more difficult to set minimum benefit levels that comfortably exceeded relative poverty levels because these benefits then exceeded the wages of workers who earned an income that was below the official poverty level. In 1981, according to the Low Pay Committee, nearly 16 percent of all male manual workers aged eighteen and over earned an income that was lower than what they would have received if they had been enrolled in the supplementary benefit program (the official social assistance program at this time). This figure would have jumped to 26 percent if overtime pay were excluded.[86] This clearly compelled policy makers to be conservative in setting social assistance levels. It also led to the introduction of a "wage stop"

---

[85] Metcalf, "The British National Minimum Wage," 173 (emphasis added). The Low Pay Commission, which was established to advise the government on the subject in 1998, was also quite clear on this: "[A] major consideration in making our recommendations was that the National Minimum Wage should be set at a level which limited the reassertion of pay differen-tials by higher workers." Low Pay Commission, *The National Minimum Wage: The Story So Far. Second Report of the Low Pay Commission* (London: CMN 4571, 2000), 21.

[86] See Chris Pond, "Low Pay – 1980s Style," *Low Pay Review* 4 (1981), 8.

for beneficiaries with large families whose social assistance income exceeded their previous wage too comfortably.[87]

At the same time, the resistance of craft and occupationally organized white-collar unions to any attempt to reduce wage differentials between their members and other workers also complicated efforts to provide adequate social protection for all workers in a more direct way. After all, when a segment of the union movement consistently opposes any attempt to reduce wage differentials between its members and other workers, it will also oppose any welfare initiative that results in risk redistribution or the creation of a redistributive contributory system. Yet, without some degree of risk or income redistribution, efforts to provide adequate social protection for all members of society cannot succeed. In the remainder of this chapter I will examine the consequences of this.

In the mid-1960s, shortly after the TUC General Council first came out against the introduction of a statutory national minimum wage, the council received a letter from Sir Lincoln Evans, formerly the general secretary of the craft union ISTC and now spokesman for the Save the Occupational Pension (STOP) action group. STOP's purpose was to prevent the introduction of the so-called Crossman scheme, a government pension plan that aimed to improve matters for the roughly 50 percent of Britain's working population that did not belong to a private pension scheme and could thus look forward only to the dismally low state pension after retirement. In his letter, Sir Evans stated that "the TUC recently declared against a legal minimum wage on the ground that it was not the business of the state to usurp the functions of the trade unions. In this its instinct was right. But if this view applies to wages, it applies with equal force to occupational pensions, which are part of the parcel of the conditions of employment, often involving considerable deductions from wages and salaries."[88] Evans ended his letter by urging the TUC to reject the Crossman scheme – just as many of its members had already done.

It is possible, of course, that Evans argued against the Crossman scheme only because of an ideological aversion to state interference with the domain of industrial relations. After all, the resistance of occupationally organized unions representing privileged workers to any redistributive welfare initiative is often defended through traditional voluntarist arguments – both by welfare state scholars and by these unions themselves.[89] Yet given the fact that the

---

[87] Under social assistance, a low-paid worker could receive more in assistance benefits then he previously earned in wages – especially when he had a large family and was therefore entitled to family supplements. To solve this problem, the entitlements of workers were subject to a "wage stop," which meant that his social assistance benefit could never exceed his previous wage. In 1966, a Labour government introduced a "wage stop" into the social insurance system as well. I will return to this at length in Chapter 4.

[88] MRC, MSS.292B/161.51/2: TUC, Letter from Sir Lincoln Evans from Save the Occupational Pension (STOP), 13 March 1970.

[89] Earlier we already saw that British unions often used traditional voluntarist arguments to explain their opposition to redistributive state intervention in the labor market. For some good

unions that represented many workers without membership of private pension schemes all supported the Crossman scheme, this is highly unlikely. The
opposition of STOP to the Crossman scheme more likely resulted from an
aversion to its redistributive features – an issue to which I will return at length
in Chapter 3.

For the Labour Party, which had produced the Crossman scheme, the actions
of STOP presented an uncomfortable truth. Just as the problem of poverty in
employment in the United Kingdom could not be solved without higher-paid
workers having to accept a lower share of the national income, so could many
lower-paid workers not obtain an adequate – or above-subsistence – income in
old age without a redistributive effort from higher-paid workers. Yet, as Evans'
letter made abundantly clear, the unions that resisted any attempt to compress
wages also had little inclination to accept the redistributive implications of the
Crossman scheme. As we will see in the following chapters, they also resisted
most of Labour's proposals to improve the financial security of less-affluent
workers against the risks of unemployment, sickness, and disability.

The case of STOP's opposition to the Crossman scheme neatly illustrates the
problem with the current scholarly tendency to emphasize union strength. It is
clearly wrong to focus only on union density when the union movement is itself
thoroughly divided on issues of welfare and wage setting. When the Crossman
scheme was put forward, British unions organized more workers than they had
ever done before. Yet this was of little help to the Labour government that
attempted to implement the scheme. On the contrary, most of the growth in
union membership was accounted for by occupationally organized white-collar
unions, which, together with many of their craft counterparts, strongly resisted
the Crossman scheme. Instead of focusing on union density rates, then, we have
to examine possible divisions within the labor union movement. The critical
issue here is whether and to what degree unions are willing to support, or strive
for, a redistributive effort between different grades of workers. In the United
Kingdom, and as we will see, many of them were not willing to do so at all.

At roughly the time when the TUC first rejected Labour's proposals for
the introduction of a statutory national minimum wage and many of Britain's
unions voiced their opposition to the Crossman scheme, two similar initiatives were under way in the Netherlands. First, in 1968, the Dutch government
introduced a statutory national minimum wage for all workers. Then, one year
later, it announced its intention to raise the flat-rate level of the state old age
pension benefit to that of the minimum wage by increasing earnings-related
contributions to the pension scheme. Both initiatives not only received full
support from the three main union federations in the Netherlands, but they
were also in fact demanded by them.[90] The "big three" did so despite the strong

---

examples of unions doing the same for the area of welfare state development, see my treatment
of labor union involvement in welfare state development in the United States in Chapter 7.
[90] For Dutch union demands for an increase in the state pension benefit, see Chapter 3. The issue of
the possible introduction of a statutory national minimum wage emerged during the late 1950s

implications of both initiatives for the distribution of income among different categories of workers. In fact, the introduction of the statutory national minimum wage was accompanied by such stringent wage-leveling efforts that the Netherlands was soon to boast one of the most equal pretax wage distributions in the Western world.[91] Moreover, it was these three union federations that proposed to raise the level of the old age pension benefit by increasing earnings-related contributions – which increased the already strong redistributive nature of the pension's contributory system. To be sure, these contributions were completely paid for by workers.

So far I have paid much attention to the British labor union movement and little to its Dutch counterpart, although both are equally important actors in the following chapters. The reason for this is that contrary to their occupationally organized British counterparts, the industrially organized unions of the Netherlands have always acted in a way that is completely in line with the prevailing view of union involvement in labor market and welfare state development. According to the plethora of existing writings on labor market development, unions are supposed to bring a redistributive agenda to the bargaining table – and this, as demonstrated by a great deal of empirical literature, is exactly what Dutch unions did.[92] According to the prevailing wisdom on

as a result of the slow collapse of the long-term incomes policy that had been introduced in the immediate postwar period. Given the preceding discussion on the introduction of a statutory national minimum wage in the United Kingdom, it is interesting to note that the three Dutch union federations were initially also quite hesitant about introduction of a statutory national minimum wage. An important reason for this seems to have been their fear that statutory legislation would undermine their ability to attract workers. Yet, in contrast to the United Kingdom, this was not enough in the end to convince them to oppose statutory interference – especially when they could not get a good enough "deal" during negotiations with employer federations. On these hesitations, see, for example, W. Verwey, "Het minimumloon – een welvaartsvaste natte vinger," *Sociaal Maandblad Arbeid* (1973), 357–62; W. J. P. M. Fase, *Vijfendertig jaar loonbeleid in Nederland. Terugblik en perspectief* (Alphen aan den Rijn: Samson, 1980), 258–61.

[91] During the late 1970s, the net level of the minimum wage in the Netherlands amounted to roughly 75 or 80 percent of average earnings for a male worker in the manufacturing industry. See, for example, M. O'Riordan, "Minimum Wages in Europe," *Low Pay Review* (1981), 5; Kees Goudswaard and Philip de Jong, "The Distributional Impact of Current Income Transfer Policies in the Netherlands," *Journal of Social Policy* 14:3 (1985), 370. For an excellent overview of how the wage-leveling efforts of the Dutch union federations affected different pay scales, see Verbond van Nederlandse Ondernemingen, *Boekje over inkomens 1970–1981. Een VNO-monografie over het in Nederland gevoerde inkomensverdelingsbeleid in de jaren 1970–1981* (Den Haag: VNO, 1981), 32. For international comparison of pretax wage divisions, see footnote 46 of this chapter.

[92] See, for example, John Windmuller, D. de Galan, and A. F. van Zweeden, *Arbeidsverhoudingen in Nederland* (Utrecht: Het Spectrum, 1983), 234; Wil Albeda, *Arbeidsverhoudingen in Nederland* (Alphen aan den Rijn: Samson, 1989), 61, 76; VNO, *Boekje over inkomens*, 31–33; Jan Pen and Jan Tinbergen, *Naar een rechtvaardiger inkomensverdeling* (Amsterdam: Elsevier, 1977), 44; Paul de Beer, *Het verdiende inkomen* (Houten/Zeventhem: Bohn Stafleu van Loghum, 1993), 64; Jan-Luiten van Zanden, "Inkomensverdeling en overheidspolitiek, 1938–1950," *Economisch Statistische Berichten* (August 1986), 768–71; J. van Wijngaarden, *Inkomensverdelingsbeleid in de verzorgingsstaat. Rechtvaardigheidscriteria voor inkomensverschillen uit arbeid* (Utrecht: Academic Thesis, 1982), 56.

welfare state development, unions are the natural supporters of welfare state development – and this, as we will see in the following chapters, is exactly what Dutch unions were. Yet this does not mean that they were such enthusiastic supporters for the same reasons that are generally put forward in the literature.

It is important to note here that the willingness and ability of Dutch industrial unions to reduce wage differentials and, as we will see, to push for redistributive welfare solutions cannot be explained by arguing that all their members stood to gain from this. All three union federations in the Netherlands organized a wide variety of different grades of workers.[93] These various groups had very different welfare state interests. While most of them probably had an interest in insuring themselves against labor market risks such as unemployment, sickness, disability, and old age, not all of them necessarily had an interest in doing so through public means. On the contrary, to achieve adequate insurance for all their members, the three union federations often opted for redistributive public solutions that were clearly to the detriment of their more privileged members. The leadership of these federations and their industrially organized union members were acutely aware of this. They nevertheless pushed forward with initiatives that aimed to reapportion risks and introduce redistributive contributory systems. In doing so, they emphasized the importance of broad worker solidarity.

Nor, for that matter, is it possible to explain Dutch labor union support for redistributive social security initiatives by viewing labor unions as mere welfare maximizers whose policies simply reflect the interests of a majority of their members. In the literature on wage bargaining, unions are generally assumed to bring a redistributive agenda to the bargaining table because of what is often called the "median voter model." This model is based on the idea that in situations in which the mean wage is higher than the median wage (which is typically the case), a majority of members will benefit from, and therefore favor, wage compression.[94] On those rare occasions when the difference between the

---

[93] Unfortunately, scholars have paid little attention to the question of to what degree unionization levels differ among different occupational categories. Most research on this is limited to the distinction between public- and private-sector workers or between manual and white-collar workers. As explained earlier, these divisions do not in fact accord closely with the variation in risk and income among workers. This makes it difficult to give a detailed account of the degree to which different "grades" of workers were represented by the three unions. The best, but certainly not a flawless, indicator of this is the educational level of unionized workers. Data on educational levels support the notion that Dutch unions organized all "levels" of workers. See, for example, Jo van Cruchten and Rob Kuijpers, "Vakbeweging en organisatiegraad van werknemers," *Sociaaleconomische Trends* (January 2007), 7–17.

[94] According to David Rueda and Jonas Pontusson, for example, "[U]nions approximate the logic of democratic decision making (one person, one vote) more closely than markets do, and whenever the mean wage exceeds the median wage, we would expect a majority of union members to favour redistributive wage demands." According to Daniele Chechi, Jelle Visser, and Herman van der Werfhorst, "Under the medium voter model and given a mean wage higher than the

stance of unions representing higher-skilled workers and the "broader confederation of the labor movement" has been noted, a similar argument has been put forward.[95] Yet such arguments cannot explain labor union support for policies such as the introduction of a statutory national minimum wage that specifically aim to improve matters for a small minority of low-paid workers – and do so at the expense of all other workers. Over the years, many scholars have noted that Dutch wage-compression policies, instead of aiming to reduce overall wage inequality, often merely sought to improve matters for those in the lowest decile of the wage distribution.[96] Many of the social security initiatives put forward by the big three in the first decades of the postwar period, as we will see, did the same.

Other initiatives put forward by them clearly had broader redistributive consequences. Yet even those often contained wage limits and contribution thresholds that severely restricted their redistributive scope. Initially, at least, these were set at such a low level that the highest income brackets were hardly affected by the introduction and expansion of social security programs. The fact that the median worker consequently hardly benefited from the redistributive consequences of welfare state expansion makes it quite difficult to explain Dutch union support for this expansion by focusing only on majoritarian interests. Throughout the period investigated in this book, and as we will see, the Dutch union movement pushed for redistributive initiatives that benefited a small group of vulnerable workers at the expense of a much larger group of workers and union members.[97] To explain their support for such initiatives, we

---

the medium, as is typically the case in earnings distributions, union policies will tend towards wage compression." Rueda and Pontusson, "Wage Inequality," 359; Daniele Chechi, Jelle Visser, and Herman van der Werfhorst, "Inequality and Union Membership: The Impact of Relative Earnings Position and Inequality Attitudes," *British Journal of Industrial Relations* 48:1 (2009), 89. See also Jonas Pontusson, David Rueda, and Christopher R. Way, "Comparative Political Economy of Wage Distribution: The Role of Partisanship and Labour Market Institutions," *British Journal of Political Science* 32 (2002), 288; Pontusson, *Inequality and Prosperity*, 3, 60–1.

[95] See Mares, *The Politics of Social Risk*, 47.

[96] See, for instance, T. B. C. Mulder, *Loonvorming in overleg. Gedragingen van het georganiseerde bedrijfsleven in Nederland na de tweede wereldoorlog* (Assen: Van Gorcum, 1956), 20; N. van Hulst, *De effectiviteit van de geleide loonpolitiek in de praktijk* (Amsterdam: Wolters-Noordhof, 1984), 258–60; Bob Reinalda, *De Dienstenbonden. Klein maar strijdbaar* (Baarn: AMBO, 1985), 36.

[97] There is some disagreement in the literature as to whether the income of the average union members is higher or lower than that of the average worker. Up to the 1980s, most scholars seem to have believed that union membership was concentrated among the higher-paid half of the earnings distribution. Following the logic of the median voter model, scholars therefore commonly argued that unionization increases worker inequality. See, for example, Friedman, "Somme Comments," 124; Rees, *The Economics*; Pettengill, *Labor Unions*, 3; George Johnson, "Economic Analysis of Trade Unionism," *American Economic Review* 65 (1975), 23–28. For some diverging views on the matter in more recent years, see Neil Millward, John Forth, and Alex Bryson, *Who Calls the Tune at Work? The Impact of Trade Unions on Jobs and Pay* (York, PA: York Publishing Services 2001); Pontusson, Rueda, and Way, "Comparative Political

have to look at their organizational logic, which emphasized class unity and broad worker solidarity. Such notions, as we will see in the following chapter, were crucially absent in the vocabulary of British craft and occupationally organized white-collar unions, whose organizational logic instead grounded in the occupational defense of wage differentials against lower paid workers.

What makes the difference between the British and Dutch labor union movement stances on redistributive welfare state development so remarkable is that it cannot be explained through differences in interests between British and Dutch unionized workers. Instead, the difference stemmed from differences in union structure, which shaped the ways in which union leaders represented workers' interests. An excellent illustration of this is the case of the skilled manual worker. In most countries, and certainly in the Netherlands and the United Kingdom, skilled manual workers have always formed the organizational backbone of the labor union movement.[98] Because of their clear "working-class" identity, the comparative literature on welfare state development generally treats them as core supporters of redistributive welfare state development. Yet the section on British voluntarism earlier in this chapter illustrated that this is not necessarily the case. Over the years, many scholars have observed that British craft unions representing skilled manual workers were the fiercest opponents to any attempt to reduce wage differentials – and the strongest supporters of voluntarism.[99]

In the United Kingdom, skilled manual workers have always organized themselves predominantly in craft unions. In the Netherlands, by contrast, they have since the beginning of the twentieth century organized themselves predominantly in industrial unions. These unions have taken a decisively different attitude toward wage compression and redistributive welfare state development than their British craft counterparts. While British craft unions are known as staunch opponents of any attempt to reduce wage differentials, Dutch industrial unions have throughout much the postwar period worked hard to achieve exactly this. Crucially, the solidaristic stance of the latter has not resulted in mass protests on the part of their skilled manual membership.

Economy of Wage Distribution," 281–308; Chechi, Visser, and Van der Werfhorst, "Inequality and Union Membership," 84–108.

[98] Skilled manual workers are undeniably part of the "working class" and are therefore presumed to be great supporters of welfare state development. Whereas scholars have at times noted that white-collar workers (whereby they often refer only to one category of white-collar workers, often named "higher-educated employees") may have less of an interest in welfare state development, they have never done so for the skilled manual worker. The preceding reference to the resistance of British craft unions to the introduction of a statutory national minimum wage already showed that this is incorrect – as will the following chapters on the involvement of British unions in welfare state development. It is also telling that the British craft unions have not always been equally strong supporters of "left" or "social-democratic" parties. See, for example, Routh, "White-Collar Unions," 167.

[99] See, for example, Lowe, *The Welfare State*, 295; Pelling, *A History*, 226; Flanders, "The Tradition," 113–14.

How are we to explain this? Part of the reason may be that industrial unions in the Netherlands were successful not only in reducing wage differentials between skilled and unskilled manual workers but also in reducing wage differentials between skilled manual workers and still higher income categories. Yet there might be more to it than interests alone. In most cases, workers themselves are not closely involved in wage negotiations. Under such circumstances, it may matter immensely whether they are represented by unions that look only to the narrow interests of one occupational category or one that emphasizes the importance of solidarity among workers. Tellingly, despite the successful wage-leveling efforts of Dutch industrial unions, their privileged members – whether white-collar or manual – have not turned *en masse* to occupational unions that oppose these efforts.[100]

Having identified the importance of union structure for the attitude of unions toward redistribution of income among different occupational categories of workers, it is now possible to move to a more detailed discussion of labor union involvement in welfare state development. One important issue here is how labor union structure affects the stances and efficacy of other important players in the welfare state debate. The preceding discussion on the introduction of the national minimum wage in the United Kingdom has offered a preview of how the political efficacy of left parties depends on the extent to which the labor union movement can unite behind their redistributive agenda. A recurring theme in the following chapters on the development of old age, unemployment, and disability insurance programs is how the British Labour Party has struggled to overcome craft and occupationally organized white-collar opposition to its public welfare initiatives. In the Netherlands, the emphasis of labor unions on solidarity between different grades of workers has made it much easier for parties on the left side of the political spectrum to implement their redistributive agenda. One of the reasons for this is surely that the solidaristic stance of the union movement increased the relative "power resources" of the left. At the same time, it can be argued that the solidaristic stance of the unions made this redistributive agenda more acceptable to groups

---

[100] Many scholars predicted that the postwar wage-leveling efforts of the big three would lead to a large increase in the numbers of privileged white-collar workers represented by independent, occupationally organized white-collar unions. See, for example, Albeda, *Arbeidsverhoudingen*, 71. Similarly, it has been argued that the attempts of the big three to organize their members along industrial lines would lead to a strong growth of independent, occupationally organized unions. See, for example, Windmuller, *Labor Relations*, 184–6. These predictions, however, have not been substantiated in a large manner. Earlier I mentioned that the big three today still represent some 80 percent of all unionized workers. It does have to be mentioned here that unionization among white-collar workers has always been very low in the Netherlands – but this was already the case long before the wage-compression efforts of the big three really got underway and is the case for low-end white-collar categories as well as for higher-educated white-collar workers. Of white-collar workers who are organized, nearly 80 percent still do so in one of the industrially organized unions – again, a number that has remained quite constant over the years. See Visser, "The Netherlands," 481.

who were naturally inclined to oppose it. One such group is the employer community. In recent years, the involvement of employer interest groups in welfare state development has received much attention from welfare state scholars. For this reason, the final section of this chapter shows how union structure affects this involvement.

UNIONS, EMPLOYERS, AND THE NOTION OF THE SOCIAL WAGE

In recent years, employer interest-group involvement in welfare state development has become a popular – and divisive – theme in the comparative and historic analysis of the welfare state. This recent surge in scholarly interest has been boosted by a series of employer-oriented writings that have raised important questions about the nature and extent of business influence on welfare state development. The main purpose of these writings has been to show that employers have played a more important and more constructive role in the introduction and expansion of social security programs than the existing literature has realized. They have done so by arguing that the welfare state not only imposes costs and labor market rigidities on employers but also provides direct and tangible benefits to them. Other welfare state scholars have raised doubts about these claims or have rejected them outright.[101]

Although this recent scholarship on employers is quite diverse, it is possible to distinguish two main variants. According to the first variant, which is part of a broader study of production regimes known as the "varieties of capitalism approach," employers might appreciate social policies when these perform a "productive function."[102] This scholarship relies heavily on the need of firms to attract skilled labor, and its authors assume that employers who rely on workers with advanced or specific skills need generous social policies to convince future workers to invest in these skills.[103] The main problem with this view is that organized employer support for welfare *state* development does not follow from this. After all, if higher wages are not sufficient to convince future workers to invest in the types of skills they need to acquire, then employers can simply create occupational provision for them. Employer support for welfare state development can result from this only when we add the much more dubious assumption that employers cannot provide sufficient

---

[101] See, for example, Korpi, "Power Resources"; Jacob Hacker and Paul Pierson, "Business Power and Social Policy: Employers and the Formation of the American Welfare State," *Politics and Society* 30:2 (2002), 277–325; Jacob Hacker, "Bringing the Welfare State Back In: The Promise (and Perils) of the New Social Welfare History," *Journal of Policy History* 17:1 (2005), 125–54.

[102] Ebbinghaus and Manow, *Comparing Welfare Capitalism*, foreword.

[103] For some prominent examples of this, see Streeck, "Beneficial Constraints"; Martin, *Stuck in Neutral*; Hall and Soskice, *Varieties of Capitalism*; Ebbinghaus and Manow, *Comparing Welfare Capitalism*; Ebbinghaus, *Reforming Early Retirement*; Iversen, *Capitalism, Democracy, and Welfare*.

insurance for their workers on their own. With this assumption, we end up with the second, and arguably much more sophisticated, variant, which states that *some* employers may have an interest in supporting social security programs, for instance, because they want to prevent wage competition through welfare benefits or because they want to off-load costs onto competitors or society as a whole.[104]

By emphasizing that employers may prefer public to private contributions when the former serves to level the playing field or to redistribute costs, this second variant has made an important contribution to the literature on welfare state development. It has done so in two major ways. First, it has demonstrated that employers, like workers and the self-employed, do not constitute homogeneous groups with similar interests. This is important because it confirms that the concept of class is not a useful tool for describing patterns of risk and resource distribution among actors in labor markets. Contrary to what power resources scholars such as Walter Korpi believe, different groups of workers, employers, and the self-employed do not dispose of similar resources; nor are they exposed to labor market risks in similar degrees.[105] As a result, they do not necessarily have the same interests. So far this new scholarship has mainly used this insight to illustrate that the process of welfare state expansion involved much potential for conflict among different groups of employers. The preceding analysis of British voluntarism has already illustrated that the potential for conflict among different groups of workers is at least equally great. The following chapters will illustrate the consequences of this for attempts to expand the boundaries of the postwar welfare state in the United Kingdom.

The second major contribution of this new scholarship is that it has laid bare a new path to welfare state reform that is based on so-called cross-class alliances between labor and powerful sections of the employer community. In his pioneering work on the importance of such alliances for the development of the postwar Swedish welfare state, Peter Swenson, for instance, described the sometimes tacit and sometimes open support of Swedish employers for the expansion of social security programs during the 1950s and 1960s. Through a sophisticated argument that is well grounded in specific historic economic circumstances such as Sweden's extremely tight labor market at the time, Swenson shows how this support among others related to the desire of major exporting firms to prevent wage competition through welfare benefits with the sheltered industries.[106] In recent years, many scholars have followed Swenson's lead by

---

[104] The main exponents of this variant are Swenson, *Capitalists Against Markets*; Gordon, *New Deals*; and Mares, *The Politics of Social Risk*.

[105] According to Korpi, "[W]e can distinguish three socio-economic classes: employers, employees, and the self-employed. Although internally quite heterogeneous, these broad categories define similarities in actors' opportunities and constraints, resources, and risks." Korpi, "Power Resources," 174.

[106] See Swenson, *Capitalists Against Markets*, 245–303.

highlighting the importance of cross-class alliances between fractions of labor and capital in the expansion of the postwar welfare state.[107]

Yet cross-class alliances – whether tacit or formal and whether based on a partial or complete alignment of interests – can also *prevent* the coming about of progressive welfare reform. This, as we will see, is exactly what happened in the United Kingdom, where powerful unions representing higher-paid workers stood side-by-side with employers in their rejection of nearly all of Labour's social security proposals during the 1950s and 1960s. This never resulted in a "formal" alliance in which these unions sought to strengthen their position by coordinating their efforts with or in other ways sought support from employer interests groups. Nor was the alignment of interests between occupationally organized unions and employer interests ever complete. On the contrary, and as explained in Chapter 3, these unions and the main employer organizations disagreed on everything *but* their opposition to Labour's proposals. Moreover, and as will be explained as well, they opposed these proposals for very different reasons. Yet there is no doubt that they both greatly appreciated each other's efforts to prevent Labour's initiatives from being implemented. And there is also no doubt that their combined efforts were to be strikingly successful.

In the industrial unions–dominated landscape of the Netherlands, there was little room for the development of such tacit alliances against progressive welfare reform. Nor was there ever a durable cross-class alliance in favor of such reform between specific groups of workers and employers. Instead, a united labor union movement managed to get most of its welfare demands implemented by either persuading employers to support its initiatives or by overcoming unified employer opposition. Sometimes the employer community immediately agreed with labor's welfare demands and initiatives. Often it first attempted to delay matters, after which labor and capital steered toward a compromise. At other times labor and capital clashed quite severely over the former's welfare demands. Either way, the labor movement managed to get most of its demands for improved public protection against labor market risks implemented. Given the Dutch labor union movement's aforementioned lack of conventional "power resources" – which resulted from its low density rate and the fact that the Labor Party was out of power during most of this period – it is important to investigate how it managed to do so. And this once more brings our attention to the formative effects of union structure.

In chapter 1 of this book, I already mentioned that the recent employer-oriented scholarship has not accompanied its critical review of the role of employers with an equally critical reexamination of labor union involvement in welfare state development. In much of the literature that has so fiercely challenged the assumption of organized employer opposition to welfare state development,

---

[107] See, in particular, Isabela Mares, *The Politics of Social Risk*; Ibidem, "Strategic Alliances and Social Policy Reform: Unemployment Insurance in Comparative Perspective," *Politics & Society* 28:2 (2000), 223–44.

blanket labor union support for its development is still taken for granted. And even those who, like Swenson and Mares, emphasize the role of cross-class alliances have failed to take note of the importance of labor's internal organizational blueprint. This neglect of the crucial importance of union structure in the employer-oriented scholarship is problematic because the stance of employer interest groups on welfare state initiatives depends to a great extent on the degree to which the labor union movement supports these initiatives. Crucially, and as illustrated later in this chapter, when employer interest groups are faced with a labor union movement that is united in its support for redistributive policies, they will display a much more accommodating stance on welfare state initiatives than when they deal with a union movement that is itself divided on this. They will do so for two reasons. First, a more unified labor union movement can more effectively apply pressure on employer groups. Second, and at least as important, under these circumstances, public welfare initiatives will be *much less costly* for employers.

To explain this, it is first necessary to note the obvious similarities between the welfare preferences of employer interest groups and those of occupationally organized unions representing privileged workers. Most important of these is the tendency of both to favor private, group-based insurance over redistributive public insurance. It follows from this that the stance of employer interest groups on public welfare initiatives may differ depending on whether or not there are powerful craft and occupationally organized white-collar unions that oppose these initiatives. One reason for this is that employer interest groups will be in a much stronger position to oppose public welfare initiatives when there are powerful unions that also oppose them. I will demonstrate this at length in Chapter 3, which deals, among other issues, with the introduction of superannuation in the United Kingdom. The chapter shows how the opposition of a powerful part of the British labor union movement to this initiative made it easier for British employer interest groups to undermine it. It did so in two ways. First, union opposition gave employers a powerful ally at the bargaining table in their dealings with representatives from the Labour Party who proposed superannuation. Second, it enabled employers to attract full attention to how bad a deal superannuation was for higher-paid workers. In the Netherlands, by contrast, employer interest groups could not capitalize on divisions within the labor union movement – because there were none. Chapter 3 shows that employers consequently found it far more difficult, and ultimately impossible, to resist redistributive public pension initiatives.

There is also a second, and perhaps more pressing, reason why the stance of employer interest groups on public welfare initiatives may differ depending on the presence of powerful unions that oppose these initiatives. Where union opposition exists, employer interest groups not only may be in a stronger position to oppose a particular welfare initiative but also may find it more imperative to do so. After all, when a union opposes a particular welfare initiative, it will also be more reluctant to accept that its members have to pay for the initiative. As a result, welfare development will be far more costly to employers in countries where unions are organized mainly on an occupational basis than in countries where they are organized mainly along industrial lines. The difference between these types of union organization lies in their effect on the degree to which labor unions accept that improvements to public benefits, such as improvements to occupational benefits, are part of the "social wage." The notion of the social wage will arise often in the following chapters, so it is necessary to spend some time on it here.

The notion of the social wage over the years has been a very popular but poorly understood concept in the welfare state literature. The general idea behind it is that unions not only care about increasing the wages of their members but also care about improving the security of their members against labor market risks such as unemployment, sickness, and disability and about enabling them to obtain an adequate income in old age. As a result, unions should be willing to accept somewhat lower direct wage increases in exchange for increases in the level or duration of public or private unemployment, disability, and old age insurance programs.[108] If unions are willing to moderate their wage demands in exchange for increases in such "nonwage benefits," then these increases will effectively be financed from the margin of pay increases, so they can be considered "deferred wages."

It is not hard to see why the notion of the social wage has proven so popular with scholars. After all, it implies that the costs of welfare state expansion can be mitigated when labor unions are willing to view social insurance programs as deferred wages. Over the years, many scholars have thus come to argue that the success of redistributive welfare state development depends on the willingness of unions to engage in a "political exchange" in which they deliver wage restraint in exchange for increased generosity of public welfare benefits.[109] The

---

[108] In *Taxation, Wage Bargaining and Unemployment*, Mares has even gone so far as to argue that "unions, as rational actors, will exercise wage moderation *only* in exchange for benefits and social services that go to union members." See Mares, *Taxation*, 12–13 (emphasis added). This is clearly not the case. Unions in fact may have many reasons to agree to moderate their wage demands, and often these have nothing to do with welfare state development. In the Netherlands, for example, the willingness of unions to moderate wage demands was strongest when the expansion of public welfare programs was slowest – namely, in the immediate postwar period. The unions were willing to do so at the time because of unemployment and export considerations – not because of their public welfare aspirations. On the contrary, it seems quite plausible that, as Dercksen et al. have argued, the priority given to low labor costs at the time induced unions to moderate their public welfare demands as well as their wage demands. See Willem Dercksen, Pim Fortuyn, and T. Jaspers, *Vijfendertig jaar SER-adviezen, deel I 1950–1964* (Deventer: Kluwer, 1982), 517.

[109] Strictly speaking, the notion of a "political exchange" is not completely accurate and can certainly be misleading. Often unions do not moderate their wage demands but simply accept a somewhat lower direct wage increase in exchange for improved security against labor market risks. In such circumstances, it would be wrong to speak of a "political exchange." What we are really referring to in such instances is the notion of the "deferred social wage." For some prominent examples of scholars who have emphasized the idea of a "political exchange" or

only problem is that they have found it difficult to explain why *some* union movements have been far more willing to engage in such political exchanges than others. Had these scholars realized the importance of union structure and been aware of the resulting differences in attitudes toward redistributive welfare development among different types of unions, they would surely have found this less difficult.

An excellent way to illustrate this is by comparing the attitudes of British and Dutch unions toward the notion of the social wage. In the Netherlands, as we will see in the following chapters, the industrially organized labor union movement has always been quite willing to view public insurance programs as deferred wages to be paid from the margin of pay increases.[110] In the United Kingdom, by contrast, the union movement has been far less willing to accept this view. Over the years, many scholars have noted the unwillingness of British unions to reduce wage claims in exchange for public welfare development.[111] Later in this chapter I will go even further by arguing that many unions in the United Kingdom typically reacted to the introduction or expansion of public welfare programs not just with an unwillingness to reduce wage claims but by *increasing* their wage demands in an effort to maintain wage differentials.

In their attempts to explain the unwillingness of British unions to reduce wage claims in exchange for public welfare initiatives, scholars have paid scant attention to the possibility that many of these unions actually had little interest in, or even opposed, these initiatives in the first place. Instead, scholars commonly argue that such initiatives were of "vital concern" to the entire labor union movement.[112] As a result, they have found it difficult to explain instances

"tradeoff" between wage moderation and public welfare development, see Peter Katzenstein, *Small States in World Markets: Industrial Policy in Europe* (Ithaca, NY: Cornell University Press, 1985), 56–7; Esping-Andersen, *The Three Worlds*, 174–6; Peter Lange, "Unions, Workers and Wage Regulation: The Rational Bases of Consent." In J. H. Goldthorpe, *Order and Conflict in Contemporary Capitalism* (Oxford: Clarendon Press, 1984), 98–123; and Mares, *Taxation*, 2–3.

[110] This willingness has been noted by many scholars and organizations such as the OECD over the years. See, for example, Organisation for Economic Co-operation and Development, *OECD Economic Surveys: The Netherlands* (Paris: OECD, 1979), 33–4; Robert J. Flanagan, David W. Soskice, and Lloyd Ulman, *Unionism, Economic Stabilization and Income Policies: the European Experience* (Washington, DC: Brookings Institution, 1983), 153; Barry Eichengreen, *The European Economy Since 1945: Coordinated Capitalism and Beyond* (Princeton, NJ: Princeton University Press, 2007), 33–4.

[111] See, for example, Douglas Ashford, *The Emergence of the Welfare States* (Oxford: Basil Blackwell, 1986), 18; Whiteside, "Industrial Relations and Social Welfare," 120–1; and Martin Rhodes, "Restructuring the British Welfare State: Between Domestic Constraints and Global Imperatives." In Fritz Scharpf and Vivien Schmidt, *Welfare and Work in the Open Economy* (Oxford University Press, 2000), 22. According to Isabela Mares, postwar efforts to "expand social benefits or services in order to offer unions incentives to moderate wage demands [were] ... relatively successful." See Mares, *Taxation*, 217–18. The following chapters will show that this was anything but the case.

[112] According to Helen Fawcett, for example, the Labour Party and the TUC during the early 1970s "engaged in a process of political exchange in order to secure wage restraint, the Labour

in which "old age pensions were raised and were guaranteed against inflation, food subsidies were introduced, the powers of the Price Commission were
extended and increased regional and housing subsidies were put in place," but
government appeals for wage moderation nevertheless "largely fell on deaf
ears."[113] The explanations offered for such instances either focus on specific
historical circumstances or center around the familiar and unsatisfactory argument of British "voluntarism."[114]

Once we realize the consequences of occupational unionism in the United
Kingdom, we do not need to resort to such arguments. We only have to realize
that neither an increase in food, housing, or regional subsidies nor any increase
in the state pension benefit or one of the other social insurance benefits was
of "vital concern" to the entire British labor union movement. Instead, these
increases were of vital concern only to unions that represented many relatively
low-paid and risk-prone workers. These were the workers who needed food
and housing subsidies to get by and who were completely dependent on the
social security system to provide adequate insurance against labor market risks.
Many other unions represented workers whose incomes were high enough to
get by without food or housing subsidies and who could rely on supplementary
occupational provision. To those unions, increases in social security programs
such as the old age pension benefit could be useful for their members. Yet this
would not be the case if these increases were mainly financed through a redistributive system of contributions and benefits that worked to the disadvantage
of their members.

To understand this, it is first necessary to point out that these members had
often already managed to achieve a more-than-adequate level of protection
against labor market risks – despite the dismally low, below-subsistence levels
of social security benefits. The reason for this was that they could add occupational provision to these public benefits. By the early 1960s, roughly one-third
of British workers could claim private severance payments when laid off, and
about half of them were entitled to occupational sick pay. Furthermore, about
half of all workers belonged to an occupational pension scheme. These occupational supplements neatly followed the logic of the social wage because
they were financed from the margin of pay increases. Thus, in exchange for

---

Party offering firm commitments *in areas vital to the concern of the trade union movement.*"
The most important of these "areas" was the public pension. See Fawcett, "Jack Jones," 158.
See also Flanagan, Soskice, and Ulman, *Unionism*, 183; Hill, *The Welfare State*, 108; Lowe, *The Welfare State*, 2; Mares, *Taxation*, 177, 205–6.

[113] Whiteside, "Industrial Relations," 121.

[114] According to Martin Rhodes, "[O]ne of the peculiarities (at least in the European context) of
the British system was the divorce between the labor movement and the social insurance system.... Combined with 'voluntarism' and organizational fragmentation in industrial relations,
this helped prevent the development of the notion of the 'social wage' in Britain." Rhodes,
"Restructuring," 22. According to Dorey, the failure "derived from their commitment to free
collective bargaining." Dorey, *Wage Politics*, 142. According to Mares, it resulted from the "low
institutional capacity of the labor movement." See Mares, *Taxation*, 205.

more generous occupational benefits, which they viewed as deferred wages, the unions that represented these workers were quite willing to accept lower direct wage increases. This, however, does not mean that they were also willing to lower their wage demands in exchange for more generous public benefits. After all, their members often had little to gain and much to lose from public welfare initiatives.

When consecutive Labour governments during the 1950s and 1960s introduced measures to improve public provision for the unemployed, sick, disabled, and elderly, they were not concerned primarily with workers who had already achieved adequate provision through a combination of public and occupational provision. Instead, and as we will see in the following chapters, they mainly aimed to increase the security of workers who could not rely on private supplements. Sometimes these workers did not have access to private supplements because they worked for firms that simply did not offer them. More often than not, a large part of the problem was also that these workers, through a combination of high risks and low wages, simply could not *afford* to obtain adequate occupational benefits. To improve matters for this group, a redistributive effort among different grades of workers was inevitable. Acutely aware of this, most of Labour's public welfare initiatives either extended the risk pool of existing schemes or introduced a system of contributions and benefits that worked more to the advantage of lower-income members. Often they did both. As we will see in the following three chapters of this study, such initiatives were vehemently opposed by unions whose members had already achieved adequate provision through a combination of public and private insurance programs – because they were the ones who stood to lose from these initiatives' redistributive features. As a result, these unions also vehemently objected to any call to moderate their wage demands in exchange for the introduction of these initiatives. On the contrary, when they did not succeed in blocking these initiatives, they often *increased* their wage demands in an attempt to restore wage differentials, which had been reduced as a result of these public welfare initiatives.

Under these circumstances, the introduction of public welfare initiatives became a very costly exercise for employers, who either had to bear the brunt of their costs or engage in fierce wage bargaining. This is why the Confederation of British Industry (CBI), which was the main representative of British employers from the mid-1960s on, even argued at one point that it was useless to ask workers to contribute to improvements to social security schemes because "in the long run these increases in employees' contributions will be reflected in wage claims, and so far as these are allowed, the whole of the initial increase ... will be met by employers."[115] Employer interest groups never complained that

---

[115] Confederation of British Industry, *Earnings-Related Social Security*, 5. See also PRO, Lab 10/1932: BEC Bulletin, 222, 22 January 1964; PRO, CAB 130/599: Tripartite talks with CBI and TUC, 5 October 1972.

unions were not willing to view occupational provision as deferred wages. On the contrary, it seems that they very much appreciated the use of occupational provision as an alternative to direct wage increases.[116]

In contrast to their British counterparts, and as will be shown in the following chapters, the mainly industrially organized labor unions of the Netherlands had few difficulties with the redistributive consequences of public welfare development. As a result, they were also much more willing to view public (like occupational) insurance as deferred wages that had to be financed from the margin of pay increases (in Dutch, called *loonruimte*). The degree to which they were willing to do so did, of course, partly depend on the particular risk at hand. While Dutch unions were quite willing to accept that improvements to public provision for the elderly and for nonoccupational injuries and sicknesses be financed from the margin of pay increases, they were much less willing to do the same for improvements in public provision for the unemployed and occupational injuries and sicknesses. Because unions blamed unemployment and occupational ailments on the employer, they felt that the employers should bear – or at least share – financial responsibility for these labor market risks. Chapter 3 will show that the willingness of Dutch unions to accept that public (e.g., occupational) provision for the elderly had to be paid for by workers themselves greatly strengthened their demands for the creation of a generous public pension. Chapter 4 will show that disagreements between employers and unions over the financial responsibility for unemployment benefits made it far more difficult to achieve quick progress for the unemployed.

Eventually, even the most reluctant Dutch unions came to accept that workers had to share financial responsibility for unemployment benefits – if only because they considered increasing the protection of *all* workers against the risk of becoming unemployed more important than the issue of who had to pay for it. It is because of considerations such as these that the involvement of the industrially organized Dutch labor union movement differed so strongly from that of its largely occupationally organized British counterpart. In the Netherlands, it was a matter of course that representatives of the three industrially organized union federations argued that part of the margin of pay increases go to improvements in the public welfare sphere.[117]

---

[116] In 1964, the BEC, for example, opposed the introduction of a public initiative on sickness and unemployment insurance because "it was necessary to have something else to offer to the unions if there was to be any chance of getting wage restraint. These various proposals on unemployment and sickness benefits were items which the employers could use in bargaining with the unions about wages, but if the Government imposed the schemes by legislation, employers would lose them as bargaining counters." PRO, Lab 10/2024: Note of a meeting with the BEC, 3 February 1964.

[117] For some examples of this, see VU, Archief Federatie van de Katholieke en Protestants-Christelijke Werkgeversverbonden, 19: Memo afkomstig van secretariaat FCWV met betrekking tot een structurele verhoging van de AOW (FED 650-SV); VU, VPCW, 180: Brief van Minister

It was also common for them to accept a lower-than-normal wage increase concurrent with the introduction of a major social security initiative. In fact, and as we will see in the following chapter, to strengthen their demands for such initiatives, they often offered this concession willingly. In the United Kingdom, it was unthinkable for the TUC to make such a concession. Its craft and occupationally organized white-collar unions would never have accepted this.

The willingness of Dutch labor unions to accept that public (e.g., occupational) provision against labor market risk was part of the social wage certainly strengthened their public welfare demands. Their stance on the social wage made public welfare development less costly and therefore more acceptable to the powerful employer community. Up to at least the late 1960s, it seems that Dutch employer interest groups were much less worried about the costs of public welfare development than were their British counterparts – even though the reach of the public welfare sphere was by then already much greater in the Netherlands than in the United Kingdom.[118] This is, of course, not to say that Dutch employers never voiced objections to public welfare expansion. On the contrary, they often did and for many reasons – which will all be mentioned in the following chapters. Yet, and as we will see, they nevertheless were far more accommodating than were their British counterparts.

Conversely, the unwillingness of unions representing privileged workers in the United Kingdom to accept that public (e.g., occupational) provision was part of the social wage severely weakened the ability of the TUC to lobby for more generous social security benefits. In contrast to its Dutch counterparts, the TUC consistently accompanied its calls for more generous public benefits with the statement that improvements either had to be paid by employers or through taxation. Although this was a rational stance, considering the opposition of much of its membership to any attempt to redistribute income or risk, the position seriously reduced the TUC's bargaining power. Employer interest groups and the Conservative Party naturally resisted any initiative that increased production costs, whether through nonwage labor costs or through taxation. The TUC's stance therefore made it very difficult for the Labour Party to improve state benefits. It also severely politicized the process of welfare state development – as we will see in the following three chapters.

van Sociale Zaken en Volksgezondheid aan SER op 20 November 1967; ARA, CSWV, 2.19.103.06, 134: Verslag van de vergadering van de Kring voor Sociaal Overleg gehouden op woensdag 7 September 1966 des namiddags om 2.15 uur ten kantore Kneuterdijk 8 (1ᵉ étage) te 's Gravenhage; KDC, Nederlands Katholiek Werkgeversverbond, 641: Commissie Sociale Verzekeringen, 1961–1967, Besluitenlijst van de vergadering van de Commissie Sociale Verzekeringen van het Nederlands Katholiek Werkgevers Verbond en het Verbond van Protestants-Christelijke Werkgevers in Nederland gehouden op woensdag 13 Oktober 1965, ten kantore Biltstraat 101 c te Utrecht.
[118] This was also noted by British employers. See PRO, Lab 10/1824: BEC Bulletin, 196, 19 December 1962.

LOOKING AHEAD

The main purpose of this chapter has been to show how union structure shapes the stance of labor unions on redistributive government intervention in the labor market. The chapter began with an analysis of the organizational blueprints of the British and Dutch labor union movements, emphasizing the distinction between the predominantly "occupational" nature of unionism in the United Kingdom and the predominantly "industrial" nature of unionism in the Netherlands. It proceeded to demonstrate how the occupational nature of union organization in the United Kingdom explains the remarkable reluctance of British unions to accept government intervention in the labor market. This section showed that the voluntarist inclinations of the British labor union movement cannot be explained without accounting for the resistance of a large part of its membership to any attempt to redistribute income among different categories of workers. The next section discussed the consequences of this for attempts to provide adequate insurance against labor market risks for all workers. Because employer interest groups have received so much attention in recent years, the final section of this chapter gave special consideration to the way in which union structure also shapes the involvement of organized employers in welfare state development.

By necessity, this chapter has paid more attention to the British labor union movement than to its Dutch counterpart. In the following chapters this imbalance will be set right. Chapters 3 through 6 of this study illustrate the importance of union structure by looking at a variety of policy contexts in the postwar development of the British and Dutch welfare states. The main purpose of Chapters 3 through 5 is to show how union structure affected the success of British and Dutch attempts to create adequate social provision for all elderly, unemployed, and sick and disabled workers. Chapter 6 is concerned with the use of social security programs for early-retirement purposes in the Netherlands. Chapter 7 summarizes the findings of this study and explores some of its implications.

3

The Development of Old Age Pensions in the Netherlands and the United Kingdom

The issue of how to organize old age pension provision has been *the* major source of contention in the postwar welfare state debate in developed nations. This is partly because of the immense growth of public and private spending on income maintenance for the elderly during the postwar years. In the immediate postwar period, public and private spending on old age pensions typically accounted for between 2 and 3 percent of the gross national product in developed nations. Today this number lies well over 10 percent.[1] Contrary to what recent discussions of an impending pension crisis might make us believe, most of this growth occurred during the first three decades after World War II. The growth in spending on income maintenance in old age has dwarfed spending related to all other labor market risks during the postwar period. Old age pension provision now typically accounts for nearly half of all public and private spending on income maintenance in developed countries.[2] This means that in

[1] For an excellent comparative overview of public spending on pensions as a percentage of gross domestic product (GDP), see Richard Minns, *The Cold War in Welfare: Stock Markets versus Pensions* (London: Verso, 2001), 9. It is more difficult to find a thorough comparative analysis of private spending on pensions as a percentage of GDP, but the difference between countries that have flat-rate benefits and those with earnings-related benefits gives us a good indicator of this. In countries with earnings-related benefits, public spending on pensions as a percentage of GDP generally lies well above 10 percent. In countries with flat-rate benefits, it generally lies well below 10 percent, but these countries have substantial private pension supplements.

[2] For an excellent comparative overview of the share of public spending on income maintenance for the elderly within all public spending on income maintenance up to the end of the period under investigation here, see Peter Flora, *Growth to Limits: The Western European Welfare States Since World War II*, Vol. 4: *Appendix (Synopses, Bibliographies, Tables)* (Berlin: Walter de Gruyter, 1987). Again, it is more difficult to find comparative data on the share of pension benefits in private spending on income maintenance. Yet there is little reason to assume that the share of pension spending would be lower in the private sphere.

terms of spending, its importance is as great as public and private spending on insurance against all other labor market risks combined.

Yet the sheer magnitude of spending on old age pension provision alone cannot explain why the matter of its arrangement has been such a major source of dispute throughout the postwar period. To understand this, it is crucial to note that much of the postwar growth in spending on old age pension provision has occurred with public pension schemes, which often have strong redistributive features. During the first three decades of the postwar period, all advanced industrial nations took measures designed to provide adequate minimum levels of public old age pension provision for all citizens. To achieve this, some of them first had to introduce public pension schemes, whereas others could improve existing public schemes by increasing their coverage and benefit levels. To create adequate benefit levels, all advanced industrial nations not only switched to pay-as-you-go financing, which made intergenerational solidarity possible, but all of them also introduced features into their schemes that were designed to redistribute income from higher to lower earnings. The degree to which they did so, however, differed markedly. As a result, advanced industrial nations also came to differ greatly in the degree to which they were able to provide adequate old age pension benefits to all citizens.

Efforts to provide all members of society with an adequate – or above-subsistence carrying level of – income in old age differ from efforts to provide adequate insurance for all against other labor market risks in one important way. Whereas, for example, allowing for adequate insurance against unemployment for all workers necessitates risk redistribution, efforts to provide all members of society with adequate income in old age center instead on direct income redistribution among different income categories. Such direct redistribution can be achieved in two different ways. One way of doing so is by financing the public pension scheme through progressive general taxation. Another way to bring about redistribution is by financing the public pension scheme through a redistributive contributory system. This, in turn, can be done in two ways. The first is by combining earnings-related contributions with flat-rate (i.e., equal absolute) benefits. The second is by introducing a minimum "floor" in a completely earnings-related scheme under which benefit levels are not allowed to fall. By redistributing part of the contributions of higher-earning members, both contributory solutions allow lower-earning members to receive more in benefits than they have paid for in insurance contributions. As a result, and as in a system based on progressive taxation, the public pension benefit consequently can reach a level that it could not reach without a redistributive effort from higher earnings.

During the first half of the twentieth century, most developed nations witnessed the emergence of a debate between proponents of a contributory public pension and those who advocated financing through general taxation. By the early postwar period, the proponents of a contributory public pension had triumphed in all but a handful of nations.[3] To its proponents, the main advantage of a contributory scheme lay in its representation of the public pension as an insurance for which all pensioners themselves had to save. Its main disadvantage was that not all workers and self-employed people earned sufficient income to put aside part of their earnings to save for an adequate income in old age. In none of the nations that had opted for a contributory system, however, did this disadvantage prompt a switch toward (greater) financing through general taxation.[4] Popular opposition to the increased income tax burden that would have resulted and fears that such a move would undermine the actuarial principles on which their pension schemes were based stood in the way of this. As a result, the only way forward was to introduce strong redistributive elements into the contributory pension schemes.

Yet efforts to improve old age pension provision for lower-earning workers by introducing a redistributive contributory system also have a major disadvantage: they rely strongly on the willingness of labor unions to accept a redistributive effort among different categories of workers. As we have already seen in Chapter 2, this willingness cannot be assumed. This chapter shows that the support of labor unions for redistributive contributory public pension initiatives depends on their organizational blueprint. It does so by analyzing efforts to provide adequate old age pension provision in roughly the first three decades of the postwar period in the Netherlands and the United Kingdom. The chapter contrasts the willingness and ability of the industrially organized Dutch union federations to push through redistributive contributory initiatives with the inability of the British Trades Union Congress (TUC) to do the same. It illustrates how the TUC's inability to promote such initiatives resulted from the opposition of its craft and occupationally organized white-collar members to any attempt to subsidize the benefits of lower-paid workers using contributions from higher-paid workers. This chapter shows the resulting amplitude of the public pension benefit in both countries. Finally, it explores how the attitudes of labor unions toward redistributive public pension initiatives shaped employer interest groups' positions on these initiatives.

---

[3] A striking aspect of old age pension provision is that all countries in which general revenues became or remained important were either British Commonwealth or Scandinavian countries. Among the countries of Western Europe, for example, only Denmark, Finland, and, to a much lesser extent, Sweden chose to finance a large part of their postwar state pension system through general taxation – a choice that is often attributed to the combination of exceptionally strong social democracy and the importance of the agricultural vote in the Nordic countries. On this, see, for example, Baldwin, *The Politics*, 137; Esping-Andersen, *Politics Against Markets*; Margaret S. Gordon, *Social Security Policies in Industrial Countries: A Comparative Analysis* (Cambridge University Press, 1989), 29–34.

[4] On the contrary, although most of the countries that had opted for a largely contributory system did allow for a small subsidy to the scheme to be paid for by general revenues, this subsidy often only decreased over the years. The United Kingdom is an excellent example of this.

SOLIDARITY VERSUS EGALITARIANISM: COMPARING PENSION
REFORM IN THE NETHERLANDS AND THE UNITED KINGDOM

The postwar histories of British and Dutch pension development lend themselves well to comparison because the two countries opted for largely similar old age pension systems in the immediate postwar period. In both countries, socialist pressure for a universal public pension, a conservative emphasis on self-help or personal responsibility, and the problem of the self-employed resulted in a universal flat-rate benefit that was mostly financed by insurance contributions. In both countries, this formula gained acceptance early on because it proved the only outcome behind which all parties could unite. The two available alternatives, a tax-financed state pension and an earnings-related contributory insurance scheme, simply aroused too much opposition from powerful segments within society. The universal, flat-rate, and mostly contributory benefit was seen in both countries as an acceptable middle ground between these two alternatives that combined the advantages of both and avoided their shortcomings.[5] A contributory system could give an old age pension benefit as a matter of right and at the same time preserve the "sense of responsibility" among workers. A small government subsidy allowed for the inclusion into the scheme of the smaller self-employed segment – a part of society to whom the problem of poverty in old age was particularly pressing. Finally, flat-rate benefits left sufficient room for further expansion of the private pension industry. Whereas the public pension was to provide an absolute minimum level of income maintenance in old age, private pension schemes offered the opportunity to obtain more generous earnings replacement.

The formula had only one major shortcoming. In principle, the contributory system presumed that flat-rate benefits were to be accompanied by flat-rate contributions, and this had the obvious disadvantage of limiting the generosity of the scheme to what the poorest-paying contributor could afford. In both countries, representatives of industry and the state were acutely aware of this problem. Yet only in the Netherlands was this problem solved in a way that eventually guaranteed all members of society an adequate income in old age. The Dutch solution came about when the union movement responded to the inadequacy of the proposed formula by proposing to combine flat-rate benefits

---

[5] It also should be pointed out that both countries already had flat-rate contributory systems in the prewar period. The Netherlands introduced an obligatory flat-rate invalidity and old age insurance pension for blue-collar workers in 1919. The same year saw the creation of a voluntary old age insurance pension for the self-employed. The British state pension scheme can be seen as a universal version of the Widows', Orphans' and Old Age Contributory Pension Act, which was introduced for blue-collar workers in 1925. Up to 1946, public-sector workers were allowed to opt out of the state pension scheme. See, in order, Cox, *The Development of the Dutch Welfare State*; Noel Whiteside, "Historical Perspectives and the Politics of Pension Reform." In Noel Whiteside and Gordon L. Clark, *Pension Security in the 21st Century: Redrawing the Public-Private Debate* (Oxford University Press, 2003); Lowe, *The Welfare State in Britain*, 131.

with earnings-related contributions. Under such a system, higher-paid contributors would end up paying more in contributions than they would receive in benefits. As a result, lower-paid contributors could receive a benefit level that was higher than they could afford to pay on their own. The TUC proposed no such redistributive solution. Instead, it entirely supported the combination of flat-rate benefits with flat-rate contributions.

Over the years, the British choice of a system of flat-rate contributions and benefits has presented scholars with quite a dilemma. There is now a strong consensus that this choice resulted in a "flawed design" that both created the inadequacy of public old age pension provision in the United Kingdom and stood in the way of attempts to improve it.[6] Yet, in attempting to explain the reasons for this choice, most scholars have not gone further than noting that all involved parties supported an "egalitarian" scheme that offered equal benefits in exchange for equal contributions.[7] Many of them also have been quite uncritical of the egalitarian rationale behind this. According to Derek Fraser, for example, the "flowering of egalitarianism" resulted from a "progressive consensus" within British society, which, in turn, was an outcome of the "spirit of the 1940s engendered by the war [that] ... dictated the necessity of the natural justice of universalism where everyone was treated in the same way."[8] Continuing this line of thinking, Hugh Pemberton recently explained the creation of Britain's egalitarian state pension by arguing that "the war contributed to a solidaristic environment."[9] In reality, the British choice to opt for a system that combined equal benefits with equal payments was hardly based on solidaristic considerations, though.[10] Nor was it a necessary outcome of the decision

---

[6] According to Helen Fawcett, for example, the "Beveridge solution" was not only "incapable of securing enough revenue to maintain the state pension at an acceptable level"; it also "created a powerful and rigid structure for social welfare ... [that] proved extremely hard to either abandon, ameliorate or reform." See Helen Fawcett, "The Beveridge Strait-jacket: Policy Formation and the Problem of Poverty in Old Age," *Contemporary British History* 10 (1996), 22. See also Howard Glennerster and Martin Evans, "Beveridge and His Assumptive Worlds: The Incompatibilities of a Flawed Design." In John Hills, John Ditch, and Howard Glennerster, *Beveridge and Social Security: An International Retrospective* (Oxford University Press, 1994); Rodney Lowe, "A Prophet Dishonoured in His Own Country? The Rejection of Beveridge in 1945–1970." In Hills et al., *Beveridge and Social Security*, 132; and Hugh Pemberton, "Politics and Pensions in Post-War Britain." In Hugh Pemberton, Pat Thane, and Noel Whiteside, *Britain's Pensions Crisis: History and Policy* (Oxford University Press, 2006), 42.

[7] See, for example, Baldwin, *The Politics*, 122; José Harris, *William Beveridge: A Biography* (Oxford: Clarendon Press, 1997), 250–1, 290; Heclo, *Modern Social Politics*, 255–6; Kevin Jefferys, "British Politics and Social Policy during the Second World War," *Historical Journal* 30 (1987), 131; and Stephan Leibfried, "Sozialpolitik und Existenzminimum: Anmerkungen zur Geschichte der englischen Entwicklung," *Zeitschrift für Sozialreform* 29 (1983), 714.

[8] Fraser, *The Evolution*, 252.

[9] Pemberton, "Politics and Pensions," 43.

[10] In this regard, it is important to note the distinction between egalitarian wage outcomes and egalitarian systems of social insurance contributions. Egalitarian wage outcomes – of which the practice of granting flat-rate instead of percentage increases is most well known – clearly have

to make the social security system universal. Instead, it resulted primarily from an aversion to redistribution.

Had there indeed been a strong postwar "solidaristic environment" in the United Kingdom, William Beveridge, the founding father of the postwar British welfare state, might not have opted for the combination of flat-rate benefits with flat-rate contributions. Perhaps he would have considered an alternative solution suggested to him in the mid-1940s by organizations such as Political and Economic Planning (PEP) and the Association of Approved Societies (AAS), which allotted flat-rate benefits in exchange for contributions graduated by income. But Beveridge did not give serious thought to this alternative, which he condemned as the "epitome of the 'Santa Claus' state."[11] It is important to point out here that in his emphasis on exchanging equal benefits for equal payments, Beveridge did not stand alone. Conservative backbenchers and employer organizations, for example, supported his recommendations only because they entailed little to no direct redistribution and did not stand in the way of the private pension industry.[12] More important, because it was a Labour government that eventually implemented Beveridge's recommendations in 1946, the TUC supported his scheme for exactly the same reasons. If the new pension scheme was to be contributory, the TUC General Council held, then it had to operate along egalitarian lines.[13]

In its emphasis on egalitarianism, the TUC differed starkly from its industrially organized Dutch counterparts. Instead of extolling the virtue of egalitarianism, the three Dutch union federations emphasized the importance of broad worker solidarity and pushed for a scheme that was similar to the one suggested by the PEP and AAS in the United Kingdom. In doing so, they clearly demonstrated their willingness and ability to push for direct income distribution among workers. Their solidaristic stance eventually led to the creation of a pension scheme that was to offer a much more generous benefit than its British counterpart. Yet it took several years of difficult negotiations to reach this outcome. While tripartite negotiations on the creation of this scheme got underway almost immediately after the end of the war, it was not until 1955 that the Algemene Ouderdomswet (AOW, General Old Age Act) established a universal public pension that combined earnings-related contributions with flat-rate benefits.

In the first three years of the postwar period, Dutch pension deliberations were quite similar to those in the United Kingdom. In the Netherlands, employer interest groups, union federations, and state representatives also

the effect of reducing income disparities between different categories of workers. Egalitarian systems of social insurance contributions – which simply grant benefits on "equal terms" – clearly do not. Instead, they serve to preserve differentials.

[11] Harris, *William Beveridge*, 409.
[12] Ibidem, 415, 424–5.
[13] MRC, MSS.292/150.5/3: Relation TUC General Council scheme and plan for social security in Sir William Beveridge's Report, 1943.

broadly rejected an earnings-related system as ill fitted to existing traditions. In the Netherlands, as in the United Kingdom, prewar labor union demands for a completely tax-financed old age pension did not return after the war. Whereas the confessional labor union federations had always rejected a tax-financed age pension because of the dependence on the state such a pension entailed, the socialist Nederlands Verbond van Vakverenigingen (NVV, Dutch Association of Trade Unions) had staunchly supported a tax-financed old age pension before the war.[14] Like the TUC, the postwar NVV altered this position when it realized that worker demands for tax financing strengthened conservative calls for means testing.[15] When the NVV and its political ally, the Dutch Labor Party, came to support the contributory approach, this paved the way for a broad consensus between labor, capital, and the state. In 1947, the government created a means-tested and completely tax-financed emergency provision for old age pensioners, but it managed to do so only on the condition that it would operate for a maximum of three years. In 1948, one year after the creation of the emergency provision, the second Van Rhijn Committee secured firm commitment from representatives of industry and the government to the creation of a universal and contributory flat-rate pension benefit, which was to leave sufficient room for voluntary provision. Like the British state pension, the Van Rhijn scheme did not attempt to provide full subsistence and promised no automatic adjustment to future wage or price increases. Because of this consensus two years before the emergency provision was due to expire, the government had good hope that it could implement a new pension act before the actual expiration date. Yet union pressure for a more generous pension benefit delayed preparation of the act for at least five years. Instead of operating for only three years, as Parliament had originally demanded, the emergency provision thus was effective for nine years.

The NVV led the way in calling for a more generous public old age benefit. The NVV had been present on the Van Rhijn Committee but criticized the group's consensus almost immediately after its publication. This, of course, led the other signatories to reproach the NVV for not knowing what it wanted,

---

[14] The confessional unions in the Netherlands had always opposed financing through general taxation for reasons of self-reliance. The Protestant CNV, for example, justified its opposition to financing from general taxation with the rationale that this would "not lift workers into a position of honour, but reduce them to beggars of the state." See Jan-Peter van der Toren, *"Van loonslaaf tot bedrijfsgenoot": 100 jaar christelijk-sociaal denken, medezeggenschap en sociale zekerheid* (Kempen: Kok, 1991), 90. See also Hertogh, "Geene wet, maar de Heer." For the support of the NVV for financing from general taxation, see Hueting, De Jong, and Neij, *Naar groter eenheid*, 95–7.

[15] To understand the prewar appeals of unions for a tax-financed pension, it is also important to realize that before the war, most workers did not pay income tax. On this, see Howard Glennerster, *British Social Policy Since 1945* (Oxford: Blackwell, 2000), 29. According to Helen Fawcett, after the war, the TUC rejected financing from general taxation not just out of fear of a return of the means test but also because it feared that the state might slash benefits in a future economic storm. See Fawcett, "The Beveridge Strait-jacket," 29.

which the federation rebuffed bluntly, stating that many of its members had disagreed with the Van Rhijn proposals from the start.[16] Over the course of the next year, the NVV leadership worked frantically to come up with a solution that could combine a contributory approach with a more generous outcome. Meanwhile, a sympathetic social-democratic minister of social affairs was preparing a public pension proposal of his own at the same time. When this minister showed little sign of interest in its plan, the NVV first turned to individual members of the Labor Party and then looked for support to its confessional union counterparts. A little over one year after publication of the Van Rhijn Report, the NVV presented the Katholieke Arbeidersbeweging (KAB, Catholic Workers Movement) and the Christelijk Nationaal Vakverbond (CNV; Christian Union Federation) with a pension plan that combined earnings-related contributions with flat-rate benefits, contained a provision for an automatic adjustment of benefit levels to price *and* wage increases, and obliged all employers and the self-employed to join an occupational pension plan. Together the flat-rate public benefit and earnings-related private benefit were intended to give all workers an old age income of at least 70 percent of their previous wages.[17]

The KAB was the first to rally behind the NVV plan. Perhaps the CNV was initially more reluctant because of one important feature of the scheme: the collection of insurance contributions by the taxation authorities must have sounded much like the introduction of a tax-financed pension benefit in Protestant workers' ears.[18] Eventually, however, the CNV was persuaded that wage-related contributions demanded collection by the taxation authorities, and the KAB) and CNV put their full weight behind the NVV plan.[19] Thus, while the TUC had earlier given its full support to an egalitarian system with equal benefits and equal contributions, the Dutch union federations, working together in the Raad van Vakcentralen (RVV, Council of Trade Union Federations), all supported a scheme based on income redistribution among workers of different wage groups.

Once the RVV presented its pension plan, it proved relatively easy to convince governing – and other – parties of its merits. One reason for this was the support unions received from another extremely influential interest group, the employer community. Ironically, the support of the employer community proved especially important in convincing governing parties to favor the NVV plan over an alternative with a distinct social-democratic signature: the plan of the social-democratic Minister of Social Affairs, Dolf

[16] IISG, NVV codelijsten 1945–1970, 1951 HM4, Notulen Sociale Commissie, 30 Augustus 1951.

[17] Dutch union federations thought 70 percent to be an acceptable number because this was what civil servants were receiving. IISG, NVV codelijsten 1945–1970, 1955 E1, Noodvoorziening Ouden van Dagen: Een serie radio-lezingen over de wettelijke ouderdomsverzekering door H. Korte Jr., Algemeen Secretaris van het NVV.

[18] See footnote 13 of this chapter.

[19] IISG, NVV codelijsten 1945–1970, 1951 HM4, Notulen Sociale Commissie, 10 October 1952.

Joekes. Like the British state pension, Joekes's plan combined flat-rate benefits with flat-rate contributions and contained no provisions for an automatic adjustment of benefits to price and wage increases. Unlike the British state pension, it entailed a deduction of the individual's resources from the public benefit. It was this latter provision that led the many different employer federations to prefer the RVV's plan over the government alternative. According to the NVV, the employer federations' main objection to Joekes's plan was that the plan "grabbed" what occupational plans remitted and thus conflicted with the highest priority of employers, which was that the public old age pension not interfere with private provision.[20] The employer federations had far fewer difficulties with the plan advocated by the unions. They could accept the combination of earnings-related contributions and flat-rate benefits because the subsistence nature of the benefit and the introduction of an income threshold over which the taxation authorities levied no contributions limited the solidarity this created.[21] Some of the members of the confessional employer federations did have strong objections to the centralized design of the scheme. Yet, during discussions in the Raad van Bestuur in Arbeidszaken (RvBA, Council of Directors in Labor Affairs), a platform designed to facilitate finding a common stance among the many employer federations on labor matters, these members were eventually persuaded by counterarguments from representatives of other employer federations, who stated that continued principled resistance against this feature of the scheme jeopardized the materialization of a consensus in industry, which could, in turn, endanger the continued existence of private pension funds. Moreover, many members of the largest employer federation at the time, the liberal Centraal Sociaal Werkgevers Verbond (CSWV, Central Social Employers' Federation), voiced appreciation for the cost-effectiveness of centralized administration.[22]

All employer federations also proved willing to accept an automatic adjustment of the public pension benefit to changes in the level of prices *and* wages. In the face of the continued willingness of unions to accept wage moderation, it must have been very difficult for employers to deny wage index linking of the old age benefit. Representatives of the CSWV justified their support for this linking by pointing to the current policy of centralized wage setting, which made an automatic linkage to the wage index cheap to administer.[23] In addition, several employers emphasized that under the present circumstances of allowing wages to rise with prices only, the index linkage made the old age pension benefit merely inflation-proof.[24] This last motivation suggests that the

[20] IISG, NVV codelijsten 1945–1970, 1951 HM4, Notulen Sociale Commissie, 30 Augustus 1951.
[21] ARA, CSWV, 2.19.103.06, 131: Notulen Kring voor Sociaal Overleg, 13 October 1953; and CSWV 2.19.103.06, 132: Notulen Kring voor Sociaal Overleg, 26 Juni 1956.
[22] VNO, F119(4) Cie Sociale Verzekering RCO 1947–1970: Notulen, 5 November 1947.
[23] ARA, CSWV, 2.19.103.06, 145: Notulen Kleine Technische Commissie Sociale Verzekering, 4 April 1955.
[24] ARA, CSWV, 2.19.103.06, 132: Notulen Kring voor Sociaal Overleg, 17 Mei 1956.

agreement to link the state benefit to increases in the level of prices *and* wages represented a compromise between the employer and union federations. The union federations celebrated the provision as a victory for those who wanted old age pensioners to benefit from future increases in prosperity[25] but later found out that this had been somewhat premature. When the policy of centralized wage setting broke down in the 1960s, they came to face a long battle with their employer counterparts over the question of whether the general old age benefit needed upgrading in line with increases in the cost of living alone or with increased prosperity (and thus higher wage) levels as well.

There was only one feature of the NVV plan that the employer federations unanimously rejected. They vehemently opposed compulsory membership in occupational plans – most of all for the self-employed. The confessional employer federations were most adamant on this – which the NVV had anticipated. The three union federations were quick to yield on this point. One reason for this was surely that they were ecstatic about the willingness of the employer federations to agree to all other points of the NVV plan. Another reason was that compulsory membership in occupational schemes also went a bit too far for some of the representatives of the CNV.[26]

The agreement between labor and capital paved the way for introduction of the AOW. As the NVV had already expected, after the KAB and its Catholic employer counterparts, the Katholiek Verbond van Werkgeversvakverenigingen (KVW, Catholic Federation of Employers' Unions) and the Algemene Katholieke Werkgeversvereniging (AKWV, General Catholic Employers' Federation), lent their support to the scheme, the governing Katholieke Volkspartij (KVP, Catholic People's Party) followed suit.[27] When criticism from the also-governing Labor Party forced Minister Joekes to withdraw his own pension proposal, the last hurdle disappeared.[28] Because Parliament sanctioned an extension of the operating period of the emergency old age provision, negotiations between representatives of unions, employers, and the state in the newly created Sociaal-Economische Raad (SER, Social-Economic Council) – which was to become a very important platform for discussions on public welfare reform in coming years – added several features to the plan. Only the two most important of these must be mentioned here. First, the negotiation partners decided to exempt the self-employed under a certain income limit from paying a premium. All workers would have to contribute. The union federations accepted this unevenness as the price they had to pay for introduction of the state benefit. Moreover, several union representatives expressed their sympathy for the

---

[25] IISG, NVV codelijsten 1945–1970, E1, Noodvoorziening Ouden van Dagen: Concept-voorlopig verslag wetsontwerp 4009 (Algemene Ouderdomsvoorziening).

[26] IISG, NVV codelijsten 1945–1970, 1952 HM4, Notulen Sociale Commissie, 8 November 1952.

[27] IISG, NVV codelijsten 1945–1970, 1952 Ec5, Noodvoorziening ouden van dagen – ongenummerde stukken, notitie inzake de ouderdomsvoorziening.

[28] See Heuting, De Jong, and Neij, *Naar groter eenheid*, 281.

hardship endured by many of the self-employed – a group of which almost one-third lived below or near the poverty line.[29]

Second, and of much more importance to future developments in the field of old age pension provision, the union federations accepted that the public benefit had to be financed exclusively by worker contributions. This meant formal recognition of the principle that public insurance benefits, like occupational insurance benefits, are deferred wages, which therefore must be paid for by workers themselves. To confessional unions, this principle was well suited to their emphasis on self-reliance. The NVV, however, like its counterpart in the United Kingdom, had long insisted that employers also should contribute to the public pension benefit.[30] In contrast to the TUC, the NVV eventually accepted complete worker financing of the scheme, though. One reason for its hesitation to accept this was that it had already agreed to keep the wages of workers artificially low for many years to facilitate the country's postwar reconstruction. This meant that complete worker financing of the act would hurt workers' pockets deeply. For this reason, the NVV and its confessional counterparts demanded, and received, wage compensation. The result was a classic example of the complexity of Dutch wage negotiations in the early postwar period. Employers agreed to provide wage compensation because the unions had shown a prolonged willingness to support wage restraint. The unions, in turn, were willing to settle for less-than-complete compensation so as not to endanger the government's stabilization policy. In the year after the creation of the AOW, employers agreed to a supplementary wage charge of 5.6 percent – a figure just below the 6.75 percent premium paid by workers – on top of the normal compensation for price and rent increases, for which employers were partly compensated by a reduction in the unemployment premium.[31]

LABOR UNIONS AND THE REJECTION OF A REDISTRIBUTIVE CONTRIBUTORY PENSION SCHEME IN THE UNITED KINGDOM

By presenting a plan based on redistribution of income among workers, the three Dutch union federations proved themselves to be far more committed allies of pensioners in need than their British counterpart, the TUC, had been. Instead of supporting the egalitarian principle of equality between worker contributions and benefits, as the TUC had done earlier, the Dutch union federations accepted that an adequate old age benefit demanded a certain degree of redistribution between higher- and lower-income workers. In the following

[29] IISG, NVV codelijsten 1945–1970, 1951 Ec5, Noodvoorziening ouden van dagen: Nota Berger, Oudedomsvoorzieningen III, 11 Juni 1951.

[30] The NVV only dropped its demands for an employer contribution to the scheme in 1952. IISG, NVV codelijsten 1945–1970, 1952, HM13, Notulen sub-commissie ouderdomsvoorziening, 16 October 1952.

[31] ARA, CSWV, 2.19.103.06, 136: Notulen Sociale Kring, 17 Juli 1956.

years, the TUC and Dutch union federations reasserted the preferences they had demonstrated earlier. In the Netherlands, the union federations continued to push for more redistribution among different grades of workers by demanding higher worker premiums and an increase in the level of the income ceiling over which no contributions had to be paid. In the United Kingdom, by contrast, the TUC's preference for equality over solidarity among workers came ever more to the fore. During the mid-1940s, its stance could be justified, with some effort, by arguing that the need to achieve an immediate increase in the living situation of existing pensioners stopped the TUC from proposing a redistributive contributory solution. Yet no such justification existed for its lack of enthusiasm for later initiatives to introduce redistributive features into the public pension scheme. The first example of such an initiative arrived quite soon after the state pension came into operation.

Despite its initial positive reception at home and abroad, the shortcomings of the Beveridge solution of combining flat-rate benefits with flat-rate contributions soon became clear. Opting for equality in worker contributions had limited the level of the state benefit to what the lowest-earning worker could afford, whereas the absence of index linking gradually eroded its dismally low real value. Inflation, an aging population, and the Labour government's decision to do away with Beveridge's recommendation for a transition period all exacerbated the shortcomings of the flat-rate contributory system. Under the circumstances, several successive governments in the immediate postwar period saw no room for benefit increases. A Conservative government first restored the real value of the state pension to its original level as late as 1955.[32]

In responding to the inadequacies of the state pension, the TUC's inability to press for worker solidarity came clearly to the fore. Realizing that unions representing well-paid workers would not accept a more redistributive social security system, the TUC continued to adhere firmly to the flat-rate contributory principle. This made a solution like the Dutch one impracticable: when Labour politicians in the early 1950s proposed to pay for uniform benefits with income-related contributions, TUC representatives were unwilling to support the idea.[33] The inability of the TUC to accept – let alone press for – redistribution of income among higher- and lower-paid workers greatly hampered its objective of achieving an adequate state pension because it could push only for an increase in the Exchequer subsidy to the scheme. Committed as the TUC was to the contributory principle for fear of a return of the means test, this was, at most, a modest demand. Even if the Exchequer subsidy had reached Beveridge's original target of 33 percent of the total costs of the scheme, in the long term this could not have produced anything resembling the standards that old age pensioners in the Netherlands, who relied only on state benefits, were enjoying at the time. More important in the short term, the demand proved

---

[32] See Hill, *The Welfare State*, 57.
[33] See Baldwin, *The Politics*, 233.

increasingly at odds with political reality. This became clear in 1951, when a friendly Labour government actually reduced the Exchequer subsidy to the National Insurance Fund in the face of rising state costs.[34]

Meanwhile, other parties contemplated alternative measures to mend the shortcomings of the flat-rate contributory approach without having to challenge the Beveridge doctrine. Faced with the prospect of a doubling in state costs owing to inflation and demographic change, the Conservatives, after their return to power in 1951, contemplated a targeting of the neediest through the means test but eventually settled for a further reduction in the Exchequer subsidy to the old age pension scheme in 1957.[35] Three years before, the Phillips Committee, a government-appointed committee charged with investigating the economic and financial problems of provision for old age, had adopted the official standpoint of the British Employers' Confederation (BEC), recommending that the retirement age be raised.[36] Even more than the Conservatives, employers took it for granted that the state pension could not provide a subsistence level in the future; the only question therefore was how to solve the scheme's financial insolvency.[37] In its evidence to the Phillips Committee, the BEC explained this as follows: "[T]hose sections of the community which are in a strong bargaining position have benefited at the expense of sections whose bargaining position has been weak. Elderly persons no longer in active employment must, in the nature of things, inevitably find themselves in this latter category."[38]

The first challenge to the actual Beveridge doctrine itself came from the Labour Party. Realizing the political impossibility of achieving an adequate minimum pension by increasing the Exchequer subsidy to the scheme, but not hampered by an inability to argue for worker solidarity, Labour's social security experts became convinced that the only viable solution to the problem of poverty in old age lay in the introduction of a redistributive contributory solution.[39] The two alternatives considered by the political right – means testing

---

[34] Ibidem, 232.

[35] See, for example, Rodney Lowe, "The Replanning of the Welfare State, 1957–1964." In Martin Francis and Ina Zweiniger-Bargielowska, *The Conservatives and British Society, 1880–1990* (Cardiff: University of Wales Press, 1996), 257. For Conservative attitudes toward social security in general during this period, see Paul Bridgen and Rodney Lowe, *Welfare Policy under the Conservatives 1951–1964: A Guide to Documents in the Public Record Office* (London: Public Record Office, 1998); and Paul Bridgen, "The One Nation Idea and State Welfare: The Conservatives and Pensions in the 1950s," *Contemporary British History* 14:3 (2000), 83–104.

[36] See Stationary Office, Report of the Committee on the Economic and Financial Problems of the Provision for Old Age (London: CMD 9333, 1954).

[37] MRC, MSS 200/3/2/c1120: Minutes committee on economic and financial problems of the provision for old age, 6 May, 1954.

[38] MRC, MSS 200/3/2/c1120: British Employers' Confederation. Government committee on the economic and financial problems of the provision for old age. Memorandum of evidence by confederation, 29 March 1954.

[39] On the political impossibility of increasing the benefit level of the state pension by increasing the Exchequer subsidy to it, see Baldwin, *The Politics*, 232; Richard C. Whiting, "Ideology

and an increase in the retirement age – were rejected out of hand as steps back.[40] As mentioned earlier, Labour was the first party to contemplate combining uniform benefits with earnings-related contributions. The TUC's lack of enthusiasm for this idea could have sufficed to shoot it down, but Labour's social security experts also must have noted its inadequacy regarding another concern: the very low level of occupational pension coverage among workers. Thus, after the TUC rejected Labour's proposal to combine flat-rate benefits with earnings-related contributions, its social security experts started to consider a solution that was also under consideration in Germany and Sweden at the time: national superannuation.

By the late 1950s, only about a third of the British working population was covered by occupational pension schemes. This privileged part of the workforce naturally comprised only higher-skilled, and thus higher-paid, workers. Most of these workers belonged to the white-collar category. Of all manual workers, only one in four could claim some degree of entitlement to pension provision at the time.[41] Although there is little information on the spread of occupational pension coverage within the manual and white-collar category, it is safe to assume that of those manual workers who could claim membership in occupational pension schemes during the late 1950s, nearly all belonged to the skilled manual category. As a result of their very low earnings, it is hard to conceive of many semi- and unskilled manual workers having been able to afford occupational pension scheme membership at the time. Often employers did not even offer them the possibility of membership in these schemes. The same distinction almost certainly applied to the white-collar category.

Labour's social security experts were well aware of the sharp differences in the abilities of different worker categories to save for supplementary occupational provision. They also noted two other shortcomings of the private pension system. First, and because of the almost complete absence of industry-wide bargaining in the United Kingdom, most pension schemes were quite small. This not only made them financially vulnerable, but it also made it more difficult to preserve pension rights after a change in employer.[42] Second, and far

and Reform in Labour's Tax Strategy, 1964–1970," *Historical Journal* 41 (1998), 1121–40; and Martin Daunton, *Just Taxes: The Politics of Taxation in Britain, 1914–1979* (Cambridge University Press, 2002), 279–302; Paul Bridgen, "A Straitjacket with Wriggle Room: The Beveridge Report, the Treasury and the Exchequer's Pension Liability, 1942–59," *Twentieth Century British History* 17 (2006), 2–3; Jim Tomlinson, "Why So Austere? The British Welfare State in the 1940s," *Journal of Social Policy* 27 (1998), 63–7.

40 See Fawcett, "The Beveridge Strait-jacket," 26; Baldwin, *The Politics*, 232.

41 See Leslie Hannah, *Inventing Retirement: The Development of Occupational Benefits in Britain* (Cambridge University Press, 1986), 56, 145.

42 In 1959, 75 percent of private pension schemes had fewer than fifty members. See Whiteside, "Historical Perspectives," 27. To deal with this problem, the BEC actually discussed the possibility of striving for the creation of industry-wide pension schemes in the mid-1950s. Like its counterparts in the Netherlands (as we will see later in this chapter), the BEC noted the other benefits of industry-wide pension schemes as well: they could help to avoid undesirable

more important to left-wing critics, workers who belonged to occupational pension schemes enjoyed very generous tax advantages. According to Labour's academic standard bearer, London School of Economics (LSE) Professor Richard Titmuss, losses to the Exchequer from the generous tax treatment of private pensions actually exceeded the costs of state expenditure on National Insurance.[43] This in itself was a problem because this, in effect, resulted in rather large tax breaks for higher-paid workers. Because of the concurrent inadequacy of the state benefit, Labour's social security experts viewed these tax breaks as intolerable.

Labour's solution to all these problems was the introduction of superannuation. In October of 1957, a Labour study group – headed by rising star Richard Crossman and under the intellectual guidance of a group of Titmuss's circle of LSE intellectuals – presented the annual Labour Party Conference with its proposal to create an earnings-related and inflation-proof state pension. The scheme contained an immediate 50 percent increase in the basic state pension and additional increases for workers depending on their previous wages. After the conference approved the scheme, Crossman worked very hard to convince the TUC of its merits. Because unions representing privileged workers resisted the scheme, he did so with only very limited success.

To many in the Labour Party, superannuation must have seemed a true panacea for the shortcomings of both state and private provision. When Richard Crossman first read about it, the concept reportedly hit him with a "blinding flash."[44] As in Sweden, where the social democrats were also preparing the creation of an earnings-related supplementary pension [resulting in the Allmän Tilläggspension (ATP) in 1959], the British Labour Party liked superannuation for its ability to spread earnings-related benefits among all workers. Unlike the Swedish case, however, superannuation came on the agenda in the United Kingdom as a means to finance an improvement in the basic state pension benefit. As a result, superannuation had a decidedly redistributive flavor; a large part of the earnings-related contributions would be used to finance a value-secured minimum rate below which no pensioner was allowed to fall.[45]

competition between employers in industry and might help to stabilize industrial relations. On the other hand, an industry-wide scheme inevitably would become subject to more claims, and unions might demand some share in its management. See MRC, MRC 200/B/3/2/c1221: Minutes General Purposes Committee BEC, 7 February 1957. In the conflict-prone system of British industrial relations, the latter argument must have mattered heavily to employers. The discussion was in any case a hypothetical one because the TUC never demanded the creation of industry-wide pension schemes – probably because unions representing privileged workers would not have accepted them.

[43] See Richard Titmuss, "Pensions Systems and Population Change," *Political Quarterly* 16:2 (1955), 163.

[44] Richard Crossman, *The Politics of Pensions* (Liverpool University Press, 1972), 12.

[45] For many poorer workers, this in fact meant that they would receive a state benefit that was higher than their previous working wage. Given the very low level of wages earned by some workers, this is hardly surprising. As we have already seen in Chapter 2, under social assistance,

Under such a scheme, the privileged members of existing occupational pension schemes would, of course, lose out. They now faced the potential replacement of their generous occupational plans with a public pension scheme that diverted a substantial part of their contributions to benefits for lower-paid workers. As a result, they vehemently opposed it.

Resistance to this plan from unions representing higher-paid workers, among which civil servant unions such as the National Association of Local Government Officers (NALGO) was especially vehement, initiated a long period of TUC ambivalence toward superannuation.[46] On the one hand, members of the TUC Social Insurance and Industrial Welfare Committee were now well aware of the political impossibility of increasing the basic pension through taxation – at least without raising the prospect of a return to means testing.[47] They also appreciated superannuation as an effective way to spread earnings-related pension schemes to all workers.[48] Yet the resistance of craft and occupationally organized white-collar unions to the redistributive features of the scheme forced the TUC to take a skeptical position on superannuation. In conversations with Labour backbenchers, TUC representatives called superannuation merely "sufficiently attractive in principle to justify detailed examination." At the same time, they made several demands that would reduce its redistributive features. First, Labour had to make sure that worker contributions were kept at a "reasonable" level. Second, and far more important, workers had to be given the option to opt out of the scheme.[49]

This latter demand in particular presented Labour strategists with quite a dilemma. On the one hand, they realized that they had to allow some degree of contracting out into existing occupational schemes in order to get craft union, and thus TUC, support for their plans. On the other hand, they realized that if too many workers contracted out, it would become impossible to finance benefit increases for lower-paid workers.[50] Crossman therefore limited the opt-out possibility in two ways. First, he allowed contracting out only into existing schemes that could match the performance of the state scheme. As TUC representatives pointed out, this effectively resulted in the death sentence for existing pension schemes because very few of them could guarantee an inflation-proof benefit or a complete transfer of existing pension rights after a

---

a low-paid worker could also receive more in benefits than he or she had previously earned in wages.

[46] On this, see MRC, MSS.292/166.21/2b: Labour Party proposals on a national superannuation scheme. Report meeting TUC and Home Policy Committee Labour Party, 7 March 1957.

[47] According to Peter Baldwin, the TUC leadership had already been aware of this back in 1953. See Baldwin, *The Politics*, 238.

[48] MRC, MSS.200/161/13: Social Insurance and Industrial Welfare Committee minutes, 13 February.

[49] MRC, MSS.292/166.21/2a: National superannuation. Proposed meeting with Labour Party, 14 May 1958.

[50] MRC, MSS.292/166.21/2b: Report meeting TUC and Home Policy Committee Labour Party, 27 February, 1957.

change in employer.[51] Second, only existing members of occupational schemes were given the possibility to contract out. According to TUC representatives, this meant that existing schemes would "wither away" because "many schemes ... depended on new entrants for their continued solvency." TUC representatives also questioned why existing schemes could not accept new members. TUC representatives concluded from this that "the Labour Party wishes the State to take over all private schemes but, for political reasons, prefers to do so in this indirect way."[52]

In the face of so much union resistance, Crossman had no alternative but to give in. In May 1958, he informed the TUC Social Insurance and Industrial Welfare Committee that the opt-out provision was to be extended to new entrants as well. After the scheme had been in operation for some years, he would see whether this option was to continue permanently.[53] Apparently, this was enough to give the scheme a cautious welcome at the TUC conference in Blackpool that year.[54] Yet the divisions within the labor movement had become painfully clear. Business groups such as the Life Offices' Association (LOA), Britain's main representative of the insurance industry, capitalized on this by showing how bad a deal superannuation was for average- and higher-income workers.[55] The Conservative government, meanwhile, referred to Labour's plans as "backdoor nationalization." This accusation proved potent in the upcoming election simply because it was close to the truth. Although mainly financed on a pay-as-you-go basis, the superannuation scheme would have strong funded elements. To some in the Labour Party at least, the appeal of superannuation therefore lay in the prospect of redirecting investment funds from private insurance companies into the hands of the state.[56] In fact, for some prominent

[51] MRC, MSS.292/161/14: Appendix, Minutes Social Insurance and Industrial Welfare Committee, 13 March 1957.

[52] MRC, MSS.292/166.21/2b: Report meeting TUC and Home Policy Committee Labour Party, 27 February, 1957.

[53] MRC, MSS.292/166.21/2b: Note of a conference between the Social Insurance and Industrial Welfare Committee with Mr. R. H. Crossman, M.P., and representatives of various unions catering to non-manual workers, 26 March 1958.

[54] For these and other objections to Labour's plans, see Baldwin, *The Politics*, 238.

[55] The LOA actively tried to "lobby in favour of private solutions" by approaching "liberal politicians and trade unionists who might support private plans." It noted that there were many unions who "were particularly anxious to protect the accrued benefits of their members." LOA: Ms. 28376/91, General meeting, 29 July 1957; Ms. 28376/96, Publicity Joint Committee, 13 March 1958; MS. 28376/90, Minutes of the Goodwill Advertising Committee, 12 June 1957.

[56] It should be pointed out here that the same party conference that accepted superannuation also adopted a nationalization platform. See Baldwin, *The Politics*, 237. The Conservative government capitalized on this by arguing that Labour wanted to collect public contributions in order to "buy off bits of British industry," that the plan amounted to "a wild attack on private insurance companies ... by the parties which always intended to nationalize the insurance companies," and that the plan would lead to "nationalization by stealth." These remarks were not without effect. Within four days of the publication of Labour's superannuation proposal, the value of life insurance companies on the London Exchange had decreased by 2.4 million pounds. See Heclo, *Modern Social Politics*, 266–7.

left-wing members, this was the only advantage Crossman's scheme held over their preferred alternative, which was a complete replacement of contributory funding to financing by general taxation.[57]

The prospect of losing large parts of the private pension industry prompted some employers into a willingness to compromise. In private discussions with Conservative ministers and Members of Parliament, representatives of the LOA went so far as to suggest the introduction of legislation to compel all employees to join occupational schemes. John Boyd-Carpenter, the Conservative Minister for Pensions and National Insurance, however, saw too many problems with this. He also did not see its necessity because he deemed a modest increase in the basic state pension as sufficient to take the heat of his party.[58] For the Conservatives, the main priority was to safeguard the financial solvency of the existing state pension scheme without touching the private pension industry. In response to superannuation, the government therefore proposed introducing a very limited measure of earnings-related contributions into the existing scheme, which, after sealing up the scheme's deficits, left room for only miniscule earnings-related benefits.[59] The plan brought little redistribution. It levied a contribution of 4½ percent only on earnings between nine and fifteen pounds per week, so workers earning less than nine pounds per week stayed on flat-rate benefits, whereas higher earnings remained untapped.[60] By spurring workers to contract out, the government further prevented any pretence of a redistributive purpose. Lower National Insurance contributions for the contracted out, more generous tax concessions to private schemes under the 1956 Finance Act, and the decision not to make the basic state pension inflation-proof all benefited private provision.

The government's solution to the shortcomings of the state pension received little sympathy from the union movement and employer community. The TUC General Council strongly criticized the increase in contributions, its use for sealing the scheme's deficit, and the continued inadequacy of the flat-rate benefit. Once more, the council wanted to have it both ways by demanding an immediate substantial increase in the state benefit, to be financed by an

[57] An incident described by Hugh Heclo neatly illustrates how far the left wing of the Labour Party stood from the TUC on pensions. Labour's left wing had voiced its opposition to superannuation during the Labour Party Conference in October 1957. Its motivation for opposing the scheme was that an earnings-related pension scheme carried the inequality of working life over to old age. Crossman's reaction to this was that "it is really for the trade unions to decide whether wages should be equal or unequal, and so long as trade unions are prepared to have unequal wages it is a little tough to ask for all pensions to be equal." See Heclo, *Modern Social Politics*, 269.

[58] See Hanna, *Inventing Retirement*, 56–7.

[59] Of the 42 million pounds in extra income this would bring, 37 million went to meet the deficit in flat-rate pension accounts, leaving only 5 million for graduated benefits.

[60] In comparison, Labour proposed to levy contributions on all earnings up to forty pounds per week. See Bridgen, "The One Nation Idea," 85.

increase in employer and Exchequer contributions.[61] Employers, meanwhile, still preferred an increase in the retirement age and condemned the government scheme as too complicated to administer.[62] Noting the opposition coming from the TUC as well, the BEC concluded that the government's scheme did not have many friends outside the Treasury.[63] Yet the government was not seeking to increase its popularity with the proposed reform; it simply aimed to address the system's insolvency without alienating too many voters.[64] In this it was quite successful. During the general elections of 1959, superannuation proved not to be the "wonderful vote-winner" Crossman had hoped it to be because a small majority of voters gave the Conservatives their third consecutive victory.[65]

In retrospect, it is possible to argue that if the Labour Party had enacted superannuation, the United Kingdom would have become one of the most advanced welfare states of the day.[66] Yet the important point is that it could not do so. Even if Labour had won the election, the concessions it had made to unions that objected to the scheme still would have prevented the scheme from being implemented in its original form. Labour's social security experts were acutely aware of this but, in contrast to the party's left wing, saw little alternative. The "Scandinavian" solution of financing the state pension by sources of income outside worker contributions certainly would have resulted in the return of the means test because there was no strong agricultural interest in tax financing in the United Kingdom. Moreover, it would not have solved the problem of the lack of private pension coverage among manual workers. Superannuation therefore did not end up in the dustbin but returned, in a somewhat modified form, when Labour regained power in 1964. Now popularly labeled the "Crossman scheme," employer, worker, and state contributions were to result in a 60 percent replacement rate on earnings up to half the national average and an additional 25 percent up to a ceiling of one and a half times the national average. The pension benefit would again be inflation-proof – or at least subject to a biennial review. To prevent opponents from accusing Labour of having a secret agenda to nationalize the pension industry, Crossman had increased the scheme's reliance on pay-as-you-go financing in which current benefits are paid for by current contributions. This assuaged fears that the scheme would generate large state-controlled savings, and there was no longer any talk of

---

[61] MRC, MSS.292B/161.10: Note for proposed meeting with Minister of Social Security, 11 October 1967.

[62] PRO, PIN 42/130: Letter from the BEC, 7 March 1960.

[63] MRC, MSS.200/B/4/2/4: BEC bulletin, 19 October 1960.

[64] According to John Boyd-Carpenter, who was the Conservative minister of pensions and national insurance at the time, superannuation "would neither win nor lose votes." See Baldwin, *The Politics*, 240

[65] See Richard Crossman, *The Backbench Diaries of Richard Crossman* (London: Hamilton, (1981), 581.

[66] See Fawcett, "The Beveridge Strait-jacket," 25–6.

government control over economic investment.[67] Finally, the option to contract out returned because it was crucial to Labour's bid to appease unions representing privileged workers.[68]

With the opposition of the latter to superannuation still fresh in their minds, Labout was reluctant at first to implement the new scheme.[69] Initially, the narrowness of Labour's parliamentary majority of four seats provided an excuse to delay implementation of the Crossman scheme. After gaining a larger majority in 1966, the less politically sensitive introduction of earnings-related supplements to sickness and unemployment benefits gave the pretext for waiting two more years. Originally planned for implementation in autumn of 1966, the pension plan thus got under way only in 1968, after Crossman personally took charge of the Department of Health and Social Security. Once more, the party worked frantically to obtain broad support for its proposals. Even more than in the late 1950s, the outcome was a useful lesson in the importance of union representation because the unions whose members already had access to occupational provision had only grown more vocal in their objections to Labour's redistributive goals. Once again, the TUC leadership struggled with the competing interests of different unions. Whereas those unions representing many workers who did not have access to occupational provision came out in clear support of the Crossman scheme, others aligned themselves closely with the business community in opposing the scheme.

The clash of interests between unions representing many lower-paid and those representing higher-paid workers came clearly to the fore in the discussions of the Social Insurance and Industrial Welfare Committee. To the representatives of the general unions, national superannuation was the only way to provide the bulk of union members with an earnings-related old age benefit because voluntary efforts had not proven successful for them. They stressed that lower-paid workers were often outside occupational pension schemes not because they wanted to but because employers had resisted the introduction of occupational schemes for them.[70] General union representatives also welcomed

[67] See Crossman, *The Backbench Diaries*, 985; ibidem, *The Diaries of a Cabinet Minister*, Vol. 3: *Secretary of State for Social Services, 1968–70* (London: Hamilton, 1977) 153–4; Barbara Castle, *The Castle Diaries, 1964–1970* (London: Weidenfeld and Nicholson, 1984), 751.

[68] In his diaries, Crossman explained his decision to do so as follows: "It was obvious that if we introduced our scheme without any provision for contracting out, all the good private schemes would have to be cancelled and there would be a terrible row.... They [the insurance industry] would tell their members that the wicked Labour government was depriving them of their pensions. This was politically very dangerous indeed.... So I announced we wanted a genuine partnership between public and private pensioneering." See Crossman, *The Politics of Pensions*, 20.

[69] According to Hugh Heclo, "[S]uperannuation was not considered sufficiently important to merit high priority among the party leadership, either after victory in 1964 and 1966 or before an election in 1970. And party leadership was in turn a function ... of apathy and misunderstanding in the British union movement, so much so that union hostility itself was an important cause of the delay that led to the plan's demise." See Heclo, *Modern Social Politics*, 279.

[70] MRC, MSS.292B/166.5/1: TUC General Council minutes, 20 August 1969.

the government's scheme for bringing "social justice" to lower-paid workers and took it for granted that a scheme based "on social principles" gave higher wage earners a somewhat lower return on their contributions than lower-paid workers.[71] Representatives of unions in which members already had access to occupational provision disagreed. They vehemently objected to the new scheme that gave lower-paid workers an advantage and urged the committee "to see that all interests were looked after without prejudice" because "these [meaning: their] interests had to be weighed against those without occupational schemes."[72] Again, these unions focused primarily on increasing the ability of workers to contract out from the state scheme into occupational schemes.

In their opposition to the Crossman scheme, these unions found a strong ally in the business community. During their first meeting with government officials, representatives from the Confederation of British Industry (CBI) – by then the only remaining employer federation in the country – made its opposition to the scheme perfectly clear. Still preoccupied mainly with the financial solvency of the National Insurance Fund, CBI representatives again proposed increasing the retirement age. An increase in the retirement age made sense, they argued, because the age at which health began to deteriorate was now much higher, and increased mechanization had lessened the rigors of work in heavy industry.[73] At minimum, the representatives stated, the government's plans must be deferred until the economic position of the United Kingdom had improved. At most, the CBI could support an increase in the Exchequer contribution, and then only to meet the growing costs of the National Insurance Fund. A higher Exchequer contribution made sense to the CBI because the government itself was to be blamed for the current problems: "As the increasing numbers of old people could presumably be attributed to the benefits of the National Health Service, which was tax-financed, the increased numbers of pensions which had to be paid as a result should also be tax-financed."[74] The absence of Labour flirtation with government control over economic investment did not make the scheme more acceptable to the CBI. On the contrary, its representatives only lamented the move to increased pay-as-you-go financing as "inflationary" and a "mortgage on the future." Provided the state's role as an investor remained small, the CBI therefore favored an increase in funded components of the scheme.[75] Like its counterparts in the Netherlands, the CBI's main priority had always been to retain occupational pension schemes. If the government decided to go ahead with the scheme, employer representatives therefore warned, the CBI would only accept this when the maximum extent of contracting out was allowed.[76]

---

[71] MRC, MSS.166.5/1: TUC, Occupational pensions, partial contracting out, 6 October 1969.

[72] MRC, MSS.292B/166.5/1: TUC General Council minutes, 20 August 1969.

[73] PRO, T 227/3081: Note of meeting with representatives from the CBI on 18 July 1968.

[74] PRO, T 227/3081: The Exchequer supplement, 13 June 1969.

[75] PRO, T 227/3081, CBI on government proposals for earnings-related social security, 19 June 1969.

[76] MRC, MSS.200/C/3/EMP/3: Government's proposals on national superannuation and social security. Summary of views of social security committee, 28 April 1969.

With both organized employers and unions representing privileged workers demanding a complete preservation of existing pension rights, the main quarrel was now over the so-called abatement, a partial contracting out of the state scheme. Because Labour realized that most occupational schemes would not be able to match the performance of the state scheme – which previously had been the condition for contracting out – it now no longer allowed for complete contracting out of the state scheme.[77] Instead, workers could give up a certain percentage of the state pension benefit in return for a reduced contribution to the state scheme. In other words, the abatement allowed occupational pensions to take over a share of the national pension. This again brought the following problem: if the abatement terms were made too lenient, the generosity of the state pension would be endangered; if the abatement terms were made too strict, many occupational schemes would not be able to survive. To Labour, an acceptable compromise was a 1 percent reduction in pension benefits in exchange for a 1.3 percent reduction in contributions. This time the TUC General Council came out firmly on Labour's side. It stated its opposition to any further increase in the level of the abatement because this would be detrimental to the income of the state fund.[78] To meet the demands of the more-privileged parts of its constituency, it simultaneously proposed making the state scheme somewhat less redistributive. While Labour had proposed giving a 60 percent replacement rate on earnings up to half the national average, resulting in a rather abrupt reduction in the marginal rate of the benefit at a relatively low level of earnings, the TUC now suggested a 40 percent replacement rate up to national earnings and, like Labour, 25 percent over higher earnings.[79] This compromise, however, convinced neither the CBI nor the objecting unions. In an official press statement, the National Federation of Professional Workers (NFPW), for example, rejected Labour's abatement as "complete nonsense."[80]

In 1969, in a powerful display of the importance of union leadership, NALGO – then the fifth largest labor union in the United Kingdom – produced a pamphlet containing the "seven major disadvantages of national superannuation." In it, NALGO's leadership explained how it had been "forced to the conclusion that the effect of the Government's proposals could be to seriously erode public service schemes, without substituting equivalent benefits." In an excellent example of how close the interests of unions such as NALGO were

---

[77] The state scheme would reach maturity in twenty-one years and was inflation-proof. Occupational schemes would never be able to match this. In addition, contracting out would be possible only for the personal pension. Widowhood and dependency benefits were to be fully provided by the state.

[78] MRC, MSS.292B/166.51/2: Issued by the press and Publications Department Congress House.

[79] MRC, MSS.292B/166.5/.2: Economic aspects of the government's national superannuation and social insurance proposals – note on memorandum by the secretary of state for social services, 2 April 1969.

[80] MRC, MSS.166.5/1: Press statement National Federation of Professional Workers, 26 July 1969.

to those of employers, the pamphlet stated, "NALGO has no quarrel with the employers or their representatives in any of the public services, whose attitude throughout has been helpful and sympathetic to staff interests."[81] As Crossman himself noted in his diary, the pamphlet had quite an impact on the "rank and file."[82] When Crossman advanced a mass meeting of NALGO members in an attempt to smooth tensions, he encountered "an atmosphere of ferocious hostility."[83] Followed by loud applause from the floor, one worker vented his frustration in a rather direct way by asking, "Is it your intention to lay your filthy hands on the lolly which is in the occupational schemes?" Crossman concluded from this that many unions were making "the wildest assertions about what was going to happen as a result of our scheme."[84] In fact, union agitation against his scheme became so fierce that it even forced a response from the TUC General Council. Just before introduction of the superannuation bill in Parliament, the TUC report carried an article subheaded, "Dick Crossman's new pension plan is being misrepresented by some, maligned by others and misunderstood by many." Although granting its own "criticisms" about certain parts of the scheme, it went on to stress that "working people can only benefit from the new state pension scheme."[85]

Matters eventually came to a head at the TUC Congress of 1969, where three white-collar unions supported a motion that criticized national superannuation for requiring members of occupational schemes to subsidize the state scheme. Perry Coldwick, the representative of the Transport Salaried Staffs' Association (TSSA) who submitted the motion, attempted to convince the congress that "this motion is no manual versus non-manual worker, no white-collar versus blue-collar motion."[86] This was true in the sense that the winners and losers in Labour's attempt at redistribution could be found in each of these categories. Many skilled manual workers were by now members of occupational pension schemes, whereas many unskilled white-collar workers remained outside the schemes. To be sure, semiskilled and unskilled manual workers rarely had access to occupational provision. Thus, although it was not a "manual versus non-manual" or "white-collar versus blue-collar motion," it certainly was an "affluent versus non-affluent" motion. The initiators of the motion did little to conceal this because they warned against attempts "to improve the position of the worse-off section of the community at the expense of those whose earnings were in the middle salary range and who were in occupational pension

[81] National and Local Government Officers Association, *National Superannuation and Social Insurance: A Statement by NALGO on the Government Proposals in the White Paper CMD. 3883* (London: NALGO, 1969), 2.
[82] See Crossman, *The Diaries*, 781.
[83] Ibidem, 639.
[84] Ibidem, 638.
[85] MRC, MSS.271/T/52/20, The Crossman scheme, 4–5.
[86] MRC, MSS.292B/784.34/3, TUC General Congress 1969, 529–30.

schemes."[87] The motion did not pass. Crossman nevertheless noted, "We really are in the soup."[88]

The leadership of the CBI had endorsed the view of its Social Security Committee that it should attempt to cooperate with – not obstruct – Labour's attempt to introduce earnings-related benefits because it was uncertain whether even a change of government could reverse existing plans.[89] It need not have worried. The Labour government introduced superannuation into Parliament in the beginning of 1970 but, to Crossman's great disappointment, lost the general elections of June 1970 before the scheme had passed the committee stage. Its Conservative successor overturned the superannuation bill and opted again for a small increase in earnings-related contributions to somewhat improve the basic pension, although not to the level of subsistence. The new government also proposed making the basic pension inflation-proof.[90] The Conservative government also proposed creating a so-called state reserve scheme that was to give workers without occupational coverage an earnings-related pension inferior to all but the worst private pensions. Under this government, requirements for recognition and preservation of pension rights were so lenient that they would do almost nothing to improve existing private pensions.[91]

In the Labour Party, this second electoral defeat naturally provoked a reconsideration of the view of superannuation as a "vote-winner." Powerful sections within the party called for a return to the Beveridge system, improving the state pension either by expanding on the Conservative solution of combining earnings-related contributions with uniform benefits or by increasing the Exchequer contribution. Union resistance to the small increase in earnings-related contributions by the Conservative government made the first a nonstarter, but the option of increased Exchequer contributions again proved quite popular with Labour's left wing.[92] Eventually, however, the moderate view prevailed, and efforts instead focused on finding ways to put superannuation more in line with the interests of higher-paid workers. To make superannuation acceptable to the higher-income strata, Labour's social security experts now accepted that they had to modify superannuation so that the state scheme would not stand in the way of private pension provision. Labour's agreeing to

---

[87] MRC, MSS.292B/445.7/1: Occupational pensions, 9 March 1970.

[88] See Crossman, *The Diaries*, 625.

[89] MRC, MSS.200/C/3/EMP/4: Social Security Committee minutes, 15 September 1969.

[90] As the TUC pointed out, the government's scheme was wholly inadequate to remove the need for supplementary benefits because the gap between the level of subsistence and the pension remained quite large: two pounds for a single pensioner and three pounds for a married couple. See MRC, MSS.292D/166.51/1: Government white paper, strategy for pensions, 13 October 1971.

[91] See Whiteside, "Historical Perspectives," 29.

[92] At the 1972 Labour Party Conference, Jack Jones, president of the Transport and General Workers' Union, submitted a motion in opposition to superannuation. The Labour leadership eventually persuaded Jones to withdraw his motion, but it had been welcomed with much enthusiasm by the left wing of the party. See Fawcett, "Jack Jones," 168.

leave private pension schemes untouched was a sharp reversal of the party's stance on pension reform because it necessitated an abdication of the party's original redistributive ambitions.

When Labour returned to power in 1974, it discarded the Conservative scheme and implemented its own renewed version of superannuation. Labour's new state earnings-related pension scheme (SERPS) differed from earlier super-annuation proposals in one major way. Instead of demanding that private schemes match the performance of the state scheme, the state now undertook to guarantee the viability of private schemes. Because SERPS guaranteed an inflation-proof benefit, this move "extended public liability in an unprece-dented fashion."[93] It also made SERPS into little more than a voluntary scheme. Within one year of its introduction, more than 10 million of the 11.5 million occupational pension scheme members had contracted out.[94] By maximizing the ability to contract out, the government successfully appeased unions repre-senting privileged workers and the CBI, but only at the expense of needy pen-sioners. With all those who lost out in redistribution contracting out, SERPS did little for the basic state pension other than making it inflation-proof, thus leaving poorer pensioners to rely on means-tested social assistance.[95] SERPS merely added 25 percent of a worker's previous best twenty years' earnings to the existing flat-rate benefit. For workers who earned a wage that was close to – or even below – subsistence, this resulted in a very meager supplement to the flat-rate benefit, which, although now inflation-proof, for married couples still came to only about 35 percent of the average earnings of a male manufac-turing worker.[96]

Some twenty years after it was first proposed, the United Kingdom had finally introduced superannuation. In terms of solidarity, SERPS was a pale reflection of what Crossman and Titmuss had proposed in the 1950s. Yet this is exactly what made it successful. Targeted as it was at the mass of the pop-ulation instead of the needy, it commanded broad societal support. After the Conservatives regained power in 1979, they therefore chose to leave it intact – at least for the moment.

UNIONS, EMPLOYERS, AND THE MOVE TOWARD FULL SUBSISTENCE PENSIONS IN THE NETHERLANDS

The protracted and difficult struggle to introduce superannuation in the United Kingdom shows that the ability of nations to achieve adequate pension

---

[93] See Whiteside, "Historical Perspectives," 31.

[94] See R. Hemming and J. Kay, "Contracting Out of the State Earnings Related Pension Scheme," *Fiscal Studies* 2 (1981), 22.

[95] The CBI noted the absence of a large increase in the basic flat-rate pension with approval. See MRC, MSS.200/C/3/EMP/5/6: Government pension proposals. Note meeting Social Security Committee, 23 September 1974.

[96] See Richard Parry, "United Kingdom." In Peter Flora, *Growth to Limits: The Western European Welfare States Since World War II*, Vol. 4: *Appendix* (New York: Walter de Gruyter, 1986), 189.

provision for all depends not on the organizational strength of labor unions but on their willingness and ability to support redistribution of income among workers. State pension provision remained inadequate in the United Kingdom not because of weak labor unionism but because craft and occupationally organized white-collar unions opposed any redistributive effort among workers. How different the situation was in the Netherlands, where union federations not only accepted that an adequate old age benefit demanded a certain degree of redistribution between more and less affluent workers but also actively pushed for this redistribution. As a result, from its inception, the Dutch public pension guaranteed a far more generous level of income maintenance for old age pensioners than the British state pension. Earnings-related contributions allowed for a much more generous benefit rate, whereas index linking guaranteed a preservation of purchasing power for the elderly or, if employers willed it (and they would eventually), allowed pensioners to share in future increases in national prosperity.

This is, of course, not to say that introduction of the AOW in 1955 completely eradicated the problem of poverty in old age in the Netherlands. Some five years after its introduction, the percentage of the elderly living in poverty had in fact only dropped from 32 to 24 percent.[97] Although the AOW is now often treated in the literature as the concluding piece of the Dutch pension system, to contemporaries, the act only provided a healthy first step in the creation of an adequate safety net of old age provision. Like its British counterpart, the Dutch state pension was not initially designed to be sufficient to live on. Instead, it was to provide an adequate pension only in combination with private pension supplements. In following years, union and employer federations continuously discussed how to improve the safety net of public and private provision in the Netherlands, with the unions putting more emphasis on public pension provision and organized employers emphasizing the importance of occupational provision. In doing so, they confirmed the preferences they had shown in the years leading up to the introduction of the AOW. The three union federations strengthened their demands for an increase in the level of the public benefit by arguing for more worker solidarity in the form of higher worker premiums and an increase in the level of the ceiling over which no income had to be paid. The employer federations fought a long but eventually unsuccessful battle to prevent such an increase. It was only when they were faced with a plan that would have resulted in an almost complete replacement of the private pension industry that they fully agreed to the demands of the union federations.

To understand the events that unfolded in the Netherlands after the introduction of the AOW, it is first necessary to point out that by the time the state pension came into operation, most workers already had access to supplementary

---

[97] NCW, 29(3): Sociale Verzekeringsfederatie, 1967–74: Kanttekeningen bij de nota van het CPB aan de SER van, 15 Januari 1969.

occupational provision. This meant that both unions and employers viewed occupational pension schemes as an integral part of the Dutch pension system. The only question, then, was how large the shares of public and private pensions were to be in the total provision of income maintenance for the elderly. All three union federations argued that the public share of total pension provision must be substantial because this was the only way to achieve adequate pension levels for all workers. The employer federations, by contrast, pushed to keep the public pension share as small as possible. They did accept that some degree of public, pay-as-you-go financing was necessary to provide a certain degree of protection against inflation.[98] Yet they wanted the public share in old age pension provision to be as small as possible in order to leave sufficient room for funded, private capital–based provision. They had at least two reasons for this. First, they felt that private pension provision furthered the personal responsibility of workers. More important, and as constantly emphasized by them, large private pension funds provided immense investment opportunities.[99] Initially, the employer federations therefore argued that the public pension should provide a subsistence benefit level only in combination with private supplements. The three union federations obviously disagreed with them on this point.

The reasons most workers already had access to supplementary occupational provision at the time of the introduction of the AOW can be found in the immediate pre- and postwar periods. As in most other European countries (but not in the United Kingdom), the prewar decision to introduce statutory legislation on an extension of collective-bargaining outcomes had provided a first impulse to bringing many workers under the tutelage of occupational pensions. Yet the high coverage rates that we see today resulted from the guided wage policy (in Dutch, *geleide loonpolitiek*) of the early postwar period.[100]

[98] KDC, KVW, 2336: Algemene Ouderdomswet, 1952–1959, Welk systeem van oudedagvoorziening door het bedrijfsleven is, indien de voorgestelde wettelijke ouderdomsvoorziening een feit wordt, gezien de huidige toestand en de verwachte ontwikkeling, gewenst?

[99] VU, FCWV, 19: Notulen Commissie Sociale Verzekering-en, 2 April 1969; ibidem, 18: Nota inzake de mogelijke structuur van een algemene aanvullende pensioenverzekering voor werknemers in Nederland, 1969; ARA, CSWV, 2.19.103.06, 134: Verslag vergadering Kring voor Sociaal, 7 September 1966.

[100] In the immediate postwar period, the goal of creating equal wage costs across companies in the same industrial sector, which was the motivation behind the 1937 act on the statutory extension of collective-bargaining outcomes, remained quite important in bringing workers under the tutelage of occupational pensions. In fact, this aim was almost equally important to the establishment of a guided wage policy in the immediate postwar period, as was the goal of achieving wage moderation. After the war, the Board of Government Mediators (College van Rijksbemiddelaars), which had an important say on wage matters in the early years of the guided wage policy, often made use of its ability to extend conditions of employment to all employers within the same sector to create new sector-wide pension funds. On several occasions, the board obliged all employers in a sector to create or raise existing pension pledges. This, among other factors, led to the creation of large industry pension funds in the steel and dock industry. Once the board simply compelled an entire industrial sector, the bulb cultivation industry, to create a pension fund. Employer federations accepted this intrusion in the

Occupational pension schemes expanded rapidly in both range and generosity during the late 1940s and 1950s because employers used the schemes to placate wage demands in the context of the guided wage policy. When tensions in the labor market mounted, employers were not allowed to increase net wage levels but were allowed to increase their pension pledges.[101] A favorable tax treatment further motivated employers' use of pension pledges as a means to satisfy worker demands. In 1950, the NVV estimated the coverage level of occupational pensions at one-third the workforce. Eight years later, the CNV estimated it at 70 percent.[102] During the same period, existing schemes also increased enormously in generosity.

In the immediate postwar period, the massive growth of occupational pension schemes was facilitated by several legislative measures. As early as 1948, for instance, the Dutch government proposed a bill enabling the minister of social affairs to compel employers and employees in specific industrial branches to, respectively, set up and join industrial pension funds. This resulted in the 1949 Wet Bedrijfspensioenfonds (Industry Pension Fund Act).[103] Then, three years later, the government proposed a bill that aimed to set strict criteria for evaluating private pension scheme performance. This resulted in the 1954 Pensioen – en Spaarfondsenwet (Pensions and Savings Funds Act).[104] Both acts passed Parliament with overwhelming majorities and received broad support from unions and employers. The union federations supported both acts because they presented a further step in the creation of adequate old age pension provision. The employer federations motivated their support by referring

---

private pension sphere because it prevented unorganized employers from gaining a competitive advantage by abstaining from collective bargaining. Worker federations appreciated it because it improved old age security for large groups of workers. See Erik Lutjens, *De wet Bpf: 50 jaar verplichte bedrijfspensioenfondsen* (Deventer: Kluwer, 1999), 15.

[101] Although adding to labor costs, increases in pension rights worked noninflationarily and improved the savings rate – which, in turn, strengthened the productive potential of the economy. On this, see IISG, NVV codelijsten 1945–1970, 1952, HM13, Notulen Commissie Ouderdomsvoorziening, 16 Oktober 1952.

[102] IISG, NVV codelijsten 1945–1970, 1951 HM4, Notulen Sociale Commissie, 21 Maart 1951; IISG, CNV, Commissie Sociale Zekerheid, 63, Ouderdomsverzekering, F5, Het vraagstuk van het aanvullende ouderdomspensioen. Uit "De Vakbeweging," 21 Januari 1958.

[103] The direct occasion for this act was the intention of creating a pension scheme in the agricultural sector. This scheme would cover at least 200,000 workers, but the government wanted to expand it further by including small employers and the self-employed, who together numbered 300,000. Parliament disagreed, however, and enabled the self-employed to opt out of participation in the 1949 Industry Pension Fund Act. For an encompassing history of the act, see Peter van Griensven, "Het sociale beleid van minister Joekes." In P. F. Maas, *Parlementaire Geschiedenis van Nederland na 1945: Het kabinet Drees-Van Schaik (1948–1951). Liberalisatie en sociale ordening* (Nijmegen: SSN, 1992).

[104] The reason the 1949 act did not set criteria was apparently that the government wanted it to get through Parliament quickly so that it could apply it to the agricultural sector, where plans were being made to set up an industrial fund. This is why the 1949 act also has been called an "emergency act." See Van Griensven, "Het sociale beleid," 639.

to the importance of private pensions for the economy.[105] To understand the latter's support for these acts, despite their natural aversion to regulation, it is important to realize that both acts were created when the future of the public pension scheme was still uncertain. The emergency old age provision had and Joekes's plan certainly would deduct individuals' resources from the public benefit, which would be extremely harmful to the growth of private pension schemes. Moreover, other equally harmful outcomes to the private pension industry were still foreseeable. For the employer federations, then, their acceptance of regulations to guarantee and extend existing occupational pension schemes served to deflect calls for an overly generous or in other ways harmful public pension.

In later years, the employer federations continuously referred to improvements in the coverage and generosity of private pension funds to counter what they disliked most: an increase in the public share of old age provision. In the first years after introduction of the AOW, the union and employer federations argued mainly over the question of whether the state benefit was to be tied to yearly increases in the level of prices or wages. At the time of introduction of the act, this had not been a strong issue. After all, the guided wage policy of the time only allowed wages to increase with price levels. When this wage policy broke down in the late 1950s, the employer federations first opposed an automatic adjustment of the public benefit to wage increases.[106] When this proved untenable, they used the automatic adjustment of the public benefit to wage increases to argue against any incremental increases in the level of the public benefit. They claimed that wage indexation meant that the benefit level would automatically approach – and eventually even come to exceed – the "social minimum" without further meddling.[107] The resistance of employer federations to incremental increases in the level of the public benefit proved unsuccessful, however. Between 1961 and 1975, the unions were able to increase its level more than twice the amount that index linking would have entailed.[108]

The first initiative for a major increase in the level of the public benefit was put forth in 1961. In that year, union, employer, and state representatives in the Sociale Verzekeringsraad (SVR, Social Insurance Council) received a request from the government for advice on whether the public benefit should be increased to a level of subsistence. All employer representatives to the council argued against doing so; all state and union representatives argued in favor of the increase. The employer representatives explained their opposition with the claim that those pensioners who could not survive on an old

[105] VNO, F119(4) Cie Sociale Verzekering RCO 1947–1970: Notulen, 27 April 1948.
[106] ARA, 2.06.064, 343: Notulen Werkgroep Financiering Sociale Verzekeringsprojecten van de Commissie Ontwikkeling Nationale Economie en de Commissie Niveau AOW-pensioenen, 20 December 1963, 5.
[107] VU, VPCW, 172: Ontwerp-advies inzake een verhoging van de AOW-pensioenen tot een sociaal minimum. Bestemd voor de vergadering van de raad van, 28 Februari 1964.
[108] See Vording 2001, 177.

age pension alone must simply resort to social assistance to subsist.[109] Internal discussions in the RvBA (Council of Directors in Labor Affairs) on the issue show that employers were, however, quite aware of the fact that this argument would convince neither the unions nor most political parties.[110] All they could do, therefore, was attempt to delay legislation on the increase in the public benefit for as long as possible.[111] They managed to do so until 1965. In that year, the government finally raised the level of the public benefit from 50 to 70 percent of the minimum wage for a married couple and to 70 percent of a full benefit for a single person. Representatives from the Verbond van Protestantsch-Christelijke Werkgevers in Nederland (VPCW, Federation of Protestant-Christian Employers) complained afterward that the government apparently had little interest in the opinion of employers. In matters concerning the public pension benefit, they argued, the government always sided with the unions.[112]

During internal discussions on the matter, the employer federations had deemed an increase in the level of the public benefit inevitable because private pension provision still was (and in the coming years would remain) insufficient to guarantee a decent supplement to the public benefit for all workers.[113] Yet, as the British example has already demonstrated, this does not in all cases mean that an increase in the state benefit to a level of subsistence is inevitable. What the employer federations did not mention, because they regarded it as self-evident, was the importance of labor union unity on the question of worker solidarity. This, among other factors, enabled the unions to found their demands for an increase in the public pension benefit on an emphasis that such an increase would be almost completely financed by workers themselves. Once more, the three union federations tied this to increased redistribution of income among workers, proposing to finance a large part of the benefit increase by removing the ceiling over which no contributions had to be paid. The Protestant CNV's motivation for this is most interesting here. Once a fierce defender of the need to adhere to strict actuarial principles, it now increasingly explored ways to reconcile its emphasis on personal responsibility with the notion of worker solidarity. This led CNV representatives to conclude that the

[109] VNO, F119(4) Cie Sociale Verzekering RCO 1947–1970: Notulen Commissie Sociale Verzekering RvBA, gehouden op vrijdag, 18 Januari 1963, ten kantore Kneuterdijk 8, te 's Gravenhage.

[110] Privately, several employer representatives admitted that a solution based on social assistance was socially not desirable. VNO, F119(4) Cie Sociale Verzekering RCO 1947–1970: Notulen Commissie Sociale Verzekering RvBA, 18 Januari 1963.

[111] ARA, CSWV, 2.19.103.06, 139: Notulen Commissie Sociale Verzekering, 25 Oktober 1963.

[112] VU, VPCW, 172: Notities betreffende SER-stuk R. no 640. Advies aan de Minister van Sociale Zaken inzake verhoging AOW- en AWW-uitkeringen tot een sociaal minimum. Geen datum.

[113] VNO, F119(4) Cie Sociale Verzekering RCO 1947–1970: Notulen Commissie Sociale Verzekering RvBA, 18 April 1963.

confessional virtue of social insurance programs' normative effect on societal structure demanded solidarity – and this meant that there was no longer any place for a ceiling.[114]

The insistence of the three union federations that workers themselves would pay for most of the demanded increase in the public benefit did not itself convince the employer federations to agree. The fact was that employer opposition to the benefit increase was not only founded on cost considerations. At least equally important, to quote a representative of the CSWV, was that "[a] further extension of the AOW [the public pension] means that a greater part of pension provision for employees is financed by public provision, which leaves less room for additional supplements provided by industry or company pension funds."[115] In other words, any increase in the level of the public benefit meant that the employer community was left with fewer opportunities to raise capital to invest. Yet, if financing the increase through worker contributions did not convince the employer federations to agree to an increase in the public pension benefit, it certainly helped to convince most political parties to support such an increase. In 1963, the employer federations had already noted that the government was leaning toward granting union demands for an increase in the public benefit. It is important to bear in mind here that this government did not include members of the Labor Party and carried a confessional liberal signature.[116]

In contrast to their stance during introduction of the public benefit in the mid-1950s, the union federations did not demand wage compensation for the increase in worker contributions that made possible the 1965 increase in public benefit level. Workers nevertheless again received some degree of compensation in 1965. During discussions on how to finance the 1965 increase, both union and employer federations were preoccupied with the effect of increased worker contributions on the purchasing power of the lower- and middle-income brackets. They had quite different reasons for this preoccupation. While union representatives worried mostly about the effect of the coming increase on the purchasing power of lower-income groups, their employer counterparts worried about the effect of the coming increase on the ability of middle-income groups to improve private pension provision.[117] To solve this problem, union representatives in the SER proposed to finance part of the public benefit increase by increasing the state contribution. Representatives of the liberal CSWV were willing to consider this proposal, but even though agricultural employers

---

[114] IISG, CNV, Commissie Sociale Verzekeringen, 66, Arbeidsongeschiktheidsverzekering, I2, Doelmatige vereenvoudiging van de uitvoering der sociale verzekering, Januari 1960.

[115] VNO, F119(4) Cie Sociale Verzekering RCO 1947–1970: Notulen, 29 Oktober 1963.

[116] From 1958 to 1972, the Netherlands was mostly governed by confessional liberal coalitions. That this did not prevent the coming about of public welfare generosity in the Netherlands has often been noted by scholars.

[117] ARA, CSWV, 2.19.103.06, 139: Notulen Commissie Sociale Verzekering, 19 Februari 1963.

supported it,[118] their confessional counterparts adamantly opposed any expansion of government financing in the pension sphere.[119] A compromise eventually came from the KAB, representatives of which proposed to compensate for part of the increase in worker contributions by financing future expenses for child benefits through taxation – instead of through contributions, as was currently the case. The confessional employer representatives eventually could support this solution – as long as it did not open the door for further government financing of social insurance schemes.[120]

Although the 1965 agreement led to a substantial increase in the level of the public pension benefit, unrest on the pension front did not subside. In subsequent years, the union federations kept pushing for an additional large increase in the level of the public benefit. They argued that the 1965 increase had simply not been enough to provide full subsistence to pensioners who did not have access to occupational provision. By the late 1960s, some 10 to 20 percent of all workers were not covered by private pension funds. For many other workers, private pension provision would result in rather meager supplementary benefits. Finally, among existing old age pensioners, a whopping 40 to 45 percent had no additional provision.[121] Another problem was that few private pension funds were able to guarantee an inflation-proof – let alone a wage- or prosperity-proof – benefit. Under the circumstances of rapid economic growth and rising inflation, this last shortcoming received increased attention. To the horror of employer federations, this attention soon brought about an increase in the public share of old age provision back on the agenda – and this time in a much more far-reaching form. Union federations, progressive or left-wing parties, and even individual employers now increasingly came to argue for what the employer federations wanted to prevent more than anything else: the introduction of a Dutch version of superannuation.

Earlier I noted that during the first decades of the postwar period, the existence of a thriving private pension industry had been a sacrosanct feature of old age pension provision in the Netherlands. There were several reasons for this. The employer community appreciated private pension funds mainly for their financial and economic value. Others appreciated them mainly because they helped to preserve workers' sense of self-reliance. The socialist NVV had realized this at an early stage. When it received criticism for its underlining of

---

[118] Employer representatives of the agricultural sector had been long-standing advocates of a state pension. The CSWV therefore worried greatly that they would side with worker representatives on this issue. ARA, CSWV, 2.19.103.06, 139: Notulen Commissie Sociale Verzekering, 22 Januari 1964.

[119] ARA, CSWV, 2.19.103.06, 133: Notulen Kring voor Sociaal Overleg, 3 Maart 1964.

[120] They could accept this because they felt that the character of child benefits was such that it resembled a state provision program more than an insurance program. VU, VPCW, 172: Kanttekeningen bij de nota van drs. J. P. de Heij, 1963.

[121] VNO, Bijlagen DB 69–123: Recente ontwikkelingen op het terrein van de pensioenvoorzieningen.

the importance of preserving the private pension industry by signing of the second Van Rhijn Report in 1948, the NVV response was: "[We] have often heard the reproof that the notion of industry pension funds conflict with our image of society. This might be true, but here also, reality is of more importance than doctrine. A people's provision for the elderly will have to deal with industry pension funds."[122] Many within the NVV also appreciated the usefulness of funded provision for the productive potential of the economy.[123] In the immediate postwar period, it therefore strove not to replace the private pension industry but to achieve worker representation on the boards of pension funds.[124]

Yet, despite this overall acceptance of the existence of private pension industry by the union movement, there had always been strong undercurrents that favored a partial or complete replacement of private pension funds by an earnings-related public pension fund. In the years leading up to introduction of the AOW, the NVV leadership, for example, noted that a group of union members was campaigning for such a solution.[125] And in 1958, after introduction of the Allmän Tilläggspension (ATP) in Sweden, both the Labor Party and the NVV investigated the possibility of grouping all existing private pension funds under the umbrella of one public fund. Employer federations were not worried about this at the time. Other political parties did not favor such a move, and the confessional union federations also were quite reluctant to support their socialist counterpart.[126] In subsequent years, however, confessional unions' dissatisfaction with the lack of progress made by private pension funds – especially on the long-standing demand of making them inflation-proof – spurred them to alter their position. Once again, the formerly conservative CNV made the sharpest reversal. In 1969, at a time when the other two union federations were still committed to leaving the private pension industry intact, the CNV came forward with a proposal to introduce a public supplement on top of the existing public benefit.[127] This almost immediately resulted in a reversal of the

[122] IISG, NVV codelijsten 1945–1970, 1951 HB 4, Notulen Commissie Sociale Verzekering, 24 Mei 1951.

[123] IISG, NVV codelijsten 1945–1970, 1953, Ec5, De plaats van de bedrijfspensioenfondsen in de toekomstige ouderdomsvoorziening, 1 November 1952; IISG, NVV codelijsten 1945–1970, 1950, H166, Notulen Sociale Commissie, 25 Augustus 1950.

[124] For an excellent overview of the organization of industrial pension funds (and thus of union representation to it), see Ronald Beltzer and Renske Biezeveld, *De pensioenvoorziening als bindmiddel. Sociale cohesie en de organisatie van pensioen in Nederland* (Amsterdam: Aksant, 2004).

[125] IISG, NVV codelijsten 1945–1970, 1950, EC7, Bedrijfspensioenfondsen: de pensioenen, 10 Januari 1950.

[126] KDC, Algemene Katholieke Werkgeversvereniging, 1500: Commissie Sociale Verzekering: Overzicht van de bestaande ouderdoms- en weduwen en wezenvoorzieningen, alsmede van de toekomstige herzieningsplannen, 1958.

[127] VNO, F118(21) Cie Sociale Zekerheid VNO: Notulen Commissie Sociale Verzekering, 4 December 1969.

stance of the other two union federations. Later in the year, the union representatives in the SER together presented a proposal to create a supplementary
public benefit for all existing pensioners, collected on a pay-as-you-go basis
and financed completely through worker contributions.[128]

It would be an understatement to say that the union proposal disturbed the
SER's employer representatives. Its introduction would be disastrous for private savings and could bring about a complete replacement of private pension
funds by a public pension fund – as the CNV had in fact already demanded.[129]
It seems that the employer federations were not quite sure what to make of the
proposal at first. In the Social Insurance Committee of the liberal Verbond van
Nederlandse Ondernemingen (VNO, Federation of Dutch Industries), which
succeeded the CSWV and several other employer federations of a liberal signature in 1968, one member saw the CNV proposal as an off-season attempt to
lure employers into voicing approval for a substantial increase in the existing
public benefit.[130] If this were indeed the case, the attempt was quite successful. Within a matter of weeks, the employer representatives to the SER made
the following counterproposal: they offered to increase the level of the existing public pension benefit by some 15 percent to that of the minimum wage,
introduce a holiday surcharge to the benefit, and oblige all workers to become
a member of an occupational pension scheme. The combination of public and
occupational benefits was to provide at least 70 percent of the last earned wage
for all workers.[131]

The authors of the combined employer proposal had to overcome substantial internal opposition. To many members of the Federatie van Katholieke en
Protestants-Christelijke Werkgeversverbonden (FCWV, Federation of Catholic
and Protestant-Christian Employers' Unions), the opposition centered mainly
on compulsory membership in pension schemes – to which they objected in
principle. The leadership of the FCWV regarded this stance as "unworkable,"
however, and argued that "[t]hose who are of the opinion that membership in
supplementary pension schemes has to remain completely voluntary have no
stance that leads to a solution in the short term that is satisfactory to the union
organizations as well. By rigidly sticking to this viewpoint, the unions will only
feel it necessary to strive for a completely centralized system."[132] Within the
VNO, there was also much skepticism toward the plan, but there the objections

[128] VU, FCWV, 18: Voorlopige conclusies ten aanzien van nieuwe pensioenvoorstellen vakbeweging, 10 Oktober 1969.

[129] VNO, F2(20) Notulen Dagelijks Bestuur, 23 September 1969; VNO, F61(3) Pensioenen 1957–
1970: Recente ontwikkelingen op het terrein van de oudedagsvoorzieningen, 1969.

[130] VNO, F118(21) Cie Sociale Zekerheid VNO: Notulen Commissie Sociale Verzekering, 4
December 1969.

[131] VU, FCWV, 18: Werkgeversstandpunt ten aanzien van oplossing pensioenvraagstuk, 17
Oktober 1969.

[132] VU, FCWV, 18: Nota inzake de mogelijke structuur van een algemene aanvullende pensioenverzekering voor werknemers in Nederland.

focused mainly on the generosity of the proposed increase in the level of the public benefit.[133] Most VNO members had much less difficulty with compulsory membership in occupational pension schemes. In fact, only a few years after introduction of the AOW, the VNO had already partially reversed its opposition to compulsory membership in occupational pension schemes. In 1958, because of "automatic" progress on private pension coverage, the leadership of the VNO questioned whether "there is still reason ... to take such a dismissive stance as taken at the time [of the creation of the AOW]. It has to be noted that we are already heading in the direction of a closing net of private provision." It also noted at the time that "from the side of the [social insurance] committee, nobody opposed this notion."[134]

Of eventual overriding importance to the leadership of all the employer federations was the fact that the government had already shown support for union demands for an increase in the public pension benefit.[135] By taking the initiative, the employer federations could at least prevent the 600 guilders plan from becoming a political issue.[136] Also important was the fact that the union federations had backed up their demands for an increase in the level of the public benefit by offering that the increase be paid completely by workers themselves. The Nederlands Katholiek Vakverbond (NKV, Netherlands Catholic Trade Union), which had succeeded the KAB, and the NVV were unwilling to support this in a formal statement, but this did not matter as long as employers supported it in coming wage negotiations. The union federations promised to endorse this as a proper stance if their members challenged it.[137] Finally, the union federations also promised to consider austerity measures in exchange for the pension proposal of the employer federations. Austerity measures proposed by the employer federations included a freezing of child benefits, the introduction of waiting days in the Sickness Act, and the introduction of deductibles (a sum that has to be paid before an insurer will pay any expenses) in the health insurance. The employer federations emphasized that austerity measures of some sort would be necessary; the costs of handing out an old age benefit at 70 percent of the last earned wage would accrue to 25 percent of total labor costs.[138]

In following years, both the union movement and organized employers lived up to their promises.[139] In late 1971, the union federations agreed to freeze

---

[133] VNO, F61(3) Pensioenen 1957–1970: Recente ontwikkelingen op het terrein van de oudedagsvoorzieningen.

[134] ARA, CSWV, 2.19.103.06, 146: Notulen Technische Commissie Sociale Verzekering, 24 Februari 1958.

[135] VNO, F2(20) Notulen Dagelijks Bestuur, 9 September 1969 and 14 Oktober 1969.

[136] VNO, F61(4) Pensioenen 1971: Nota pensioenverzekering – AB 71–12.

[137] VNO, F118(21) Cie Sociale Zekerheid VNO: Notulen Commissie Sociale Verzekering, 6 November 1969.

[138] VNO, F75(105) VUT-regelingen 1970–1985: Rapport inzake consequenties van vervroegd pensioneren in het kader van oplossingen voor oudere werknemers.

[139] Only one promise that could not be kept; attempts to make membership in occupational pension schemes compulsory for all workers proved to be too difficult. After a very long series of

child benefits for the first and second child if the resulting savings were used to improve occupational pension provision.[140] The employer federations, in turn, accepted a limited degree of pay-as-you-go financing in the private pension sphere to make inflation-proof benefits possible.[141] This and a host of other measures greatly improved the generosity and reliability of old age pension provision in the Netherlands. Most important was, of course, the increase in the level of the public pension benefit. Within several years, the public pension benefit came to be tied firmly to the level of the minimum wage. This paved the way for an automatic improvement of the public benefit that even exceeded average wage increases. By the time SERPS was introduced in the United Kingdom, the Dutch public pension offered a benefit to married couples that approached 80 percent of the net average earnings of a male worker in the manufacturing industry.[142] By comparison, and as mentioned before, the corresponding number in the United Kingdom lay close to 35 percent.

A FINAL NOTE ON EMPLOYERS

The preceding histories of postwar pension reform in the Netherlands and the United Kingdom have demonstrated the importance of union structure to the success of efforts to provide all members of society with an adequate income in old age. At the same time, these histories tell us much about the ways in which union structure impacts employer interest-group stances on public pension initiatives. In the preceding two chapters I noted the growing prominence of recent writings on organized employers in the debate on welfare state development. Because of this growing prominence, the last section of this chapter

---

negotiations, this goal disappeared from the agenda of employer and worker federations in the early 1980s. There are several reasons for why this never succeeded. First, it proved quite difficult to oblige the last group of workers to join occupational pension schemes because these often worked part time, had long interruptions in employment, or worked in small companies without (membership in) pension schemes. Second, the increase of the AOW benefit to that of the minimum wage and consecutive improvements in pension coverage reduced the necessity of providing this final group with private supplements. In the Netherlands today, worker coverage in occupational pension schemes is well over 90 percent. See Beltzer and Biezeveld, *De pensioenvoorziening*, 8.

[140] VNO, F119(5): Cie Sociale Verzekering RCO: Notulen Commissie Sociale Verzekering RvBA, 25 November 1971.

[141] VU, FCWV, 18: Nota inzake het pensioenvraagstuk afkomstig van de Commissie Sociale Verzekeringen van de Stichting van de Arbeid, 30 Oktober 1969.

[142] This percentage came about because the benefit was tied to the national minimum wage, which at its peak in the early 1980s, according to estimates by various authors, equaled 80 percent of the average earnings of a male worker in the manufacturing industry. On the level of the public pension benefit, see, for example, Goudswaard and De Jong, "The Distributional Impact," 370. On the level of the minimum wage, see Goudswaard and De Jong, "The Distributional Impact," 370; Verbond van Nederlandse Ondernemingen, *Boekje over inkomens*, 32; Paul de Beer, *Het verdiende inkomen*, 66.

dwells on the stance of British and Dutch employer interest groups toward the organization of old age pension provision.

As a result of differences in their organizational blueprints, the stance of British and Dutch labor unions, and of different British labor unions for that matter, toward the organization of old age pension provision differed substantially. No such differences emerge when we compare the stance of British and Dutch employer interest groups. In both countries, all employer interest groups were concerned mainly with ensuring that the new public pension was to interfere as little as possible with the development of the private pension industry. In the United Kingdom, employer interest groups supported the creation of a universal state pension because its effect on private industry was limited. In the Netherlands, the employer federations preferred the more generous NVV scheme to that of the government for exactly the same reason. In the periods following the creation of the British and Dutch state pensions, all activities of British and Dutch employer organizations continued to revolve around their objective of keeping the private share of old age pension provision as large as possible and the public share as small as possible. British employer groupings opposed superannuation because they regarded it as a threat to their private pension industry. Dutch employer federations opposed an increase in the level of the flat-rate public benefit for the same reason.

In the years after introduction of universal contributory benefits, employer interest groups in both countries were faced with quite different challenges to their private pension industries. As a result, they responded in different ways. In the United Kingdom, employer interest groups were faced with superannuation, a scheme that, if enacted in its original form, would have replaced most of the private pension industry. In the Netherlands, by contrast, the employer community initially only faced union demands for increases in the rate of the flat-rate public benefit. Such increases, which were to be financed by raising the level of earnings-related contributions, certainly would have left less room for the development of occupational pensions. Yet they did not raise the prospect of an almost complete replacement of private provision by public provision. Compared with its Dutch counterpart, then, the British business community was faced with a much more serious challenge to its activities in the area of old age pension provision.

In their opposition to Labour's superannuation proposals, the BEC, LOA, and later CBI were supported by unions representing privileged workers who also opposed superannuation. There is no doubt that these business groups and unions greatly appreciated each other's resistance to Labour's proposals. As noted earlier, unions such as NALGO did not hesitate to emphasize this publicly. Although there is no evidence that business groups and labor unions such as NALGO ever sought to coordinate their activities, their combined opposition was sufficiently consistent and successful to be described as a powerful, albeit tacit, "cross-class alliance" that prevented the coming about of superannuation – at least in its original, redistributive form. At the same time, it should be acknowledged that British business groups and craft union movement rejected superannuation for very different reasons and, as a result, also had strongly conflicting goals.

British business groups opposed superannuation because it posed a challenge to the private pension industry and because they feared that its introduction would prove quite costly to employers. This latter concern was strongly reinforced by the behavior of craft unions, which were mainly concerned that superannuation would result in a redistribution of income among different grades of workers. Because these unions were strongly opposed to such redistribution, they made it clear that they would make up for possible losses by demanding higher wage increases during subsequent wage negotiations. Thus, if implemented, superannuation surely would complicate wage negotiations. It also meant that employers likely would have to carry most of its costs. In a published reaction to the Crossman scheme, the CBI expressed its worries about this, stating that "in the long run these increases in employee's contributions will be reflected in wage claims, and so far as these are allowed, the whole of the increase will be met by employers."[143] This certainly reinforced the CBI's opposition to Labour's pension initiatives. It also explains why it demanded that any increase in the state pension benefit, if inevitable, be financed through general taxation.

In the Netherlands, by contrast, the employer community did not have to worry that it would have to carry most of the costs of public pension development. On the contrary, and for reasons explained in Chapter 2, the union movement there was increasingly willing to accept that increases in public provision for retired workers had to be financed by workers themselves. During negotiations over introduction of the AOW in the early 1950s, the unions had still demanded a partial wage compensation for this worker-based financing. At the time, the employer federations were willing to give this compensation because the unions had shown a consistent willingness to support wage restraint. When the guided wage policy that had produced this wage restraint broke down, the employer federations were no longer willing to give, but the union federations also no longer demanded such compensation. The 1965 increase in the state benefit was completely paid for by workers – who, however, received some compensation through the replacement of contributory financing of child benefits by financing through general taxation. Five years later, no compensation was granted.

The willingness of Dutch unions to accept that improvements to the public pension benefit had to be paid for by workers themselves did not spur any greater willingness by the employer federations to agree to such improvements. The reason for this was that any improvement to the public pension benefit left less room for the development of the lucrative private pension industry. (In

---

[143] Confederation of British Industry, *Earnings-Related Social Security* (Newcastle: Hindson Reid Jordison, 1970), 5.

this respect, old age pension insurance is quite different from insurance against other labor market risks.) Yet, if it did not prompt employer federation sympathy for an increase in the public pension benefit, the union stance certainly made it more difficult for employers to resist such an increase in public benefit provision. Again, the contrast with the United Kingdom is significant. There the TUC was forced to argue for a limited – and, in any case, politically unfeasible – increase in Exchequer contribution to the scheme. In the Netherlands, by contrast, union demands for a benefit increase funded by worker contributions received a very favorable reception in political circles. It is no coincidence, then, that employer federations such as the VPCW complained that the government – even though it was dominated by confessional and liberal parties – often chose to side with the position of the unions.

4

The Development of Unemployment Insurance
in the Netherlands and the United Kingdom

Efforts to provide all workers with adequate protection against the risk of unemployment differ from efforts to create adequate universal old age pensions in one important way. While the latter center on direct income redistribution among different occupational categories, the former also lean heavily on indirect redistribution through risk reapportioning. This difference can be attributed to the specific nature of unemployment. The risk of unemployment is such that different categories of workers are exposed to it to quite different degrees. Some workers occupy relatively secure positions and thus can insure themselves against the risk of becoming unemployed on relatively favorable terms. Other workers are much more prone to the risk of becoming unemployed and thus cannot do the same. Risk pooling allows such workers to achieve insurance against unemployment on the same terms as less risk-prone workers. After all, when all workers join in a common risk pool, "good" risks effectively subsidize "bad" risks.

The greater importance of risk reapportioning does not make the redistributive logic behind efforts to provide all workers with adequate protection against the risk of unemployment different from efforts to create adequate universal old age pensions, though. Whether "directly" or "indirectly," such efforts require a redistributive effort between different categories of workers. Moreover, the winners and losers in risk reapportioning are largely the same as the winners and losers in direct income redistribution because workers who are more exposed to the risk of unemployment are often lower paid as well. Thus worker solidarity affects unemployment insurance development in the same way it affects old age pension development: in order to provide all workers with adequate protection against the risk of unemployment, workers with stronger positions in the labor market have to support the welfare efforts of less-fortunate workers.

Because worker solidarity is again of central importance here, the main narrative of this chapter will follow a similar pattern to that of Chapter 3. In the Netherlands, the three industrially organized union federations actively pressed for more risk reapportioning and the introduction of a redistributive contributory system. Faced with the opposition of its craft and occupationally organized white-collar membership against this, the Trades Union Congress (TUC) leadership could not do the same. As we will see in the following pages, British craft and occupationally organized white-collar unions were as opposed to risk reapportioning as they were to the introduction of a redistributive contributory system. As a result, the Netherlands proved far more successful than the United Kingdom in providing all workers with adequate insurance against labor market risks during the postwar period.

In their attitudes toward improving the generosity of the public unemployment insurance program by increasing its redistributive features, British unions differed to a great extent both from Dutch unions and between themselves. The employer communities on both sides of the channel were, conversely, in full agreement on the point: they full-heartedly opposed any attempt to redistribute risks to enhance public unemployment benefits. It is not hard to see why this was the case. Employers have always regarded unemployment as the most problematic social risk. Much more than other welfare dependents, the unemployed tend to be labeled as unwilling, not unable, to work. This popular perception, as well as the notion that unemployment is "uninsurable," meant that many nations only introduced public unemployment insurance schemes several decades after the introduction of public insurance programs against all other labor market risks.[1] The Netherlands is a good example of this. It only introduced a public unemployment insurance scheme in 1949, almost half a decade after the introduction of the first social insurance program.[2] Both during and after its creation, Dutch employer federations insisted that it had to operate according to strict actuarial principles so that its costs and possible misuse would be limited as much as possible.

In any event, the Dutch employer federations were far less successful than their British counterparts in their opposition to an increase in risk reapportioning and the introduction of a redistributive contributory system. Dutch employer federations' inability to prevent what they described as "excessive solidarity" in the operation of public unemployment insurance tells us much about the importance of the organizational blueprint of unions to the success of efforts to create adequate security for all. It suggests that when a union movement is united in its support for an extension of risk reapportioning

---

[1] See, for example, Jens Alber, *Vom Armenhaus zum Wohlfahrtsstaat* (Frankfurt: Campus, 1982), 49.
[2] For an excellent overview of the introduction of the most important social insurance programs in the Netherlands, see Cox, *Development of the Dutch Welfare State*.

and the introduction of a redistributive contributory system, employer interest groups eventually have to cede to this. If, on the other hand, as with the
British case, many unions also oppose such measures, matters are quite different. In the United Kingdom, the employer community and privileged part of
the union movement agreed that the unemployment insurance scheme must
operate according to strict actuarial principles. As a result, the degree of risk
reapportioning remained far more limited than in the Netherlands. Moreover,
and contrary to in the Netherlands, the system of contributions and benefits
did not come to work to the advantage of lower-paid workers.

The British and Dutch postwar old age pension development histories that
were analyzed in Chapter 3 lent themselves well to an illustrative comparison
because both countries initially opted for the same formula. The initial consideration of a flat-rate contributory system in the two countries made it possible
to begin Chapter 3 with a direct comparison of early postwar efforts to create
adequate old age security for all members of British and Dutch society. Such a
direct comparison is not possible in this chapter. In fact, the British and Dutch
approaches to unemployment insurance development differed from the start. The
British extended the flat-rate contributory system that we now all know as the
"Beveridge approach" to the public unemployment insurance scheme, whereas
the Dutch opted for a "Bismarckian system," in which unemployed workers
were entitled to earnings-related benefits in exchange for earnings-related contributions. This makes it necessary to discuss the postwar histories of unemployment insurance development in the two countries one at a time.

In Chapter 3 we saw that a flat-rate contributory system has the obvious
drawback of limiting the generosity of the scheme to what the poorest-paying
contributor can afford. When all contributors are entitled to a benefit at an
equally low level, this creates a problem for the less affluent because they do
not have the means to add private provision to this. This is why the Nederlands
Verbond van Vakverenigingen (NVV, Dutch Association of Trade Unions)
and the British Labour Party both proposed combining flat-rate benefits with
earnings-related contributions in, respectively, the late 1940s and early 1950s.
When the British Labour Party proposal failed, Labour moved toward a complete break with the Beveridge approach by proposing national superannuation.
Chapter 3 has shown how the inability of the Labour Party to push through
a redistributive solution led to the introduction of a limited earnings-related
supplement to the existing flat-rate pension benefit. The first part of this chapter shows that attempts to improve the British public unemployment insurance
scheme had quite similar results.

Yet if the Beveridge approach comes up short in caring for less-fortunate
workers, then so does the Bismarckian system. When workers receive an unemployment or old age benefit that is a percentage of their previous wages, the
lowest-paid workers inevitably end up with benefits that are too low to live
on. After all, for those who earn a wage that is already close to subsistence,
any decrease in that income might be disastrous. The only way to fix this is

by entitling the lowest-paid workers to a benefit that closely approaches their previous wages. Such a move certainly functions redistributively because the lowest-paid workers then will be entitled to a higher percentage of previous earnings than will higher-paid workers. Chapter 3 demonstrated that the British Labour Party's first two superannuation proposals attempted to enact precisely this type of redistribution. The second part of this chapter shows, among other things, how the Dutch union federations successfully pressed for such a solution during the 1960s.

TOWARD SUPERANNUATION FOR THE UNEMPLOYED IN THE UNITED KINGDOM

When William Beveridge came to head the Committee on Social Insurance and Allied Services in June 1941, his main task was to propose ways to create a unified system in which all programs and services were organized and financed in the same way. Beveridge set about this task by proposing the establishment of a single National Insurance Fund that would entitle all the retired, sick, disabled, and unemployed to the same flat-rate benefit.[3] In Chapter 3 we saw that both the union movement and the employer community supported Beveridge's choice of a flat-rate contributory public pension. In addition, the TUC and its employer counterparts also agreed on the need to organize the public unemployment insurance program along egalitarian lines. As with the public old age pension, the union movement and employer community had been accustomed to a flat-rate contributory unemployment system since the beginning of the twentieth century. And as with the public old age pension, neither the privileged part of the labor union movement nor the employer community would have accepted an alternative scheme. As a result, it was not just the state old age pension benefit that turned out to be inadequate in coming years; the flat-rate benefit proved just as inadequate for the sick, disabled, and unemployed as it was for the elderly.

Considering the very low level of the national insurance benefit, it is not surprising that after introduction of the 1946 National Insurance Act, discussions of the state unemployment insurance program, like discussions of the state old age pension, focused mainly on the inadequacy of the benefit. Even the proposed solutions to the inadequacy of the benefit were quite similar. By the mid-1950s, all involved parties had developed their own notions on how to solve this problem. As with the state old age pension, the Conservatives played with the idea of introducing a means test.[4] In contrast to the state old age pension, they received support for this from the employer community. The

---

[3] Beveridge proposed making an exception only for industrial injuries – and Chapter 5 will analyze his reasons for this.

[4] See Paul Bridgen, "The State, Redundancy Pay, and Economic Policy-making in the Early 1960s," *Twentieth Century British History* 11:3 (2000), 247.

British Employers' Confederation (BEC), for example, argued that "unemployment is not, properly speaking, an insurable risk in the sense in which old age and sickness are." Any benefit therefore had to be "adjusted to need ... thus making it subject to a means test."[5] The TUC vehemently opposed this and instead pushed in vain to raise benefit levels through a tax-financed increase to the National Insurance Fund.[6] As for the Labour Party, its own solution was national superannuation. From the moment Labour adopted the superannuation platform in the mid-1950s, it aimed to extend the earnings-related principle to public unemployment and sickness insurance schemes as well. It pressed ahead with a reform of the public old age pension scheme first only because it felt that the problem of inadequate old age pension benefits was more pressing.[7] Once reform there had been achieved, Labour anticipated the addition of earnings-related supplements to the unemployment and sickness benefits as well because "it would [then] be quite impossible for any democratic government to resist the argument that the sick and the unemployed must be kept in an inferior status."[8]

As it turned out, the Labour Party did not provide the spark for the introduction of the earnings-related principle into state unemployment and sickness insurance programs. Instead, this initiative emerged from a complex series of negotiations among the BEC, the TUC, and the Conservative government over the issue of redundancy during the early 1960s. After it defeated Labour during the general election of 1959, thereby shelving the superannuation issue momentarily, the Conservative government had presented a plan to introduce a national redundancy fund that would entitle all redundant workers to severance payments. As we will see, the Conservative government's initiative was motivated more by economic than social considerations. The BEC countered the government's proposal by suggesting instead a public earnings-related supplement to the flat-rate public unemployment benefit. In this the BEC was

---

[5] MRC, MSS 200/C/3/EMP/3/114: BEC, Report of Employment and Manpower Standing Committee, 1962.

[6] Because the National Insurance Fund offered equal benefits to the retired, the (non–industrially injured) sick and disabled, and the unemployed, an increase in the "National Insurance Benefit" raise the income not only of the elderly but also of the sick and the unemployed as well. The National Insurance Fund continued to hand out more or less equal flat-rate benefits to the retired, the sick, and the unemployed until the mid-1970s. The subsequent period witnessed an increasing degree of differentiation, in which the unemployed were affected the most. For the development of the benefit rates of the most important social security programs between 1951 and 1981, see Parry, "United Kingdom," 189. For an excellent overview of events during the 1980s, see Paul Pierson, *Dismantling the Welfare State? Reagan, Thatcher, and the Politics of Retrenchment* (Cambridge University Press, 1994).

[7] The problem of poverty in old age affected far more people than the problem of poverty in unemployment. On the severity of the problem of poverty among old age pensioners, see Brian Abel-Smith and Peter Townsend, *The Poor and the Poorest* (London: Bell, 1965).

[8] MRC, MSS.292B/163.3/1: Labour Party, Labour's plan for short term benefits. I: The principles of Labour's approach, January 1963.

supported by the TUC. After winning the general election of 1964, a new Labour government eventually introduced both.

One striking feature of the introduction of the earnings-related principle into the unemployment and sickness insurance plans is that the move was to a large extent rooted in economic considerations. Of course, social considerations also played a role in its introduction; after all, it was a Labour government that eventually carried through the 1965 Redundancy Payments Act and 1966 National Insurance Act, of which the latter introduced earnings-related benefits. Yet the public justification for its introduction was that it addressed Britain's comparatively lackluster postwar economic performance. When the Conservative government had come forward with its plan to introduce a national redundancy fund in the early 1960s, it believed that the fund's introduction would boost the performance of the British economy. At the time, the BEC – and later the TUC – argued that earnings-related unemployment benefits would be better for the British economy. No one claimed that earnings-related sickness benefits also would help the economy. Yet, with the exception of organized employers, all those involved felt that the unified nature of the British insurance system required equal treatment of the unemployed, sick, and disabled (the British sickness insurance scheme dealt with both non-work-related disabilities and sicknesses). Thus the economic considerations that brought about the introduction of earnings-related unemployment benefits also indirectly led to the introduction of earnings-related sickness benefits.

The next section of this chapter begins with a detailed account of the economic rationale behind the introduction of the earnings-related principle into the unemployment and sickness insurance programs. Through this account, I critique a notion that has become quite popular in the last few years: the idea that public welfare policies can serve a productive or economic function, which can, in turn, inspire organized employer support for welfare state development. This notion has become especially popular among scholars espousing the "varieties of capitalism" approach to the study of political economy.[9] In *Varieties of Capitalism*, for example, Peter Hall and David Soskice argued that "many kinds of social policies actually improve the operation of markets and enhance the capacities of firms to pursue distinctive strategies, thereby inspiring active support in the business community."[10] Likewise, Bernhard Ebbinghaus and Philip Manow argued in *Comparing Welfare Capitalism* that "welfare states do not always institute 'politics against markets' as is commonly assumed: social policies can also serve a productive function."[11] In the varieties of capitalism literature, many examples of the supposed productive functions of social

---

[9] For an overview of this literature, see footnote 99 of Chapter 2.

[10] It is important to note that Hall and Soskice explicitly referred to public policies because they later argued that this "calls for a reinterpretation of the welfare state." Hall and Soskice, *Varieties of Capitalism*, vi, 50.

[11] Ebbinghaus and Manow, *Comparing Welfare Capitalism*, foreword.

policies relate to the use of public benefits for redundancy purposes.[12] For this reason, the British debate over the introduction of a national redundancy fund and the introduction of earnings-related benefits during the 1960s is ideally suited to explore this argument.

In Chapter 2 of this work I expressed my main criticism of the idea that employer interest groups may support the development of public welfare policies when these serve a productive or economic function. That is, when employers appear to like the "productive" or "economic" function of public welfare policies, what they actually like are the policies' redistributive effects. After all, if firms want to "persuade" workers to invest in skills or shed redundant workers without getting into conflict with unions, they can simply do so by providing occupational provision for this. Employers will only prefer public solutions if they result in redistribution between them and their competitors. Yet this will, of course, give other employers very good reason to oppose such solutions. As we will see in the following section, the British employer community was acutely aware of this redistributive logic. As a result, it vehemently opposed the Conservative government's plans. The BEC only introduced a plan for earnings-related unemployment benefits because it felt that this would be less costly than introducing a national redundancy fund. In the event, however, it had to accept the introduction of both.

THE ECONOMIC BENEFITS OF UNEMPLOYMENT COMPENSATION

The idea of improving financial provision for the unemployed as a means to reform the labor market arose in the United Kingdom during the early 1960s. It resulted from concerns over the relatively lackluster postwar performance of the British economy. The country's relative decline in economic productivity worried Britons increasingly in the first decades of the postwar period, and by the early 1960s, a strong consensus had emerged on the need to accept a greater degree of state intervention to deal with this.[13] During this decade, consecutive Conservative and Labour governments implemented a series of measures designed to improve the functioning of the British economy. Many of these aimed to improve the operation of the labor market. The 1960s period, among others, saw the introduction of legislative and other measures aimed at increasing labor mobility, furthering a greater dispersion of economic activity, and

---

[12] In *Reforming Early Retirement in Europe, Japan, and the USA,* Bernhard Ebbinghaus, for example, aimed to show that the use of public welfare policies for redundancy purposes is "not a case of politics *against* markets ... but that it functions as politics for markets, facilitating the restructuring of production systems." Bernhard Ebbinghaus, *Reforming Early Retirement,* 3.

[13] For some excellent works on this, see, for example, Peter A. Hall, *Governing the Economy* (Oxford: Polity Press, 1986); Astrid Ringe and Neil Rollings, "Responding to Relative Decline: The Creation of the National Economic Development Council," *Economic History Review* 53 (2000), 331–53; Hugh Pemberton, "Relative Economic Decline and British Economic Policy in the 1960s," *Historical Journal* 47:4 (2004), 989–1013; Keith Middlemass, *Power, Competition and the State,* Vol. 2: *Threats to the Post-war Settlement* (London: Macmillan, 1990).

creating a permanent incomes policy.[14] Most of these measures are of no concern to this chapter because they only peripherally affected the development of the British welfare state. The one major exception to this is the arena of financial protection for the unemployed. Improved protection against the financial consequences of unemployment, consecutive Conservative and Labour governments argued in the 1960s, might increase labor mobility, thereby leading to a more efficient use of labor within firms, and might even increase the chances of creating a permanent incomes policy. To understand this, it is necessary to examine the immediate pretext for improving financial protection against unemployment: the need to take away workers' fear of redundancy.

As in other countries in which automation and competition with low-wage foreign competitors resulted in structural losses of jobs, the pressure to do something about redundancy had been mounting in the United Kingdom since the 1950s. At first, this stemmed mainly from social concerns, but with time, the comparatively lackluster performance of the British economy – which grew at a much lower rate than most continental European economies – brought in economic considerations as well. Policy makers increasingly saw workers' fear of redundancy as contributing to the weak performance of the British economy. By causing "strikes, restrictions, or resistance to change," this fear seemed to act – as the BEC, for one, argued – "as a break on industrial expansion."[15] As the performance of the British economy deteriorated further, the need to fix the problem was felt with increasing urgency. One possible solution was to ameliorate workers' fear of redundancy by improving financial provision for the unemployed. The rationale for this was simple: by increasing workers' protection against the financial consequences of redundancy, it was hoped that workers would become less resistant to industrial change. In other words, 'buying off' workers who stood to lose from automation and the closing of plants in declining sectors could lessen union resistance to these changes. This not only would improve labor mobility and workplace flexibility but also might improve the relationships between labor, capital, and the state, thereby even introducing the prospect of future wage restraint.[16]

According to Paul Bridgen, the idea of using improved compensation for unemployment to facilitate industrial change first arose in the Treasury in 1961.[17] From there it spread to other ministries and tripartite advisory councils such as the National Joint Advisory Council (NJAC) and later the National Economic Development Council (NEDC).[18] Within the Treasury, officials

---

[14] For an overview, see Ringe and Rollings, "Responding," 331–53.
[15] MRC, MSS 200/C/3/EMP/3/114: BEC 63/135, Payments for redundancy, 1963.
[16] See Bridgen, "The State," 239, 243.
[17] For an excellent overview of governmental discussions on the economic benefits of reform in this area, see Bridgen, "The State," 233–58.
[18] The NEDC was a tripartite platform that was created as a "corporatist response" to British relative decline. It was abolished by Margaret Thatcher in the mid-1980s. For an overview of its history, see Ringe and Rollings, "Responding to Relative Decline," 331–53.

focused on the question of how to attain the transfer of labor from declining sectors of the economy to growing sectors without provoking massive union protests against the (temporary) job losses that would then certainly occur. Initially, Treasury officials only looked to "voluntarist" solutions. An obvious solution was to give so-called severance payments to redundant workers, which were lump-sum or weekly payments as compensation for the termination of employment after several years of good service. In some industries, severance payments were already an established practice. Officials hoped that instigating the spread of this practice represented a solution to the problem of redundancy that fitted well with the voluntarist framework of the British industrial relations system – and to which, thus, employer interest groups and unions would not object.

Of course, this solution of furthering the use of severance payments through voluntary means had the obvious limitation of depending on the benevolence and financial health of individual employers. The latter was especially a problem because employers who operated in industries where redundancy occurred most often also were least able to afford severance payments. Because of this, the need for a legislative initiative slowly gained acceptance in government circles. Several additional factors played a role in this growing realization of the need for state action. Most important among these was that the Conservative government began to link progress on redundancy to the achievement of an incomes policy. Following the 1961 sterling crisis, the Conservative government became convinced that a successful economic policy required introduction of a permanent incomes policy. To attain such a policy, the government clearly needed union support. By promising to improve the "security and status" of workers, the government hoped to secure the cooperation of unions in the creation of a permanent incomes policy. In the summer of 1962, the government announced its intention to implement a "package" of measures aimed at improving the status and security of workers. Among the first items to be covered was redundancy.[19]

Once the government was willing to move beyond voluntary measures, two alternatives presented themselves. Initially, government officials only explored severance payments. The National Economic Development Office (NEDO), the secretariat of the NEDC, later contributed another alternative to the discussion: the introduction of earnings-related contributions and benefits into the unemployment insurance program.[20] Both options had their problems. An important problem with the former was that mere legislation obliging employers to make severance payments would not suffice because the employers who were most prone to end up making severance payments also were least likely able to afford them. A solution through the severance-payments route therefore required the creation of an employer-financed national fund. Such a scheme, of

[19] See Bridgen, "The State," 242–44.
[20] Ibidem, 244.

course, would be deeply unpopular with employers who were less likely to deal with redundancy; after all, they would end up at the losing end. Officials also were well aware of another problem with the severance-payments route. To make the scheme affordable, it would have to be limited to redundant workers. Yet any attempt to do so certainly would be arbitrary.[21]

As problematic as the severance-payments route was, however, the government considered it much more feasible than the alternative of reforming the unemployment insurance scheme. One of the problems with unemployment insurance reform was that many inside the Conservative Party were now advocating a move toward "selective targeting" (read: introducing a means test for the neediest).[22] An expansion of the unemployment insurance scheme with a contributory approach would run exactly contrary to this aim and therefore would increase already-existing divisions within the Conservative Party over welfare issues. Even more important, unemployment insurance reform would be a lengthy affair, and Conservative Prime Minister Harold Macmillan desperately wanted to achieve some measure of progress before the coming general election. Thus, when in the beginning of 1963 Macmillan announced his intention to create a scheme to deal with redundancy, there was little doubt that he referred to the creation of an employer-financed national fund that would hand out severance payments.

By opting for the creation of a "national redundancy fund" instead of earnings-related unemployment benefits, Macmillan might have closed the ranks within the Conservative Party, but he did so at the cost of incurring the wrath of the employer community. Its participation in the NJAC and the NEDC meant that the BEC had been closely involved in deliberations over the problem of redundancy. It certainly shared the government's concerns over worker resistance to dismissal owing to redundancy. It therefore had little difficulty with ministerial attempts to encourage the voluntary use of severance payments. The BEC supported the handing out of severance payments to reward years of good service and liked the additional benefit of reducing union resistance against dismissal.[23] This does not mean that the BEC also supported introducing compulsory severance payments, though. On the contrary, it had very solid financial and economic reasons to oppose such legislation.

---

[21] PRO T311/106, Maude to Harding, 18 March 1963.

[22] See Bridgen, "The State," 247. On the Conservative split over social security in general, see Bridgen and Lowe, *Welfare Policy under the Conservatives*, 11–15; Lowe, "The Replanning," 257; and Bridgen, "The One Nation Idea and State Welfare," 83–104.

[23] This is not to say that the BEC also shared the government's concerns over a lack of labor mobility, however. On the contrary, many employers were of the opinion that "rather than mobility of labour being sluggish, turnover was far too large." See MRC, MSS.200/B/4/2/3: BEC Bulletin, 29 January 1958. In previous years, the BEC had therefore actively explored ways to reduce labor mobility. See MRC, MSS 200/3/2/c1120: Letter from Linoleum and Felt Base Employers' Federation to BEC on 18 December 1953; MRC, MSS.200/B/4/2/2: BEC Bulletin, 14 November 1956.

The BEC did not believe that compulsory severance payments would contribute to a healthier economy for several reasons. If the goal was to increase labor mobility, BEC representatives warned government officials, the legislation would be counterproductive. First, the BEC questioned whether compulsory severance payments would make workers more willing to accept their dismissal. After all, workers primarily feared the financial consequences of long-term unemployment, and severance payments did little about that. Moreover, many redundant workers now left voluntarily, whereas they would no longer do so when large sums were at stake.[24] Second, even if compulsory severance payments reduced union resistance to redundancy, they would do so with substantial financial costs. These costs might, in turn, deter employers from discharging surplus labor, thereby reducing – instead of increasing – labor mobility.[25] It is unclear whether the BEC believed this reasoning would also hold under the operation of a national redundancy fund. Because the goal of such a fund was to redistribute the costs of severance payments between employers who were more and those who were less prone to having to deal with redundancy, all employers likely would have to contribute equally to the fund regardless of risk incidence. Under such circumstances, employers would more likely be encouraged to release workers than deterred.[26] Although the BEC must have realized this, it kept arguing that statutory severance payments would decrease labor mobility long after the government's announcement to set up a national redundancy fund.[27]

The BEC was equally skeptical about the government's belief that compulsory severance payments – or, for that matter, any other initiative aimed at increasing the security of workers – might convince unions to support a permanent incomes policy. On the contrary, it feared that such legislation would only complicate future wage negotiations. The reason for this was explained at length in the preceding two chapters. As shown in those two chapters, the industrially organized unions in the Netherlands had come to accept that public – like private – insurance against labor market risks had to be financed in principle by workers themselves. As a result, the costs of public welfare development could often be (partially) offset during wage negotiations. In the United Kingdom, it was unthinkable for unions to lower their wage demands in exchange for public welfare development. As a result, public welfare development only gave

[24] MRC, MSS.200/C/4/61: British Industry, 4, 16 April 1965; MRC, MSS.200/B/3/3/264.1A: Note on the fifth meeting of the labour group of the FBI economic study committee, held at the FBI Offices on Monday, 5 October, 1964; MRC, MSS 200/C/3/EMP/3/115: Notes on redundant workers (severance payments) bill.

[25] PRO, Lab 10/2024: Note of a meeting with the BEC, 3 February 1964.

[26] This was also pointed out by officials from the Ministry of Labour at the time. See Bridgen, "The State," 241. See also Chapter 6 on this.

[27] See PRO, Lab 10/1932: Note for the record, redundancy and wage-related unemployment benefits, 8 November 1963; PRO, Lab 10/2024: Note of a meeting with the BEC, 3 February 1964; MRC, MSS.200/B/4/2/4: BEC Bulletin, 18 December 1963.

employers less room for maneuvering during wage negotiations. As the BEC put it, "legislation ... would weaken the bargaining power of employers in their dealings with the unions." This was so because "these various proposals ... were items which the employers could use in bargaining with the unions about wages, but if the Government imposed the schemes by legislation, employers would lose them as bargaining counters."[28]

Finally, the BEC questioned the government's plan in two other respects. At the time, severance payments normally only applied to workers whose jobs had become redundant because of structural change. Legislation might make it more difficult to distinguish between dismissal because of redundancy and "normal" cases of dismissal. Already unions were trying to call every dismissed worker redundant, and they would certainly become more insistent on this when large sums were at stake.[29] The result could be twofold. First, instead of improving the relationship between the two sides of industry, a statutory obligation to hand out severance payments in case of redundancy might actually increase industrial conflict.[30] Second, and far more important, the scheme would be extremely costly. Government officials could only admit that they shared the BEC's concerns on the latter point because many of them had already expressed doubts about the scheme for exactly this reason.[31]

It was the latter concern that eventually spurred the BEC into action. In private, BEC representatives expressed strong doubts about the ability of a national redundancy fund to bring about any of the benefits for which the government hoped. In fact, they privately dismissed the whole notion that improved financial provision against redundancy, or unemployment in general, for that matter, could improve the operation of the labor market. The only problem with labor mobility, they reasoned, was the lack of movement from declining to new industries. To stimulate this, investments in industrial training and housing facilities would be much more fruitful.[32] Likewise, if high wages were a problem, it was best not to raise the costs of labor further.[33] The BEC leadership was smart enough, however, to refrain from expressing the full depths of its skepticism in public. Realizing the inevitability of some kind of

---

[28] PRO, Lab 10/2024: Note of a meeting with the BEC, 3 February 1964.

[29] A representative of the Shipbuilding Employers' Confederation expressed his feelings on this in a straightforward manner: "It looks as though we are now well and truly saddled with the word 'redundancy' but I must confess that I shall continue to fight a rearguard action in the hope that someday we will talk of unemployment or shortage of work, without trying to cover up our thoughts by using fancy words!" MRC, MSS 200/C/3/EMP/3/114: Letter from the Shipbuilding Employers' Federation to the BEC on 25 February 1963.

[30] MRC, MSS.200/C/4/61: British Industry, 4, 16 April 1965. See also PRO, Lab 10/2024: BEC draft bulletin, 19 September 1963.

[31] PRO, Lab 10/1932: Meeting with the BEC on wage-related unemployment benefit, background notes, no date. See also PRO T311/106, Maude to Harding, 18 March 1963.

[32] MRC, MSS 200/B/3/3/264.1A: EPP 64/113, Paper on redundancy and mobility for consideration by the members of the labour group of the FBI economic study committee, October 1964.

[33] Ibidem.

legislative initiative to improve financial provision for unemployed workers, it instead tried to convince the government that an earnings-related unemployment scheme was much preferable to a redundancy payments scheme. Although problematic in its own right, the former had one important advantage over the latter: its financial cost would be much lower.

In the summer of 1962, the BEC General Purposes Committee considered for the first time deflecting pressure for the creation of a national redundancy fund by proposing to increase the generosity of the state unemployment insurance program. It set up a special working committee to consider such an increase. The main conclusion of this committee was that the outcome of such a move would be quite uncertain. If the BEC proposed increasing the level of the unemployment benefit, the committee warned, it might end up with higher unemployment insurance *and* severance-payments costs.[34] As a result, the BEC leadership decided to limit its actions to warning the government about the probable adverse consequences of statutory legislation on severance payments. At the time, many BEC officials still felt that they would be able to dissuade the government from passing such legislation.[35]

When it finally became clear that the government was indeed committed to the introduction of a national redundancy fund, the BEC changed course. In June 1963 it came forward with a detailed plan to add earnings-related supplements to the flat-rate unemployment benefit. In discussions with government officials, BEC representatives underscored the economic advantages of an earnings-related unemployment scheme by arguing that such a plan would encourage flexibility in labor distribution and improve industrial relations by removing the fear of redundancy. As a result, they argued, "wage related supplements to unemployment benefit ... would be a positive contribution to economic growth."[36] At the same time, they emphasized that a national redundancy fund might increase industrial trouble and deter employers from discharging labor surplus – thereby impeding the goal of improving labor mobility.[37]

In reality, the BEC very much doubted whether its plan would either help to increase labor mobility or facilitate the relationship between employers and the unions. In private, members of the BEC Social Insurance and Employers' Liability Standing Committee and the working party on redundancy policy admitted that "the Confederation was by no means convinced of their efficacy, but ... they were thought to be a considerable improvement on the idea of statutory severance payments."[38] One of the most important improvements to the

---

[34] MRC, MSS 200/C/3/EMP/3/114: BEC 63/135, Payments for redundancy, 1963.

[35] MRC, MSS 200/C/3/EMP/3/114: BEC 62/376, Draft report to General Purposes Committee, 18 September 1962.

[36] MRC, MSS.200/B/4/2/4: BEC Bulletin, 18 December 1963.

[37] PRO, Lab 10/1932: Note for the record, redundancy and wage-related unemployment benefits, 8 November 1963.

[38] MRC, MSS 200/C/3/EMP/3/115: Social Insurance And Employers' Liability Standing Committee and Working Party on Redundancy Policy, Minutes of joint meeting held at 36 Smith Square, Westminster, S.W.1., on Wednesday, 29 January 1964, at 2.30 p.m.

idea of statutory severance payments was probably that workers and the state would also be more likely to contribute to a national insurance solution, which would reduce the costs of employers.

If the BEC had stood alone in its opposition to the government's redundancy plan, it might have been forced to reconcile itself with the situation. This was not the case, however, because the confederation found a very influential ally in the TUC. By the time the government announced its intention to introduce legislation, the BEC and TUC had already achieved a striking degree of consensus over the problems at hand. While both acknowledged that fear of redundancy might lead workers to resist industrial change, neither felt that this justified abandoning the voluntary practice of labor union negotiation. Like the BEC, the TUC had great doubts about the ability of statutory legislation on severance payments to take away workers' fears of redundancy. Moreover, it shared the BEC's belief that legislation was too blunt an instrument. Not only would it be difficult to distinguish between normal dismissal and dismissal because of redundancy, but different kinds of redundancy also required different degrees of compensation.[39] Most important, statutory legislation on severance payments conflicted with the interests of some of the most powerful members of the TUC: the unions representing workers who already had achieved rights to redundancy severance payments through voluntary collective bargaining.

To the Conservative government, the TUC's dismissal of its proposal may have come as a surprise. To Labour backbenchers, it did not. Some two years before the Conservatives announced their intention to create a national redundancy scheme, the Labour Party had already approached the TUC with an alternative of its own. At the time, economic considerations had not yet entered political party agendas. Labour's initiative therefore arose purely from social concerns. Under Labour's proposal, employers would have been obliged to pay their workers at least one-half of normal earnings for the first month of either redundancy or sickness. The TUC Social Insurance and Industrial Welfare Committee had reacted quite dismissively to this proposal. When Labour representatives to the committee explained the need for it through the low coverage rates of redundancy schemes, they were told that the TUC "strictly opposed legislation, because this might hurt the position of unions during negotiations over collective agreements."[40] While "fully recognizing the need for extending redundancy and service payments," the members of the committee emphasized that "this should be done by encouraging trade union negotiation."[41] To replace labor union negotiation by legislation, they warned,

---

[39] MRC, MSS.292B/161.1: TUC Social Insurance Committee and Industrial Welfare Committee, Minutes of first meeting, January 11, 1962. While the BEC was afraid that too many workers would receive severance payments, the TUC feared that an arbitrary definition of redundancy would exclude workers. TUC, MSS.292B/108.2/1: NJAC (general council side), 23 April 1963.

[40] MRC, MSS.292B/161.1: TUC Social Insurance and Industrial Welfare Committee, Minutes of seventh meeting, 12 April 1961.

[41] MRC, MSS.292B/161.5: TUC Social Insurance and Industrial Welfare Committee, Fourth meeting, 8 January 1964.

would "give rise to many fundamental problems which did not appear to have been considered by the Labour Party."[42] According to the BEC, these problems were that "better results from the standpoint of trade unions would often be obtained on this subject by local negotiation."[43] Of course, those who could get better results were workers with a strong position on the labor market and who consequently already had negotiated rights to severance payments in case of redundancy. For other workers, voluntary negotiation had already proven to be much less advantageous.

During the early 1960s, less than one-third of all workers had secured a right to receive severance payments when laid off.[44] Among the remainder, many could hardly rely on labor union negotiation to provide coverage against the risk of becoming redundant. The combination of low wages and a high-risk incidence of becoming redundant put occupational provision against redundancy out of reach for many workers. For such workers, their only hope for any improvement lay in the creation of a public scheme. In such a scheme, they would be able to share their risks with less-risk-prone workers. Of course, this gave less-risk-prone workers a good incentive to oppose the creation of a public scheme. After all, and as mentioned earlier, in a common risk pool privileged workers end up subsidizing the welfare efforts of less-privileged workers. For unions representing privileged workers, it made no difference that employers would bear the full costs of the scheme. In discussions of the TUC Sub-Committee on Sickness and Unemployment Benefits, representatives of these unions argued that employers would use the costs of the scheme as an argument to oppose future wage increases. Because risk reapportioning meant that the amount of foregone wage increase would be much higher under a state scheme than under occupational provision, the introduction of a national redundancy fund was therefore not in the interests of workers who currently had access to severance payments.[45] Under pressure from unions in which members stood to lose from risk reapportioning, the TUC declared that it could not accept a public scheme.

[42] MRC, MSS.292B/161.1: TUC Social Insurance and Industrial Welfare Committee, Minutes of seventh meeting, 12 April 1961.

[43] MRC, MSS 200/C/3/EMP/3/113: BEC letter to secretaries of member organisations on security of employment, 23 February 1959. For the view of TUC itself, see MRC, MSS.292B/161.2: TUC Sub-Committee on Sickness and Unemployment Benefits, Minutes of the second meeting, 14 February 1962; and MRC, MSS.292B/163.1: TUC Sub-Committee on Sickness and Unemployment Benefits, 9 May 1962.

[44] Some scholars even estimate it at one-sixth. For this estimate and the generosity of existing schemes before introduction of the Redundancy Payments Act, see Stanley Parker, *Effects of the Redundancy Payments Act* (London: HMSO, 1971), 4; Hilda Kahn, *Repercussions of Redundancy* (London: Allen and Unwin, 1964), 21–4; Santosh Mukerjee, *Through No Fault of Their Own: Systems for Handling Redundancy in Britain, France and Germany* (London: MacDonald, 1973), 53.

[45] MRC, MSS.292B/161.2: TUC Sub-Committee on Sickness and Unemployment Benefits, Minutes of the second meeting, 14 February 1962.

Whereas the unions representing workers who already had access to severance payments opposed the creation of a public scheme because they could achieve better results through voluntary wage negotiation, others also found reason for skepticism. In discussions with government officials, TUC representatives admitted that many workers certainly had a lot to gain from statutory severance payments. Yet, they stressed, such workers undoubtedly had even more to gain from proper financial provision for long-term unemployment. This represented an important problem because the TUC feared that legislation on severance pay would provide the government with an "alibi for doing nothing on insurance benefits."[46] The TUC had long argued for a government- or employer-financed increase to the national insurance benefit level, and it feared that an additional statutory levy on all employers would complicate this goal. In a meeting with the Minister of Pensions, TUC representatives pointed this out and added that countries with statutory service payments often also had very inadequate social security provisions.[47] Because of its opposition to statutory severance payments, the TUC came out in cautious support for the BEC's alternative. While remaining firm on the need to raise the flat-rate national insurance benefit first, it carefully hinted that it might also accept the introduction of earnings-related supplements.[48]

Bolstered by the TUC's support, the BEC put the government under extreme pressure. If the government did decide to move ahead with its scheme, BEC representatives warned, it would receive "a strong reaction" from its members. "Not only would the die-hards be opposed to them," the director of the confederation, George Pollock, argued, "but also the more progressive elements."[49] In personal conversations with government officials, Pollock urged the government to accept the BEC proposal.[50] Unhampered by ideological bonds with the present government, the TUC was able to voice its discontent more bluntly. According to TUC General Secretary George Woodstock, the government's proposals "sprang from immediate political considerations and not from a genuine desire to provide greater security of income for workpeople."[51]

With both the BEC and TUC strongly opposed to the introduction of a national redundancy fund, government policy drifted. The sheer strength of

---

[46] PRO, Lab 10/1835: Memorandum by Barnes, 16 September 1963. See also MRC, TUC MSS292B-108.2/1: NJAC (general council side), 23 April 1963.

[47] MRC, MSS.292B/161.5: TUC, National Joint Advisory Council to the Ministry of Labour (general council side), Third meeting, 18 December 1963. See also MRC, MSS.292B/161.5: TUC Social Insurance and Industrial Welfare Committee, Fourth meeting, 8 January 1964.

[48] The exact wordings of the TUC were that "first priority should be given to an increase in the basic rates of unemployment and sickness benefit. They would consider graduated schemes once this was done." MRC, MSS.200/C/3/EMP/3/115: TUC attitude on severance payments legislation, 5 February 1964.

[49] PRO, Lab10/2034: Meeting with D. Taylor, 2 September 1963.

[50] PRO, Lab10/2034: Meeting with D. Taylor, 8 October 1963.

[51] TUC, MSS.292B/108.2/2: NJAC (general council side), 18 December 1963.

this opposition certainly influenced the government, and many inside the bureaucracy openly preferred the BEC's alternative.[52] Yet the introduction of the earnings-related principle into the unemployment insurance scheme was equally controversial. Many inside the Conservative Party opposed this because they wanted to move toward selective targeting instead. Moreover, there were those who, like the BEC, were as skeptical about the economic benefits of an earnings-related scheme as they were about the economic benefits of statutory severance payments.[53] As a result, the government was utterly divided. Some in Parliament wanted to go ahead with the statutory redundancy scheme. Others preferred an earnings-related scheme. Still others wanted to do both. Finally, there were those who began to question the idea of reform altogether.[54] According to Paul Bridgen, the issue divided the cabinet to the core.[55] The government certainly found it impossible to come up with a concrete proposal before the general election of 1964 – this despite having worked on the redundancy issue for three years. All it could do was promise to make a decision after it had renewed its mandate.

Matters were taken out of the government's hands when it lost its parliamentary majority to the Labour Party after the 1964 election. Having already shown a commitment to introduce statutory severance payments *and* the earnings-related principle, the new Labour government found it much easier to achieve progress than did its Conservative predecessor. To accommodate the TUC, it first raised the level of the National Insurance Benefit – although not to a level of subsistence. In less than a year after the election, it also introduced the Redundancy Payments Act.[56] Organized employer and union objections to this were of no avail. In clear and ironic terms, the Minister of Labour informed them that "he appreciated the strength of the case in logic for dealing with earnings-related unemployment insurance benefits before dealing with severance payments. The review of the social insurance scheme would, however, take a good deal of time, and provision to encourage mobility of labor and acceptance of change were urgently needed. He could not hold out any prospect of severance pay legislation being deferred, but social insurance proposals would be prepared as quickly as possible."[57]

In the end, the National Insurance Act that introduced the earnings-related principle into the national insurance scheme passed Parliament in the beginning of 1966, some one-and-a-half years after Labour regained power. The

---

[52] See Bridgen, "The State," 248–50.
[53] PRO, Lab 10/2024: Note of a meeting with the BEC, 3 February 1964.
[54] PRO, Lab 10/1932: Internal memo, 26 November 1963.
[55] See Bridgen, "The State, 254.
[56] The scheme implemented by Labour did not differ greatly from the one prepared by the Conservatives. On its exact features, see Lawrence S. Root, "Britain's Redundancy Payments for Displaced Workers," *Monthly Labor Review* (June 1987), 18–23.
[57] MRC, MSS.200/C/3/EMP/3/115: BEC 65/28, Government proposals for legislation on severance pay for redundant workers, Note by confederation, 20 January 1965.

new Labour government, led by Harold Wilson, presented this feat as a part of its strategy to modernize the British economy.[58] Because Labour's ambition to improve financial provision for the unemployed long predated any discussion of such provision's utility for economic modernization, it is safe to assume, however, that social considerations were at least of equal importance to the new government. It is even possible that economic arguments primarily served as rhetoric, designed to put pressure on the BEC and TUC.[59] If this was the case, though, one can hardly blame Labour. After all, even its "natural ally" was almost as opposed to an earnings-related unemployment scheme as it had been to statutory severance payments.

THE INTRODUCTION OF THE EARNINGS-RELATED SUPPLEMENTARY SCHEME

Despite its support for the BEC's proposal, the TUC was not enthusiastic about an earnings-related unemployment scheme. In fact, the TUC – much like the BEC itself – had supported the BEC's scheme mostly because its members agreed that the "proposal of a comprehensive wage related National Insurance Scheme is greatly preferable to the alternative suggestion of a National Redundancy Fund."[60] Once more, the TUC's hesitancy stemmed primarily from the position of its craft and occupationally organized white-collar unions. These unions had no more interest in earnings-related unemployment benefits than in superannuation or the national redundancy scheme, and they feared the redistributive consequences of an extension of the unemployment insurance program. As had been the case with superannuation and the national redundancy scheme, their resistance first came to the fore in discussions with Labour when the latter was still in the opposition.

Intensive discussions between Labour and the TUC over the possible introduction of the earnings-related principle into the state unemployment insurance program began in the early 1960s.[61] In their first meeting with Labour officials, the representative of unions representing privileged workers immediately made it clear that "no part of an insured person's wage related contributions should

---

[58] See Glennerster, *British Social Policy*, 97–8.

[59] Based on this, Howard Glennerster remarked, "One is struck, rereading the discussions of the day, how completely topsy-turvy and transitory are the arguments to justify social policies." Glennerster, *British Social Policy*, 98.

[60] MRC, MSS.292B/161.3: TUC Social Insurance and Industrial Welfare Committee, Minutes of fifth meeting, 13 February 1963.

[61] Labour had already informed the TUC of its intention to introduce the earnings-related principle into unemployment – and sickness – insurance in the mid-1950s. At first, though, discussions between Labour and the TUC focused mainly on superannuation. They only started seriously discussing the idea of extending the earnings-related principle to other national insurance schemes in 1962, at roughly the time when the Conservative government put forward its severance payments scheme.

be used to pay for flat rate benefits."[62] In fact, the representative made it clear that they disliked the idea of an earnings-related scheme even without direct redistribution between higher- and lower-paid workers. To understand this, it is necessary to revisit the difference between saving for retirement and insuring against the risk of unemployment. Unlike the risk of becoming dependent in old age, the risk of unemployment is a much greater concern for some workers than for others. This gives less-risk-prone workers good reason to resist participating in public insurance against unemployment because such participation would entail subsidizing the welfare efforts of more-risk-prone insurance plan members. If less-risk-prone workers do want to insure themselves, they would do far better to pool their insurance with equally risk-prone workers in occupational schemes. In fact, some might not even need to insure themselves against the risk of becoming unemployed at all.

Representatives of craft and occupationally organized white-collar unions used exactly this logic when they argued against Labour's plans. Anne Godwin, the representative of the Clerical and Administrative Workers' Union (CAWU), simply stated that "sickness and unemployed benefits differed from retirement pensions in that the contingencies against which they were intended to give protection, affected the higher-paid less than the lower-paid." This made it "undesirable to put too heavy a burden directly on those with the smallest risk."[63] Another representative to the TUC Social Insurance and Industrial Welfare Committee warned that "many higher paid workers would resent a high level of contributions for benefits which might mean little to those in tolerably secure positions."[64] The problem was also that many workers could already claim occupational coverage. To them, "wage related National Insurance benefits would mean little ... except increased contributions."[65]

There were, of course, representatives – namely those of general unions – who bemoaned the absence of occupational provision for most workers. There were also those who emphasized that Labour's wage-related proposal was the only way to raise flat-rate benefits.[66] Yet the TUC did not yield on its preference for a flat-rate system of national insurance over an earnings-related system. Labour representatives were told that the TUC's main priority remained to obtain an increase in the national insurance benefit so that any additional

[62] MRC, MSS.292B/161.2: TUC Sub-Committee on Sickness and Unemployment Benefits, Minutes of the fourth meeting, 9 May 1962.

[63] MRC, MSS.292B/161.2: TUC Sub-Committee on Sickness and Unemployment Benefits, Minutes of the second meeting, 14 February 1962.

[64] MRC, MSS.292B/161.1: TUC Social Insurance and Industrial Welfare Committee, Minutes of first meeting, 11 January 1962.

[65] MRC, MSS.292B/161.2: TUC Sub-Committee on Sickness and Unemployment Benefits, Minutes of the second meeting, 14 February 1962.

[66] MRC, MSS.292B/161.2: TUC Sub-Committee on Sickness and Unemployment Benefits, Minutes of the fourth meeting, 9 May 1962.

provision could be left to labor union negotiation.[67] In response, the Labour representatives pointed out how close the stance of the TUC was to that of the Conservative government. Douglas Houghton, who would later become a minister in the new Labour government, was right on the mark when he stated that "the trade unions might be in danger of accepting the [Conservative] Government's view that state provision should be limited to the most basic social needs and that the establishment of higher standards should be left to private individuals and groups."[68]

When Labour and TUC representatives renewed their discussions over the earnings-related principle some two to three years later, the TUC took a more positive stance. In these later talks, Labour representatives were told that the TUC "welcomes and supports the principles of the Labour Party's proposals for a comprehensive scheme of wage-related national insurance benefits and contributions."[69] To understand this, it is necessary to note that in the meantime, the TUC had already supported the BEC's earnings-related unemployment scheme. When the new Labour government adopted the main principles of this scheme, the TUC simply continued to support it. Second, even when Labour and the TUC first discussed the earnings-related principle, many of the latter's members already acknowledged that only an increased contribution from workers could raise the unemployment benefit.[70] Third, and by far most important, the BEC's scheme was acceptable to unions representing privileged workers because it met their most pressing demand: there was to be no direct redistribution between higher and lower incomes.

The proposal of the new Labour government was to add an earnings-related supplement, amounting to one-third of weekly earnings between nine and thirty pounds, to the existing flat-rate benefit. The supplement would be paid for six months.[71] Entitlement to the earnings-related supplement depended

---

[67] Of course, this had to be financed – preferably by increasing the Exchequer contribution or otherwise by increasing the employer contribution to the National Insurance Fund. Perhaps the TUC preferred the former to the latter because of the effect of the latter on wage negotiations. See the following discussion between Labour and the TUC on the introduction of a national redundancy scheme for this.

[68] MRC, MSS.292B/161.2: TUC Sub-Committee on Sickness and Unemployment Benefits, Minutes of the second meeting, 14 February 1962.

[69] MRC, MSS.292B/161.7: TUC Social Insurance and Industrial Welfare Committee, Second meeting, 11 November 1964.

[70] Most TUC members had acknowledged this long before. MRC, MSS.292B/161.2: TUC Sub-Committee on Sickness and Unemployment Benefits, Minutes of the fourth meeting, 9 May 1962.

[71] In the BEC's scheme, this earnings band was set at 9 and 18 pounds – which was similar to the bounds of the Conservative government's pension scheme. As far as the duration of the scheme was concerned, the BEC had considered a period ranging from three to six months. The TUC had demanded a duration of one year. MRC, MSS.292B/161.6: Note of meeting with the Minister of Pensions and National Insurance, the Minister of Labour and representatives of the British Employers' Confederation at the House of Commons, on Wednesday, 13 May 1964, at 5:15 p.m.

strictly on the number of weekly contributions paid, with contributions set at 2 percent of weekly earnings. Unemployed workers could only claim the maximum benefit level after a contribution record of ten years. In such a system, there was to be little solidarity between more- and less-privileged workers. First, earnings over one-and-a-half times average earnings (which meant an income higher than thirty pounds per week because average earnings equaled roughly twenty pounds per week at the time) were excluded from the scheme. Second, the scheme was specifically designed to limit redistribution between more- and less-privileged workers. It did so in two ways. First of all, unlike with superannuation, no part of earnings-related contributions would be used to finance an increase in the flat-rate benefit. This ensured that there would be no direct redistributive effort between higher- and lower-paid workers. Second, and equally important, more-risk-prone workers had a much lower chance of completing the contributory record that was needed to achieve the maximum earnings-related benefit than did less-risk-prone workers. This also ensured that risk redistribution would be limited.

All these measures did secure craft and occupationally organized white-collar acquiescence, but they also ensured that the earnings-related unemployment scheme did little to improve the situation for those who needed it most, namely, the lower-paid and more-risk-prone workers. By excluding all earnings below nine pounds, the scheme was no improvement for workers who earned less than half the national average. They remained completely dependent on the dismally low national insurance benefit. For some of the workers who earned just a little more than half the national average, the situation was arguably even worse. Not only did the scheme bring them little improvement, but they also could lose out by participating in it. The reason for this was that the new scheme did not improve the benefit level of the lower-paid family man with several children because his benefit would be subject to a wage stop. He would, however, have to contribute to the scheme. As a result, to a lower-paid family man with several children, the scheme simply presented an increase in taxation levels by 2 percent, for which he received nothing in return. To understand this, it is necessary to look at the problem of "excessive benefiting" that worried policy makers so much. This problem arose from the combination of a flat-rate scheme with an earnings-related supplementary scheme – and was worsened by the problem of low pay in the United Kingdom.

In Chapter 3 and the beginning of this chapter, I emphasized that all involved parties in the United Kingdom, including the TUC and BEC, supported the notion that the national insurance system had to operate along egalitarian lines and thus was to levy equal contributions in exchange for equal benefits. They allowed for only one major exception to the egalitarian principle. Welfare recipients who had families to support were entitled to a higher benefit than welfare recipients without dependents. This exception arose out of necessity because the low level of the flat-rate national insurance benefit affected welfare recipients with a wife and children most seriously. Wife and child supplements could

TABLE 4.1. *The Unemployment Benefit as a Percentage of Weekly Earnings under the National Insurance Scheme in 1965*

Weekly Earnings (£)	Single	Married, No Children	Married, One Child	Married, Two Children	Married, Three Children
10	40	65	78	85	93
12	33	54	65	71	78
14	28	46	56	61	67
18	22	36	43	47	52
20	20	32	39	43	47
30	13	22	26	28	31

Source: MRC, MSS292B/161.6: TUC, Level of wage related national insurance benefit, 16 April 1964, several appendices. Calculation of percentages by author.

raise the total benefit dramatically. While a single welfare recipient received around four pounds in 1965, his married counterpart with three children could claim over nine pounds. Table 4.1 illustrates the effect of wife and child supplements. Benefit levels are given as a percentage of previous earnings for workers who earned between ten pounds (or half the average earnings at the time) and thirty pounds (or one-and-a-half the average earnings) per week. A secondary purpose of this table is to show how inadequate the national insurance benefit was for welfare recipients.

Yet the main purpose of Table 4.1 is not to illustrate the inadequacy of the unemployment benefit. Instead, it is to show that for unemployed workers who had earned just over half the national average earnings and who had several family members to support, the national insurance benefit already closely approximated previous earnings. For instance, an unemployed worker who had a wife and three children to support was entitled to a benefit that amounted to 93 percent of his previous earnings. This meant that the introduction of an earnings-related scheme on top of the flat-rate benefit would entitle some workers to a total benefit that even more closely approached their previous earnings. Table 4.2 illustrates this problem. Under the combination of the flat-rate benefit and earnings-related supplements, an unemployed worker with a wife and three children who had previously earned ten pounds per week was entitled to a benefit that equaled 97 percent of his previous wage. As the table shows, other unemployed workers with dependents (provided that their previous wages were sufficiently below the national average) also were entitled to benefits that closely approximated their previous earnings (and thus one-and-a-half times the national average), the flat-rate benefit.

It is needless to say that the prospect of some benefit recipients receiving "excessive benefiting" worried the BEC very much. The confederation had already anticipated this problem in its own scheme and had devised a solution for it: that is, the flat-rate benefit and earnings-related supplement were not

TABLE 4.2. *The Unemployment Benefit as a Percentage of Weekly Earnings under the National Insurance Scheme and the Earnings-Related Supplementary Scheme*

Weekly Earnings (£)	Single	Married, No Children	Married, One Child	Married, Two Children	Married, Three Children
10	43	68*	81*	89*	97*
12	42	63	73*	79*	87*
14	41	58	68*	73*	78*
18	39	53	60	64	68*
20	38	51	57	61	65
30	37	45	49	52	54

*Subject to either the BEC or Labour's maximum benefit threshold.
Source: MRC, MSS292B/161.6: TUC, Level of wage related national insurance benefit, 16 April 1964, several appendices. Calculation of percentages by author.

together to exceed two-thirds of previous earnings.[72] Severely pressured by the BEC and apparently itself worried about excessive benefiting, Labour adopted this feature in its own scheme, although it raised the limit to 85 percent of previous earnings. Whereas the BEC regarded the 85 percent threshold as too high, the TUC resisted the introduction of a maximum benefit level altogether. Its protests, however, were of no avail. When the TUC complained that many low-wage families would now receive no supplement, despite having paid benefits, the government merely responded that it understood the problem but that "it had not however been possible to find a solution in time.... Further enquiries were undertaken by the Ministry."[73]

The BEC also used the issue of excessive benefiting as an argument against the extension of the earnings-related principle to the sickness insurance scheme. In resisting this, however, the confederation stood alone.[74] The BEC leadership felt that it had nevertheless been successful in keeping the scheme as lenient as

[72] MRC, MSS.200/C/3/EMP/3/115: Social insurance and employers' liability standing committee and working party on redundancy policy, Minutes of joint meeting held at 36 Smith Square, Westminster, S.W.1., on Wednesday, 29 January 1964, at 2:30 p.m.

[73] TUC, MSS.292B/161.8: Need for increased family allowances, 13 July 1966.

[74] The BEC gave several reasons for its opposition to extending the earnings-related principle. Among its arguments were the notions that the sick normally had a job to which to return, which meant that this did not relate to the question of redundancy; that half the working population was already covered by an occupational sick pay scheme; that earnings-related sickness benefits would have no effect on labor mobility; that an extension of the earnings-related principle would lead to inflation; and that it would lead to increased absenteeism. PRO, Lab 10/1932: Note of second meeting with BEC, 7 February 1964; MRC, MSS.200/C/3/EMP/5/1: CBI social insurance committee, Minutes of meeting held at 21 Tothill Street, London, S.W.1., on Wednesday, 6 October 1965, at 2:30 p.m; MRC, MSS 200/C/3/EMP/3/115: Social insurance and employers' liability standing committee and working party on redundancy policy, Minutes of joint meeting held at 36 Smith Square, Westminster, S.W.1., on Wednesday, 29 January 1964, at 2:30 p.m.

possible. Income below nine and above thirty pounds was excluded altogether, benefits averaged only 50 percent for most recipients, with the exception of lower-paid workers with large families, and on the BEC's insistence (despite fierce resistance from the TUC), the Labour government had introduced a waiting period of twelve days before the earnings-related supplement could be paid. These features may not have made application of the earnings-related principle to the sickness insurance scheme palatable to the BEC, but it at least made it bearable. Most important to the BEC was the introduction of a waiting period, which, according to its estimates, would cut annual sickness claims by at least 4 million.[75] As a result, the BEC leadership was not discontented with the new scheme. Most important to the organization was that the scheme "did not involve large additional expenditure; the additional unemployment and sickness contributions by employers would come to about thirty million pounds, or one-fifth of one percent of the wages bill and could have been much more."[76]

Although presented by the Labour government as an important step forward for all workers, introduction of the 1966 National Insurance Act did little for those who needed it most: the low-paid workers who were most susceptible to the risk of becoming unemployed. Not only were the lowest-paid workers not entitled to earnings-related supplements, but the introduction of a long waiting period ensured that workers who were often unemployed also did not qualify for the supplements. Moreover, the supplements were paid out for a limited period only. This meant that they did nothing to improve matters for the long-term unemployed. Despite the limited nature of the scheme, the Conservatives criticized its costs and effect on the willingness of the unemployed to seek work. This line of reasoning led a Conservative government to abolish the supplements in 1982.[77]

FROM BISMARCK TO THE SOCIAL INSURANCE IN THE NETHERLANDS

In the Netherlands, early postwar thinking on public protection against the financial consequences of unemployment developed in a completely different direction from the United Kingdom. Instead of opting for a system that combined flat-rate benefits with flat-rate contributions, as the British had done, the Dutch created a system that offered earnings-related benefits in exchange for earnings-related contributions. To a large extent, the choice of a completely earnings-related system in the Netherlands can be explained in the same way as the choice of a totally flat-rate system in the United Kingdom: this was simply

---

[75] MRC, MSS.200/C/3/EMP/5/1/: New national insurance legislation, 23 August 1965.

[76] MRC, MSS.200/C/3/EMP/5/1/: Extract from minutes of November 1965 council meeting.

[77] See Frans Pennings, *Benefits of Doubt: A Comparative Study of the Legal Aspects of Employment and Unemployment Schemes in Great Britain, France and the Netherlands* (Deventer: Kluwer, 1990), 62.

what workers and employers had been accustomed to before the war. Until the introduction of the 1949 Werkloosheidswet (WW, Unemployment Act), there had technically been no public unemployment insurance program in the Netherlands. Yet the state had given large subsidies to union-operated unemployment funds. In addition, many employers had offered so-called reduced-pay schemes (*wachtgeldregelingen*) to unemployed workers. Employers were not obliged to create reduced-pay schemes, but because state subsidies almost completely financed them, many had started doing so in the 1930s.[78]

The WW created a public unemployment insurance program that resembled prewar semipublic protection from the financial consequences of unemployment in two important ways. First, it offered the same percentage of previous earnings as had the prewar reduced-pay schemes. Married men and breadwinners were entitled to 80 percent of their previous wages; unmarried men and women, as well as nonbreadwinners of eighteen years and older, were entitled to 70 percent of their previous wages; and the rest to 60 percent of previous wages. Second, the new insurance comprised two separate schemes. Depending on their contributory records, workers were first entitled to "reduced pay" for a minimum of eight weeks (it was up to the unions and employers of a specific industry to decide whether benefits should continue for a longer period).[79] After their entitlement to reduced pay had ended, unemployed workers were, again depending on contributory records, entitled to unemployment benefits for thirteen weeks (or twenty-one weeks if a worker was not entitled to reduced pay but was entitled to the unemployment benefit).[80] In terms of benefit levels, the two schemes were quite similar; the only difference in this respect was that under the reduced-pay scheme, employers were allowed to supplement the percentages given earlier, whereas they were not in principle

---

[78] See P. Schrage and E. Nijhoff, "Een lange sisser en een late knal? De ontwikkeling van de Nederlandse werkloosheidsvoorziening in West-Europees perspectief: een terreinverkenning." In W. P. Blockmans and L. A. van der Valk, *Van particuliere naar openbare zorg en terug? Sociale politiek in Nederland sinds 1880* (Amsterdam: NEHA, 1992), 38–42.

[79] The responsibility for administration of unemployment insurance in the Netherlands lay with so-called industrial insurance boards (*bedrijfsverenigingen*), which comprised representatives of unions and employers in a particular industry. It was up to these boards to decide whether or not to grant reduced pay for more than eight weeks. I will return to the importance of the industrial insurance boards in Chapter 6.

[80] In comparison, in 1946, the duration of the British unemployment benefit was set at a minimum of 180 days. Based on the contribution record of a worker, the duration could be extended by 130 days. In 1953, the additional duration was increased to 312 days. In 1966, the minimum duration level was increased to twelve months. The duration of the British unemployment insurance program thus was much longer than that of its Dutch counterpart. This does not mean that the long-term unemployed were necessarily worse off in the Netherlands. Nearly all unemployed workers in the Netherlands were entitled to the relatively generous Sociale Voorzieningen A and B (Social Provisions A and B), which served to complement the unemployment insurance program. See the following paragraph on this. For a good, detailed comparison of the features of the British and Dutch unemployment insurance programs, see Pennings, *Benefits of Doubt*, 33–89, 295–389.

allowed to do so under the unemployment scheme.[81] In terms of financing, eligibility criteria, and, as shown earlier, duration, the two schemes differed quite substantially.[82]

Unlike the 1955 Algemene Ouderdomswet (AOW, General Old Age Act), which created a pension scheme that combined flat-rate benefits with earnings-related contributions, the 1949 WW did not posses specific features designed to aid lower-paid workers. In fact, the strict "Bismarckian system" that was initially chosen in the Netherlands limited redistribution as much as did the flat-rate Beveridge scheme on which the British unemployment insurance program was based. First, there was to be no direct redistribution between higher- and lower-paid workers in the form of a redistributive contributory system. Second, the insurance program was specifically designed to limit risk redistribution in three ways. First, a wage limit excluded all workers who earned more than a 120 percent of the modal wage – and who consequently stood a much lower risk of becoming unemployed.[83] Second, entitlement to a benefit strictly depended on a contribution record of 156 days in the previous twelve months for the reduced-pay scheme and 78 days in the previous twelve months for the unemployment scheme.[84] Third, the contribution level of the

---

[81] If individual employers decided to grant private supplements to the state unemployment benefit, these in principle had to be subtracted from the state benefit. Yet the industrial insurance boards that were responsible for operation of the unemployment scheme were allowed to make exceptions to this rule. As we will see in Chapter 6, these exceptions were made quite frequently. ARA, CSWV, 2.19.103.06, 146: Verslag van de vergadering van de Technische Commissie Sociale Verzekering, gehouden op 18 December 1957, ten kantore van de Metaalbond.

[82] The government had chosen to differentiate between the reduced-pay and unemployment schemes because it felt that the goals of the former differed from those of the latter. Workers who received reduced pay were seen as a part of the industrial labor reserve, whereas workers who received an unemployment insurance benefit were regarded as part of the general labor reserve. The employer federations disagreed with this line of reasoning and, for administrative reasons, preferred the creation of a single unemployment scheme. ARA, CSWV, 2.19.103.06, 130: Kort verslag van de vergadering van de Kring voor Sociaal Overleg, gehouden op woensdag 5 Januari 1949, des namiddags te 2.15 uur, ten kantore van het Centraal Sociaal Werkgevers-Verbond, Kneuterdijk 8, te 's-Gravenhage.

[83] To avoid the fact that price increases or increases in the level of prosperity would draw more workers out of the unemployment insurance pool, the level of the wage limit was linked to price and wage increases. In coming years, the union and employer federations would often struggle over whether the level of the wage limit should increase with prices, wages, or neither. ARA, CSWV, 2.19.103.06, 146: Verslag van de vergadering van de Technische Commissie Sociale Verzekering, gehouden op 27 September 1958; ARA, CSWV, 2.19.103.06, 139: Verslag van de vergadering van de Commissie Sociale Verzekering van het CSWV, gehouden op 22 Oktober 1963, ten kantore van de Vereniging van Tricot- en Kousenfabrikanten te Utrecht; VNO, F119(4) Cie Sociale Verzekering RCO 1947–1970: Verslag van de vergadering van de Commissie Sociale Verzekering van de Raad van Bestuur in Arbeidszaken, gehouden op 29 oktober 1963, ten kantore van het Nederlands Katholiek Werkgevers-Verbond, Raamweg 32 te 's Gravenhage.

[84] This was roughly similar to the case in the United Kingdom. See Anthony Ian Ogus and Eric M. Barendt, *The Law of Social Security* (London: Butterworth, 1982), 67.

reduced-pay scheme differed per industrial insurance board. This meant that if the unemployment level in a certain industry was higher than in other industries, employers and workers in that industry also had to pay higher contribution levels.

To a certain extent, the limited redistributive nature of the 1949 WW can be seen as the outcome of organized employer pressure for an adherence to strict actuarial principles. Yet it also should be noted that the three union federations seem to have had little difficulty at the time in accepting this. This may have been because the three union federations worried as much about the costs of the new unemployment insurance programs as did the employer federations.[85] This became evident in the ferocity of discussions over who would pay for its costs. In debates before introduction of the WW, the three union federations kept arguing that employers were responsible for involuntary unemployment and therefore had to bear the brunt of the costs of the unemployment insurance scheme. The employer federations naturally disagreed and wanted workers to share its costs equally.[86] The discussions ended with a clear victory for the employer federations. The reduced-pay scheme was to be financed by employers and workers on a fifty-fifty basis; the unemployment scheme was to be financed by employers and workers, who each financed 25 percent of the costs, and the state, which provided the rest. In coming years, the three union federations and their employer counterparts would continue to clash over who was to bear the (increased) costs of the scheme. In this, discussions over unemployment insurance development differed greatly from discussions over an increase in the generosity of the state old age pension – which, the unions acknowledged, had to be financed by workers themselves.

There was another reason why the union federations at the time were willing to accept the notion that the new unemployment insurance program had to follow strict actuarial rules. The fact was that some of their union members insisted on this. The public official unions, for example, took serious issue with their inclusion in the unemployment insurance program. Because their members enjoyed relatively secure positions, they objected to their having to

---

[85] ARA, CSWV, 2.19.103.06, 130: Kort verslag van de vergadering van de Kring voor Sociaal Overleg, gehouden op woensdag 5 Januari 1949, des namiddags te 2.15 uur, ten kantore van het Centraal Sociaal Werkgevers-Verbond, Kneuterdijk 8, te 's-Gravenhage.

[86] The unions did demand wage compensation in exchange. The employer federations at first rejected this, resulting in a stalemate that was solved in a rather strange way: a majority in the SER (which excluded at least some employer representatives) spoke out in favor of wage compensation on the condition that employers were then allowed to pass on its costs through price increases. See C. M. J. Ruijters, "Sociale Zaken." In M. D. Bogaarts, *Parlementaire geschiedenis van Nederland na 1945: De periode van het kabinet-Beel (1946–1948)* (Den Haag: Sdu, 1989), 663. It is important to note the distinction between state unemployment insurance development and the development of state insurance against old age, sickness, and disability in this regard. While the unions were willing to accept that workers themselves pay state insurance against all the other major labor market risks, they were not willing to do the same for state insurance against unemployment.

contribute to the insurance program at all – let alone on an equal basis.[87] This, among other things, led them to support the unions favoring premium differentiation between industries. Especially within the NVV, many argued against a uniform contribution level for all industries.[88] As a result, the union federations were willing to go along with the employer federations on this. Parliament eventually stood in the way, however. A parliamentary majority could accept premium differentiation between industries for the reduced-pay scheme but wanted the unemployment scheme's contribution levels to be uniform across industries.[89]

The initial willingness of the union federations to adhere to "sound" actuarial rules soon made way for an interpretation that stressed the importance of worker solidarity. The industrial consensus on premium differentiation melted away first. As early as 1951, the members of the NVV Committee on Social Insurance Programs already agreed that "there is no reason why a worker who, through no fault of his own, works in a branch of industry with unfavorable risk, should pay a much higher premium than a worker who happens to work in a branch with more favorable risk."[90] The other union federations now also took this position and opposed renewed attempts by employers to extend premium differentiation between industries to the unemployment scheme.[91]

Worker solidarity-based considerations also partly guided union efforts to abolish the wage limit. In the run-up to introduction of the WW, the union and employer federations argued intensely over the question of whether or not higher-paid workers should be excluded from the scheme. At the time, the union federations had been willing to give in partially. While accepting that the much lower risk of unemployment for higher-paid workers required the introduction of a wage limit, they insisted that the limit be set at a much higher level than the one demanded by the employer federations. The amount on

[87] ARA, CSWV, 2.19.103.06, 130: Kort verslag van de vergadering van de Kring voor Sociaal Overleg, gehouden op 14 Oktober 1947 ten kantore van het Centraal Sociaal Werkgevers-Verbond, Kneuterdijk 8, te 's-Gravenhage.

[88] Some of them continued to do so after the NVV leadership itself had already changed its stance. IISG, Codelijsten van het NVV-Commissiearchief 1945–1967, 322 Socialecie 1956–1961, Kort verslag van de 42e^e vergadering van de Sociale Commissie van het NVV, gehouden op woensdag 24 Juni 1954 om 19.00 uur ten kantore van het NVV.

[89] ARA, CSWV, 2.19.103.06, 3: Algemeen Bestuur, circulaires 1948/49: Standpunt van het CSWV met betrekking tot de aanhangige plannen tot invoering ener wachtgeld- en werkloosheidsverzekering.

[90] IISG, NVV notulen 1908–1975. Codelijsten 1945–1970, 1951 HB 4, Commissie Sociale Verzekering NVV (Kleine Commissie): Kort verslag van de twaalfde vergadering van de Sociale Commissie van het NVV, gehouden op donderdag 24 Mei 1951 om 19.30 te kantore van het NVV.

[91] ARA, CSWV, 2.19.103.06, 146: Verslag van de vergadering van de Technische Commissie Sociale Verzekering gehouden op woensdag 5 December 1956 des voormiddags om 10 uur ten kantore van de Vereniging van Tricot- en Kousenfabrikanten te Utrecht.

which the two sides of industry eventually agreed was clearly a compromise.[92] Throughout the 1950s and early 1960s, the union federations worked actively to first raise and then completely abolish the wage limit.[93] Their efforts met with complete success in 1964. From that year on, all workers were included in the unemployment insurance program regardless of their income.[94]

The willingness of the Dutch union federations to push forward with redistributive solutions was expressed not only in their pursuit of an increase in risk sharing. After succeeding in getting rid of the wage limit in 1964, the three union federations also pressed for direct income redistribution among workers with the introduction of a redistributive contributory system. The three did so because they felt that the earnings-related system was much less able to accommodate lower-paid workers than higher-paid workers. For many lower-paid workers, they argued, even a benefit of 80 percent of their previous wages was too low to live on. After all, for those who earned a wage that was already close to subsistence, any loss of income was detrimental.[95] To solve this problem, the union federations proposed granting the lowest-paid workers a benefit equal to their previous wages – or, in other words, to give a minimum benefit level equal to the net minimum wage. To do so would result in direct income redistribution between the lowest- and higher-paid workers because it would entitle the former to a higher percentage of previous earnings (a full 100 percent) than the latter, whereas both would continue to pay the same percentage of earnings-related contributions. According to the Sociaal-Economische Raad (SER, Social-Economic Council), this move would increase the financial security of approximately 12 percent of all workers aged twenty-three and over.[96]

---

[92] The compromise was 6,000 guilders (which equaled to 120 percent of the modal wage), whereas the employer federations had argued for setting the wage limit at 4,000 or 4,500 guilders. The employer federations later complained that the agreed-upon limit was much too high. ARA, CSWV, 2.19.103.06, 130: Kort verslag van de vergadering van de Kring voor Sociaal Overleg, gehouden op 14 Oktober 1947 ten kantore van het Centraal Sociaal Werkgevers-Verbond, Kneuterdijk 8, te 's-Gravenhage.

[93] For the Protestant CNV, this was again more difficult to reconcile with its emphasis on strict actuarial rules. It eventually solved this dilemma by arguing that "Talma's [one of the confessional founding fathers of the Dutch public insurance system] idea of social insurance having a normative effect on societal structure demands solidarity: this means that there is no place for a wage limit." IISG, CNV, Commissie Sociale Verzekeringen, 66, Arbeidsongeschiktheidsverzekering, I2, Doelmatige vereenvoudiging van de uitvoering der sociale verzekering, Januari 1960.

[94] There was, of course, a threshold over which no contributions were levied, just as the level of the benefit was also limited by a threshold. In 1968, the threshold for contributions for the unemployment, sickness, and disability insurance programs was set at 15,350 guilders. See SER, *Eerste advies over de programmering van de sociale verzekering op de middellange termijn* (Den Haag: SER, 1970), bijlage V, 1.

[95] For this line of reasoning, see the SER's advise on the matter. SER, *Advies inzake de invoering van een minimumdagloon in de Werkloosheidswet en de Wet Werkloosheidsvoorziening, 14 Juni 1968* (Den Haag: SER, 1968), 3–8.

[96] SER, *Advies inzake*, 6.

The idea of introducing a minimum benefit level first arose in discussions over reform of the state disability and sickness insurance programs in the early 1960s. Like the state unemployment insurance program, these insurance plans combined earnings-related contributions with earnings-related benefits. This meant that the same reasoning with regard to lower-paid workers applied to them as well. The main difference between these two insurance programs and the state unemployment insurance program was that the former dealt with recipients who were rarely accused of an unwillingness to work. Whereas a worker's unemployment often was seen as resulting from idleness, an unwillingness to work, or moral shortcomings, disability and sickness were seldom attributed to personal flaws.[97] This made introduction of minimum benefits into the state disability and sickness insurance programs much less controversial than their introduction into the state unemployment insurance program. It also should be noted here that lower-paid workers were far more frequently accused of being unwilling to work than higher-paid workers. From the perspective of employers at least, this made it crucial to retain as great a margin as possible between benefits and wages for the lowest income categories.

The employer federations initially opposed the introduction of a minimum benefit level into all three insurance programs. They did so by taking the principled stance that an insurance program did not have to cover living costs completely; that was what social assistance was for.[98] In practice, the employer federations were somewhat less hostile to the introduction of a minimum benefit level into the disability insurance program than in the other two insurance schemes. This was partly because the disability insurance scheme catered mostly to people expected to remain outside employment for long periods. This was clearly not the case with the sickness and unemployment insurance programs.[99] Thus, in discussions on introduction of the reform of the state disability insurance program, the employer federations did not resist introduction of a minimum benefit level for very long. When the 1966 Wet op Arbeidsongeschiktheidsverzekering (WAO, Act on Disability Insurance) passed Parliament, it already included a minimum-benefit provision. The 1966 Ziektewet (Sickness Act), which, as we will see in Chapter 5, created an insurance for short-term sicknesses and disabilities, did not include such a provision. Yet it did give the unions and employers responsible for its operation the right to supplement the state benefit. As we will see in Chapter 6, they came to use this *en masse*.

---

[97] This would slowly change during the 1970s and 1980s, when the Dutch sickness and disability insurance programs were used *en masse* to shed redundant workers. See Chapter 6 on this.

[98] VNO, F119(4) Cie Sociale Verzekering RCO 1947–1970: Verslag van een gecombineerde vergadering van de Commissie Sociale Verzekering van het CSWV en de Raad van Bestuur in Arbeidszaken, gehouden op 25 Januari 1966, ten kantore Kneuterdijk 8 te 's Gravenhage.

[99] See SER, *Advies inzake de invoering van een minimumdagloon*, 10.

The employer federations resisted the introduction of a minimum benefit level into the unemployment insurance program most fiercely, for the reasons noted earlier. Even as they argued against a minimum benefit level, however, they realized that they would probably not be able to prevent its introduction. Not only did the unions support it, but so did the government. In fact, by the time the unions came forward with their proposal to introduce a minimum benefit into the earnings-related social insurance scheme, the government was already considering raising the rate of social assistance to the level of the minimum wage. This meant that those without work who had previously earned a wage equal to or a little higher than the national minimum wage would receive a higher benefit when on social assistance than when drawing the unemployment benefit – as, it should be noted, was then the case in the United Kingdom.[100] Realizing this, the employer federations acknowledged that their case was quite weak.[101] After being outmaneuvered in the SER on the need for a minimum benefit, the employer federations eventually succeeded in getting worker representatives to agree that it would apply only to breadwinners.[102] The employer federations could celebrate their partial victory only temporarily, however, because Parliament later decided that the minimum benefit should apply to all categories of workers.

Despite the opposition of the employer federations, in the late 1960s, the government introduced a minimum benefit level into the unemployment insurance program, sickness insurance scheme, and the newly created unemployment provision. This meant that all unemployed, sick, and disabled workers who were entitled to an unemployment benefit could look forward to a benefit that was at least as high as the net minimum wage. As mentioned in Chapter 3, the net minimum wage, in turn, would approach 80 percent of average earnings in the coming years.[103] In comparison, in the United Kingdom, the flat-rate public unemployment benefit continued to float somewhere between 20 and 40 percent of average earnings depending on child and family supplements.[104] To this, unemployed British workers who had previously earned wages that were below average earnings could often add neither private nor public supplements.

The introduction of a minimum benefit level completed a series of measures for which the unions had pushed since almost immediately after the WW came into effect. Although it had initially been based on strict actuarial principles, the Dutch public unemployment insurance program eventually came to display

[100] Ibidem, 4.
[101] ARA, CSWV, 2.19.103.06, 140: Verslag van de vergadering van de Commissie Sociale Verzekering van het CSWV op 27 November 1967, ten kantore Kneuterdijk 8, 's-Gravenhage.
[102] VNO, F119(4) Cie Sociale Verzekering RCO 1947–1970: Verslag van de vergadering van de Commissie Sociale Verzekering van de Raad van Bestuur in Arbeidszaken, gehouden op 14 Juni 1968, ten kantore van het Verbond van Nederlandse Ondernemingen, Prinses Beatrixlaan 5 's Gravenhage.
[103] See Goudswaard and De Jong, "Income Transfers in the Netherlands," 370.
[104] See Parry, "The United Kingdom," 189.

several features specifically designed to improve matters for lower-paid workers. Abolition of the wage limit made sure that all workers were subject to the redistributive effects of risk pooling, whereas introduction of the minimum benefit level produced direct income redistribution among workers. Both measures, it should be noted, took a long time to be fully implemented. So the Netherlands was among the last countries with an earnings-related unemployment insurance program to abolish the wage limit.[105] And the introduction of a redistributive element into the unemployment insurance scheme's contributory system came over a decade after emergence of a consensus on the need to combine flat-rate old age pension benefits with earnings-related contributions. Many reasons can be given for the late introduction of specific measures aimed at improving matters for lower-paid workers into the unemployment insurance program. Among the most important reasons is surely that the unions had focused first on two other important objectives.

For a long time after the introduction of the 1949 WW, the union federations focused almost exclusively on two objectives. The first was to increase the level of the unemployment insurance benefit for all recipients. The second was to increase the duration of the unemployment insurance benefit for all recipients. While agreeing that these two objectives had priority, the three union federations disagreed on which of the two was more pressing. While the NVV wanted to first increase the duration of the benefit, the Christelijk Nationaal Vakverbond (CNV, Christian Union Federation) preferred raising the level of the benefit first.[106] For nearly a decade and a half after the introduction of the WW, the employer federations managed to prevent both. It was not until 1964 that the unions saw improvements, and then these came simultaneously on both fronts. In that year, the duration of the unemployment benefit was increased by five weeks, and the benefit was raised to a uniform level of 80 percent. This outcome resulted after several years of fierce negotiations between employer and union representatives in the SER and again an intervention by Parliament on behalf of the union federations.

[105] By the early 1960s, among the nations of northwest Europe with earnings-related unemployment insurance programs, only the Netherlands and the Federation Republic of Germany still had wage limits. The level of the wage limit was much higher in Germany than in the Netherlands, however. See SER, *Advies over verlening van de maximumuitkeringsduur werkloosheidsverzekering* (Den Haag: SER, 1962), 29.

[106] This difference seems to have resulted from different tactical considerations. While the NVV emphasized that a decision to increase the duration of the benefit could be reversed more easily, the CNV emphasized that an increase in the duration of the benefit would be easier to obtain than an increase in the industrial injuries scheme. NVV, Codelijsten van het NVV-Commissiearchief 1945–1967, 322 Socialecie 1956–1961, Kort verslag van de 74ᵉ vergadering van de Sociale Commissie van het NVV, gehouden op woensdag 20 Februari 1957, om 19.00 uur ten kantore van het NVV. IISG, CNV, Commissie Sociale Verzekeringen, 68, Werkloosheidsverzekering, J5, Advies inzake verlenging uitkeringstermijn Werkloosheidswet en/of verhoging van de uitkeringspercentages, 6 Juni 1957. See also ARA, CSWV, 2.19.103.06, 139: Verslag van de vergadering van de Commissie Sociale Verzekering van het CSWV, gehouden op 7.11.1961 ten kantore van het CSWV.

The issue of the benefit rate of the unemployment insurance program is of particular interest to us here because it shows that the employer federations were quite willing to deviate from a strict interpretation of actuarial rules when this was in their interests. When the representatives of union and employer federations negotiated creation of the WW in the late 1940s, they had, as we saw earlier, agreed to grant different benefit percentages depending on marital status, sex, and age. Both parties must have been aware of the incompatibility of this solution with sound actuarial rules. They nevertheless pushed forward with this plan because it represented the only solution acceptable to them. The employer federations had deemed a benefit rate of 80 percent of the previous wage as far too costly. The union federations, in turn, could not accept a lower uniform rate because married men and breadwinners had already been entitled to a benefit level of 80 percent of their previous wages before the war.[107] When the union and employer federations agreed on percentages of 80, 70, and 60 percent for different categories, Parliament agreed. The Minister of Social Affairs successfully resisted a Communist motion to set the benefit at a uniform level of 80 percent by arguing that unions and employers had already decided otherwise.[108]

In following years, the union federations continued to strive for a uniform benefit rate of 80 percent of the previous wage. The two confessional union federations in particular found it easy to do so by arguing that the actuarial nature of the unemployment insurance program demanded a uniform percentage for all categories of workers.[109] Not surprisingly, the confessional employer federations were more susceptible to this argument than were their liberal counterparts. While admitting privately that it was "incorrect" to combine a uniform premium with benefit differentiation, the liberal Centraal Sociaal Werkgevers Verbond (CSWV, Central Social Employers' Federation) in 1957 went so far as to state that it believed "for reasons of principle, that in a social insurance program, a uniform premium does not have to result in a uniform benefit."[110] This stance, of course, did not comport with its emphasis on a strict adherence to actuarial rules on other issues related to the unemployment insurance program. Nor did it align with its initial reaction, made some five

---

[107] ARA, CSWV, 2.19.103.06, 3: Algemeen Bestuur, circulaires 1948/49: Standpunt van het CSWV met betrekking tot de aanhangige plannen tot invoering ener wachtgeld- en werkloosheidsverzekering; ARA, CSWV, 2.19.103.06, 3: Algemeen Bestuur, circulaires 1948/49: Verslag van de vergadering van het Algemeen Bestuur van het Centraal Sociaal Werkgevers-Verbond, gehouden op 5 Februari 1948, des n.m. te 2 uur, ten kantore Kneuterdijk 8, 's-Gravenhage.

[108] See Ruijters, "Sociale Zaken," 1420.

[109] KDC, Algemene Katholieke Werkgeversvereniging, 1500: Commissie Sociale Verzekering van het Katholieke Verbond, 1954–1960, Nota voor de Commissie Sociale Verzekering van het Katholiek Verbond van Werkgeversvakverenigingen, September 1954.

[110] ARA, CSWV, 2.19.103.06, 146: Verslag van de vergadering van de Technische Commissie Sociale Verzekering, gehouden op donderdag 20 Juni 1957; ARA, CSWV, 2.19.103.06, 146: Verslag van de vergadering van de Technische Commissie Sociale Verzekering, gehouden op donderdag 20 Juni 1957.

years earlier, to the NVV's proposal to combine earnings-related contributions with flat-rate benefits in discussions over the introduction of the state old age pension. The CSWV's reaction then had been that the actuarial nature of the pension demanded adherence to the principle that "when the benefit is uniform, the contribution must be uniform as well."[111] Of course, the CSWV did eventually support the NVV's old age pension plan for the simple reason that it was greatly preferable to the government's means-tested alternative. Liberal employer representatives were definitively more opportunistic in their adherence to actuarial rules than were confessional employers. Chapter 3 has already mentioned this, and Chapter 6 will illustrate this more dramatically.

The employer federations eventually agreed to discuss the possibility of an increase in the level of the unemployment benefit as part of a complete review of the operation of the state unemployment insurance program, which also addressed an issue that was of importance to them.[112] They never agreed, however, to set the benefit level at 80 percent of previous earnings for all recipients. After several years of negotiations, the union and employer federations eventually agreed to a compromise that had been devised by the NVV. In this compromise, all workers who were entitled to an unemployment benefit, with the exception of those under twenty-one years of age and those who were not married, would be able to claim a benefit of 80 percent of their previous wages and would be able to do this for twenty-six instead of twenty-one weeks (the union federations had initially demanded an extension of up to thirty-four weeks). Against the wishes of the employer federations, Parliament later decided to do away with the exception for the unmarried and for those under twenty-one years of age.[113]

In the same year when negotiations between the union and employer federations resulted in increases in the duration and benefit level of the unemployment insurance program, a government initiative created a new earnings-related state provision for the unemployed. In later years, when the problem of long-term unemployment became more severe, this provision turned out to be very

---

[111] ARA, CSWV, 2.19.103.06, 131: Kort verslag van de vergadering van de Kring voor Sociaal Overleg, gehouden op 13 October 1953 des namiddags te 2.15 uur in Restaurant Garoeda, Kneuterdijk 18a, Den Haag.

[112] The review also looked into the possibilities of merging the reduced-pay and unemployment schemes – which had been a long-standing wish of the employer federations. They had several reasons to pursue this, and one of these was their goal to get rid of the uniform premium in the unemployment scheme. Union opposition to this and the fear that the government would use a merging of the two schemes as an excuse to diminish its share in the financing of the unemployment insurance program eventually made this unfeasible. ARA, CSWV, 2.19.103.06, 146: Verslag van de vergadering van de Technische Commissie Sociale Verzekering, gehouden op 19 Maart 1957, ten kantore van dr. W. G. J. Ten Pas te Amsterdam; ARA, CSWV, 2.19.103.06, 146: Verslag van de vergadering van de Technische Commissie Sociale Verzekering, gehouden op 22 Mei 1957.

[113] ARA, CSWV, 2.19.103.06, 146: Verslag van de vergadering van de Technische Commissie Sociale Verzekering, gehouden op donderdag 20 Juni 1957.

important for the financial security of unemployed workers. After 1976, as a result of new legislation, the provision was also used by employers to shed redundant workers in large numbers. A short investigation into the creation of the provision is merited in this chapter. Its use to shed redundant workers will be investigated in Chapter 6, which deals with the use of several social security schemes to shed redundant workers in the Netherlands.

FROM GRANT TO RIGHT: INTRODUCTION OF THE
UNEMPLOYMENT PROVISION

For the sake of simplicity, this chapter has thus far treated the unemployment insurance program as the only form of financial compensation against unemployment besides social assistance. This depiction is somewhat misleading, however, because a third alternative did exist: the so-called Sociale Voorzieningen A en B (Social Provisions A and B). These provisions constituted a mixture between a "Bismarckian" (or earnings-related) insurance scheme and a social assistance program. Created in 1952, the Sociale Voorzieningen A en B enabled the unemployed to preserve income maintenance for several months after they could no longer claim the unemployment insurance benefit. Like the unemployment insurance scheme, the Sociale Voorzieningen A offered a benefit of 80, 70, or 60 percent of previous wages for twenty-one weeks. After that period, the Sociale Voorzieningen B entitled unemployed workers to benefits of 75, 60, or 45 percent of previous wages for an indefinite period. The Sociale Voorzieningen A also resembled an insurance program in that unemployed workers could only claim a benefit if they met certain qualification criteria. Workers needed to have a working history of at least thirteen weeks in the previous twelve months to qualify for a Sociale Voorzieningen A benefit. Workers did not have to meet certain qualification criteria to be able to claim the Sociale Voorzieningen B benefit. The actuarial characteristics of the Sociale Voorzieningen A en B were combined with two characteristics that are normally attributed to social assistance programs. First, benefits were means-tested.[114] Second, they were completely state-financed. Technically, both provisions were therefore part of the social assistance system.

The Sociale Voorzieningen A en B are often left out of the literature on Dutch welfare state development because they were of little significance in the Dutch system of compensation for the financial consequences of unemployment. From 1958 to 1962, the financial costs of operating the Sociale Voorzieningen A en B constituted only about 8.5 percent of the costs of operating the state unemployment insurance program.[115] The main reason for this lay

[114] A means test deducted two-thirds of income from work from the benefit of Sociale Voorzieningen A (Social Provision A). Sociale Voorzieningen B (Social Provision B) applied a means test to both capital and income from work. In case of a breadwinner, half the income of the other members of the family was deducted. See Pennings, *Benefits of Doubt*, 311.

[115] The total costs of the unemployment insurance program in these years was 1,000.8 million guilders compared with only 85.5 million for Sociale Voorzieningen A en B. For an overview

in the almost complete absence of long-term unemployment among workers at the time. The Sociale Voorzieningen A en B are only mentioned in this chapter because they developed into a much more generous addition to the unemployment insurance program in the 1960s and 1970s. In 1964, the government passed the Wet Werkloosheidsvoorziening (WWV, Unemployment Provision Act), which transformed both provisions into a more generous provision that operated separately from the social assistance scheme. Then, in 1976, the duration of the benefit was extended by five years for elderly workers. Of these two steps, the second is of far more interest to us here and therefore deserves a separate treatment in Chapter 6.

Introduction of the WWV resulted from dissatisfaction with the inclusion of an earnings-related benefit into the social assistance system. Both Parliament and the union federations informed the government of their objections to the inclusion when the latter contemplated a major reform of the social assistance system in the late 1950s.[116] This represented a dilemma for the government. On the one hand, it believed that a supplement to the unemployment insurance program could not be omitted. On the other hand, it felt that long-term unemployment was different and therefore needed to be treated differently from short-term unemployment. The government's solution was to introduce a new provision that would operate separately from both the unemployment insurance and social assistance programs. It also briefly considered increasing the duration of the unemployment insurance scheme but shied away from this after employer and worker federations reached a compromise on an extension of the unemployment insurance program by five weeks. To contradict that, the government feared, would unduly complicate matters. Moreover, since neither union nor employer federations would be willing to pay for an improved version of the Sociale Voorzieningen A en B, the government felt that a separate scheme – in provision form – was most suitable.[117]

The union federations applauded introduction of the WWV mainly for two reasons. First, the new scheme lacked a means test and even allowed for the granting of private supplements as long as the total benefit did not exceed a recipient's previous wage level.[118] Second, workers could claim a benefit on

of the costs of Sociale Voorzieningen A en B from 1958 to 1962, see SER, *Advies inzake het voorontwerp van een Wet werkloosheidsvoorziening* (Den Haag: SER, 1964), 5.

[116] For the union federations, the main problem was the means-tested nature of both provisions and the low benefit rates of Sociale Voorzieningen B. IISG, NVV, Codelijsten van het NVV-Commissiearchief 1945–1967, 322 Socialecie 1959–1961, Kort Verslag van de 99e vergadering van de Sociale Commissie van het NVV, gehouden op woensdag 19 November 1959, om 19.00 ten kantore van het NVV.

[117] ARA, Ministerie van Sociale Zaken, afdeling Sociale Bijstand 1945–1967, 5.068.5008, nr. 168: Advies inzake het voorontwerp-Wet Werkloosheidsvoorziening, 26 Juni 1964.

[118] Initially, this was not allowed, but within one year after the WWV came into operation, private supplements no longer had to be deducted from the unemployment provision benefit. Both the labor unions and organized employers supported this. ARA, CSWV, 2.19.103.06, 28: Resumé van de Contactvergadering van directeuren en secretarissen der aangesloten

fairly lenient terms. Not only was a working history of only six consecutive weeks or sixty-five days in the previous year sufficient to claim a benefit, as a matter of principle, the voluntarily unemployed also were entitled to a benefit. This leniency stemmed from the government's intention of charting a "middle course" between the two predecessors of the new unemployment provision. Under the Sociale Voorzieningen A, a worker could claim a benefit only if he or she had a working history of thirteen weeks and was involuntarily unemployed. The Sociale Voorzieningen B, on the other hand, granted benefits to all workers – including the voluntarily unemployed and those with no working history. The employer federations naturally argued that a non-means-tested provision demanded stricter qualification rules than a means-tested provision. Others who shared this opinion included the government-appointed members of the SER and the government officials of the Vereniging van Directeuren van Overheidsorganen voor Sociale Arbeid (Association of Director-Generals of Government Bodies for Social Work). The government officials of the latter body argued for stricter qualification rules because even the probation period was often longer than six weeks.[119] The arguments of employers and skeptical government officials, however, were of no avail. The government insisted that fairness demanded a middle course between the two predecessors of the new unemployment provision.[120]

Whereas the union federations saw the lenient nature of the new unemployment provision in a positive light, the employer federations regarded it as the act's main shortcoming. The employer federations had little difficulty with the level and duration of the provision's benefit, although these were quite generous: the benefit was set at 75 percent of the previous wage, and the duration was set at two years.[121] To them, the main problem with the act lay in the ease with which workers could claim an unemployment benefit. In the years leading up to introduction of the act, the employer federations had therefore urged the government to either make the benefit means-tested (and thus part of the social assistance system) or dependent on a long working history (as was a real insurance). In the end, however, it turned out to be neither of the two.[122] Even more

---

werkgeversverenigingen, gehouden op 18 Oktober 1965, ten kantore Kneuterdijk 8 (1ᵉ étage) te 's-Gravenhage.

[119] ARA, Ministerie van Sociale Zaken, Afdeling Sociale Bijstand 1945–1967, 5.068.5008, nr. 168: Brief van Verenigingen van Directeuren van Overheidsorganen voor Sociale Arbeid, 29 Februari 1964.

[120] ARA, Ministerie van Sociale Zaken, Afdeling Sociale Bijstand 1945–1967, 5.068.5008, nr. 168: Concept-wijziging van het Algemeen gedeelte van de Toelichting op de Wet Werkloosheidsvoorziening.

[121] To be precise, the level of the benefit was supposed to be 95 percent of the level of the unemployment insurance benefit. This is why the government initially decided on the numbers of 75, 65, and 55 percent of previous wages for different categories of workers. It raised these to the uniform level of 75 percent when the level of the unemployment insurance benefit was raised to a uniform level of 80 percent.

[122] The employer federations would have preferred a solution within the social assistance system and thus a continuation of the means test. ARA, CSWV, 2.19.103.06, 28: Resumé van de

regrettable to the employer federations was that the voluntarily unemployed were also entitled to a benefit. In the years after the unemployment provision came into operation, the employer federations put much work into rectifying this latter feature. It soon became clear that they had good reason to do so.

Responsibility for operation of the unemployment provision was given to the local authorities, in contrast to centralized administration of the unemployment insurance scheme. To prevent misuse of the new scheme, these authorities were allowed to hand out lower benefits or debar "undeserving" workers altogether. In practice, however, this almost never happened. In 1966, only two years after the act's introduction, an unemployment survey conducted in the city of Geldrop showed that as many as 35 percent of all recipients of an unemployment provision benefit were voluntarily unemployed. More important, almost half of all recipients were under thirty, and the vast majority of them had little motivation to return to work.[123] Faced with these numbers, and after fierce pressure from the employer federations, the government decided to limit entitlement to the unemployment provision on this point. From 1972 on, entitlement extended only to the involuntarily unemployed – as was the case with the state unemployment insurance scheme. The union federations opposed the 1972 amendment to the WWV. Although acutely aware of the act's misuse, they simply did not deem this as important enough to warrant a reversal of improvements made to the social security system.[124]

Compared with the long and complicated history of union attempts to improve the level and duration of the unemployment insurance benefit, the generosity and ease of establishment of the unemployment provision seem remarkable. This shows us two things. First, it shows us how effective the employer federations were for a long time in resisting an increase in the generosity of the unemployment insurance scheme. Part of the reason why the unemployment provision could be created so easily was surely that it was a provision and not an insurance program, which enabled the government to bypass both the union and employer federations. Whereas the government was obliged to consult the "social partners" on matters relating to social security, it did not have to do so on matters relating to (tax-financed) social provision reform. Initially, the government therefore did not even want to consult the main corporatist body in the Netherlands, the SER, on its plans to reform the Sociale Voorzieningen A en

---

Contactvergadering van directeuren en secretaressen der aangesloten werkgeversverenigingen, gehouden op 24 Augustus 1964 ten kantore Kneuterdijk 8.

[123] NCW, 31(5): Cie Sociale Verzekeringen 1971–1975: Nota de gemeenten en de werkloosheidsvoorziening, 3.

[124] Characteristic of this is the reaction of the Sociale Verzekeringsraad (SVR, Social Insurance Council) to the accusation of large-scale fraud in the social security system: "Although the Council is of course not in the least indifferent to the size of the fraud … [it] considers it more important to prevent social insurance laws from being discredited or provoking irritation." VNO, Misbruik/oneigenlijk gebruik sociale voorzieningen, F64(4): Persbericht Ministerie van Sociale Zaken, 9 Juni 1975.

B. It only did so after another counseling body that did not contain union and employer representatives, the Raad van State (Council of State), emphasized that "such a move will not be understood politically."[125] Second, it illustrates the importance of timing. Both the first major reform of the WAO and the WWV came about in the mid-1960s and thus at the pinnacle of a long period of high economic growth, low unemployment, and an all-but-complete absence of long-term unemployment. Under these circumstances, the government did not have to worry about the affordability of the unemployment provision, which might explain in part why the provision turned out to be so generous.

This golden era of high growth and low unemployment would soon come to an end, however. The first signs of this were already present in the mid-1960s. The closing of state mines and the first restructuring measures in the ship-building and textile industries during the period gave the government a first taste of what was to come in the 1970s and 1980s. Under these circumstances, the unemployment provision, which initially applied to only a small group of workers, grew steadily in importance. In fact, and as we will see in Chapter 6, it eventually came to fulfill a function that far exceeded its original purpose.

---

[125] ARA, Ministerie van Sociale Zaken, Afdeling Sociale Bijstand 1945–1967, 5.068.5008, Nota van de Centrale Revisie en Contact Instantie, 26 Februari 1964.

5

The Development of Disability Insurance in the Netherlands and the United Kingdom

This chapter looks at the last common source of economic misfortune against which the welfare state provides protection: disability. Unlike old age and unemployment, disability is never treated as a single risk. All countries distinguish in some way between different disabilities, and some go quite far in this. First, there are often separate policies for disabilities resulting from sickness, accident, and old age. Second, most countries distinguish between work-related and non-work-related accidents and sicknesses. Third, there may be different policies for the short- and long-term disabled. Fourth, many countries have different disability policies for workers and for the self-employed. This chapter is concerned with all policies that compensate for disability during a person's working life, which means that several policies are to be covered here. In the United Kingdom, the two main distinctions in the postwar period were between short- and long-term disabilities and between work-related and non-work-related disabilities. In the postwar Netherlands, only the distinction between workers and the self-employed remained important.

In most countries, work-related disability programs represent the oldest form of social security.[1] The Netherlands and the United Kingdom are no exceptions. The Dutch Industrial Injuries Act (Ongevallenwet, 1901) and the British Workmen's Compensation Act (1897) had passed their respective parliaments more than a decade before the next social security initiatives were put forward in the two countries. The early passing of these work-related disability programs is not a coincidence. Work-related disabilities differ from non-work-related disabilities, old age, and unemployment in that responsibility for provision against them lies fairly incontestably with employers. Employers are generally accepted to bear full responsibility for the working conditions of their workers and thus for any work-related accidents and sicknesses. Because

[1] See Alber, *Vom Armenhaus*, 49.

of this reasoning, the establishment of work-related disability programs related more to the struggle for worker emancipation than did the introduction of any other social security program. For labor unions, the absence of financial compensation for work-related disabilities was a grave injustice that urgently needed to be rectified. Unions' ability to do so at least partly reflected the growing strength of worker organizations in late nineteenth- and early twentieth-century Europe. By the end of the first two decades of the twentieth century, all industrialized European countries had introduced work-related disability programs that without exception were funded by employers and often were far more generous than other social insurance programs.

Yet work-related disability programs, however generous, can at most play a minor part in catering for the disabled. After all, the vast majority of accidents and sicknesses are not related to paid work. Employers cannot be held responsible for dealing with their employees' non-work-related sicknesses and accidents. This means that the issue of worker solidarity, and thus of union organization, is again of central importance in this chapter. Since not all workers have an income or risk profile that grants them adequate insurance against all types of disabilities on their own, efforts to provide all workers with adequate insurance against disability during their working lives demand a redistributive effort among different grades of workers. As we will see, the Netherlands and the United Kingdom, as a result of differences in the stance of their labor union movements, again differed to a great extent in the degree to which such a redistributive effort came about.

Because worker solidarity is again of central importance here, it should not come as a surprise that Dutch efforts to provide adequate financial provision for all disabled people were far more successful than were British efforts to do so. By the mid-1960s, the Netherlands had created a system that offered very generous treatment to all disabled people regardless of cause, duration, or contributory record. In the United Kingdom, by contrast, only disabled people who incurred their injury at work could count on generous treatment. Indeed, the inability of the British welfare state to provide adequate care for the much larger group of people with non-work-related disabilities is one of its major failings. Compared with their equivalents in most continental European countries, and certainly in the Netherlands, British state benefits designed to provide for non-work-related disabilities were much less generous in terms of benefit levels and entitlement rules. This manifested in a much higher level of poverty among the British disabled than among their continental European counterparts.[2]

---

[2] On the (comparative) failure of the British welfare state to provide for non-work-related disabilities, see, for example, Irene Loach and Ruth Lister, *Second Class Disabled* (London: Disability Alliance, 1978); Richard Berthoud, *Disability Benefits: A Review of the Issues and Options for Reform* (York, PA: York Publishing Services, 1998); Alan Walker and Lucy Walker, "Disability and Financial Need – The Failure of the Social Security System." In G. Dalley, *Disability and Social Policy* (London: PSI, 1991).

The continued inadequacy of state provision for the financial consequences of non-work-related disabilities has been one of the most marked features of the postwar British welfare state. This makes it quite remarkable that welfare state scholars have paid so little attention to the causes of this inadequacy. While most treatments of postwar British welfare state development give ample reasons for Beveridge's decision to grant preferential treatment to people with work-related disabilities, few even raise the question of why state provision for people with non-work-related disabilities remained so poor. Between roughly the late 1950s and late 1960s, the Labour Party – first from opposition and later when in government – proposed several initiatives to improve state provision for people with non-work-related disabilities. Unfortunately, these initiatives have attracted little academic interest. The first part of this chapter, which deals with the United Kingdom, will look at these initiatives in great detail.

A similar charge of omission can be made with regard to scholarship on the Netherlands. While scholars have paid much attention to the operation of the Dutch disability insurance system after its 1960s reform, there has been no systematic investigation to date of how this reform came about. As a result, we know much about the consequences of the system's generosity but little about its causes. The most common explanation for the system's generosity is that it was reformed quite late, which means that its most generous features were introduced at a time of continuously high economic growth.[3] There are at least two reasons why this explanation is insufficient. First, if reform had taken place at an earlier stage, union pressure probably would have resulted in new reform measures in later years – after all, this had been the case with the state old age pension and unemployment insurance programs. The outcome might then have been equally generous. Second, and more important, the explanation based on timing can be turned upside down. As will be shown in the second part of this chapter, which deals with the Netherlands, the late moment of reform was itself at least partly *the result* of the commitment of all involved parties to increasing the disability system's generous features.

This lack of systematic investigation of the introduction of the 1966 Ziektewet (Sickness Act) and Wet op Arbeidsongeschiktheidsverzekering (WAO, Act on Disability Insurance) in the Netherlands also has had another consequence. In their (often very brief) treatments of the introduction of these acts, both academic and popular writings have attributed a very important role to Gerard Veldkamp, who, as Minister of Social Affairs at the time, presided over their creation. Some scholars have even described both acts as his "brainchild."[4] This chapter emphasizes that Veldkamp's role in the 1966 disability insurance reform

[3] See, for example, Van der Veen, "De ontwikkeling," 35; Coen Teulings, Romke van der Veen, and Willem Trommel, *Dilemma's van sociale zekerheid: een analyse van 10 jaar herziening van het stelsel van sociale zekerheid* (Amsterdam: VUGA, 1997), 9.
[4] See Peter Kerklaan, "De lange houdbaarheid van de ongevallenwet in Nederland 1901–1967," *Tijdschrift voor Sociale en Economische Geschiedenis* 3:4 (2006), 86.

was much more minor than often suggested. It is certainly true that Veldkamp had been a long-standing supporter of this reform (he had already argued for reform of the kind that eventually came about in 1966 in his 1949 dissertation).[5] And as Minister of Social Affairs, he certainly did share responsibility for its specific features. Yet it is crucial to realize that the 1966 reform measures were principally the outcome of a long process of discussions between representatives of labor union federations, employer federations, and the state that had begun in the immediate postwar period. The decision to grant all disabled people equally generous treatment regardless of risk, cause, and contribution record resulted from an agreement between the union and employer federations on the need to do so. Once the "social partners" reached agreement on the main features of the 1960s reform, Parliament closely followed their recommendations.

The second part of this chapter investigates the events leading up to the 1966 reform that created such a generous disability insurance system in the Netherlands. The chapter ends with a brief look at the last major formal extension of this system: the introduction of the 1976 Algemene Arbeidsongeschiktheidswet (AAW, General Disability Act), which extended the disability scheme with a flat-rate insurance benefit for the self-employed. Chapter 6 looks at one important consequence of the 1966 reform: the massive use of the disability insurance system to get rid of redundant workers. The first part of this chapter examines the United Kingdom. This part begins by comparing the British welfare state's treatment of work-related and non-work-related disabilities. It then looks at the stance of British unions on Labour's attempts to improve state provision for people with non-work-related disabilities. We set the stage for the United Kingdom discussion by returning to the Beveridge reforms of the late 1940s.

THE TRADES UNION CONGRESS AND THE INDUSTRIAL PREFERENCE

When Beveridge undertook his review of the social security system, the risk of disability posed a particular problem for him. As mentioned earlier, Beveridge's task was to put forward ways to create a unified system in which all programs and services were organized and financed in the same way. To achieve this, he proposed the creation of a single National Insurance Fund that would entitle all social security recipients to the same flat-rate benefit. Beveridge took it for granted that those unable to work because of old age, unemployment, or non-work-related disabilities (as mentioned in Chapter 4, the British sickness insurance program covered all non-work-related injuries and sicknesses) should receive the same treatment. His only dilemma was how to approach

---

[5] Gerard Veldkamp, *Individualistische karaktertrekken in de Nederlandse sociale arbeidsverzekering: een critisch onderzoek naar de grondslagen der sociale arbeidsverzekering* (Alphen aan den Rijn: Samsom, 1949).

work-related disabilities. As in other countries, workers who incurred disabilities at work were accustomed to preferential treatment. This manifested in two ways. First, the disabled who incurred their disability at work could claim a much higher benefit than other social security recipients. Second, and also in contrast with other social security benefits, entitlement to compensation for work-related disabilities did not depend on a worker's contributory record. A worker could claim a benefit even if his or her disability occurred on the first day of work. In fact, workers did not have to contribute to work-related disability insurance at all because employers were considered solely responsible for the cost of work-related disability benefits.

For Beveridge, the main dilemma was whether social security recipients who incurred their disability at work should subsequently continue to receive higher benefits than other social security recipients. On the one hand, he felt that social justice demanded equal compensation for all interruptions of earnings. To quote Beveridge himself, "If a workman loses his leg in an accident, his needs are the same whether the accident occurred in a factory or in the street."[6] On the other hand, Beveridge felt that there were several compelling reasons to hand out higher benefits to the industrially disabled than to the elderly, unemployed, or otherwise disabled. In his report, he gave three such reasons. Two of these were economic arguments, whereas the third was of a social or moral nature. First, Beveridge believed that only very generous compensation against work-related disabilities would encourage people to work under dangerous conditions. This made high work-related disability benefits a matter of national interest because many industries that were vital to the community also were especially dangerous. Second, Beveridge hoped that generous compensation for work-related disabilities would reduce instances of employers being sued in tort and found liable even when they were not morally at fault.[7] Third, and despite his opinion that the consequences of both types of disabilities were quite similar, Beveridge believed that there was a fundamental moral difference between disabilities occurring while working under orders and non-work-related disabilities.[8]

Beveridge solved his dilemma by proposing to retain the "industrial preference," as the more generous treatment of people with work-related disabilities is often called in the United Kingdom, only for long-term victims of

---

[6] William Beveridge, *Social Insurance and Allied Services: Report* (London: HMSO, 1942), 38–9.
[7] Beveridge could not have known at the time that this would have little effect. In fact, lawsuits increased steeply in the early postwar years. On this, see Richard Lewis, "Tort and Social Security: The Importance Attached to the Cause of Disability with Special Reference to the Industrial Injuries Scheme," *Modern Law Review* 43:5 (1980), 526. It has been estimated that about 16 percent of persons receiving industrial injury benefits also received damages under the 1948 legislation permitting suits as an additional remedy. In some other countries, the right to sue the employer was abolished for those covered by work-related disability programs. See Gordon, *Social Security Policies*, 143–4.
[8] For an overview of Beveridge's views on this, see Beveridge, *Social Insurance*, 39.

work-related disabilities. In his proposal, workers suffering from work-related disabilities would have to rely only on the national insurance sickness benefit during the first thirteen weeks of their disability. If they were still disabled after this period, they would receive a generous work-related disability supplement to the sickness benefit. The sickness benefit would be set at the same level as the unemployment and old age pension benefits. Unlike the unemployment benefit, but like the old age pension benefit, there was to be no limit to how long recipients were entitled to a sickness benefit. As with the unemployment and old age pension benefits, entitlement to a sickness benefit would depend on strict contribution criteria. Those disabled who incurred their injury at work would not have to meet certain contribution criteria.

Beveridge considered his solution to be both morally just and cheap – because only 10 percent of work-related disabilities lasted longer than thirteen weeks.[9] The new Labour government agreed with Beveridge on the latter count but nevertheless opted for a total preservation of the industrial preference. Among the most important reasons for this was undoubtedly that the Trades Union Congress (TUC) strongly opposed Beveridge's recommendation to retain the industrial preference only for the long-term disabled.[10] To the TUC, it was imperative to "distinguish between industrial accident and disease and other causes of interruption of earnings both in respect of the basis of fixing compensation [meaning: the level of the benefit] and in the method of meeting the costs."[11] It therefore argued for the complete preservation of the industrial preference using a range of arguments that will be explained at length below.

Under Labour's 1946 National Insurance (Industrial Injuries) Act, workers with work-related disabilities never had to depend on just the sickness benefit. Instead, they could first claim a flat-rate – but generous – industrial injury benefit for a maximum period of six months. If the disability lasted longer than this period, they were entitled to an industrial disablement pension. The disablement pension fully followed insurance standards: the level of the benefit depended solely on the extent of the disability.[12] In contrast to the workmen's compensation benefit, which it replaced, the disablement pension was set at a flat-rate level. If a worker remained fully disabled, he or she could claim the full disablement pension in combination with the sickness benefit. If a worker remained partially disabled, he or she could claim a percentage of the flat-rate benefit level and combine this with income from work or from other sources. A special hardship allowance was available for those who were not fully disabled

---

[9] See Beveridge, *Social Insurance*, 40.

[10] For the TUC's dissatisfaction with this feature, see MRC, MSS.292/150.5/2: Deputation to Sir William Jowit on the Beveridge Report, 12 August 1943.

[11] MRC, MSS.292/150.5/3: Relation of Trade Union Congress General Council scheme and plan for social security in Sir William Beveridge's Report, 1943.

[12] In this, the new disablement pension differed from its counterparts in most other countries, which handed out benefits on the basis of previous earnings – instead of on the basis of the extent of disability.

but still could not return to work at their previous or an equivalent job. This allowance could be quite generous. At maximum, it could increase the level of the industrial disablement pension by 40 percent.[13] The industrial disablement pension was paid in either the form of a weekly pension (when the disability exceeded 20 percent) or a gratuity (when the disability fell between 1 and 20 percent).[14] In principle, the benefit was payable for life and thus did not have to end when the recipient reached the retirement age.

Compared with the national insurance scheme (but not compared with its continental equivalents), the industrial injuries scheme was extremely generous. When involved in an accident at work, a worker would first receive an industrial injury benefit that was 70 percent higher than the national insurance benefit. After six months, the disablement pension added about one-third of average earnings to the sickness benefit, which amounted to only one-fifth of average earnings. Those who had become disabled for the long term because of non-work-related accidents or sicknesses could only claim the sickness benefit. Often they could not even claim that. While all people with work-related disabilities were eligible for a benefit, regardless of contributions paid, entitlement to the non-work-related sickness benefit depended on a strict contribution record.[15] If claimants failed to meet the contribution criteria, and they often did, their only option was to draw on the means-tested national assistance.[16] Finally, unlike the industrial injuries scheme, the national insurance scheme only granted benefits to the fully disabled. Table 5.1 illustrates the relative generosity of the industrial injuries scheme in terms of benefit levels. The table shows that a fully disabled male worker received a significantly higher benefit when his disability resulted from work-related activities – especially after six months. Child and family supplements could decrease the difference between

---

[13] The maximum level of the special hardship allowance was the amount needed to raise a 60 percent disablement pension to a full pension. Another way to understand the generosity of the special hardship allowance is to note that it accounted for almost 40 percent of the total cost of all disablement pensions.

[14] At first, workers could only claim the disablement pension when they were at least 20 percent disabled. After fierce criticism of this by the TUC, the government changed this to 1 percent in 1953.

[15] Under the 1946 National Insurance Act, a claimant could only draw a sickness benefit when "(1) not less than 26 contributions have been paid between entry into insurance and the day for which benefit is claimed; (2) Not less than fifty contributions or their equivalent have been paid by or credited to the claimant in respect of the last complete contribution year before the year of the claim." Moreover, "[a] person who paid less than 156 contributions since entry into insurances ceased to be entitled when period of incapacity has extended to 132 days, but may re-qualify after he or she has paid a further 13 weeks of contributions." Douglas Potter, *The National Insurance Act, 1946 with General Introduction and Annotations* (London: Butterworth, 1946), 3.

[16] As late as 1991, more than one-third of all disabled who incurred their disability outside work did not qualify for a contributory benefit. See Susan Lonsdale and Mansel Aylward, "A United Kingdom Perspective on Disability Policy." In Leo Aarts, Richard V. Burkhauser, and Philip R. de Jong, *Curing the Dutch Disease: An International Perspective on Disability Policy Reform* (Aldershot: Avebury, 1996), 96.

TABLE 5.1. *Weekly Benefit Level of a Fully Disabled Male Worker in Shillings, 1959*

Type of Benefit	Single	Married	Married, One Child	Married, Two Children
Sickness benefit	50	80	95	102
Industrial injury benefit	85	85	100	107
Industrial disablement pension	135	135	135	135

Source: Pentti Korvenmaa, *Social Welfare Administration in the United Kingdom and in the Netherlands* (The Hague: Ministry for Social Work, 1959), 4–8.

the sickness and industrial injuries benefits paid for the first six months. After this, however, even a single disabled male worker who incurred his injury at work received almost twice in benefits (namely 185 shillings) as a married worker with two children who incurred his or her injury outside work (he or she received 102 shillings).

A particularly useful way to illustrate the comparative generosity of the industrial injuries scheme is by comparing the consequences of work-related and non-work-related disabilities on the income of a lower-paid worker. Lower-paid workers provide a clear illustration because they seldom had the opportunity to add occupational provision to the benefit they received from the state – a problem to which I will return at length below. If a poorer worker suffered from a work-related accident or sickness, he or she could always look forward to a benefit that closely approached or even exceeded his or her previous wage. If he or she remained disabled for longer than six months, the combination of an industrial disablement pension and sickness benefit could even result in a benefit that far exceeded the previous wage. To Beveridge and the TUC, but not to employer interest groups, such an outcome was acceptable in light of the national importance of providing adequate protection from disabilities that resulted from work done under orders or in dangerous industries.[17] If the disability occurred outside work, however, the outcome was at most a below-subsistence national insurance sickness benefit. Supplementary benefits for the disabled who incurred their disabilities outside work were as good as nonexistent until the 1970s. When supplementary benefits did become available, their level was quite insufficient, and they were often either obscure or hard to obtain.[18] The consequence of this

[17] This apparently remained the case in later years. As we saw in Chapter 4, when Labour introduced the earnings-related supplement into the unemployment and sickness insurance programs, it introduced a wage limit for national insurance claimants to prevent them from receiving a benefit that exceeded their previous wages. No such limit applied to industrial injury claimants. MRC, MSS.200/C/3/EMP/5/1: National insurance – proposals for wage-related unemployment and sickness benefits, Summary of comments by member employer organisations, 1965

[18] See Peter Alcock, *Poverty and State Support: Social Policy in Modern Britain* (Harlow: Longman Group, 1987), 101–3.

was an exceedingly high poverty rate among the victims of non-work-related disabilities.[19]

The relatively generous treatment of people with work-related disabilities naturally led to a considerable amount of resentment by those disabled who themselves could claim only a meager sickness benefit or, even worse, had to rely on means-tested national assistance. Over the years, individual (Labour) politicians, lawyers, and social security experts also came to criticize the industrial preference.[20] By the 1960s, they were joined by several organizations that actively lobbied for equal generosity for all disabled people, regardless of the cause of the disability. Most important among these lobbyists was the Disablement Income Group, which gained a formal charter as the Disability Alliance in 1973. In the 1970s, the chairman of this alliance, the renowned poverty scholar Peter Townsend, repeatedly called for the creation of a "Dutch system," which gave generous provision for all disabilities, whether or not they were work-related.[21]

Among the many groups that called for equal treatment of all people with disabilities regardless of cause, one organization remained conspicuously absent. This organization was the TUC. Over the years, several commentators have noted that the TUC "depressingly failed to refer to this question" and even "jealously defended the industrial preference."[22] Yet none of them ever looked into the reasons for the absence of the TUC among the groups calling for equal treatment of all disabled people regardless of the cause of their disability. Nor did they ever investigate the involvement of the labor union movement in the development of state provision for people with disabilities in general. This is remarkable because the TUC's position was of crucial importance to the failure of British efforts to establish adequate provision for all disabled people.[23]

---

[19] For good overviews of this, see, for example, Amelia I. Harris, Elizabeth Cox, and Christopher R.W. Smith, *Handicapped and Impaired in Great Britain* (London: HMSO, 1971); Peter Townsend, *Poverty in the United Kingdom* (Harmondsworth: Penguin, 1979); J. Martin, H. Meltzer, and D. Elliot, *OPCW Report 1: The Prevalence of Disability Among Adults* (London: HMSO, 1988).

[20] See, for example, Lewis, "Tort and social security," 514–31; Alan Walker and Peter Townsend, *Disability in Britain: A Manifesto of Rights* (Oxford: Martin Robertson, 1981); Ogus and Barendt, *The Law of Social Security*; Harry Calvert, *Social Security Law* (London: Sweet and Maxwell, 1987). See also Department of Health and Social Security, *Social Security Act 1975: Reform of the Industrial Injuries Scheme* (London: HMSO, 1981), 2.

[21] See, for example, the Disability Alliance, *The Case for a Comprehensive Income Scheme for Disabled People* (London: Disability Alliance, 1975). See also MRC, MSS.200/C/3/EMP/5/5: Social Security Committee, Summary of the proposals of the Disablement Income Group, 3 July 1972.

[22] See Patrick Atiyah, *Accidents, Compensation and the Law* (London: Weidenfeld and Nicolson, 1975), 610; and MRC, MSS.292D/161/1: Draft of *New Society* article on industrial injuries discussion document, 24 March 1980.

[23] MRC, MSS.200/C/3/EMP/5/1: National insurance – proposals for wage-related unemployment and sickness benefits, Summary of comments by member employer organisations, 1965.

The TUC first gave serious consideration to the issue of the possible equal treatment of all disabled people regardless of cause during the early 1940s, when Beveridge consulted the confederation on its ideas for a reform of the existing social security system. At the time, as mentioned earlier, the TUC strongly opposed the idea. Like Beveridge, the TUC emphasized that only generous compensation for work-related disabilities would encourage people to work under dangerous conditions. To the TUC, it was also noteworthy that work-related disabilities occurred while working under orders. This made employers fully responsible for the costs of work-related disabilities, which, in turn, enabled workers to demand near-to-full compensation for loss of earnings. The old Workmen's Compensation Act had entitled disabled workers who incurred their injury or sickness at work to half their previous earnings. In the years leading up to the introduction of the 1946 National Insurance (Industrial Injuries) Act, the TUC demanded that this be raised to at least two-thirds of previous earnings.[24]

To the TUC's disappointment, first Beveridge and later the Labour government that implemented Beveridge's proposals did not share the TUC's views on the need to increase the benefit level for people with work-related disabilities to two-thirds of previous earnings. In fact, they did not opt for a benefit that replaced earnings at all. Instead, the 1946 National Insurance (Industrial Injuries) Act entitled workers who became disabled at work to a flat-rate benefit given as a compensation for loss of faculty. The TUC eventually could accept this outcome because the flat-rate benefit was set at a very generous level and because compensation for loss of faculty meant that workers could still receive a benefit if they continued to work.[25] Another one of Beveridge's recommendations that eventually became legislation (as we have seen, his recommendation to maintain the industrial preference for only the long-term disabled did not) was far more difficult for the TUC to swallow. To the TUC's utter dismay, Beveridge recommended making workers and the state responsible for the financing of the industrial injuries scheme – and the Labour government agreed.

This final feature of the new industrial injuries scheme conflicted both with workers' sense of justice and with established practice – in the United Kingdom as well as overseas. For the TUC, this regrettable feature was only tolerable for three reasons. First, employers continued to pay the largest share of the costs. Second, the low risk of work-related disability made the costs to workers sufferable.[26] Third, and most important, "in return for his contribution,

---

[24] MRC, MSS.292/150.5/2: Workmen's Compensation and Factory Committee and Social Insurance Joint Committee – memorandum on certain phrases of the Beveridge Report, 4 January 1942.

[25] It nevertheless objected to it. MRC, MSS.292/150.5/3: Relation of Trade Union Congress General Council scheme and plan for social security in Sir William Beveridge's Report, 1943.

[26] For example, in 1955, there were, on average, 200,000 injury benefit and industrial disablement pension recipients compared with almost 1 million recipients of the national insurance sickness benefit. This proportion was probably similar in the mid-1940s. See Parry, "United Kingdom," 200.

the employee will receive a greatly improved system of compensation, with higher benefits, administered impartially and on a non-profit making basis."[27] The TUC nevertheless continued to press for a completely employer-financed industrial injuries scheme in ensuing decades.[28] It is quite possible that this may have been part of the reason for its continued support for the industrial preference because the creation of a single scheme for all disabled people certainly would make it more difficult to restore individual employer liability for work-related disabilities.[29]

At the same time, there was a growing awareness within the ranks of the TUC that the enormous difference in benefit levels for work-related and non-work-related disabilities was hard to defend from both legal and social angles. Privately, TUC members eventually even came to admit that "a separate IIS [industrial injuries scheme] could be seen as increasingly anachronistic and that the objective should be to move towards provision of the same benefits for all disabled people, regardless of the cause of disability, and this would not be helped by further emphasizing the separation of the IIS."[30] The acceptance of this view in principle did not mean, however, that the TUC ever actually came close to seeking abolition of the industrial preference. It might have done so if it did not have another, much more forcible reason to refrain from this: its awareness of the financial consequences of the abolition of the industrial preference.

Although realizing that treating different disabled groups differently based on cause of disability was problematic, the TUC also realized that any attempt to treat non-work-related disabilities as generously as work-related disabilities

---

[27] MRC, MSS.292/171.7/4: Industrial Injuries Act, 1946.

[28] As late as 1981, the members of the TUC stated that "the whole contribution for industrial injury benefits should be met by employers, so that the costs of compensating workpeople injured while working in dangerous jobs and industries would be reflected in the price which the community has to pay for the products of these industries." MSS.292D/160.11/2: Note of the fifth meeting of the TUC social security review working party held on 23 January 1981, at Congress House. See also MRC, MSS292D/161/6: Royal Commission on compensation for personal injury, Draft evidence – injuries in the course of employment; MRC, MSS292D/161/6: Minutes of the fourth meeting (1973–1974) held at Congress House on Wednesday, 9 January 1974.

[29] As late as 1983, the TUC Social Insurance Committee "took the view that the strongest factor in having separate schemes is that this approach enables the costs of benefits for disablement from different causes to be allocated to the different sources of risk. In the case of the IIS [industrial injuries scheme], all costs should be borne by employers and contributions adjusted according to accident records of particular industries, and of particular employers as compared with the average in their industry." MRC, MSS.292D/160.11/3: Development of the National Insurance Scheme: Benefits for unemployment, incapacity and disablement, Second draft, 1983.

[30] MRC, MSS.292D/160.11/2: Note of the fifth meeting of the TUC social security review working party held on 23 January 1981, at Congress House. See also MRC, MSS.292B/163.3/1: Industrial Injuries Act, Note for meeting with Mr. Swingler, Minister of State for Social Security, 7 January 1969; MRC, MSS.292D/161/5: Minutes of the sixth meeting (1973–1974) held at Congress House on Wednesday, 13 March 1974, at 2:00 p.m.

would require substantial additional contributions. After all, non-work-related accidents and sicknesses far exceeded in frequency and number those that occurred in or because of work. In 1970, for example, on average, almost 1.5 million disabled people claimed a sickness benefit or social assistance, whereas only 300,000 disabled people received a benefit from the industrial injuries scheme.[31] It would be extremely costly to entitle all the additional 1.5 million disabled people to a benefit like that enjoyed by the 300,000 industrial injuries scheme claimants. This was the main reason that the TUC continued to defend the industrial preference. It simply understood that the costs of extending the generous work-related disability benefit would not be met.

Without an accompanying increase in contributions, equal treatment of all disabilities would only result in a redistribution of income between non-work-related and work-related disability claimants. Moreover, because the former far exceeded the latter in number, the outcome in terms of benefit levels would be much closer to the level of the sickness insurance program than to that of the industrial injuries scheme. This meant that matters would improve only slightly for victims of non-work-related accidents and sicknesses. Victims of work-related accidents and sicknesses would, on the other hand, experience a vast decline in income. The same TUC members who had previously admitted that the industrial preference was now anachronistic realized this very well. They therefore advised against abolition of industrial preference because "abandonment of the IIS would not increase the total resources available for compensating injury and disability, and would mean a level down of existing benefits for workpeople injured at work."[32]

The important point here is that only a substantial increase in contributory efforts could bring about a significant improvement in the plight of victims of non-work-related disabilities. Without such an increase, the abolition of the industrial preference would bring them little improvement. Yet such an increase was hard to achieve in the United Kingdom because of the resistance of unions representing privileged workers to any attempt to redistribute income among different categories of workers. Redistribution would be crucial to attain adequate insurance against the risk of non-work-related disability. After all, not all workers (or the self-employed, because the sickness benefit was not limited to workers) had high enough income to afford the substantial increase in contributions that was necessary to grant those disabled who had incurred their disability outside work an evenly generous benefit on evenly generous terms as currently enjoyed by the disabled who had incurred their disability at work. The next section of this chapter illustrates this.

---

[31] See Parry, "United Kingdom," 400–1.
[32] MRC, MSS.292D/160.11/2: Note of the fifth meeting of the TUC social security review working party held on 23 January 1981, at Congress House.

THE EVOLUTION OF PUBLIC PROTECTION FROM
NON-WORK-RELATED DISABILITIES IN THE UNITED KINGDOM

A popular view among welfare state scholars is that Beveridge only attended to those disabled in war and work, not to others.[33] Perhaps it would be more accurate to say that with the exception of war- and work-related disabilities, Beveridge paid more attention to the needs of the affluent than to those of the less affluent. It is important to point out here that the industrial injuries scheme could be so generous because it was based on solidarity through risk redistribution. All workers and employers paid the same contributions even though they differed greatly in their exposure to the risk of work-related disability. Manual workers were much more prone to incurring work-related disabilities than were white-collar workers, and manual workers operating in dangerous industries were much more likely to experience work-related disabilities than their counterparts who worked in less-dangerous industries. A similar distinction, of course, can be applied to employers operating in more- and less-dangerous industries.[34]

In light of the national importance of providing adequate protection from disabilities incurred while working under orders or in dangerous industries, Beveridge apparently did not worry about the uneven distribution of risk through the industrial injuries scheme.[35] It was surely also important that work-related disabilities posed only a small risk. Throughout the period under investigation here, the industrial injuries scheme accounted for at most 3.5 percent of the total cost of social security expenditure. The sickness scheme, by comparison, even though it was much less generous, generally accounted for some 10 percent of the total social security cost during the same period.[36] Of course, this percentage would increase sharply if the sickness scheme were to hand out equally generous benefits and on equally generous terms as in the industrial injuries scheme. More important, such a move would also sharply increase redistribution between different categories of workers.

By now it should come as no surprise that the inadequacy of state security against the risk of non-work-related disability mainly posed a problem

---

[33] War-related cases of disability received an even more generous treatment than work-related disabilities. For this and the view described earlier, see, for example, Lowe, *Welfare Policy in Britain*, 159.

[34] Risk redistribution was, in fact, far more important for employers because they paid most of the industrial injuries scheme's costs. On the importance of risk redistribution among employers, see Mares, *The Politics of Social Risk*.

[35] The TUC did, however. It had always argued for premium differentiation because it deemed it "not fair to pay the costs of accidents out of a fund by people who have little or no risk of accidents." MRC, MSS292/155.5/4: Fifth joint meeting of the Social Insurance and Workmen's Compensation Committees, held on Wednesday, 1 October 1941.

[36] See Lowe, *Welfare Policy in Britain*, 129.

for the less affluent. As had been the case with unemployment and old age, Beveridge's solution of providing only a public minimum of protection against non-work-related disabilities, which then could be supplemented by more generous private provision, worked very well for the more-affluent part of working Britain. The problem lay primarily with the more-risk-prone and lower-paid workers – and those self-employed – who did not have the means to add private provision to the state sickness benefit. Some fifteen years after the creation of the 1946 National Insurance Act, this group still accounted for about half of all workers. The other half could count on occupational sick pay, although at quite various levels of generosity. Thus the "two nations" that Titmuss spoke about in the mid-1950s applied not only to income in old age but also to disability as well.[37]

Just as the spread of occupational pensions and severance payments had complicated efforts to improve matters for the elderly and unemployed who relied solely on the national insurance benefit, the existence of occupational sick pay stood in the way of attempts to improve state provision against non-work-related disabilities. Workers with adequate occupational provision had little to gain from improved state provision and therefore refused to pay for it. As a result, the TUC once more could do nothing beyond call for an Exchequer-financed increase of the national insurance benefit. It certainly could not support Labour's ideas for improving matters for the disabled who incurred their injuries outside work and did not have the means to add private provision to the national insurance sickness benefit. Two of Labour's ideas were mentioned in Chapter 4 as being linked to improved state security for the financial consequences of unemployment.

As mentioned several times earlier, since the mid-1950s, Labour's conviction that a contributory solution was the only acceptable way forward had generated several ideas that centered on earnings relation. In approaching the risk of non-work-related disability, Labour's initial priority was to grant earnings-related benefits to short-term cases. Chapter 4 examined extensively the TUC's reaction to Labour's plan, launched in the late 1950s, to impose a statutory obligation on employers to pay workers at least one-half of normal earnings during the first month of redundancy or sickness. It gave an even more extensive treatment of another initiative taken by Labour at roughly the same time, which was its plan to add earnings-related supplements to the flat-rate unemployment and sickness benefits for a maximum of six months. The TUC General Council initially expressed its "strong objection" to both proposals.[38] It is tempting to refer back to the reasons given for this. Yet, because this has already been done at length in Chapter 4, it is enough here to state that the unions that represented privileged workers opposed the redistributive consequences of exchanging voluntary provision for statutory provision.

---

[37] See Titmuss, "Pension Systems," 91.
[38] MRC, MSS,292B/163.3/1: Industrial Agreements, payments during sickness, 25 July 1961.

Chapter 4 also showed why the TUC eventually did support introduction of the earnings-related principle into the sickness and unemployment schemes in the mid-1960s. Solidarity with less-privileged workers certainly had little to do with this. On the contrary, the absence of direct redistribution between higher- and lower-income workers and the inclusion of all earnings below nine pounds ensured that the earnings-related scheme was of little use to the poorer national insurance contributors.

Some three years after Labour introduced the earnings-related supplementary scheme, it came up with a much more complete plan to combat hardship in disability. In 1969, it published a white paper in which it promised a "new deal" for the disabled.[39] The goal of this new deal was twofold. First, it aimed to further improve public protection for short-term cases of disability. Second, it aimed to improve matters for an up-to-then-forgotten group, the long-term disabled. To achieve these two different goals, the new deal consisted of two different proposals. The first entailed a statutory obligation on all employers to pay a minimum level of sick pay to their workers during the first four weeks of disability. The second proposal entailed the introduction of fully earnings-related benefits for the long-term disabled into Crossman's pension scheme. This "invalidity pension" would be paid after six months, or twenty-six weeks, as was the case with the industrial disablement pension. The government was somewhat unclear about what would happen for recipients during the twenty-two weeks between employer-paid sick pay and the granting of the invalidity pension. Most likely the outcome in terms of generosity would be more or less similar to the situation as it was then in the first six months of disability. Minor adjustments, however, were likely. Most important of these was that the existing flat-rate sickness benefit and earnings-related supplement might be replaced by a single benefit, which could turn out to be somewhat more generous for the lower-income brackets.

As expected, the employer community, now represented mainly by the Confederation of British Industry (CBI), fiercely opposed Labour's plans. The CBI especially disliked the proposed statutory obligation to pay workers a minimum level of sick pay during the first four weeks of disability. It deemed this to be costly and unfair to employers and feared that it would increase absence rates – especially among lower-paid workers.[40] Moreover, as a matter of principle, the CBI condemned the proposal as a further departure from the concept of relating statutory provision to need and a further move toward a completely earnings-related scheme.[41] Fortunately for the CBI, it did not stand

---

[39] See Department of Health and Social Security, *The New Pensions Scheme: Latest Facts and Figures with Examples* (London: HMSO, 1969), 1.

[40] MRC, MSS.200/C/3/EMP/5/3: CBI working party on sickness benefit, Friday, 4 October 1968, 10.30 a.m.

[41] MRC, MSS.200/C/3/EMP/5/3: CBI Social Security Committee, Meeting held on Thursday, 25 April, 1968, at 14.30 hours at 21 Tothill Street, S.W.1.

alone in its criticism of Labour's plans. As with many of Labour's attempts to improve state provision for the risks of unemployment and old age dependency, the Labour government might have been able to implement its new deal for the disabled if the employer community had indeed stood alone in its criticism of it. Yet this was once more not the case. Again, the TUC also made known its own disapproval of Labour's plans. Like the CBI, it was particularly unhappy with Labour's statutory sick pay proposal.

It is important to remember here that Labour had already approached the TUC once with a similar proposal in the late 1950s. At the time, the TUC had rejected Labour's proposal for a statutory obligation on employers to pay their workers at least half of normal earnings during the first month of redundancy or disability. When Labour later refurbished that plan, several years of thinking had resulted in some minor alterations. First, introduction of the 1965 Redundancy Payments Act obviously made it unnecessary to go beyond a statutory obligation to hand out sick pay. Second, the obligation was no longer to hand out half of normal earnings. Instead, employers would now have to pay a full 100 percent on earnings up to nine pounds and 50 percent on further earnings up to twenty-one pounds. Third, the employer-paid sick pay would no longer only replace the national insurance sickness benefit; it also would replace the industrial injury benefit. None of these alterations enticed the TUC to support the plan this time, however. In fact, the last alteration only increased the TUC's opposition to the proposal.

The main goal of Labour's proposal was clearly to improve matters for workers who incurred injuries outside work and did not have the means to add occupational provision to the sickness benefit. It did so mainly at the expense of workers who could claim occupational sick pay. This can be illustrated as follows: Table 5.2 compares the generosity of Labour's sick pay scheme with that of the national insurance sickness scheme in terms of earnings replacement for workers who earned half of national average wages, two-thirds of the national average, the national average wage, and one-third more than the national average.

As we can see, the generosity of Labour's sick pay scheme exceeded that of the combined flat-rate sickness benefit and earnings-related supplement for nearly all income brackets. The improvement was greatest for the lowest-earning claimants – especially if they had few or no dependents. Only workers who earned more than a third more than the national average and had two or more children would lose out – and then only slightly (instead of a 52 or 54 percent earnings replacement rate, they would receive a replacement rate of 50 percent).

Yet this did not mean that Labour's statutory sick pay actually brought a net improvement to all workers. The reason for this is that the preceding table excludes a major source of security against loss of income owing to disability, namely, occupational sick pay. By the late 1960s, over half of all workers could claim at least some degree of occupational provision for sick pay. For many

TABLE 5.2. *Benefit as a Percentage of Previous Earnings under Labour's Sick Pay Proposal and the Existing National Insurance Scheme (NI) during the First Four Weeks of Sickness or Disability*

Weekly Earnings (£)	Labour Plan	NI When Single	NI When Married, No Children	NI When Married, One Child	NI When Married, Two Children	NI When Married, Three Children
11	91	47	72	85*	85*	85*
15	80	43	62	72	76	80
22	68	40	53	60	63	67
30	50	37	45	49	52	54

*Wage limit applied.
Sources: Calculated from DHSS, *Explanatory Memorandum on the National Superannuation and Social Insurance Bill 1969* (London: HMSO, 1969), 44–52; DHSS, *Social Insurance Proposals for Earnings-Related Short-Term and Invalidity Benefits* (London: HMSO, 1969), 15–23.

of them, the combination of the flat-rate sickness benefit, the earnings-related supplement, and occupational provision resulted in a full 100 percent earnings replacement.[42] Those workers had great cause to oppose Labour's sick pay proposal. Not only would Labour's plan bring no improvement for them, but it also would make it far more difficult for them to achieve future wage increases or improvements in occupational provision. After all, and as explained at length in Chapter 4, introduction of a statutory obligation for employers to provide sick pay to all their workers would result in a substantial increase in wage costs for employers. Faced with a substantial increase in total wage costs, employers would be more resistant to any further increases in total wage costs. The final result would be that even workers who did not profit from Labour's scheme would find it more difficult to achieve generous outcomes during wage negotiations.[43]

To a large extent, the TUC's opposition to Labour's 1969 statutory sick pay proposal thus can be explained in the same way as its rejection of Labour's statutory sick and redundancy pay proposal in the late 1950s and the TUC's attempts to stop the 1965 Redundancy Payments Act. All these initiatives ran contrary to the interests of unions representing privileged workers because they could achieve better results through voluntary negotiation. The unions came out in strong opposition to Labour's sick pay proposal.[44] This in itself was probably enough of a reason for the TUC leadership to oppose Labour's

[42] MRC, MSS 200/C/3/EMP/3/114: BEC62/130, Unemployment benefit, 27 July 1962.
[43] See Chapter 4 on this.
[44] MRC, MSS.292B/163.3/3: Letter from Transport Salaried Staff's Association, National superannuation and social insurance, short-term benefits, 8 July 1969. For earlier statements of TUC unions on the uselessness of legislation on sick pay for the higher paid, see MRC, MSS.292B/161.2: TUC Sub-Committee on Sickness and Unemployment Benefits, Minutes of the second meeting, 14 February 1962.

TABLE 5.3. *Benefit as a Percentage of Previous Earnings under Labour's Sick Pay Proposal and the Industrial Injury (II) Benefit during the First Four Weeks of Sickness or Disability*

Weekly Earnings (£)	Labour Plan	II When Single or Married	II With Two Children	II With Three Children	II With Four Children
11	91	72	92	101	109
15	80	62	77	83	87
22	68	53	63	67	71
30	50	48	55	58	61

Sources: See Table 5.2.

proposal. At the same time, the TUC also had its doubts about the effect of Labour's sick pay proposal on another category of workers, namely, those who had incurred their injury or sickness at work.

Whereas unions representing privileged workers agitated against Labour's statutory sick pay proposal mainly because of its effect on voluntary negotiation, others had difficulties with the outcome of the proposal for some of the workers who had incurred their injuries at work.[45] Labour wanted statutory sick pay to replace both the national insurance sickness benefit and the industrial injury benefit during the first four weeks of disability. Although this would result in an improvement for some workers with work-related disabilities, many such workers with large families would lose out. Table 5.3 compares the generosity of Labour's sick pay benefit with that of the industrial injury benefit in terms of earnings replacement for several different income brackets. In the existing situation, an industrial injury actually resulted in a benefit that exceeded the previous wage for a low-paid worker with three or more children. This would end under Labour's statutory sick pay scheme. Many workers with two or more children would receive a lower benefit under Labour's scheme. As Table 5.3 shows, this was the case both for workers with very low earnings and for those with relatively high earnings.

The TUC feared that at least some of the workers with work-related disabilities would lose out under other parts of Labour's new deal for the disabled as well. One such worry related to the consequences of the introduction of the invalidity benefit for the loss-of-faculty concept. In the existing situation, workers who incurred their injury at work received a disablement pension if their disability lasted longer than six months. They were able to combine this disablement pension with the flat-rate sickness benefit. If this flat-rate sickness benefit were replaced by a fully earnings-related invalidity benefit after six

---

[45] MRC, MSS.292B/163.3/3: Letter from Transport Salaried Staff's Association, National superannuation and Social Insurance, short-term benefits, 8 July 1969. MRC, MSS.292B/166.51/3: Industrial injuries scheme, 9 July 1969.

months, the TUC feared that the government might very well decide to make the disablement pension less generous.[46] Government attempts to reassure the TUC General Council on matters such as these were far from successful. When the government was overly vague or made contradictory remarks, that even augmented the concerns of the TUC. This was clearly the case with the question of what would happen in the twenty-two weeks between statutory sick pay and granting of the invalidity benefits. The government was quite unclear on this. While emphasizing that "the existing ... injury benefit preference over sickness benefit will be retained," it also noted that "the effect will be to draw the two benefits more into line."[47] Needless to say, such contradictory remarks did not convince the skeptics within the TUC.

Although worries about keeping the disablement pension high and the question of the twenty-two-week gap continued to resurface in the TUC's discussions with the government, it was quite clear that the TUC's main gripe with the new deal for the disabled related to the statutory sick pay proposal.[48] Thus this proposal was the first to go. In July 1969, the General Council informed its members that "the Government recognise that there are substantial objections to the statutory sick pay scheme ... and have decided not to proceed with it."[49] By withdrawing the statutory sick pay proposal, Labour sacrificed most other parts of the new deal as well. Only the invalidity benefit eventually made it – although only circuitously, as part of State Earnings-Related Pension Scheme (SERPS). Perhaps this benefit came through because it represented the least ambitious part of the new deal. As in for example Germany and Austria, Labour's earnings-related invalidity pension was part of the pension scheme. Yet, contrary to these countries, eligibility conditions were not eased in a major way. The full earnings-related addition given to the flat-rate benefit by the SERPS required a buildup period of twenty years.[50] If a worker became disabled before then, SERPS would do little for him or her. This left many national insurance contributors out in the cold because the risk of dis-

[46] MRC, MSS.292B/166.51/1: Industrial injuries scheme, Comments on ministry paper, October 1968.

[47] See Department of Health and Social Security, *The New Pensions Scheme*, 15. On the TUC's dissatisfaction with this, see MRC, MSS.292B/166.51/1: Industrial injuries scheme, Comments on ministry paper, October 1968.

[48] MRC, MSS.292B/163./1: Industrial Injuries Act, Note for meeting with Mr. Swingler, Minister of State for Social Security, 7 January 1969. MRC, MSS.292B/173.26/1: Note for meeting with Mr. S. Swingler on Thursday, 19 December 1968. MRC, MSS.292B/166.51.2: Note of a meeting with deputation from TUC at 10.30 a.m. on Thursday, 16 January 1969. MRC, MSS.292B/166.51.2: Note of a meeting with TUC deputation on Monday, 21 July 1969.

[49] MRC, MSS.292B/161.13: Government's proposed earnings-related scheme short-term benefits, 9 July 1969.

[50] To compare, in Austria and Germany, insurance against non-work-related disabilities was also part of the general pension scheme, but this pension was payable to the disabled after a minimum of five working years.

ability is such that it often occurs before the disabled worker has had time to build up adequate contributions.

The demise of the new deal clearly illustrates the limits of what governments can do to improve public protection when both the union movement and the employer community oppose interference with voluntary bargaining. After 1969, large-scale attempts to tackle the problem of disability in a unified way were a thing of the past in the United Kingdom. Faced with the unwillingness of unions to accept its redistributive consequences, Labour no longer attempted reform of state disability insurance, whereas the Conservatives never had this ambition to begin with. In the 1970s, both parties turned instead to more modest improvements. In 1971, a Conservative government introduced a small attendance allowance for long-term disabled workers whose disability required constant attendance. In the same year, it introduced a flat-rate invalidity pension that was to replace the sickness benefit after a disability of six months. The invalidity pension was somewhat more generous than the sickness benefit, especially for those with children and those whose disability occurred early in working life. At some 35 percent of average earnings, this benefit still hardly compared with what those disabled outside work could rely on in most continental European welfare states, however – let alone in the Netherlands. Moreover, the Conservative government did not ease eligibility conditions, which left many long-term disabled workers dependent on the means-tested supplementary benefit. When Labour returned to power in 1975, it introduced a noncontributory invalidity pension for this group. The only merit of this pension was that it ended the reliance of many long-term disabled workers on the means test. Because it was tax-financed, the benefit was exceedingly meager: it gave out only about 20 percent of average earnings.

The introduction of SERPS, the contributory and noncontributory invalidity pensions, and the attendance allowance in no way diminished public pressure for more generous provision for non-work-related disabilities. The Disablement Income Group, for example, kept arguing for a Dutch-style system in which the benefit level depended on neither the cause of disability nor the contribution record.[51] Yet the stance of the CBI and the TUC on the issue made these calls quite unrealistic. Characteristic of their apathy toward the plight of non-work-related disabled people was their response to the introduction of the noncontributory invalidity pension. Whereas the CBI was content that it could play a dead bat on this issue, the TUC accompanied its welcome of this initiative with the warning that there should be improvements for the industrially disabled as well.[52]

---

[51] MRC, MSS.292D/160.31/2: RD 940, Comments by Peter Townsend on the proposals for a disablement income, November 1973; MRC, MSS.200/C/3/EMP/5/5: Social Security Committee, Summary of the proposals of the Disablement Income Group, 3 July 1972.

[52] MRC, MSS.200/C/3/EMP/5/5: Social Security Committee, Summary of the proposals of the Disablement Income Group, 3 July 1972. MRC, MSS.292D/160.31/2: TUC Social Insurance Committee and Labour Party's Social Policy Sub-Committee joint meeting, 24 January 1974.

TOWARD A SINGLE DISABILITY INSURANCE PROGRAM FOR ALL DISABLED PEOPLE IN THE NETHERLANDS

It is not a coincidence that the Disablement Income Group always looked to the Netherlands among all possible countries with state pension schemes as the country that had got it right on the disability issue. At the time when Peter Townsend started his campaign for a comprehensive solution to the problem of poverty in disability, the Dutch had just enacted legislation that did exactly that. In 1965, the second chamber of the Dutch Parliament unanimously passed a Ziektewet and WAO that had several unique features. Most important among these was that entitlement to a benefit no longer depended on the cause of disability, its duration, or the contributory record. From July 1, 1967, on, every sick and fully disabled worker could count on a benefit of at least 80 percent of his or her previous wages for as long as the sickness or disability prevented him or her from working. If 80 percent of the previous wage turned out to be lower than the minimum wage, then the worker was entitled to a benefit at minimum-wage level. The disability scheme offered a benefit to the partially disabled as well – even to those who were only 15 percent disabled. Finally, if partial disability prevented a worker from finding a new job, then he or she was entitled to a higher – which often meant a full – benefit. For Townsend, the Dutch example must have seemed like a true panacea, especially after the Dutch enhanced the disability scheme in 1976 with a flat-rate insurance benefit for the self-employed.

Of course, this panacea came at a price. After all, the Dutch sickness and disability schemes could only provide such generous protection against all sorts of disabilities because they operated in a highly redistributive manner. This explains why the creation of a comprehensive solution to the problem of poverty in disability was possible in the Netherlands and not in the United Kingdom. Again, the main difference lay in the stance of the British and Dutch labor union movements on redistribution of income and risk among different categories of workers. Without the willingness and ability of the Dutch union federations to press for redistribution of income and risk between more- and less-privileged workers, the Dutch solution to providing for the disabled would not have been so successful. At the same time, it must be noted that the Dutch employer federations were remarkably cooperative toward the demands of the union federations for a more generous treatment of all types of disabilities. In Chapter 4, I showed that both British and Dutch employer interest groups were quite averse to the creation of a generous public unemployment insurance program. Although both accepted the need for a basic level of public protection for the unemployed, they also agreed that this protection remain as minimal as possible. In contrast to their British counterparts, the Dutch employer federations were willing to accept a much more generous level of public protection for the disabled. The reasons for this willingness will be discussed later.

For now, it is sufficient to say that the Dutch employer federations were already willing to do so in the immediate postwar period.

Had Townsend embarked on his campaign in the immediate postwar period, some twenty years before he actually did so, then he would hardly have given the Netherlands a second glance. At that time, there was nothing particularly generous about the Dutch system of public insurance for disabilities. Moreover, it was even more fragmented than the one he was used to. Table 5.4 shows the extent of this fragmentation by comparing some important features of the three compulsory insurance programs that comprised this system in the early postwar period. As in the United Kingdom until 1946, all workers whose disability occurred on the job were entitled to a separate benefit until reaching retirement age. This benefit was provided through the industrial injuries insurance program. The Dutch industrial injuries insurance program offered a benefit that was even more generous than that of its British counterpart, equaling 80 percent of previous wages in the first six weeks of disability and seventy percent after this. As in the United Kingdom, entitlement to a work-related disability benefit did not depend on the contributory record. As in the United Kingdom until 1946, the benefit was completely financed by employer contributions.

In contrast to in the United Kingdom, there also were separate policies for workers unable to work because of a non-work-related sickness and those unable to work because of a permanent non-work-related disability. This latter distinction made matters quite complex in the Netherlands. If a worker suffered from a non-work-related sickness, then he or she could claim a benefit under the Ziektewet. This act was generous in the sense that it entitled sick workers to a benefit that equaled 80 percent of their previous wages – a level even higher than the industrial injuries benefit after six weeks – regardless of their contributory records. Yet the sickness benefit lasted for only six months, and large groups of disabled workers were not entitled to it. First, only the disabled who worked in an "enterprise" could claim a sickness benefit. This meant that housing staff and those who were employed in the so-called free professions could not. Second, and perhaps more important, only workers who suffered from a "sickness" were entitled to it. The Ziektewet did not define what a "sickness" was, and case law defined it merely as a development that was subject to change. This meant that a worker was not entitled to a sickness benefit when it immediately became clear that his or her disability would be permanent. Of course, this led to a lot of bickering over the question of whether or not a disability could be regarded as permanent, and case law on this was quite inconsistent.[53]

If a worker was sick for longer than six months (after which the sickness was automatically regarded as permanent), was unable to work because of a permanent non-work-related disability instead of a sickness, or was simply

---

[53] J. van Bruggen and B. C. Slotemaker, *Commentaar op de Ziektewet. Handboek voor de practijk* (Deventer: Kluwer, 1935), 80–3.

TABLE 5.4. *Public Insurance Against Disability in the Netherlands in the Early Postwar Period*

	Industrial Injuries Act (Ongevallenwet)	Sickness Act (Ziektewet)	Invalidity Act (Invaliditeitswet)
Year	1901	1929	1919
Purpose	Insurance against work-related sicknesses and injuries	Insurance against non-work-related sicknesses	Insurance against non-work-related (and permanent) invalidity
Scope	All workers, with separate acts for the shipbuilding and agricultural sectors	Workers in "enterprises" (as defined by act)	All workers
Benefit	80 percent of the former wage for six weeks; then 70 percent; partial benefits were possible; duration indefinite	80 percent for a maximum period of six months	3 percent of the previous wage for each of fifty weekly contributions; duration indefinite
Entitlement	No contributory requirements	No contributory requirements	When at least 150 weekly contributions had been paid
Contributor	Employer	Employer and worker	Employer and worker
Financing	Funded	Pay as you go	Funded

not covered by the sickness benefit, then he or she could only hope to receive a benefit under the Invaliditeitswet (Invalidity Act). In contrast to the other two insurance schemes, entitlement to an invalidity benefit depended solely on the contributory record. Workers were only entitled to a benefit if they had contributed to it for at least three years, and the level of the benefit depended on the number of contributions paid. This meant that only workers whose disability occurred when they were close to retirement age could count on a pension benefit that could provide them with an above-subsistence-level income. Others either did not receive a benefit at all or received a benefit that was quite inadequate. Unlike the industrial injuries pension, the invalidity scheme did not hand out benefits to the partially disabled. Like the sickness insurance program, it was financed by employers and workers on a fifty-fifty basis.

When the second Van Rhijn Committee, comprising representatives of the state, the labor union federations, and employer federations, reexamined this system in the immediate postwar period, they naturally confronted the question of whether it would not be preferable to replace it with a unified system that treated all disabilities in the same way.[54] As had happened only a few years before in the United Kingdom, all involved parties quickly dismissed this idea at the time. The reasons given for this were quite similar to those seen in the United Kingdom. First, and most important, all parties agreed that such a system was unaffordable. Second, and following from this, they agreed that the risk of work-related disability deserved special, more generous treatment. On both points, the union federations were in full agreement with their employer counterparts. As late as 1954, the NVV's Social Insurance Committee still spoke out against a single disability insurance program that did not distinguish between different causes because, among other reasons, it deemed such a system to be too costly, and because it believed that the industrial preference was still very popular among its members.[55] Why, then, did the NVV, together with its confessional counterparts and the main employer federations, eventually commit itself to the creation of exactly such a system? The reason for this lay in its commitment to improving matters for, in particular, those disabled who incurred disabilities outside work. With these improvements under way, the division of work-related and non-work-related disabilities into different policies simply became unnecessary.

The first of these improvements was made as early as 1947, when the government increased the maximum duration of the sickness benefit from six months to one year. One year later, the second Van Rhijn Committee recommended increasing the maximum duration of the sickness benefit by another year, to two years. It also recommended granting the sickness benefit to all disabled people regardless of cause. The main purpose of these two recommendations was to improve matters for the disabled who currently had to rely on the contributory invalidity pension. Under the Van Rhijn proposal, they would be able to count on near-to-complete earnings replacement under the noncontributory sickness benefit for the first two years. The recommendations also served to improve matters for the disabled who were entitled to an industrial injury benefit. They had previously received 80 percent of their previous wages during the first six weeks of disability and 70 percent after that. The proposal of the second Van Rhijn Committee effectively meant that this initial six-week period would increase to two years.

The committee also proposed increasing the generosity of the invalidity scheme, thus improving matters for long-term victims of non-work-related disabilities. It proposed doing so in three ways. First, it proposed allowing the invalidity insurance program to continue when a worker received a sickness benefit. Because it also proposed increasing the maximum duration of the sickness benefit to two years, this would effectively reduce the qualifying period for

---

[54] See A. van Rhijn, *Rapport inzake de herziening van de sociale verzekering* (Den Haag: Staatsdrukkerij, 1948), 18–19.

[55] ARA, CSWV, 2.19.103.06, 145: Verslag Vergadering Kleine Technische Commissie Sociale Verzekering, 11 October 1954.

entitlement to the invalidity benefit from three to one working year. Second, it proposed setting the level of the benefit at 70, 60, and 50 percent of the previous wage during, respectively, the first, second, and all ensuing years. This would particularly improve matters for workers who incurred a permanent non-work-related disability at an early age. Under the existing scheme, the level of the benefit depended completely on the number of years a worker had contributed to the scheme, which disadvantaged younger workers. Finally, the committee proposed granting an invalidity benefit to partially disabled workers as well.[56]

It is important to remember how generous these proposals were. By proposing the extension of the maximum duration of the sickness benefit to two years while retaining its noncontributory nature and extending it to all disabled workers regardless of cause, the second Van Rhijn Committee offered the majority of disabled workers the prospect of near-to-complete earnings replacement. Although its members were not yet willing to do the same for the disabled whose disability lasted for longer than two years, the committee's proposed improvements for this group also went quite far. This shows us that as early as 1948, the Dutch union and employer federations were already committed to a series of measures that was more far-reaching than those later rejected by their British counterparts in the 1960s.

Despite this early consensus on the need to make far-reaching improvements to public insurance for disabilities, serious discussions on disability insurance reform only got underway in the mid-1950s. Until that time, all efforts simply focused on the more-pressing matter of old age pension reform. If both issues were to be addressed at the same time, both union and employer federations feared, then the creation of a new old age insurance scheme might be delayed, especially because the two issues were closely linked.[57] Thus only after the issue of the organization of the old age pension was solved did the union and employer federations turn their attention to disability insurance reform. But when they finally did, they proceeded in a remarkably swift manner.

---

[56] See Van Rhijn, *Rapport inzake*, 18–24.

[57] This close linkage resulted from the lack of distinction between disabilities that resulted from injuries and those that resulted from old age in the existing social insurance system. At the time, most continental European social insurance systems did not really distinguish between the two, and the Netherlands was no exception. A look at the Invalidity Act can illustrate this. The Dutch invalidity insurance program was in every sense an insurance for old age and invalidity. Beyond the fact that it only provided sufficient benefits for those disabled who incurred their injuries quite late in their working lives, it also contained a separate old age insurance program. The question of what to do with this old age insurance program after introduction of the General Old Age Act was indeed one of the most difficult issues faced by representatives of the labor unions, employer federations, and the state in the early 1950s. On the origins of the Invalidity Act, see Hoogenboom, *Standenstrijd en zekerheid*. On union and employer federations' fears that the simultaneous handling of disability insurance and old age insurance reform might delay progress on the latter, see SER, *Advies inzake de herziening van de invaliditeitsverzekering* (Den Haag: SER, 1957), 1.

Because the inadequacy of the invalidity insurance program posed the most pressing problem, the union and employer federations first focused on reforming this insurance program. In June 1952, Minister of Social Affairs Dolf Joekes formally asked the recently created Sociaal-Economische Raad (SER, Social-Economic Council) for advice on the possibilities for reform of the invalidity insurance scheme. This was followed by another request by Joekes's successor, Ko Suurhoff, in December 1955. The SER turned its attention to a reform of the invalidity insurance scheme immediately after the February 1954 publication of its advice on the creation of the Algemene Ouderdomswet (AOW, General Old Age Act). By then, the second Van Rhijn Committee's recommendations for improving the benefit levels of the invalidity insurance program were considered insufficient. Union representatives demanded and employer representatives were willing to go along with a permanent maximum benefit level of 70 percent of the previous wage. With its proposed creation of four disability classes with intervals of 25 percent, the SER presented quite a generous solution for the problem of partial disability. Furthermore, the council recommended making the invalidity benefit wage-proof, which entailed a conversion to pay-as-you-go financing. Finally, entitlement to the new invalidity scheme would not depend on a minimum contributory record. To avoid misuse, however, administrators were given the right to refuse benefits to a claimant if his or her disablement occurred within one year of beginning to work and could be traced back to his or her state of health before that period. The council published its advice on January 11, 1957.

It is important to point out here that all members of the SER lent their full support to the preceding recommendations. From the side of the union federations, this is not so surprising. Chapters 3 and 4 showed the remarkable commitment of the Dutch labor union movement to improving matters for all old age pensioners and unemployed workers. It only makes sense that this commitment extended to improving matters for all disabled workers as well. The ease with which the employer federations were willing to go along with the demands of the labor union movement is more surprising, however. Chapters 3 and 4 showed how reluctant the Dutch employer federations were to accept generous outcomes and deviation from strict actuarial principles in the areas of public old age and, particularly, unemployment insurance development. On the issue of public disability insurance reform, they were much more willing to accept this. How can we explain this? The reason may have been that an increase in the generosity of the public disability insurance program was simply less threatening to them.

First, unlike old age pension provision, insurance for disabilities did not generate large private savings. The opposition of the Dutch employer federations to attempts to improve the general old age pension after its creation mainly resulted from their realization that any such improvement would leave less room for development of the lucrative private pension sector. The employer federations had no such reason to oppose an extension of the disability insurance system. This might explain why they so easily accepted the conversion from a funded system to a pay-as-you-go system for both the industrial injuries insurance and the invalidity insurance programs.[58] Second, as mentioned in Chapter 4, the disabled – unlike the unemployed – did not struggle with the stigma of being unwilling to work. Disabled workers simply were not able to work. The employer federations' opposition to a further extension of the public unemployment insurance program in the 1950s was not only motivated by concerns over costs; they also feared its implications for the willingness of the unemployed to find a new job. Such fears were absent with regard to public insurance against disabilities. On the contrary, one of the reasons why the employer federations supported giving benefits to the partially disabled as well was that such a move might keep more people at work.[59]

Internal discussions among employer representatives in the social insurance committees of the Centraal Sociaal Werkgevers Verbond (CSWV, Central Social Employers' Federation) illustrate the difference in attitudes toward public insurance for unemployment and for disabilities. When one employer representative suggested lowering the level of the invalidity benefit when the disability persisted for a longer period – as the second Van Rhijn Committee had suggested in 1948 – several other employer representatives voiced their opposition to this. In particular, they refuted the argument that such a progressive lowering of the invalidity benefit made sense because the relationship of the disabled worker with his or her previous position grew steadily weaker over the years. The consensus was that such an alteration in benefit levels could only be defended if there were a change in the level of disablement. Of course, things were different regarding unemployment. With unemployment insurance, a progressive lowering of the benefit level was considered quite reasonable.[60]

If the advice of the SER had led to an immediate follow-up, then a reformed invalidity insurance scheme could have been operating before the end of the decade. Yet, as with the proposals of the second Van Rhijn Committee almost a decade before, there was no such immediate action. This time the reason for the delay was that the generosity of the SER's plan created doubts about the need to retain separate invalidity and industrial injuries schemes. If the invalidity scheme offered benefit levels equal to those of the industrial injuries scheme,

---

[58] On the need to accept pay-as-you-go financing for the industrial injuries scheme as well, see ARA, CSWV, 2.19.103.06: Verslag van de vergadering van de sociale kring, 12 Juni 1963.

[59] This alone cannot explain why they were willing to go along with the creation of four disability levels instead of two, as was the case in most countries, however. There was indeed some fear on the side of employers over whether or not so generous a solution for the partially disabled would be too costly. The fact that medical specialists advised this was the eventual decisive factor. There seems to have been a strong belief that good medical specialists would ensure that the costs would not get out of hand. ARA, CSWV, 2.19.103.145: Verslag Vergadering Kleine Technische Commissie Sociale Verzekering, 17 Januari 1955; ibidem, 22 April 1955; Verslag Vergadering Kring voor Sociaal Overleg, 17 September 1959.

[60] ARA, CSWV, 2.19.103.06, 145: Verslag Vergadering Kleine Technische Commissie Sociale Verzekering, 7 Februari 1955.

an increasing group of employer, union, and state representatives wondered, then why not merge them into a single disability insurance program?

In preparing their advice, the members of the SER had already given serious thought to the option of merging the invalidity and industrial injuries schemes into a single disability insurance program. They decided in the end that they, the SER, would offer no official opinion on such a merger. Two of the reasons for this have already been mentioned. First, there was still some fear in both union and employer circles over the costs of such a merger. Second, and related to this, they agreed that the creation of a single disability insurance program for all long-term disabled workers conflicted with the still very popular notion of the industrial preference.[61] Of course, the SER's generous plan for the invalidity scheme was also expensive; moreover, it surely conflicted with the notion of the industrial preference. This makes it quite unlikely that these two considerations were decisive. Much more important probably was the desire to achieve rapid progress for existing invalidity insurance claimants. The union federations in particular emphasized that the introduction of a single insurance plan for all the long-term disabled raised many issues, and arranging it therefore would be a lengthy affair.[62]

Not all union and employer representatives to the SER agreed with its decision to focus only on reform of the existing invalidity insurance scheme, disregarding the possibility of a merger between the industrial injuries and invalidity insurance plans. From the moment that the union and employer federations turned their attention to the issue of disability insurance reform in 1954, there were those who argued that the SER should advise merging the invalidity and industrial injuries schemes into a single disability insurance program. Some of them stressed that such an outcome was desirable; others stressed that it simply made sense. A good example of the former was Jan Mulder, secretary of the largest employer federation at the time, the CSWV. In a meeting of the CSWV's Social Insurance Committee in October 1954, Mulder said that he had "serious objections to ... combining an industrial injuries scheme with high benefits and an invalidity insurance program with lower benefits." When other members of the CSWV interpreted this as a plea for the creation of a single insurance program for all disabled workers regardless of cause, he did not deny this.[63] A good example of the view that a merger between the two schemes just made sense came three months later when another member of the CSWV's Social Insurance Committee stated that he saw no reason to oppose a merger of the

---

[61] ARA, CSWV, 2.19.103.06, 145: Verslag Vergadering Kleine Technische Commissie Sociale Verzekering, 11 October 1954.

[62] IISG, NVV, Codelijsten Commissiearchief 1946–74, 318, Stukken socialecie 1954–56: Nota inzake enkele vraagpunten betreffende de toekomstige Invaliditeitsverzekering, 13 Augustus 1954; IISG, CNV, Commissie Sociale Verzekeringen, 64, GI, Raam voor een ontwerp-advies inzake de herziening van de invaliditeitsverzekering, geen datum.

[63] ARA, CSWV, 2.19.103.06, 145: Verslag Vergadering Kleine Technische Commissie Sociale Verzekering, 11 Oktober 1954.

invalidity and industrial injuries schemes if they would eventually offer the same benefit levels anyway.[64] In subsequent months, other employer representatives repeatedly voiced their approval for a merger of the invalidity and industrial injuries schemes into a single disability insurance program.[65]

It is difficult to pinpoint exactly when the union and employer federations committed themselves to the creation of a single disability insurance scheme for all the long-term disabled. The records of union and employer federations' social insurance committees from both the run-up to and the aftermath of the SER's statement give the impression that the employer federations displayed a willingness to do so somewhat before their union counterparts did. The reason for this may have been that union leaders were more fearful that the creation of a single disability insurance scheme would be a complicated, and therefore lengthy, affair. Since the goal of rapid progress on existing invalidity insurance claims was less important to employers, this consideration simply did not receive much attention in employer circles. For employers, all that mattered was that the invalidity and industrial injuries schemes had come to resemble each other closely, which lent appeal to the administratively cheaper solution of merging both schemes into a single disability insurance program.[66]

The latter argument of expediency eventually proved decisive for both the union and employer federations. In March 1958, the Sociale Verzekeringsraad (SVR, Social Insurance Council, which dealt with technical issues regarding social security) released advice in which it argued for a merger of the invalidity, industrial injuries, *and* sickness insurance schemes into a single disability insurance program.[67] Although the task of this council had been to advise the Minister of Social Affairs on a technical issue related to operation of the

---

[64] ARA, CSWV, 2.19.103.06, 145: Verslag Vergadering Kleine Technische Commissie Sociale Verzekering, 17 Januari 1955.

[65] ARA, CSWV, 2.19.103.06, Verslag Vergadering Kleine Technische Commissie Sociale Verzekering, 7 Februari 1955; ARA, CSWV, 2.19.103.06, 145: Verslag Vergadering Kleine Technische Commissie Sociale Verzekering, 22 April 1955.

[66] This resemblance was not only the result of the SER's advice on reform of the state invalidity insurance program. During contemporaneous discussions on a reform of the industrial injuries scheme, it had become clear that the employer federations were not able to prevent the introduction of a uniform contribution level for all companies. Hitherto, contribution levels differed depending on a company's risk incidence. As far as the employer federations were concerned, this undermined the whole idea of the *"risque professional,"* thus taking away an important reason to distinguish between different causes of disability. ARA, CSWV, 2.19.103.06, 146: Verslag Vergadering Kleine Technische Commissie Sociale Verzekering, 24 Februari 1958.

[67] Whereas the SER focused on sociopolitical aspects of social security, the functions of the Social Insurance Council were to supervise and to advise on technical social insurance issues. As with the SER, union federations, employer federations, and the government appointed one-third each of the Social Insurance Council members. For an overview of the events leading up to the creation of the Social Insurance Council, see P. G. T. van Griensven, "Sociale Zaken: spanning tussen het sociaal wenselijke en het economisch mogelijke." In J. J. M. Ramakers, *Parlementaire geschiedenis van Nederland na 1945: Het kabinet-Drees II (1951–1952); In de schaduw van de Koreacrisis* (Nijmegen: SSN, 1997); and Cox, *The Development of the Dutch Welfare State.*

industrial injuries scheme, its union, employer, and state members had felt that they could not abstain from tackling the more important issue of the future relationship between the industrial injuries scheme and the invalidity and sickness schemes.[68] In its advice, the SVR acknowledged that some remaining differences between the future invalidity scheme and the industrial injuries scheme would complicate efforts to merge them, but it stressed that none of these differences was insurmountable.[69] Two years later, the SER also voiced its support for the creation of a single disability insurance program. The SER's statement differed from the earlier SVR's statement only in that the former wanted the disability insurance program to cater only to the long-term disabled. All short-term disabled workers would first receive a benefit from a separate (but greatly improved) sickness insurance program.[70]

To ensure that the introduction of a single disability insurance program did not impede their goal of rapid progress on existing invalidity benefit claims, the union federations pressed for the introduction of a temporary supplement to the invalidity benefit. The Interimwet Invaliditeitsrentetrekkers (Temporary Act for Invalidity Beneficiaries) that granted this supplement came into operation in 1962 and operated for five years. Like the later WAO, it created a benefit equal to 80 percent of the previous wage for a fully disabled worker with an average wage and an even higher level for fully disabled workers in the lowest income brackets. In contrast to the WAO, however, it only entitled a worker to benefits if he or she had contributed to the invalidity insurance program for

For an overview of the council's functioning, see Johanens Th. J. van den Berg, Max G. Rood, and Teun Jaspers, *De SVr 40 jaar: einde van een tijdperk, een nieuw begin?* (Deventer: Kluwer, 1992).

[68] This technical issue related to the question of how transfer of implementation of the industrial injuries scheme to the newly created industrial insurance boards should be arranged. For the council's actual advice, see Sociale Verzekeringsraad, "Interimadvies overdracht uitvoering ongevallenverzekeringen aan de bedrijfsverzekeringen van 3 Oktober 1958." In Sociale Verzekeringsraad, *Advies inzake een arbeidsongeschiktheidsvereniging* (Den Haag: SVR, 1960).

[69] Among the issues mentioned were how to deal with differences in (1) partial disability levels (the revised invalidity scheme would have four disability levels; the industrial injuries schemes had twenty), (2) coverage levels (the industrial injuries scheme had a somewhat different definition of the term "worker"), (3) financing (employers were allowed to deduct half their invalidity insurance premium; they were not allowed to do the same with their industrial injuries premium), and (4) provision for medical treatment (the invalidity insurance scheme provided for this; the industrial injuries scheme did not). See Sociale Verzekeringsraad, *Advies inzake*, 79–92.

[70] There are two main reasons why the SER wanted to retain a separate sickness insurance scheme. First, all parties agreed that the sickness insurance contribution levels should differ among industries. As we will see later, both the union and employer federations were divided over whether the new disability insurance scheme should have uniform or different contribution levels across industries. Second, they both wanted to retain a wage limit for participation in the sickness insurance scheme. They did not want to retain a wage limit in the new disability insurance program. For both reasons, see ARA, CSWV, 2.19.103.06, 145: Verslag Vergadering Kleine Technische Commissie Sociale Verzekering, 22 April 1955.

at least a year and the disability impaired at least two-thirds of the worker's work capacity.[71]

With their prediction that the merger of the invalidity and industrial injuries insurance schemes into a single disability insurance program would be a lengthy affair, the union federations had been quite right. It would take until 1967 before the new disability insurance program, accompanied by a reformed sickness insurance scheme, came into operation. Hesitation over the creation of a single disability insurance scheme as opposed to reforming existing schemes, outstanding differences between the invalidity and industrial injuries schemes, and other issues, including questions over the exact role of the future Gemeenschappelijke Medische Dienst (GMD, Common Medical Service) together delayed decision making for several years.[72] This delay, however, did not work to the detriment of the future scheme's generosity. While in 1957 the SER had thought 70 percent of the previous wage to suffice for the full benefit level, this was later raised to 80 percent. The coming years also saw the addition of a minimum benefit level for those fully disabled workers whose benefit was lower than the recently introduced minimum wage. Furthermore, the new disability insurance plan was to have no wage limit (all existing insurance plans against disability did) and as many as eight disability levels, and entitlement to a disability benefit was to commence with the beginning of employment.

It is important to emphasize here that as with the recommendations of the second Van Rhijn Committee and the SER's advice of 1957, these generous features cannot be understood as the outcome of a victory of "labor" over "capital." They rather testify that the Dutch employer federations were very willing to accept generous outcomes for public insurance for the financial consequences of disability. When the chairman of the CSWV's Social Insurance Committee asked for committee members' opinions on the union demand to set the maximum benefit level at 80 percent of the previous wage, he found that they did not object to this. All members agreed that a benefit level of 70 percent of the previous wage was simply insufficient for a fully disabled worker.[73]

---

[71] For details of the act, see W. van Uden, "Interim-regeling voor invaliditeitsrentetrekkers," *Sociale Zorg* 24 (1962), 405–9.

[72] The latter issue in particular proved quite divisive, with the confessional/nonconfessional cleavage proving almost as important as the cleavage between union and employer federations. The KAB and CNV, for example, shared many employers' aversion to a centralized medical service. Some within the CSWV, on the other hand, preferred a centralized service. ARA, CSWV, 2.19.103.06, 146: Verslag van de vergadering van de Technische Commissie Sociale Verzekering gehouden op woensdag, 9 Oktober 1956, des voormiddags om 10 uur ten kantore van de Vereniging van Tricot- en Kousenfabrikanten te Utrecht; ARA, CSWV, 2.19.103.06, 146: Verslag van de vergadering van de Technische Commissie Sociale Verzekering, gehouden op, 3 April 1959, te 's-Gravenhage.

[73] ARA, CSWV, 2.19.103.06, 132: Verslag Vergadering Kring voor Sociaal Overleg, 30 Januari 1958; ARA, CSWV, 2.19.103.06, 145, Verslag Vergadering Kleine Technische Commissie Sociale Verzekering, 22 April 1955. Also important was that the sickness insurance scheme itself offered 80 percent of the previous wage.

The employer federations also could accept the abolition of entitlement conditions and the wage limit. In fact, they had already considered supporting abolition of the wage limit in discussions over the 1957 statement pushing reform of the invalidity insurance scheme. The argument against the wage limit had then been that higher-paid workers also needed protection against non-work-related disability, which made voluntary insurance insufficient for them.[74]

The employer federations were a bit more hesitant to lend their support to the decision to create eight different disability levels. In previous discussions over reform of the invalidity insurance scheme, they had already expressed concerns over a system with four disability levels. At the time, medical specialists had judged that a gradation into four disability levels was the maximal level of refinement that could be achieved for insuring non-work-related disabilities.[75] Now the union federations wanted to expand four disability levels to eight. Despite their hesitation, however, the employer federations were eventually willing to consent to this. Of much importance in this was that the industrial injuries insurance scheme contained as many as twenty disability levels. Moreover, employers seem to have held a sincere (but as we will see in Chapter 6, quite naive) belief that further refinement of invalidity levels would help to keep more disabled workers at work.[76]

The employer federations were even more hesitant to accept the introduction of a minimum benefit level into the disability insurance program. Not only did they dislike the redistributive consequences of this, but they also regarded it as unnecessary and costly.[77] Because it applied only to persons who were expected to remain outside employment for a long period, employers eventually could agree to the introduction of a minimum benefit level into the disability insurance program.[78] But the employer federations vehemently opposed its introduction into the sickness insurance program. As we saw in Chapter 4, they managed to stall its introduction there for roughly five more years – also because the union federations were at least for the moment quite content with a clause in the 1966 Ziektewet that entitled unions and employer who were responsible for its operation to grant a supplement to the state benefit. In practice, this meant that the sickness benefit level of 80 percent of the previous wage was only a minimum norm.

[74] ARA, CSWV, 2.19.103.06, 145: Verslag Vergadering Kleine Technische Commissie Sociale Verzekering, 22 April 1955.
[75] The main problem here was that the exact level of a non-work-related disability was often far more difficult to determine. For the opinion of medical specialists, see VU, VPCW, 155: Ontwerp-advies inzake de herziening van de invaliditeitsverzekering, 7 December 1956.
[76] ARA, CSWV, 2.19.103.06, 146: Kort Verslag Vergadering Technische Commissie Sociale Verzekering, 21 Mei 1958.
[77] ARA, CSWV, 2.19.103.06, 140: Verslag van de vergadering van de Commissie Sociale Verzekering van het CSWV op, 14 December 1965, ten kantore Kneuterdijk 8, 's-Gravenhage. (26)
[78] See SER, *Advies inzake de invoering van een minimumdagloon*, 10.

The employer federations were most unwilling to give in to union demands on one final issue. In the years leading up to the 1966 disability insurance reform, employer and union federations were completely at odds over the issue of whether or not contribution levels should differ among industries. This issue had already led to much discussion during the preparation of the SER's 1957 advisory statement on reform of the invalidity insurance scheme. Whereas the employer federations had emphasized the importance of adhering to actuarial principles, which together with the industry-based implementation of the invalidity insurance plan demanded premium differentiation between industries, the union federations argued for solidarity among industries.[79] At the time, the employer federations had been willing to yield because of the non-work-related character of the invalidity insurance plan; thus the SER's 1957 statement expressed unanimous support for uniform contribution levels across industries. The employer federations were much less willing to give in, however, on the new disability insurance scheme. Because the new disability insurance scheme was to cover work-related disabilities as well, they were far more adamant that contribution levels reflect actual business risks. Only when contribution levels were allowed to differ among them, the employer federations argued, would industries be motivated to keep contribution levels as low as possible.[80] The union federations, on the other hand, supported uniform contribution levels because they felt that it would be unfair if a worker paid higher contribution levels only because he or she worked in a more dangerous industry.[81]

The union and employer representatives to the SER eventually reached a compromise agreement in which the costs of a disability benefit would be shared equally among industries only after the benefit had been handed out for at least two years. Both sides agreed that the contribution levels of the reformed sickness insurance scheme differ among industries. Because they also agreed to reduce the duration of the sickness benefit from one year to six months, the result was that industries would themselves be responsible for bearing the costs of the first two-and-a-half years of a worker's disability, whereas the costs of longer-term disabilities would be shared among them.[82]

---

[79] Reflecting its confessional emphasis on the importance of adhering to actuarial principles, the CNV was a bit more hesitant about this than the NVV. During internal discussions, the CNV expressed its willingness to support the NVV's plea for uniform contribution levels across industries only if the opportunity for premium differentiation would be granted and if the invalidity insurance scheme were part of a broader disability insurance scheme, also encompassing the sickness and industrial injuries schemes. IISG, Codelijsten NVV-Commissiearchief 1945–1967, 318: NVV Socialecie 1954–1956: Notitie voor de leden van het Dagelijks Bestuur inzake de Invaliditeitsverzekering, 9 April 1956.

[80] ARA, CSWV, 2.19.103.06, 146: Verslag Vergadering Technische Commissie Sociale Verzekering, 20 Mei 1959;

[81] VNO, Arbeidsongeschiktheidsregelingen, F5(6): Nota Raad van Bestuur in Arbeidszaken, 30 December 1963.

[82] Two reasons were given for the decision to reduce the duration of the sickness benefit from one year to six months. First, this made it possible to grant partial benefits at an earlier stage (the

The employer federations were quite content with this outcome because this initial period covered "ninety-eight to ninety-nine percent" of all disability costs.[83] Unfortunately for them, Parliament, on the insistence of Minister of Social Affairs Gerard Veldkamp, did not adopt this compromise. The new disability insurance program would have uniform contribution levels across industries from the start. To pacify employer federations, Parliament decided to set the duration of the sickness benefit at one year.

Parliament did adopt all other recommendations of the SER. It had merely decided against the contributions compromise because it deemed it too administratively complex. Nevertheless, the employer federations were furious. In the years after the creation of the new disability insurance program, their insistence on the introduction of premium differentiation into the plan only increased. As we will see in Chapter 6, they had good reasons for this insistence.

THE GENERAL DISABILITY ACT AND INCLUSION OF THE SELF-EMPLOYED

With the introduction of the 1966 Ziektewet and WAO, the problem of poverty in disability all but completely disappeared from the Netherlands. Those groups for whom state provision had previously been quite inadequate, including workers who incurred injuries off the job, the partially disabled, and workers in lower-income brackets, now all received more-than-adequate treatment. There was only one group left for whom disability still posed the prospect of financial ruin: the self-employed. However generous the 1966 Ziektewet and WAO were in other respects, they only covered employed workers. It would take another full decade before a separate state disability insurance program for the self-employed came into operation. Until then, the only benefit that the self-employed could fall back on if their disabilities resulted in loss of income was means-tested social assistance.

Several factors accounted for the long delay in establishing disability insurance coverage for the self-employed. The first involved the classical argument that the element of force that accompanied a compulsory insurance program would be felt more sharply by the self-employed than by other workers. This argument carried great weight in all social insurance arenas – after all, there had only been a consensus on inclusion of the self-employed in the public old age pension scheme because the problem of poverty in old age was so pressing for this group. Yet this argument against inclusion was deemed extra important concerning the risk of disability because disability did not always result

sickness insurance scheme did not hand out partial benefits). Second, those disabled who were not covered by the sickness insurance scheme (meaning: higher-paid workers) would thus be able to enjoy a benefit at an earlier stage. ARA, 2.06.064, 628: Advies over een arbeidsongeschiktheidsverzekering, 9 December 1960.

[83] ARA, CSWV, 2.19.103.06, 132: Verslag Vergadering Kring voor Sociaal Overleg, 29 Mei 1959.

in a loss of income for the self-employed. An additional problem here was that the self-employed formed a very diverse group, comprising agricultural laborers, entrepreneurs of small- and midscale businesses, and practitioners of the so-called free occupations. For agricultural laborers, disability nearly always resulted in a loss of income. For entrepreneurs and practitioners of the free occupations, however, this was not always the case. Thus, whereas the former were quite eager to see the introduction of a compulsory insurance program (and preferably one in which they could share their risk with employed workers or other self-employed categories less prone to the risk of disability), the latter two categories were not so eager to see its introduction. As late as 1963, official hearings with representatives of small- and middle-scale businesses generated only haphazard support for the introduction of a disability insurance program for this group. The representatives of the free occupations even stated their own complete disinterest in it.[84]

Another important reason for the delay was that the establishment of disability insurance for the self-employed raised many difficult questions about such a scheme's financing, implementation and relationship to the disability insurance scheme for workers. The last issue in particular delayed progress for many years. After the SER turned its attention in the mid-1950s to disability insurance reform, several successive governments voiced a preference for an insurance scheme that included both workers and the self-employed. The union and employer federations, as well as representatives of the self-employed, however, strongly opposed this. This was so because workers and the self-employed had different disability insurance preferences. Whereas the former desired, for instance, earnings-related benefits, the latter preferred the less-expensive alternative of flat-rate benefits.[85] The self-employed who were eager to be covered by a state disability insurance scheme, meanwhile, were forced to wait in the wings when the government (temporarily) shelved its plans for the creation of universal insurance program. For the government, the union federations, and the employer federations, disability insurance for employed workers simply came first.

After introduction of the 1966 Ziektewet and WAO, it still took more than a full decade before the self-employed also were covered by a disability insurance program. The complete indifference of the union and employer federations to extending coverage to the self-employed certainly contributed to this long delay. In the early 1970s, for example, the union federations proposed delaying the introduction of the Algemene Arbeidsongeschiktheidswet (AAW, General Disability Act), which had been scheduled for 1972, by several years because they considered other social security initiatives to be more important.

[84] VU, VPCW, 21: Notitie inzake de arbeidsongeschiktheidsverzekering voor zelfstandigen, geen datum; ARA, CSWV, 2.19.103.06, 139: Verslag Commissie Sociale Verzekering, 9 Mei 1963.
[85] VNO, F119(4) Cie Sociale Verzekering RCO 1947–1970: Verslag Vergadering Commissie Sociale Verzekering van de Raad van Bestuur in Arbeidszaken, 12 Juli 1963.

Just before the act's eventual introduction, the employer federations thought about doing the same.[86] It is quite likely that the latter did so at least partly from their dissatisfaction with one redistributive feature of the act: like the AOW, the AAW entitled the self-employed to a flat-rate benefit in exchange for earnings-related premiums that were bound to a certain maximum level. In the years leading up to the act's introduction, the employer federations had voiced strong disapproval of this feature.[87]

The AAW came into operation in 1976. The act entitled the self-employed to a flat-rate benefit if the disability lasted for more than fifty-two weeks (the act covered only long-term disability) and the disablement exceeded more than 25 percent of their earnings capacity.[88] The level of the benefit was set at the same level as the minimum benefit level of the disability insurance scheme for workers. The introduction of the AAW ended a long period of discussion over improving the state disability insurance system and, with that, the social security system as a whole.

[86] VNO, F118(21) Cie Sociale Zekerheid VNO: Verslag Vergadering Commissie Sociale Verzekering, 7 April 1976.
[87] VNO, F118(24): Verslagen Sociale Raad VNO: Verslag Vergadering Sociale Raad, 6 Mei 1971.
[88] The WAO granted a benefit to a worker when he or she was at least 15 percent disabled. The employer federations had pressed for this higher minimum disability level for the AAW. They had tried, but failed, to increase the higher minimum disability level for the worker's insurance program as well. VNO, F118(21) Cie Sociale Zekerheid VNO: Verslag Vergadering Commissie Sociale Verzekering, 7 Januari 1971.

6

Union Solidarity and the Use of Social Security for Early Retirement Purposes in the Netherlands

The preceding three chapters examined the development of state insurance for dependency stemming from old age, unemployment, and disability in roughly the first three decades of the postwar period. By the end of this period, most ambitious reforms of the British and Dutch social security systems had been carried through, albeit with quite varying degrees of success. From the 1970s on, the focus of policy makers in both countries slowly shifted from improving the social protection net to stabilizing its costs. Efforts to improve state protection from economic misfortune in the labor market now focused on one group in particular: elderly workers who had not yet reached the retirement age. With the return of mass unemployment in the 1970s and 1980s, elderly workers became a particularly vulnerable group, and both countries responded to this with measures that – either intentionally or unintentionally – encouraged the withdrawal of older workers from the labor market. They did so in quite different ways and consequently to quite different degrees, though. In the Netherlands, elderly workers withdrew from the labor market to such a great extent that by the mid-1990s, fewer than 15 percent of men worked until the official retirement age of sixty-five years.[1] In the United Kingdom, elderly workers left the labor market to a more limited degree. There, in the mid-1990s, about 30 percent of men were still at work by the age of sixty-four.[2]

The mass withdrawal of elderly workers from the labor market in the Netherlands was facilitated by three very generous institutional arrangements that are known in the literature as *early-exit pathways*. These exit pathways both allowed workers to retire early on generous terms and made it easier

---

[1] See Willem Trommel, *Korter arbeidsleven: de wording van een rationele mythe. Loopbaan, arbeidsmarkt en verzorgingsstaat in neo-institutioneel perspectief* (Den Haag: Sdu, 1995), 3.

[2] See Richard Blundell and Paul Johnson, "Pensions and Labor Market Participation in the United Kingdom," *American Economic Review* 88:2 (1998), 168.

for employers to release them. In this chapter, I look at the development of these three early-exit pathways. In the fourth and final part of this chapter, I analyze the introduction of industry-wide early retirement schemes (called Vervroegde Uittreding [VUT]) in the early 1980s. In the second and third parts of this chapter, I analyze how the state disability and unemployment insurance schemes developed into mass early-exit pathways in, respectively, the early and late 1970s. In the case of the disability insurance program, this development was to a large extent an outcome of the decision to incorporate labor market considerations into the disability assessment. In the case of the unemployment insurance program, it was to a large extent an outcome of the decision to release unemployed workers over a certain age from the obligation to look for work and the decision to extend the duration of the benefit for this group.

These decisions, which transformed the disability and unemployment insurance programs into mass early-exit pathways, are of extra importance to us here because they had two very different consequences. On the one hand, they increased the security of workers from the financial consequences of redundancy. On the other hand, they made it easier for employers to *declare* workers to be redundant. Over the years, this latter consequence has received much attention from scholars, especially from those who have assigned employers a more proactive role in the development of welfare states. Some scholars have even gone so far as to suggest that this labor-shedding consequence was not just an unintended side effect of an expansion of social rights but an actual goal of these measures.[3] In this chapter, I argue strongly against this view. The employer practice of labor shedding through the state disability and unemployment insurance schemes was nothing more than an unintended side effect of measures aimed at improving the security of workers from the financial consequences of redundancy. While the Dutch union federations had demanded the introduction of these measures for social reasons, their employer counterparts had been quite hesitant to accept them, especially because they feared that firms would use these measures to restructure at the expense of other companies and of society at large. Similarly, introduction of the industry-wide early retirement schemes in the early 1980s was greeted with much enthusiasm by the labor union movement – and with great reluctance by the employer community.

In the United Kingdom, lower benefit levels and stricter entitlement rules prevented social security schemes from developing into early-exit schemes on a large scale. The United Kingdom also did not experience the introduction of state- or industry-wide early retirement schemes that could have provided workers of all income ranges with the ability to retire early in a voluntary manner. As a result, older British workers left the labor market to a much smaller extent than did their Dutch counterparts. In the following section I describe how this fits into the arguments set forth in previous chapters.

---

[3] See, for example, Mares, "Enterprise Reorganization"; Mares, *The Politics of Social Risk*, 213–46; Hall and Soskice, *Varieties of Capitalism*, 50; and Ebbinghaus, *Reforming Early Retirement*.

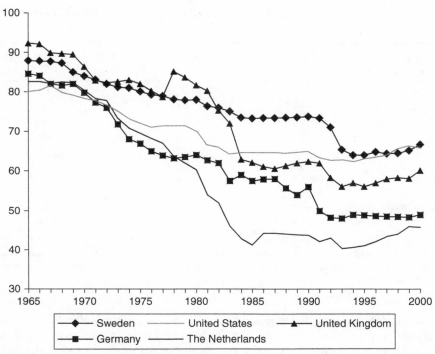

FIGURE 6.1. Labor Force Participation Rate of Men Aged Fifty-Five to Sixty-Four in Various Countries (in percent). (*Sources:* OECD, *Labour Force Statistics.* Paris: OECD, various years. Calculations by author.)

EXPLAINING THE EXTRAORDINARY EXIT OF ELDERLY WORKERS FROM THE DUTCH LABOR MARKET

When the golden years of high economic growth and low unemployment ended in the 1970s, all industrial economies experienced a sharp drop in the participation rate of the elderly in the labor market. In some economies, however, older workers withdrew from the labor market to a much greater extent than in others. Figure 6.1 shows the extent to which the labor force participation rate of men over age fifty-five declined in four European countries and the United States between 1965 and 2000. The figure shows that the decline started in the late 1960s and accelerated rapidly from the mid-1970s on. More important to us here, the figure shows that the withdrawal of the elderly from the labor market was most pronounced in the Netherlands, whereas the United Kingdom experienced a much more modest decline. The labor force participation rate of male older workers remained relatively high in the United Kingdom until the late 1970s, after which it dropped rapidly, to just under the level of the United States, but far above that of Germany and the Netherlands.

TABLE 6.1. *Composition of the Labor Force of Older Men in Various Countries, 1989*

Country	Age	Labor Force Participation Rate (%)	Part-Time Work Rate (%)
Sweden	60–64	62.7	30.7
	55–59	87.1	6.5
USA	60–64	54.2	18.8
	55–59	78.8	10.7
UK	60–64	53.5	8.1
	55–59	77.4	2.9
Germany	60–64	34.2	3.9
	55–59	78.6	1.4
The Netherlands	60–64	24.5	25.9
	55–59	65.3	15.2

Source: Klaus Jacobs and Martin Rein, "Early Retirement: Stability, Reversal, or Redefinition." In Frieder Naschold and Bert de Vroom, *Regulating Employment and Welfare. Company and National Policies of Labour Force Participation at the End of Worklife in Industrial Countries* (Berlin: Walter de Gruyter, 1994), 29.

The low labor market participation of older men in the Netherlands becomes even more pronounced when we note the high rate of part-time work for this group. Table 6.1 breaks the labor force participation rates of men in the five countries down into age groups of sixty to sixty-four and fifty-five to fifty-nine in a given year and adds to this the part-time work rate for these groups. The figure shows that the Netherlands in 1989 not only had the lowest participation rate for both age ranges but also had one of the highest part-time work rates. Of the roughly 25 percent of men who were still in the workforce between the ages of sixty and sixty-four, a further 26 percent only worked part time. Of the roughly 65 percent of men who belonged to the workforce between the ages of fifty-five and fifty-nine, some 15 percent worked part time. In the United Kingdom, in contrast, part-time work remained a rare phenomenon among older male workers. There, only about 8 percent of men who were still in the workforce between the ages of sixty and sixty-four worked part time. Of those men who were still in the work force between the ages of fifty-five and fifty-nine, only about 3 percent worked part time.

To be sure, the high part-time work rate among older workers in Sweden partly accounts for the high employment rate of older workers there. More than in other countries, older workers in Sweden did not leave the workforce entirely but continued to work part time until they reached the official pension age. Whereas a Dutch or German worker, for example, often drew a five-year partial pension, under which he or she received five years of part-time pay but actually worked full time during the first two-and-a-half years and then retired completely from the company, Swedish workers continued to work throughout the entire five years. Another important reason for the exceptionally high labor force participation rate of older workers in Sweden lay in the presence of labor market reintegration programs, including sheltered jobs and subsidized employment, for this group.[4]

Why did elderly male workers withdraw from the labor market to a vastly greater extent in the Netherlands than in other countries? Why did their counterparts in the United Kingdom do so to a much more modest degree? Apart from the near-nonexistence of Swedish-style labor market reintegration programs in the United Kingdom and the Netherlands, these questions can be answered by looking at the degree to which social security and other arrangements in the countries facilitated the early exit of workers.[5] To understand this, it is necessary to distinguish between "pull" factors, which refer to the effects generous arrangements have on the ability and willingness of workers to withdraw from the labor market, and "push" factors, which refer to the effect generous arrangements have on employer practices regarding layoffs. Let us explore these factors.

Imagine a situation in which an older male manual worker is about to lose his job due to redundancy in, say, the early 1980s. If this worker lived in the Netherlands, then he was entitled to an unemployment benefit of at least 75 percent of his previous wage for a period of at least two-and-a-half years. If he was older than fifty-seven and a half, legislation passed in 1976 allowed him to draw this benefit until he reached the official retirement age without having to look for a new job. If he was somewhat younger but suffered from a minor disability, incorporation of a labor market consideration article in the Wet op Arbeidsongeschiktheidsverzekering (WAO, Act on Disability Insurance) meant that he could draw a full disability benefit (which equaled at least 80 percent of the previous wage) until he reached the official retirement age. In other words, if our older worker became unemployed in the Netherlands, he stood a very good chance of being able to retire early on quite generous terms. Things were quite different, however, if he lived in the United Kingdom. There, our older worker most likely could look forward to a state unemployment benefit that equaled some 30 percent of the average wage and to several weeks of

---

[4] See Gunnar Olofsson and Jan Petersson, "Sweden: Policy Dilemmas of the Changing Age Structure in a 'Work Society.'" In Frieder Naschold and Bert de Vroom, *Regulating Employment and Welfare: Company and National Policies of Labour Force Participation at the End of Worklife in Industrial Countries* (Berlin: Walter de Gruyter, 1994); Anne-Marie Guillemard and Martin Stein, "Comparative Patterns of Retirement: Recent Trends in Developed Societies," *Annual Review of Sociology* 19 (1993), 481.

[5] Up to the early 1980s, many older unemployed workers did benefit from specific reemployment measures realized in the 1970s. A good example of such a measure was the "30 percent wage subsidy regulation," which subsidized the labor costs of the unemployed who had a poor employment outlook due to age. This subsidy was abolished in 1981. See Willem Trommel and Bert De Vroom, "The Netherlands: The Loreley Effect of Early Exit." In Naschold and De Vroom, *Regulating Employment and Welfare*, 58–9.

severance pay. Together these benefits were seldom enough to end his reliance on the labor market. And even if he were content with this combined income (which could be the case if he either had previously earned very low wages or was able to supplement the state benefit with generous private supplements), he still could not retire early on an unemployment benefit because the duration of this benefit was much shorter than in the Netherlands, and he did have the obligation to continue to look for a new job.

Of course, there were some alternatives to drawing an unemployment benefit. If our worker belonged to a private occupational pension fund, then he could decide to draw his private pension early – especially if his employer was prepared to make him a good offer. Yet not many British manual workers had access to private pension savings, and even fewer could afford to draw from these early. From 1977 on, it also would have been possible for our worker to receive a flat-rate early retirement pension from the so-called job-release scheme if he were close to reaching the official retirement age and provided that his employer was willing to recruit a replacement from the employment register. However, even if his employer were willing to do so, the chances of our manual worker actually drawing such a benefit were slim: at between one-fourth and one-third of the previous wage, the level of the benefit was so low that it could replace earnings only for the lowest-income workers.[6] Finally, our manual worker also could end up on social assistance. Between 1981 and 1983, a Conservative government freed all income support recipients over the age of sixty from the obligation to register as unemployed, with the exception of those who received a partial income support benefit as a supplement to an unemployment benefit. It also granted them automatic access to the "long-term rate" of income support, which was 25 percent higher than the normal rate.[7]

In sum, if our older male manual worker became redundant in the United Kingdom, then there was a large chance that he simply could not afford to retire early. In a poll taken in the late 1980s, Westergaard, Noble, and Walker showed that among British male workers who became redundant over the age of sixty, almost 40 percent were actively in search of work immediately after losing their job, whereas only about 35 percent withdrew from the labor market completely. Among the rest, some 12 percent were unemployed and not actively seeking

---

[6] The scheme first applied only to workers who were within one year of reaching the official retirement age. Although the minimum entry age was lowered in consecutive years, the scheme never became popular. Between 1977 and 1983 (when the scheme was made voluntary), only 195,000 workers participated. See Frank Laczko and Chris Phillipson, "Great Britain: The Contradictions of Early Exit." In Martin Kohli, Herman van Gunsteren, and Anne-Marie Guillemard, *Time for Retirement: Comparative Studies of Early Exit from the Labor Force* (Cambridge University Press, 1991), 50.

[7] See Bernard Casey and Stephen Wood, "Great Britain: Firm Policy, State Policy and the Employment of Older Workers." In Naschold and De Vroom, *Regulating Employment*, 379. See John Westergaard, Ian Noble, and Alan Walker, *After Redundancy: The Experience of Economic Insecurity* (Cambridge: Polity Press, 1989).

work, 7 percent were on a sickness or injury benefit,[8] and another 6 percent had found new part-time or full-time work.[9] No such surveys were taken in the Netherlands because all redundant workers of this age group could retire there on a benefit of at least 75 percent of their previous wages.

There is little doubt that the more generous nature of social security arrangements in the Netherlands provided redundant older workers there with a more comfortable level of protection from the financial consequences of redundancy than their British counterparts could enjoy. At the same time, however, the generous nature of social security arrangements in the Netherlands also *increased* the number of redundancies there. The reason for this is that the very existence of generous social security arrangements made employers less reluctant to declare workers redundant. After all, when generous benefits can buy labor union consent for downsizing, and collective funding makes it possible to redistribute the costs of these benefits onto competitors or to society at large, it becomes much easier for employers to release less-productive workers. There is clear evidence that in both the Netherlands and the United Kingdom, social security arrangements have had an impact on employment practices.[10] As a result of the more generous nature of the Dutch social security system, though, this impact was much greater there. I will return to this issue at length in the next two sections of this chapter.

As a result of the combination of these "pull" and "push" factors (which, as we have seen above, often cannot be distinguished from one another), the number of social security recipients in the Netherlands soared all the way from the 1970s up to the first half of the 1990s. The number of social security recipients was highest during the 1980s. Throughout that decade, more than 40 percent of all Dutch male workers aged fifty-five to sixty-four received a disability, sickness, or unemployment benefit. In 1985, at its peak, the number exceeded 50 percent.[11] In comparison, the percentage of British workers aged fifty-five

---

[8] During the 1980s, the number of men aged fifty-five to fifty-nine and sixty to sixty-four who were deemed unable to work because of disability rose by two-thirds and one-half, respectively. Interestingly, most of this increase can be explained by the already-disabled's staying disabled longer – instead of an increase in the number of workers who became disabled. See Casey and Wood, "Great Britain," 365.

[9] See Westergaard, Noble and Walker, *After Redundancy*, 107.

[10] In the case of the United Kingdom, the redundancy payment legislation discussed in Chapter 4 is widely considered to have influenced employment practices. According to Bill Daniel, for example, "managers found that when lump sum payments were available to workers, then many individual workers were not adverse to the idea of redundancy." See Bill Daniel, "The United Kingdom." In Michael Cross, *Managing Workforce Reduction: An International Survey* (London: Croom Helm, 1985), 73. The response to this by successive governments was to make it more costly for firms to call workers redundant by lowering the refund employers received for the redundancy payments they made. The refund was first lowered in 1969 and was abolished completely for all but the smallest firms in 1986.

[11] For a full overview of the magnitude of social security arrangements to withdraw older workers from the workforce in the Netherlands during the 1980s, see Wetenschappelijke Raad voor

to sixty-four who received social security benefits throughout the 1980s never exceeded 19 percent.

One pathway that provided an important "pull" factor (as well as a minor "push" factor, as we will see in the fourth section of this chapter) in the Netherlands has not yet been mentioned here: the early retirement route. Up to the mid-1980s, nearly all workers who retired early in the Netherlands did so through either the unemployment or disability/sickness route. After this period, two developments changed this. First, the number of older workers who received social security benefits first stabilized during the mid-1980s and then dropped sharply from the early 1990s on. This was the result of a series of social security reforms aimed at reducing the inflow into the disability insurance program in particular. Second, an ever-larger group of workers came to retire early through one of the industry-wide early retirement schemes that were the result of collective bargaining. This latter development is of much interest to us here because it meant that more and more workers came to retire early not necessarily because their employer deemed them redundant but rather because they themselves wanted to do so. Table 6.2 illustrates the growing importance of this private exit pathway. By 1992, more male workers aged sixty to sixty-four left the labor market through one of the industrial early retirement schemes than through the disability route.[12] In that year, over 40 percent of all male workers aged sixty to sixty-four received an industrial early retirement pension.

Again, in the United Kingdom, far fewer workers had the opportunity of retiring early voluntarily. In contrast with the Netherlands, the United Kingdom never saw the creation of collectively funded early retirement schemes. As a result, only workers with access to a private pension provision could even consider retiring early – and this was about half the working population. There were, of course, some employers who offered early retirement pensions, but these were often only available to workers with access to private pension savings. This meant that in the United Kingdom, only the more fortunate workers had the option of retiring early by voluntary means.[13] To compare, in 1979, it was estimated that some 80 percent of Dutch employees were covered by collective agreements making provision for some form or other of early retirement.[14]

Regeringsbeleid, *Een Werkend Perspectief. Arbeidsparticipatie in de jaren negentig* (Den Haag: SDU, 1990).

[12] In 1992, 126,800 male workers aged sixty to sixty-four received a disability benefit compared with 148,000 who received an early retirement benefit. See Centraal Bureau voor de Statistiek, *Sociaal-Economische Maandstatistiek* (London: Augustus, 1993), 55, 62.

[13] See Laczko and Phillipson, "Great Britain," 235-7.

[14] See Bernard Casey and Gert Bruche, *Work or Retirement? Labour Market and Social Policy for Older Workers in France, Great Britain, the Netherlands, Sweden and the United States* (Aldershot: Gower, 1981), 126.

TABLE 6.2. *The Use of Different Early Retirement Pathways among Male Workers in the Netherlands, 1980–1992, by Number of Participants as a Percentage of the Age Groups Fifty-Five to Fifty-Nine and Sixty to Sixty-Four*

Year	Disability	Unemployment	Bargaining for Early Exit	Total
Ages 55 to 59				
1980	30.0	0.8		30.8
1984	31.9	7.0		38.9
1988	32.8	5.7		38.5
Ages 60 to 64				
1980	40.5	0.8		41.3
1984	42.3	10.1	16.8	69.2
1988	39.7	9.5	33.3	82.5
1992	37.4	9.1	42.6	89.1

Sources: Willem Trommel and Bert de Vroom, "The Netherlands: The Loreley Effect of Early Exit." In Naschold and De Vroom, *Regulating Employment and Welfare*, 58 for the period 1980–1988. The 1992 data for age group sixty to sixty-four were obtained through the author's calculations based on CBS, *Sociaal-Economische Maandstatistiek* (1993, various months); OECD, *Labor Force Statistics* (Paris: OECD, 1993); and Hendrika Lautenbach and Marc Cuijpers, "Meer ouderen aan het werk," *Sociaal-Economische Trends* (2nd quarter 2005), 13.

To summarize the preceding findings, British workers withdrew from the labor market to a much more moderate degree than did their Dutch counterparts because of the absence of generous (semi-)public early-exit pathways in the United Kingdom. But what, then, explains the absence of such pathways for British workers? To understand this, we need only to revisit the previous chapters of this book. In earlier chapters I illustrated the continued inadequacy of state insurance for old age, disability, and unemployment in the United Kingdom in the 1950s and 1960s. I also explained how this inadequacy resulted from the unwillingness of large sectors of the labor union movement to accept redistribution of income and risk between different categories of workers. The return of high unemployment rates in the 1970s did not suddenly make these labor unions more willing to accept this. As a result, the only major policy response was the introduction of the job-release scheme in 1977, as described earlier. Social security benefits were not improved, there was to be no incorporation of labor market considerations into the invalidity benefit, and the state unemployment insurance program did not adjust to grant special treatment to workers over a certain age. Considering the defeat of nearly every Labour initiative to improve public provision for old age, unemployment, and disability in a redistributive contributory manner one decade earlier, it is hard to imagine how such measures could have been introduced in the United Kingdom. When Labour returned to power after a four-year absence in 1974, it needed all its powers of persuasion to get the Trades Union Congress (TUC) and employer interest groups to accept the State Earnings Related Pension Scheme – Labour's final, watered-down version of superannuation.

In the Netherlands, the situation was dramatically different. There, three decades of successful labor union pressure for solidarity between higher and lower income levels had resulted in a very generous welfare state by the time unemployment again became a major policy concern. When the Dutch labor union movement was faced with the economic woes of the 1970s and 1980s, it reacted by demanding more public protection from the financial consequences of unemployment. As a result, three major early-exit pathways emerged in the Netherlands in the 1970s and 1980s. The following three sections of this chapter analyze the emergence of these pathways. The first section deals with the pathway that has received the most attention from scholars: the disability insurance route.

THE DUTCH DISABILITY INSURANCE PROGRAM AND EXIT FROM THE LABOR MARKET

When then Minister of Social Affairs Gerard Veldkamp presented "his" WAO (Act on Disability Insurance) to Parliament in April 1963, he voiced the expectation that the number of sickness and disability benefit recipients eventually would stabilize at 150,000 to 200,000.[15] In reality, this number was surpassed within three years after the act came into operation. At its peak in the early 1990s, the number of disability benefit recipients in the Netherlands reached almost 1 million – which equated to one in ten Dutch workers of working age.[16] Figure 6.2 shows how exceptionally large the number of disability benefit recipients was in the Netherlands by 1990. While the number of disability benefit recipients was exceptionally large in the Netherlands across all age groups, it was staggeringly high among older workers. For every active labor market participant aged sixty to sixty-four, there were two disability benefit recipients in the same age group. In the United Kingdom, the opposite was the case: active labor market participants outnumbered disability benefit recipients there by two to one. In the United States and Sweden, the ratio of active labor market participants to disability benefit recipients for the age group of sixty to sixty-four lay much closer to the British than to the Dutch pattern. In Germany, the ratio fell almost exactly in between that of the United Kingdom and that of the Netherlands.

This huge increase in the number of Dutch disability benefit recipients after introduction of the WAO cannot be understood without accounting for the

[15] See Willem Velema, "De kroongetuige. Hoe het WAO-drama voorkomen had kunnen worden." In J. G. Hibbeln and Willem Velema, *Het WAO-debacle: De fatale missers van wettenmakers en uitvoerders* (Amsterdam: Van Arkel, 1993), 15.

[16] See Leo Aarts, Richard Burkhauser, and Philip de Jong, *Curing the Dutch Disease: An International Perspective on Disability Policy Reform* (Aldershot: Avebury, 1996), 1.

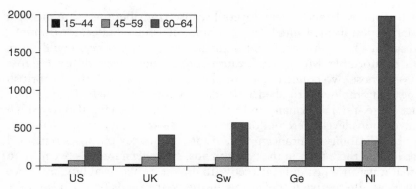

FIGURE 6.2. Disability Benefit Recipients per 1,000 Active Labor Market Participants by Age in Various Countries in 1990. (*Source:* Leo Aarts, Richard Burkhauser, and P. de Jong, "Introduction and Overview." In ibidem, *Curing the Dutch Disease.* Aldershot: Avebury, 1996, 4–5.)

prevalent use of this act to shed redundant workers – a development that was not foreseen by Veldkamp. It has been estimated that up to 1987 (when the insurance program underwent its first major reform), some 50 percent of all disability insurance enrollment was related to worker redundancy.[17] Judging from the preceding graph, this percentage may even be on the conservative side. It is now a well-known fact that almost immediately after its introduction, employers started to make use of the state disability insurance program as an alternative to the costly dismissal route.[18] Labor unions agreed to this because the outcome was so generous for workers (the unemployment benefits lasted only for two-and-a-half years and were granted on the condition that a worker looked for new work; a disability benefit could be granted indefinitely and did not involve the need to look for work). As mass dismissals became more common during the 1970s, use of the state disability insurance program as an alternative to dismissals also became more common. Since most redundant workers who ended up on disability benefits belonged to an older age group, this in practice transformed the insurance program into an early retirement pathway.

But what, then, explains the prevalent use of the public disability insurance program to shed workers in the Netherlands? Why did the same not occur in other countries? Part of the answer to these questions lies in the generosity of the WAO, described at length in Chapter 5. This act's generosity made its use as an alternative to dismissals quite attractive – to workers because of

---

[17] See Wolter Hassing, Jan Van Ours, and Geert Ridder, "Dismissal Through Disability," *De Economist* 145:1 (1997), 29–30.

[18] The disability insurance program was apparently used for this purpose for the first time during the closing of the mines in Limburg. See Frans Messing, *De Nederlandse economie, 1945–1980: Herstel, groei, stagnatie* (Haarlem: Fibula-Van Dishoeck), 230.

its high benefit levels and to employers because contributions were uniform among industries. In the United Kingdom and the United States, for example, lower disability benefits meant that a smaller range of workers could retire on them comfortably. Moreover, because contribution levels differed across industries in those two countries, it would have been less attractive for British and American employers to shed redundant workers through the disability insurance route. Yet, in Germany and Sweden, disability benefits also were high and contributions levels were uniform among industries. Nevertheless, the use of the public disability insurance program for redundancy purposes remained far more limited there than in the Netherlands. To understand this, we have to realize that it was not just quite attractive to use the public disability insurance program as an alternative to dismissals in the Netherlands. It was also quite easy to do so.

The ease with which the public disability insurance program could be used as an alternative to dismissals stemmed from two more or less uniquely Dutch features. First, in the Netherlands, the responsibility for running the disability insurance program lay almost completely with unions and employers – not with the state. The decision on whether or not to award a social security benefit to a claimant was made by industrial insurance boards (*bedrijfsverenigingen*), which consisted of representatives of labor unions and employers in a particular industry. Government supervision of these boards was quite weak due to a number of factors, all rooted in the confessional desire to limit government involvement in the administration of social security as much as possible.[19] Second, the WAO contained a so-called labor market consideration clause (*verdisconteringartikel*) that allowed partially disabled workers to receive a full benefit if their partial disability stood in the way of finding new work.[20] This clause lent itself particularly well to the aim of shedding older workers. Because workers of this age group were rarely able to find new work after losing their jobs, the ensuing administrative practice was that they needed to be only marginally handicapped in order to receive a full benefit. This made it quite easy for employers to release older workers through the disability insurance program simply because minor handicaps were quite common in this age group. As early as 1971, the chairman of the Verbond van Nederlandse Ondernemingen

---

[19] For a lengthy treatment of how this desire shaped the structure of the Dutch social security system, see Van Griensven, "Sociale Zaken"; Doreen Arnoldus, *In goed overleg? Het overleg over de social zekerheid in Nederland vergeleken met België, 1967–1984* (Amsterdam: Aksant, 2007).

[20] While the Swedish and German public insurance programs for non-work-related disability also allowed for the incorporation of labor market considerations, this was only for older workers. In 1970, Sweden introduced a labor market consideration clause in its *förtidspensionering* for workers aged sixty-two and older. It lowered the age limit to sixty in 1976 and abolished the clause completely during the early 1990s. In Germany, court decisions in 1969 and 1976 introduced labor market considerations into the public disability insurance program for older workers.

(VNO, Federation of Dutch Industries) Social Security Committee already noted that larger companies in particular made full use of this opportunity. When the need for dismissals arose, the personnel and medical departments often decided together which employees could be released through the disability insurance program.[21]

According to the conventional literature on Dutch welfare state development, employers could only misuse the labor market consideration clause for labor shedding purposes because industrial insurance boards employed this clause in a way that diverged from its original meaning.[22] At center stage in this claim stands the statement, made by the Federatie van Bedrijfsverenigingen (FvB, Federation of Industrial Councils, the umbrella organization of industrial insurance boards) in 1973, that from then on, industrial insurance boards would assume that poor employment opportunities of partially disabled workers were the result of discrimination unless the opposite could be proven. The conventional literature has described this decision as either a "very broad interpretation" or as a "fundamental alteration" of the original meaning of the labor market consideration clause.[23] In the more popular discourse, this decision has come to be known as the outcome of a "mammoth alliance" (*monsterverbond*) between labor unions and employer interest groups.[24]

Because recent writings on the role of employer interest groups in welfare state development have paid much attention to the role of so-called cross-class alliances between labor unions and employer interest groups in favor of welfare state development, it is worth taking a look at this accusation.[25] After all, if labor unions and employer interest groups had indeed broadened the labor market consideration clause beyond its original meaning, then it becomes quite tempting to believe that they did so at least partly with the purpose of shedding redundant workers. The description of the 1973 statement of the FvB as the outcome of an "alliance" between labor unions and employer interest groups certainly adds substance to this notion.

---

[21] VNO, F119(5): Cie Sociale Verzekering RCO: Kort verslag vergadering Commissie Sociale Verzekering Raad van Bestuur in Arbeidszaken, 12 Maart 1971.

[22] De Vroom and Blomsma, for example, argued that "it has been the very broad interpretation by the Industrial Insurance Boards of the relevant instruments that made disability regulation a tool of labor-market policy." Bert de Vroom and Martin Blomsma, "The Netherlands: An Extreme Case." In Kohli et al., *Time for Retirement*, 107.

[23] For this, see, respectively, De Vroom and Blomsma, "The Netherlands"; and Duco Bannink, "Het Nederlandse stelsel van sociale zekerheid. Van achterblijver naar koploper naar vroege hervormer." In Willem Trommel and Romke van der Veen, *De herverdeelde samenleving. De ontwikkeling en herziening van de Nederlandse verzorgingsstaat* (Amsterdam University Press, 1999), 67. See also Romke Jan van der Veen, *De sociale grenzen van beleid. Een onderzoek naar de uitvoering en effecten van het stelsel van sociale zekerheid* (Leiden: Stenfert Kroese, 1990), 77

[24] VNO, F119(5): Cie Sociale Verzekering RCO: Verslag Vergadering Commissie Sociale Verzekering Raad van Bestuur in Arbeidszaken, 12 Maart 1971.

[25] See, for example, Peter Swenson, "Bringing Capital Back," In ibidem, *Capitalists Against Markets*; Mares, *The Politics of Social Risk*; Gordon, *New Deals*; ibidem, *Dead on Arrival*.

Yet a close examination of the events leading up to 1973 does not bolster the idea that the federation's statement was in any way the outcome of an alliance between labor unions and employer interest groups – let alone with the purpose of shedding redundant workers in mind. Moreover, the federation's statement did not constitute a "fundamental alteration" of the labor market consideration clause. It is even doubtful whether it constituted a "very broad interpretation" of the clause. Instead, it can be explained entirely as evolving directly from the central purpose of the labor market consideration clause, which was to make sure that partially disabled workers did not have to apply for an unemployment benefit – or even worse, social assistance – when they were not able to find a suitable job after becoming partially handicapped. It is for exactly this reason that the federation's statement received full political support in 1973. The only parties who had doubts about it at the time were the employer federations.

To understand the issue at hand here, it is first necessary to briefly sketch the background of the labor market consideration clause – which was not outlined in Chapter 5. The labor market consideration clause entered the WAO because it had been part of the industrial injuries scheme. Like most of its foreign equivalents, the Dutch industrial injuries scheme contained a clause that gave medical officers some leeway in determining the level of disability in order to deal with situations in which a strict medical assessment would result in an unjust outcome. Chapter 5 showed that this also was the case in the United Kingdom, where the clause was used quite often.[26] When the decision was made to merge the Dutch invalidity and industrial injuries schemes into a single disability insurance program, there was a strong consensus that the labor market consideration clause of the industrial injuries schemes should be incorporated into the new insurance scheme. Although the employer federations did express their fear that the incorporation of this clause in an act that also applied to non-work-related disabilities might lead to very high numbers of disability benefit recipients, they supported its inclusion in the WAO.[27] In fact, as early as 1955, the employer federations had already voiced their opinion that beyond the purely medical assessment, age and "labor market invalidity" would have to factor into determining the level of disability if there were to be a single disability insurance scheme for all disabled workers.[28] Thus came about section 21, paragraph 2, subsection a of the WAO, which stated: "In determining the level of disability, one ought to pay as much attention as practicable to the decreased ability to find work that is caused by the disability."[29]

---

[26] See my discussion on the importance of the special hardship allowance in Chapter 5.

[27] ARA, CSWV, 2.19.103.06, 142: Verslag vergadering Werkgroep Bovenwettelijke Uitkeringen, Commissie Sociale Verzekeringen, 23 September 1964.

[28] ARA, CSWV, 2.19.103.06, 145: Verslag vergadering Kleine Technische Commissie Sociale Verzekering, 17 Januari 1955.

[29] See Article 2, lid 2, sub a, of the WAO.

The speed with which the employer federations agreed to transfer the industrial injuries' labor market consideration clause to the new disability insurance program can be explained at least in part by the rosy labor market situation at the time. When the WAO passed Parliament in February 1966, contemporaries could look back on nearly two decades of uninterrupted growth and low unemployment. They had good reason to believe that this situation would continue indefinitely. At the same time, however, economic difficulties in certain sectors of the economy, such as textiles and shipbuilding, already provided a preview of what lay ahead. In these sectors, the need for redundancy was slowly increasing, and with that, increased use of the disability insurance program as an alternative to dismissals. As a result, the labor market consideration clause was a source of concern almost immediately after the WAO came into operation.

Initially, it seems that the Gemeenschappelijke Medische Dienst (GMD, Common Medical Service), which advised the industrial insurance boards on determination of a claimant's disability level, employed the labor market consideration clause in more or less the same way as formally endorsed by the FvB in 1973.[30] Concerns over the staggering increase in the number of full disability benefit recipients soon led it to alter its stance, however. On November 12, 1970, a study group of the GMD judged that the labor market consideration clause was being used too frequently because the inability of partially disabled workers to find new work often could not be proven to be related to their handicap. From then on, the study group decreed, medical officers were to advise a higher disability level only if a partially disabled worker could prove that his or her inability to find new work was the direct result of his or her handicap. This severely limited the use of the labor market consideration clause because this was often very difficult to prove. As a result, many more workers were declared 50 to 60 percent disabled, and these were then rarely ever able to find new work.[31]

The new line of conduct of the GMD soon resulted in parliamentary questions to then Minister of Social Affairs Bauke Roolvink, whose answer was, "In certain cases, the determination of a less-than-full disability percentage occurs too swiftly.... In my opinion, an employee who loses his position through a disease or disability should receive a full disability benefit until the moment in which he finds new employment and it has been shown that he can perform the new labor permanently."[32] The minister also requested that the Sociale

30 A good sign of this is that the proportion of full beneficiaries was already as high as 90 percent in 1970. See Leo Aarts and Philip de Jong, "The Dutch Disability Program and How It Grew." In Aart, Burkhauser, and De Jong, *Curing the Dutch Disease*, 39.

31 UWV, Archief GMD: Verslag bespreking delegaties Federatie van Bedrijfsverenigingen en de Gemeenschappelijke Medische Dienst over de toepassing van artikel 21, lid 2, sub a van de wao, 30 Maart 1973.

32 Philip de Jong and Pieter Vos, *Het wao-debat: de centrale regelingen en de praktijk bij bedrijven* (Amsterdam: Welboom Bladen, 1994), 22.

Verzekeringsraad (SVR, Social Insurance Council) provide him with information on the matter. The SVR then turned to the FvB for advice.

In the meantime, a study group of the FvB had already launched an investigation into the new line of conduct of the GMD. Its conclusion was that neither the act itself nor case law justified the GMD's strict interpretation.[33] During the course of 1971, another study group tested the view of the GMD by examining use of the labor market consideration clause in the industrial injuries scheme. As it turned out, GMD medical officers always employed the labor market consideration clause unless intermediation by an officer resulted in the actual redeployment of a partially handicapped worker. This study group therefore concluded that the GMD was following the disability criteria of the invalidity scheme (which had not contained a labor market consideration clause) more closely than the criteria of the industrial injuries scheme. The correct interpretation of the labor market consideration clause was, this study group argued, that a partially disabled worker should receive a full benefit when employers did not offer him or her work, regardless of the reason for this. Only when a worker refused a suitable job was it reasonable to refrain from applying the labor market consideration clause.[34]

During 1971 and 1972, representatives from the SVR, the GMD, and the FvB together discussed a new code of conduct. This eventually resulted in a circular issued by the FvB on May 25, 1973, that stated that from then on, industrial insurance boards must assume that poor employment outlooks for partially disabled workers resulted from discrimination unless the opposite could be proven. Thus medical officers employed the labor market consideration clause in this way until its abolition in 1987.

In reading the course of events just described, it becomes quite difficult to escape the conclusion that the FvB's broad interpretation of the labor market consideration clause was correct. The FvB's interpretation of the labor market consideration clause did not differ from the one employed by medical officers under the industrial injuries clause and, more important to the FvB, was in line with the parliamentary comments of then Minister of Social Affairs Roolvink.[35] Moreover, the FvB's interpretation also seemed to have accorded with jurisprudence of the Centrale Raad van Beroep (Central Court of Appeal), which had issued the verdict on July 7, 1972, that if a partially handicapped worker could only be reemployed with intensive counseling, he or she should be considered fully disabled.[36]

---

[33] UVW, Archief FvB, doos 78: Notulen vergadering bestuur Federatie van Bedrijfsverenigingen, 14 April 1971.

[34] SVR, SVR-advies dd. 19–2-1979 (B22doos14): De verdiscontering van de WW bij vaststelling van de mate van arbeidsongeschiktheid a.b.i. art. 12 lid 2, AAW.

[35] Roolvink had been replaced by Jacob Boersma by the time the federation issued its circular. On the importance of ministerial consent for employer and union representatives, see, for example, UWV, Archief GMD: Notulen vergadering Gemeenschappelijke Medische Dienst, 12 Januari 1971.

[36] Admittedly, the court had also come out against the continuation of a full benefit until the resumption of work, which made its verdict somewhat ambivalent. For a good overview of case

This does not, of course, mean that all involved parties were content with the FvB's circular. Employer representatives to the FvB and SVR certainly were not.[37] Yet, in the words of the chairman of the combined Social Insurance Committee of employer federations, these representatives grudgingly admitted that "on reading the relevant documents, the Act itself and that which has been written regarding its introduction, one has to conclude that the receipt of an unemployment and disability benefit should only rarely be combined. The reason for this is that during the granting of a disability benefit, account should be made for labor market considerations."[38] In private, the members of the combined Social Insurance Committee of employer federations also admitted that although frequent use of the labor market consideration article was undesirable, it did seem inevitable: in practice, employers did not hire partially disabled workers.[39] Finally, employer representatives were also aware that part of the problem lay with employers themselves because they had used the act to downsize their workforces.[40] Based on these considerations, employer representatives to the FvB and SVR lent their blessing to the FvB's circular. Yet they did so only on the condition that the scope of medical officer mediation between employers and partially disabled unemployed workers would be increased.[41]

In their emphasis on the need to improve medical officers' ability to mediate between employers and partially disabled unemployed workers, the employer federations received full support from their union counterparts – although these certainly did not believe that the new code of conduct on the labor market consideration clause must depend on this expanded meditation. Such an

law on the issue, see Saskia Klosse, *Menselijke schade: vergoeden of herstellen? De werking van (re)integratiebepalingen voor gehandicapten in de Bondsrepubliek Duitsland en Nederland* (Antwerpen: Maklu 1989), 396–9.

37 The employer representative Habermehl, for example, initially argued for a "middle way" between a pure medical assessment and the assumption that there was a connection between the handicap and unemployment unless proven otherwise. Yet the federation's new line of conduct was prompted by the realization that it was seldom possible to prove whether or not there was a connection between the two. Under such circumstances, the federation argued that the benefit of the doubt had to be given to the claimant. For some time the employer representatives also argued for a code of conduct by which the labor market consideration clause would be used only for partially disabled workers over age forty-five. See, for example, UVW, Archief FvB, doos 78: Notulen vergadering bestuur Federatie van Bedrijfsverenigingen, 14 April 1971, and 9 Februari 1972.

38 VNO, F119(5) Cie Sociale Verzekering RCO: Verslag vergadering Commissie Sociale Verzekering Raad van Bestuur in Arbeidszaken, 10 November 1972.

39 VNO, F119(5) Cie Sociale Verzekering RCO: Verslag vergadering Commissie Sociale Verzekering Raad van Bestuur in Arbeidszaken, 10 November 1972.

40 VNO, F118(21) Cie Sociale Zekerheid VNO, Verslag vergadering Commissie Sociale Verzekering, 6 Januari 1972.

41 UWV, Archief GMD: Verslag van de bespreking tussen delegaties van de Federatie van Bedrijfsverenigingen en de Gemeenschappelijke Medische Dienst over de toepassing van artikel 21, lid 2, sub a van de WAO, 30 Maart 1973; VNO, F118(21) Cie Sociale Zekerheid VNO: Verslag vergadering Commissie Sociale Verzekering, 4 Oktober 1973.

expansion soon proved unfeasible, however, because of two factors. First, there seems to have been a clash of competencies between the GMD and employment exchange centers. At the time, medical officers did sometimes mediate between partially handicapped unemployed workers and employers, but what employer and union federations wanted was to set up a separate mediation apparatus for the GMD. The new Minister of Social Affairs, Jacob de Boer, apparently saw no need for this, though, because employment exchange centers could, in his opinion, fulfill this role.[42] Second, and far more important, the inflow of partially handicapped workers into the disability insurance scheme increased so rapidly that the GMD simply did not have the capacity to guide all partially handicapped workers to new work. As early as 1971, officers of the GMD had admitted that those over forty-five years of age received little to no career reentry guidance.[43] When the number of unemployed increased further after the outbreak of the first oil crisis in 1973, and with that the use of the disability insurance program for redundancy purposes increased, the GMD became even more overwhelmed.

If the outbreak of the first oil crisis gave employer federations good reason to withdraw their support for use of the labor market consideration article, the minister's refusal to set up a separate mediation apparatus for the GMD finally gave them a good excuse to do so. In a report presented to the Minister of Social Affairs in late 1974, the employer representatives to the SVR stated their objection to the current use of the labor market consideration article. Because they had themselves agreed that broad interpretation of the labor market consideration article was correct one year earlier, they realized that it would be futile to attempt to challenge this.[44] As a result, they called for a statutory change of the clause.

On examining the trajectory of the costs of the public disability insurance scheme, it is not difficult to see why the employer federations did so. At the time of introduction of the WAO, contributions were set at a little over 4 percent of a worker's wage. Within several years, this percentage had risen to over 9 percent, and the employer federations feared that the number could double in years to come, also because the state disability insurance program would be accompanied by a flat-rate insurance program for the self-employed in the near future.[45] Yet there evidently was another side to this story as well. All involved parties were well aware that under the current circumstances, a partially disabled and unemployed worker with a remaining work capacity of less than

[42] VNO, F119(5): Cie Sociale Verzekering RCO: Verslag vergadering Commissie Sociale Verzekering Raad van Bestuur in Arbeidszaken, 12 Oktober 1973; ibidem, 11 April 1973.

[43] UVW, Archief FvB, doos 78: Notulen vergadering bestuur Federatie van Bedrijfsverenigingen, 12 December 1973.

[44] VNO, F119(5), Cie Sociale Verzekering RCO: Verslag vergadering Commissie Sociale Verzekering Raad van Bestuur in Arbeidszaken, 14 Juni 1974.

[45] VNO, Arbeidsongeschiktheidsregelingen, F5(6): Nota VNO en NCW aan de leden van de Tweede Kamer van de Staten-Generaal, 19 Februari 1975.

50 percent had zero chances of finding new work even if he or she were still young.[46] Under such circumstances, the union federations argued, the financial consequences of the use of the labor market consideration clause simply had to be accepted.[47]

Judging from the lack of governmental response to the employer federations' plea for a statutory change of the labor market consideration clause, the government sided with the union federations on this. During the parliamentary treatment of the Algemene Arbeidsongeschiktheidswet (AAW, General Disability Act) that was to create a flat-rate insurance program for the self-employed, the government merely admitted to having its doubts about "the practice that had grown by now," to which it did not add whether it referred to the broad interpretation of the labor market consideration clause or to the massive inflow into the disability insurance program in general. Significantly, though, the government did add that it could see no immediate cause for legislative changes.[48] The employer federations also failed to convince the government, let alone their union counterparts, to go along with two other proposed measures to stem the increase in the number of disability benefit recipients. First, while they argued for limiting the use of the labor market consideration clause for partially disabled workers, they argued against inclusion of the labor market consideration clause in the flat-rate disability insurance scheme for the self-employed altogether.[49] Second, they continued to argue for the introduction of premium differentiation across industries into the WAO – as they had also done in the run-up to creation of the act.[50]

The latter proposal shows that the employer federations were quite concerned about the redistributive effects of companies' use of the disability insurance scheme to shed redundant workers. In Chapter 5, I showed that in the run-up to creation of the act, the employer federations had insisted on premium differentiation to prevent exactly this.[51] Another sign of the employer federations' concern about this instance of redistribution can be found in their fierce opposition to the practice of allowing firms to offer private supplements to the public disability benefit. To smooth the process of releasing redundant staff through the public disability insurance program, firms often offered private supplements for a few years so that workers could – at least initially – enjoy full earnings replacement. The employer federations fiercely opposed this

[46] UWV, Archief GMD: Verslag bespreking delegaties Federatie van Bedrijfsverenigingen en de Gemeenschappelijke Medische Dienst over de toepassing van artikel 21, lid 2, sub a van de WAO, 30 Maart 1973.

[47] UVW, Archief FvB, doos 78: Notulen vergadering bestuur Federatie van Bedrijfsverenigingen, 7 Februari 1973.

[48] See Klosse, *Menselijke schade*, 411–14.

[49] Ibidem, 413.

[50] VNO, F118(21) Cie Sociale Zekerheid VNO: Verslag vergadering Commissie Sociale Verzekering, 6 Maart 1974; ibidem, 4 Januari 1978.

[51] See the final pages of the section on the introduction of the 1965 Sickness Act and Act on Disability Insurance.

practice because they felt that it contributed to the transfer of normal company risks from one firm to another.[52] They failed completely to stop this practice, however. By the late 1970s, nearly all collective agreements covering more than 5,000 workers included provisions for the granting of private supplements in case of sickness, disability, or unemployment.[53]

It would take quite some time before the employer federations' objections to established industry practices were heard by the government. In 1981, the government added a third clause to the labor market consideration article, giving the industrial insurance boards the ability to limit the use of this article to a certain time period. Yet they could still only do so if they could show that the inability of a partially disabled worker to find new work had nothing to do with his or her disability. As a result, the effect of the introduction of this third clause was quite limited. In 1987, the government finally abolished the labor market consideration article altogether. In the same year it also lowered the level of the worker benefit to 70 percent of the previous wage. It is beyond the scope of this chapter to examine these measures at length; they can be explained in part by the growing need to curb public expenditure and, in the case of abolition of the labor market consideration article, by the rosier labor market situation at the time. While these measures certainly lessened the inflow into the disability insurance recipient ranks, at least after some time,[54] they did not raise the labor market participation rates of older workers. For older workers, two early-exit pathways still remained: the unemployment insurance route and the industry-wide early retirement schemes. The latter early-exit pathway grew ever more popular in the late 1980s. In the final section of this chapter I will analyze the development of this "private" pathway. In the following section I analyze how the Dutch public unemployment insurance program developed into a major early-exit route.

EARLY EXIT THROUGH THE DUTCH UNEMPLOYMENT SYSTEM

Dutch employer federation concerns over the effect of generous social insurance schemes on the labor-shedding behavior of individual firms may have

---

[52] ARA, CSWV, 2.19.103.06, 145: Verslag vergadering Kleine Technische Commissie Sociale Verzekering, 7 Februari 1955; Ibidem, Commissie Sociale Verzekering, 10 November 1967; VNO, F119(4) Cie Sociale Verzekering RCO 1947–1970: Verslag Commissie Sociale Verzekering, 30 Januari 1967.

[53] Loonbureau, *Bovenwettelijke uitkeringen. Bepalingen inzake toekenning van (aanvullende) uitkeringen bij arbeidsongeschiktheid, overlijden en werkloosheid zoals geregeld in de cao's voor bedrijfstakken met meer dan 5.000 werknemers* (Den Haag: Loonbureau, 1978).

[54] After abolition of the labor market consideration article in 1987, many industrial insurance boards continued to apply labor market considerations to their disability estimates. It would take a new round of reforms before this practice was completely stemmed. See, for example, Teulings, Van der Veen, and Trommel, *Dilemma's van sociale zekerheid*, 80–1; W. C. Kers, *Afvloeiing of herintreding: WAO-toetreding voor en na de stelselherziening 1987* (Den Haag: VUGA, 1996), 3, 17.

become more pressing after the WAO came into operation, but they were in no sense new. The argument that too generous a benefit might prompt firms to release their workers more easily had already surfaced during the preparation of the 1949 Werkloosheidswet (WW, Unemployment Act).[55] And as soon as the WW came into effect, employers from industries with lower levels of unemployment complained that construction companies in particular drew huge amounts of money from the general unemployment fund.[56] By the mid-1960s, the Centraal Sociaal Werkgevers Verbond (CSWV, Central Social Employers' Federation) was well aware of the complaint that firms in certain industries transferred normal company risks to the general unemployment fund.[57] In many cases this constituted a clear misuse of the public unemployment insurance scheme. In November 1967, representatives of the Federatie van Katholieke en Protestants-Christelijke Werkgeversverbonden (FCWV, Federation of Catholic and Protestant-Christian Employers' Union) noted that individual employers sometimes contacted regional employment offices with the request that older workers be released from the obligation to look for new jobs.[58] At the time, all employer federations fiercely condemned this practice.[59]

Some ten years later, however, the employer federations supported introduction of legislation that did exactly that. In 1976, Parliament passed the Wet tot Uitbreiding Uitkeringsduur WWV voor Ouderen (Act on Extension of the Unemployment Benefit Duration for the Elderly), which did two things. First, it extended the duration of the unemployment benefit by a maximum of five years for all workers whose entitlement to an unemployment benefit ended when they were sixty years or older. This meant that a male worker who became unemployed at the age of fifty-seven and a half (the normal duration of the unemployment benefit was two-and-a-half years) could enjoy an unemployment benefit until he reached the official retirement age. Second, it released this age group from the obligation to look for new work. As a result, for workers who were at least fifty-seven and a half years old when their unemployment began, the unemployment benefit had become a semiofficial early retirement pension.

The introduction of the 1976 act was a costly affair that strongly undermined the actuarial principles on which the unemployment insurance program was based. All employer federations nevertheless lent their full support to it.

[55] See Ruijters, "Sociale Zaken," 1424.

[56] ARA, CSWV, 2.19.103.06, 145: Verslag vergadering Kleine Technische Commissie Sociale Verzekering, 10 Maart 1954.

[57] ARA, CSWV, 2.19.103.06, 134: Verslag vergadering Kring voor Sociaal Overleg, 13 Januari 1967.

[58] Then Minister of Social Affairs Bauke Roolvink was also aware of this and sent a furious letter to the SVR to address this form of misuse. VU, FCWV, 18: Brief Ministerie Van Sociale Zaken en Volksgezondheid aan de Sociale Zekerheidsraad, 16 November 1967.

[59] VNO, F119(4) Cie Sociale Verzekering RCO 1947–1970: Verslag Vergadering Commissie Sociale Verzekering Raad van Bestuur in Arbeidszaken, 19 Oktober 1967.

How can we explain this? It is again tempting to believe that the desire of some companies to release redundant workers more easily played a role in this. And indeed, it seems that at least some employers appreciated this side effect of the 1976 act. When the work group on collective dismissals of the VNO discussed the coming introduction of the act, its members agreed that it "on the one hand, provides a solution for employers in these times of reorganization and company closures." They were well aware, however, of the act's downside: "on the other hand, the employer federations should guard against an increase in the burden of collective expenses, which will inevitably be the result of the statutory change." The work group's members concluded that the employer federations found themselves right in between "Scylla and Charybdis."[60]

The preceding description illustrates the clear limitations of some of the arguments made by recent writings on employer interest in welfare state development. Generous public provision against unemployment certainly can make it easier for firms to shed redundant or less-productive workers, but it can do so only at the expense of firms that have less need to shed workers. This makes it somewhat misleading to argue that such instances can be viewed as example of the ways in which the welfare state can "improve the operation of markets" or has "productive purposes."[61] If there are gains to be achieved at all, then these, by definition, will be redistributive; gains for the few must be financed through higher contribution levels or an increase in taxation, which inevitably will come at the expense of others. It is for exactly this reason that both British and Dutch employer federations always insisted on premium differentiation across industries. It is also for this reason that the Dutch employer federations came to regret their support for introduction of the labor market consideration clause in the WAO. And finally, it is for this reason that the employer federations most likely would not have supported introduction of the 1976 Act on Extension of the Unemployment Benefit Duration for the Elderly if they had not felt that introduction of this act was inevitable and that their support for this act could at least prevent the worse alternative: an extension in the duration of the unemployment benefit for all workers.

Several years before, one aspect of the 1976 Act had already been subjected to debate. Earlier I noted that individual companies sometimes contacted regional employment offices with their requests that older workers be released from the obligation to look for new jobs. In the late 1960s, this practice briefly took a more structured form, when the SVR discussed the introduction of so-called nonactivity arrangements for older workers in the textile industry. As mentioned

---

[60] VNO, F30(5): Kort verslag vergadering Werkgroep Collectief Ontslag, 19 November 1975.

[61] In a work on early retirement reform, Bernhard Ebbinghaus, for instance, aimed to "show that early retirement is not only a case of politics against markets ... or the expansion of social rights in response to market vagaries but also that it functions as politics for markets, facilitating the restructuring of production systems." Ebbinghaus, *Reforming Early Retirement*, 3. For the citations, see Hall and Soskice, *Varieties of Capitalism*, vi; Ebbinghaus and Manow, *Comparing Welfare Capitalism*, foreword.

briefly earlier, the Dutch textile industry was one of the first industries to come under serious strain mainly because of increased competition from low-cost industries in developing countries. By the late 1960s, the situation had become so dire that major layoffs seemed unavoidable. To prevent mass unrest in an industry that was already in economic difficulty, union and employer representatives in the textile industry had agreed to use the unemployment insurance scheme as an early retirement pension by allowing workers from the age of sixty-two and a half and older to retire early with generous benefits. These workers would be relieved of the obligation to look for new jobs, and their public unemployment benefits would be complemented with private supplements to a full 100 percent of their previous wages during the first year of unemployment and to 95 percent in the second year. They also agreed on a one-time bonus almost equal to the minimum wage and on continuation of the occupational pension buildup.[62] In 1967, this agreement came under review of the tripartite SVR.

Despite the nonactivity arrangements' obvious unlawfulness (both the WW and the WWV stated clearly that unemployment benefits could only be granted if a worker were actively in search of new work), the SVR was divided over the issue. After a short discussion in the Board of Governors on Labor Affairs, in which only the chairman of the CSWV briefly considered agreeing to the measure on an ad hoc basis, all employer federations agreed that the nonactivity arrangements were unacceptable. Many reasons were given for this. First, the practice clearly constituted misuse of the public unemployment benefit. Second, the granting of ad hoc support would inspire other sectors to copy the practice. Third, it would be completely unfair to other industries – whether or not these were also in distress – if the textile industry were able to reorganize its workforce at the expense of the unemployment fund.[63] Union representatives to the SVR agreed on the unlawfulness of the measure but nonetheless supported it for social considerations. They also argued that by releasing less-productive older workers, more-productive younger workers could be taken on in their stead. The latter argument does not seem to have impressed the SVR's employer representatives, considering, for instance, that the whole point of the measure was to reduce the size of the workforce.[64] The SVR's state representatives apparently sided with the labor unions on the matter because the SVR eventually did give permission for introduction of the nonactivity arrangements.[65]

---

[62] VU, FC, 18: Brief Federatie van Katholieke en Protestants-Christelijke werkgeversbonden aan de betrokken vakorganisaties, 24 Oktober 1967.

[63] VNO, F119(4) Cie Sociale Verzekering RCO 1947–1970: Verslag vergadering Commissie Sociale Verzekering Raad van Bestuur in Arbeidszaken, 19 Oktober 1967.

[64] VU, FC, 18: Brief Federatie van Katholieke en Protestants-Christelijke werkgeversbonden aan de betrokken vakorganisaties, 24 Oktober 1967; ARA, CSWV, 2.19.103.06, 140: Verslag vergadering Commissie Sociale Verzekering, 10 November 1967.

[65] VNO, F119(4) Cie Sociale Verzekering RCO 1947–1970: Verslag vergadering Commissie Sociale Verzekering CSWV, 10 November 1967.

Several years later, when the employer federations were debating the Act on Extension of the Unemployment Benefit Duration for the Elderly, they faced what was essentially the introduction of nonactivity arrangements on a much larger scale. In this case, the plan was to release all unemployed workers from the age of fifty-seven and a half and older from the obligation to look for work. This naturally raised the question of whether or not the employer federations should again make a stand against this "illegitimate" use of the social insurance program. As one employer representative noted, this was what they had done in the late 1960s, and the financial impact of the current plan would be many times greater.[66] After much hesitation, the employer federations nevertheless gave their support to introduction of the 1976 act. They had two reasons to do so.

First, and most important, they realized that some kind of improvement of the existing unemployment insurance legislation was inevitable. The problem of rising unemployment not only made this a top priority to the labor union movement, but it also strengthened the unions' demands. Realizing this, the employer federations came to regard introduction of special measures for the elderly as a lesser evil. By supporting introduction of this act, they hoped to at least be able to prevent an increase in the duration of the unemployment benefit for all workers regardless of age – an additional demand of the labor unions. Second, introduction of this legislation could help to stem the even less-desirable practice of shedding workers through the public disability insurance scheme. It is hard to say how important this second consideration was to the employer federations, however. In discussions in the Social Security Committee of the VNO, only the committee's chairman noted that by giving support to this plan, the employer community could both deflect union calls for an increase in the duration of the unemployment benefit for all workers *and* help to remove hidden unemployment from the public disability insurance program. Several other members responded by asking whether such a division of unemployment and disability would make any difference in practice. One member even questioned the morality of sending older unemployed workers with partial handicaps to the unemployment insurance program.[67]

The employer federations also hoped to use introduction of the 1976 act as leverage for their attempts to introduce stricter job-search requirements for workers drawing an unemployment benefit. At the time, workers drawing unemployment benefits were only required to look for and accept "suitable

---

[66] VNO, F79(14) Werkloosheidsrgelingen 1921–86: Consequenties uitbreiding uitkeringsduur Wet Werkloosheidsvoorziening (WWV) ten behoeve van oudere langdurig werklozen.

[67] Interestingly, this same member had several years earlier argued that his fellow employer representatives should not make such a large fuss about the introduction of nonactivity arrangements into the textiles sector because this was greatly preferable to releasing workers through the public disability insurance program. For this, see VNO, F118(21) Cie Sociale Zekerheid VNO: Verslag vergadering Commissie Sociale Verzekering, 2 Oktober 1969. For the discussion over the 1976 act, see ibidem, 2 April 1975.

jobs," which were defined as jobs that not only paid wages that were equal to those of their previous jobs but also involved similar work activities or skill levels. The employer federations rightly emphasized that the current interpretation of the suitable job clause hindered economic efficiency and opened the door for abuse.[68] The union federations responded that their members would never accept a stricter definition of the concept, and the unions refused even to consider establishment of a committee to investigate the matter.[69] It would take many years before the government even dared to address this issue.[70]

The employer federations were more successful in preventing an increase in the duration of the unemployment benefit for all workers. Important to this was that the state representatives to the Sociaal-Economische Raad (SER, Social-Economic Council) sided with the employers on this during preparation of a formal advice on the matter. In the end, the SER presented a divided report to the Minister of Social Affairs in late 1975. While all members of the SER agreed to an increase in the duration of the unemployment benefit for workers aged seventy-five and a half and older, a minority, consisting only of union representatives, argued for measures to improve matters for all long-term unemployed.[71] The employer federations also successfully fought off another union demand, which was to expand the range of the new act to the formerly self-employed as well.[72]

In summary, a close examination of the introduction of the 1976 act gives little evidence for the idea that the stance of the employer federations toward the act was shaped in a major way by their appreciation for its effect on companies' ability to release redundant workers. The main motivation for their support was clearly to prevent introduction of more far-reaching proposals. As we saw earlier, the employer federations did realize that by making it easier to dismiss workers, the act provided a solution for companies who needed to downsize their workforces. Yet they also realized the financial consequences of this. This latter effect – increased collective costs – continued to worry the employer federations, but not to such an extent that they felt it necessary to press their members to abstain from taking advantage of the redundancy-related possibilities provided by the act. The opinion of the Executive Committee of the VNO, for example, was simply that "once the

---

68 KDC, Algemene Katholieke Werkgeversvereniging, 1500: Commissie Sociale Verzekering van het Katholieke Verbond, 1954–1960, Nota inzake enkele principiële wijzigingen, welke in de Werkloosheidswet dienen te worden aangebracht, geen datum.

69 VNO, F118(21) Cie Sociale Zekerheid VNO: Verslag vergadering Commissie Sociale Verzekering, 4 Juni 1975.

70 For more on this, see Inge Pardaan, *Passende arbeid: een beschouwing vanuit de sociale wetgeving rond werkloosheid, ziekte, arbeidsongeschiktheid en bijstand en kijkend naar regulieren, seizoens- en gesubsidieerde arbeid* (Deventer: Kluwer, 1997).

71 VNO, F30(5) Kort verslag vergadering Werkgroep Collectief Ontslag, 3 September 1975.

72 VNO, F118(21) Cie Sociale Zekerheid VNO: Verslag vergadering Commissie Sociale Verzekering, 6 Augustus 1975.

arrangement is there, it should be possible to make use of it." The VNO's work group on collective dismissals agreed that "it is not the purpose of the employer federations to urge their members to be reticent about the use of the current legislation." It added to this that "when firms do use the possibilities offered by this legislation, then they should also accept the resulting increase in collective burden and contributions."[73]

The 1976 Act on Extension of the Unemployment Benefit Duration for the Elderly continued to function in more or less its original form until after the turn of the twenty-first century. It thus operated for much longer than the labor market consideration clause in the WAO, which was abolished in 1987. One reason for this difference was surely that even after introduction of the 1976 act, the public unemployment insurance program remained a much less popular early-exit pathway than public disability insurance. Earlier we saw the importance of public disability insurance as an early-exit pathway in the 1980s and early 1990s. In the latter decade, it was industry-wide early retirement schemes that became increasingly important.

THE INTRODUCTION OF INDUSTRY-WIDE EARLY
RETIREMENT SCHEMES

The preceding two sections showed that the practice of labor shedding through the public disability and unemployment insurance programs emerged as an unintended side effect of an expansion of social rights. Introduction of the industry-wide early retirement schemes (known in the Netherlands as *VUT-regelingen*) differed from this in that these schemes were specifically designed to withdraw older workers from the labor market. One of the main arguments for their introduction was that they could create jobs for younger workers by encouraging older workers to leave the labor market early. They never really came to fulfill this aim, however. Once older workers were given the opportunity to retire early, they certainly starting doing so in mass numbers, but companies more frequently responded to this by downsizing than by hiring new workers to fill the vacant positions.[74] Thus what began as a solution to the youth unemployment problem soon became a subsidized early-exit pathway for older workers and another instrument for employers to downsize their workforces.

Just as labor union pressure for an extension of social rights had resulted in the transformation of public disability and unemployment insurance schemes into early-exit pathways, labor unions were again the driving force behind

---

[73] VNO, F30(5): Kort verslag vergadering Werkgroep Collectief Ontslag, 3 September 1973.

[74] An investigation of the use of early retirement schemes at the large steel factory Hoogovens in 1981, for example, showed that in 71 percent of cases, early exit did *not* lead to the hiring of a new employee. See Paul van Ginneken, *VUT. Vervroegde uittreding en ontwikkeling* (Den Haag: Ministerie van Sociale Zaken, 1981), 28.

the introduction of industry-wide early retirement schemes. The idea of these schemes came from the Nederlands Katholiek Vakverbond (NKV, Netherlands Catholic Trade Union Federation), which issued a pamphlet in 1974 entitled, "Jong voor Oud" ("Young for Old"), in which it argued for introduction of a job-replacement scheme that could serve the double aim of granting certain older workers the ability to retire early and of reintegrating younger unemployed workers into the workforce. The scheme would give workers aged sixty-two and a half and older the option of leaving the workforce voluntarily in exchange for a benefit similar to the one currently granted to unemployed workers. Companies would then have to hire an unemployed worker to fill the vacancy, who would be appointed by the regional employment office. The NKV argued that the scheme would not be costly because it did not alter the number of workers who received benefits; it merely replaced older workers with younger workers. The unemployed worker did not have to be given exactly the same function that had been performed previously by the retired older worker.[75]

From the start, there was much skepticism about the feasibility of replacing early-retiring workers by younger workers. Among the skeptics were members of the committee of government-appointed external experts who investigated the NKV plan in 1975. This committee concluded that any attempt to force employers to replace early-retiring workers with younger workers would encounter fierce opposition, not in the least from the employer federations, whereas voluntary adherence most likely would result in far more "exits" than "entries." Partly from this latter prediction, it also criticized the NKV's low estimate of the scheme's cost. Within this generally skeptical evaluation of the NKV's plan, it did note that the scheme could add to the well-being of older workers with rough employment histories. Based on the latter consideration, it cautiously advised experimentation with a voluntary version of the scheme.[76]

It is difficult to say what the attitude of the union movement and employer community was toward the idea of introducing voluntary early retirement schemes. While the employer federations were downright skeptical about their ability to address the problem of unemployed youth, they were again – as had been the case with introduction of the Act on Extension of the Unemployment Benefit Duration for the Elderly described earlier – aware that these schemes could help certain industries to restructure. On several occasions, members of the VNO noted that introduction of early retirement schemes could raise productivity by "clearing out" the number of employees.[77] Counter to this benefit,

---

[75] VNO, F75(105) VUT-regelingen 1970–1985: Discussie-nota sociaal pensionen, gepubliceerd door N.K.V. op 22 Januari 1975.

[76] See A. de Boon, *Rapport van de commissie van externe adviseurs terzake van vervroegd uittreden van oudere werknemers* (Den Haag: Ministerie van Sociale Zaken, 1975).

[77] VNO, F75(105) VUT-regelingen 1970–85: Interim-rapport werkgroep aan bestuur Stichting van de Arbeid, 8 September 1977; ibidem, Regelingen van vervroegd uittreden, 9 Juni 1978; ibidem, Rapport inzake consequenties van vervroegd pensioneren in het kader van oplossingen voor oudere werknemers, geen datum.

however, stood several probable adverse effects. First, introduction of early retirement schemes would be costly because it certainly would not be possible to limit them to certain groups of older workers.[78] Second, the schemes would result in a further deterioration of the ratio of active to inactive workers. Finally, once workers were given the option of retiring voluntarily, it was quite possible that the most productive older workers also would run off. On this last problem, employer representatives noted again the record of misuse of the public disability insurance scheme.[79]

Another problem with determining the overall attitude of organized industry toward introduction of early retirement schemes is that different industries seem to have regarded them quite differently. For example, while the executive committee of the VNO both emphasized the early retirement schemes' costs and the afore-mentioned problem of the most productive workers retiring early, some industries believed that early retirement might very well be self-financing.[80] To the executive committee of the VNO, three other considerations were eventually of overriding importance. First, the committee realized that union pressure for introduction of collective early retirement arrangements would only increase in the future.[81] Second, it realized that the government's intention to cut back collective expenditure (in late 1977, a coalition of liberals and Christian-Democrats announced for the first time a plan to take serious measures against the ongoing increase in collective expenditure) presented the union movement with a financial predicament, meaning that something might have to be offered to the unions in return for expense curbing.[82] Third, despite its skeptical stance toward the idea of introducing collective early retirement schemes, it greatly preferred this to some of the other ideas for redistributing labor that were circulating at the time.

It is important to mention here that the NKV's proposal was by no means the only plan that aimed to tackle the problem of unemployment by redistributing

---

[78] VNO, F75(105) VUT-regelingen 1970–85: Rapport inzake consequenties van vervroegd pensioneren in het kader van oplossingen voor oudere werknemers, geen datum. It should be noted here that this makes it remarkable that the employer federations nevertheless proved willing to go ahead with the creation of these schemes. According to Isabela Mares, the most important consideration of employer organizations with regard to the development of early retirement schemes is that of retaining control over which workers stop working and when. A comparison of the attitudes of the Dutch employer federations toward the use of the public disability insurance program for redundancy purposes and the development of industry-wide early retirement schemes suggests otherwise. See Mares, "Enterprise Reorganization," 299; ibidem, *The Politics of Social Risk*.

[79] VNO, F75(105) Vut-regelingen 1970–85: Regeling van vervroegd uittreden, 9 Juni 1978.

[80] VNO, F7(111) Cie Arbeidsduur 1975–89: Kort verslag vergadering Commissie Overleg Ploegendiensten/Arbeidsduur, 22 September 1977.

[81] VNO, F7(111) Cie Arbeidsduur 1975–89: Kort verslag vergadering Commissie Overleg Ploegendiensten/Arbeidsduur, 4 Augustus 1977.

[82] VNO, F7(11) Cie Arbeidsduur 1975–89: Kort verslag gecombineerde vergadering Commissie Arbeidsduur (RvBA) en de Adviescommissie Beleid Ouderen (RNWV), 18 Mei 1978.

labor. Among other ideas were the introduction of part-time work on a large scale, a shorter workweek, more vacation days, and a lowered retirement age. While the labor union movement resisted the idea of stimulating part-time work, the employer federations resisted all other ideas. The employer federations resisted a shorter workweek and more vacation days because these would apply to all workers instead of just older workers, which made them far more costly. They also feared that these measures would be cumulative because the labor union movement was determined to introduce a collective arrangement for early retirement.[83] The labor unions also preferred early retirement to a shorter workweek and more vacation days.[84] In sum, among all the ideas put forward to redistribute labor, the idea of introducing early retirement schemes was the only one on which labor unions and organized employers could agree.[85]

Based on all the preceding considerations, the employer federations cautiously stated their willingness to consider the introduction of early retirement schemes. They agreed, however, only under certain conditions. First, they demanded that employers be allowed to dismiss a request for early retirement by a worker when this would have large-scale negative consequences for the firm's operation. Second, they demanded that an early-retired worker not be allowed to perform paid labor of any sort. Finally, and by far most important, the employer federations insisted that early retirement schemes had to be completely private in character. The employer federations fiercely resisted the introduction of a public early retirement scheme because this would result in huge transfers of income between industries, and because a national scheme would be more difficult to terminate. The second condition seems to have been most problematic for the union federations. They preferred a public scheme for the same reason the employer federations opposed it. Without a redistributive effort across different industries, the union federations feared, some industries might not be able to afford early retirement schemes.[86] In the end, however, the union federations were forced to give in. The early retirement schemes were to be based on industry-wide funds that would be financed on a pay-as-you-go basis. The industrial insurance boards would be responsible for their operation.

[83] VNO, F7(11) Cie Arbeidsduur 1975–89: Kort verslag gecombineerde vergadering Commissie Arbeidsduur (RvBA) en de Adviescommissie Beleid Ouderen (RNWV), 18 Mei 1978; ibidem, Verslag vergadering Commissie Arbeidsduur, 19 Juni 1980.

[84] VNO, F7(11) Cie Arbeidsduur 1975–89: Conclusies vergadering Commissie ABO/Arbeidsduur, 12 Oktober 1979.

[85] The executive committee of the VNO described it as follows: "If a choice has to be made between all the instruments aimed at redistributing labor ... an arrangement aimed at voluntary early unemployment [it refused to call it early retirement – DON] ... would be preferable." VNO, F75(105) VUT-regelingen 1970–85: Notitie ten behoeve van de Centrale Commissie Arbeidsvoorwaardenbeleid, 15 Juni 1978.

[86] VNO, Cie Arbeidsduur 1975–89: Kort verslag vergadering Commissie Overleg Ploegendiensten/Arbeidsduur, 14 Juli 1977, en 2 September 1977; VNO, F75(105) VUT-regelingen 1970–85: Interim-rapport werkgroep aan bestuur Stichting van de Arbeid, 8 September 1977.

Despite their insistence that older workers be allowed to retire early only on a temporary basis, the employer federations seem to have had little difficulty with the redistributive impact of the early retirement schemes on the income of younger and older workers. They also agreed to the continuation of both private and public pension buildup throughout a worker's period of early retirement.[87] State interference with the early retirement schemes remained as limited as possible. The state only interfered with them in two ways. First, it could extend the use of early retirement schemes to an entire sector through its ability to declare a collective agreement binding. Second, the government decided in 1979 that early retirement schemes should be treated like private pensions, which meant that the benefits, not the contributions, would be taxed.

In 1976, the building, metal, and dock industries and the education sector were the first to experiment with early retirement schemes. In these sectors, sixty-three- and sixty-four-year-old workers were allowed to retire early on a benefit of about 80 percent of their previous wages. This experiment confirmed what the employer organizations and the committee of external experts had already suspected: in only about 15 percent of cases did firms refill vacant positions with unemployed workers.[88] The experiment also demonstrated that early retirement was extremely popular among workers. As a result, the use of early retirement schemes soon spread in range and scope. By 1979, it was estimated that some 80 percent of Dutch employees were covered by collective agreements making provision for some form or other of early retirement.[89] The age limit also dropped rapidly. By the mid-1980s, it was very normal for a sixty-year-old worker to retire early on a early retirement benefit. In some industries, workers even could retire at the age of fifty-five.[90]

For about the first ten years, early retirement apparently operated to the satisfaction of both workers and firms. From the late 1980s on, however, large firms in particular became more critical of the scheme. Among the reasons for this were concerns over the scheme's costs, a growing paucity of qualified workers, and the absence of employer control over the exit route.[91] But the schemes' immense popularity among workers made it quite resistant to change. The trend of early exit through the VUT only stabilized from the mid-1990s on, and it would take until the turn of the century for a government to announce serious measures to stem the rampant use of the early retirement schemes. These measures, however, are far beyond the scope of this chapter.

---

[87] VNO, F75(105) VUT-regelingen 1970–85: Interim-rapport werkgroep aan bestuur Stichting van de Arbeid, 8 September 1977.

[88] See Trommel, *Korter arbeidsleven*, 68.

[89] See Casey and Bruche, *Work or Retirement*, 126.

[90] See Trommel, *Korter arbeidsleven*, 70.

[91] See De Vroom and Blomsma, *The Netherlands*, 22.

7

Conclusions and Implications

The comparative literature on welfare state development has long emphasized the crucial role played by labor associations in the creation and reform of social policies in advanced industrial countries. Yet, and possibly because of its long-standing tendency to emphasize class divisions, there has been far too little attention paid to the wide variety in labor union attitudes toward the redistributive consequences of welfare state development. For over a decade now, class-oriented accounts such as the power resources approach have been subjected to intense criticism. To date, however, this has not resulted in a fundamental reinterpretation of organized labor's role in the development of the postwar welfare state. As noted earlier, even the most sophisticated institutionalist and employer-oriented accounts of recent years have paid little attention to the very diverse and often conflicting nature of workers' demands for security against labor market risks. As a result, scholars have largely continued to view labor unions as the natural supporters of the welfare state. There consequently still is a strong consensus that the presence of an organizationally strong labor union movement increases the political efficacy of left parties.

This book has challenged this view of the involvement of organized labor in welfare state development. Through an extensive analysis of over four decades of postwar welfare state development in the United Kingdom and the Netherlands, this book demonstrated that labor union support for redistributive welfare state development cannot be taken for granted. Depending on the risk and income profiles of their members, unions value public welfare solutions, and especially their redistributive consequences, in quite different ways. Rather than viewing welfare state development as a political victory of labor over capital, the analysis therefore investigated the circumstances under which labor unions are willing and able to redistribute income and risk within the labor category. It demonstrated that this willingness and ability crucially depend on the way in which the unions organize workers. Criticizing the preoccupation with labor union's organizational strength that has characterized much of the literature on welfare state development, this book consequently argued for the importance of labor's organizational blueprint as an explanatory variable for welfare state outcomes.

The analysis proceeded from the recognition that workers differ greatly in terms of income and exposure to labor market risks. A major purpose of the welfare state is to diminish these differences so that all workers are adequately insured against labor market risks such as unemployment, sickness, disability, and old age. In their greater ability to redistribute risks and resources between societies' more- and less-privileged members, public welfare solutions generally differ strongly from private ones. It is for this reason that unions representing only skilled, and thus higher-paid, less-risk-prone workers often prefer private to public welfare solutions – or favor a combination of private and public insurance plans against labor market risks that involves no redistribution between more- and less-privileged workers. In this they differ strongly from unions that also represent lower-skilled, and thus lower-paid, more-risk-prone workers. To make sure that *all* their members can achieve adequate insurance against labor market risks, such unions are far more willing to consider redistributive welfare solutions that result in a leveling of income and risk among different groups of workers.

Focusing on the postwar development of the British and Dutch welfare states, this book demonstrated how differences in union structure related to the very different welfare trajectories followed by the two countries. In the Netherlands, the three industrially organized labor union federations were the main initiators of plans that aimed to increase the generosity of public welfare programs through risk redistribution and systems of contributions and benefits that benefited lower-paid workers at the expense of higher-paid workers. In the United Kingdom, the Trades Union Congress (TUC) never pushed for redistributive contributory welfare initiatives. Moreover, it gave at most lukewarm support to the redistributive initiatives put forward by various Labour governments. The reason for this lack of enthusiasm lay in the "craft" or "occupational" nature of many of its union members. These unions represented workers who stood to lose from the redistributive consequences of such initiatives and thus organized against them. As a result, and even though it organized a relatively high percentage of all workers, the British union movement did anything but increase the political efficacy of the Labour Party.

In the Netherlands, by contrast, the presence of a large industrial union movement made sure that redistributive public welfare development there did not depend on the presence of a left-dominated government. The landmark 1966 Ziektewet (Sickness Act) and Wet op Arbeidsongeschiktheidsverzekering (WAO, Act on Disability Insurance), as well as various acts that increased the generosity of the unemployment insurance scheme and state pension in the 1960s, all passed Parliament under confessional-liberal governments. All these acts either introduced or strongly increased the redistributive nature of public provision against labor market risks. They all came about after strong and pro-longed pressure from the labor union movement and were prepared in detail during discussions between union representatives and their employer counter-parts. The unions managed to impose these acts, often in the face of substantial employer opposition, despite organizing for European standards a relatively low percentage of workers. Much more important than their organizational strength, then, was that they were united in their support for redistributive welfare state development.

Dutch employers were reluctant to accept or were outright opposed to some of the unions' welfare demands. To other demands, including quite redistribu-tive ones, they gave their strong support. This lends support to some of the employer-oriented writings of recent years, which have argued that the role of organized employers in welfare state development has been much more complex, and at times also much more supportive, than previous writings have made it out to be. Indeed, the analysis showed that welfare state development in neither of the two countries constituted a political victory of labor over capital. Much more important for the success of postwar welfare state initiatives was whether they could count on the undivided support of the labor union movement. In short, welfare state development progressed depending on the willingness of labor associations to redistribute income and risk within the labor category. When this was the case, organized employers were often, but not always, quite willing to accept an expansion of public protection against labor market risks.

At the same time, the analysis gave little support to the argument, put forward by another variant of the recent employer-oriented literature, that employers may support public welfare initiatives because they appreciate their "productive" function. Focusing on, respectively, the introduction of a redundancy payments scheme in the United Kingdom and the use of social security schemes for redundancy purposes in the Netherlands, Chapters 4 and 6 dealt with this argument at length. Although the introduction of redun-dancy payments was defended by both Conservative and Labour govern-ments as a way to improve labor mobility, Britain's employer organizations were quite opposed to the scheme. And the use of social security schemes for redundancy purposes in the Netherlands was made possible only because of a series of decisions that were defended by the union movement out of social considerations – and were strongly opposed by the major employer interest groups. In both countries, then, organized employers realized very well that any "productive" benefits associated with public welfare development could only come about through a substantial redistributive effort among different firms. Following recent work by Isabela Mares, it also would seem para-doxical that Dutch employers were least opposed to the expansion of the one scheme over which they had least control – the industry-wide early retire-ment funds. The reason for this was quite conventional: industry-wide early retirement schemes were neither public nor permanent and did not constitute a misuse of social security.

In the overall, Dutch employers were far more supportive of redistributive public welfare state development than were their British counterparts. This, too, can be explained to a large extent through differences in the organizational structure of the British and Dutch labor union movements. The preceding analysis showed that union structure impacts employer interest-group stances on welfare state development in two important ways. Both of these result from the way in which union structure shapes the stances of national labor union movements on redistributive welfare state development. First, when a large part of the labor union movement opposes redistributive welfare initiatives, employer interest groups are in a much stronger position to oppose them as well. Second, when many unions oppose such initiatives, they also will resist paying for these initiatives, making them quite costly for employers. When unions, by contrast, support redistributive welfare initiatives, they will be far more willing to accept that such initiatives have to be financed out of the margin of pay increases, thereby substantially reducing their cost to employers.

Events surrounding attempts to expand the public old-age insurance program in both countries illustrate this well. In the United Kingdom, the opposition of craft and occupationally organized white-collar unions greatly strengthened the opposition of employer groups and the pension industry to Labour's superannuation proposals. Not only did union opposition give these groups a powerful ally at the bargaining table, but it also enabled them to direct attention to how bad a deal superannuation was for higher-paid workers. At the same time, employer interest groups in the United Kingdom realized very well that unions that opposed superannuation because of its redistributive consequences would do anything in their power to restore lost wage differentials at the bargaining table. This meant that if superannuation were to be implemented, it would severely complicate wage bargaining for employers. The consequences of this greatly worried employer interest groups and hardened their opposition to superannuation.

In the Netherlands, by contrast, employer interest groups were faced with a union movement that was united in its support for redistributive welfare state development. This facilitated the coming about of a much more cooperative stance from employers in two ways. First, as the years progressed, Dutch unions were increasingly willing to accept that public, like private, insurance for labor market risks was part of the social wage, which had to be financed out of the margin of pay increases (in Dutch: *loonruimte*). This made public welfare development much less costly, and therefore more palpable, to employers. At the same time, however, it also made it more difficult for them to resist public welfare initiatives. It simply proved quite difficult for the employer federations to resist public welfare initiatives when the union movement offered that the costs of such initiatives be borne by workers themselves. This, as we have seen, was even the case when governments were dominated by "friendly" liberal and confessional parties.

OCCUPATIONAL UNIONISM AND THE EMERGENCE
OF DIVIDED WELFARE STATES

The issue of how labor unions value redistributive welfare state solutions is crucial for welfare state outcomes in all industrialized countries. The importance of union structure is therefore by no means limited to the development of the Dutch and British welfare states alone. The dominance in those countries of, respectively, industrial and occupational unionism and the fact that their welfare patterns do not easily fit into the explanatory framework of class-oriented approaches such as the power resources approach have made the Netherlands and the United Kingdom ideally suited to illustrate the importance of labor union structure to welfare state outcomes. Most other advanced industrial nations, at first sight, fit more neatly into an explanatory framework that focuses on labor's relative power resources. Yet this does not warrant the current preoccupation of scholarly investigations of those nations with union strength. A couple of examples can illustrate that the organizational structure of national labor union movements mattered to the welfare trajectories of other countries as well.

An excellent case in point here is Sweden. In the comparative literature on welfare state development, scholars often attribute the generous nature of the Swedish welfare state to the organizational strength of the labor union movement there. But what if the extraordinary organizational strength of the Swedish labor union movement had been combined with an equally strong entrenchment of occupational unionism as in the United Kingdom? In that case, the outcome might very well have been a much less generous or "solidaristic" welfare state. Moreover, it is important to bear in mind that the relationship between Sweden's high union density level and its generous welfare state features is in no way unidirectional.[1] The relationship between the (overall) vertical nature of union organization in Sweden and its generous welfare state features does, by contrast, seem quite straightforward. In Chapter 2, I discussed the overall vertical nature of union organization in Sweden and its importance for wage-bargaining outcomes there. Its importance for welfare state outcomes no doubt has been equally important.

The need for a reinterpretation of the role of labor union involvement in welfare state development is most pressing in nations in which occupational unionism is strong. This inevitably brings our attention to the Anglo-Saxon world. As explained in Chapter 2, occupational unionism also exists in the countries of continental Europe and to a greater extent in some of these countries than in others. In many of these countries, occupational unionism has left its mark on the course of welfare state development. Earlier in this book I noted Esping-Andersen's acknowledgment of the importance of craft unionism

---

[1] On this, see, for example, Lyle Scruggs, "The Ghent System and Union Membership in Europe, 1970–1996." *Political Research Quarterly* 55:2 (2002), 275–97.

in Denmark to welfare outcomes there. Likewise, to understand the long persistence of special insurance schemes for white-collar workers in Belgium,
Germany, and Switzerland, for example, we have to account for the separate
organization of white-collar workers there.[2] Yet, and as noted earlier, in none
of these countries has the importance of occupational unionism been as great
as in the Anglo-Saxon world. As a result, the consequences of occupational
unionism for welfare state outcomes also have been much greater there.

Because of its prominent position in the welfare state debate, the United
States forms an excellent case in point here. Like its counterpart in the United
Kingdom, the American labor union movement has throughout the twentieth
century been known for its powerful occupationally organized unions. As in the
United Kingdom, the origins of occupational unionism in the United States lie
in the early emergence of craft unions that catered only to certain professions
of skilled, and thus relatively privileged, manual workers. From the moment
lower-skilled manual workers also started to organize *en masse*, this has led to
great divides within the American labor union movement. These divides arguably have been even greater there than in the United Kingdom. In the United
States, craft unions not only prohibited lower-skilled workers from joining them,
but in the first decades of the twentieth century, the craft-organized American
Federation of Labor (AFL) actually worked actively to obstruct lower-skilled
workers from unionizing in separate, industrially organized unions. It often did
so in collaboration with employers.[3] Moreover, during the 1930s, the AFL dis-
solved hundreds of federal unions and distributed its skilled members among
craft unions.[4] Thus, whereas the Dutch union federations and many of their
continental European counterparts worked actively to organize all workers on
an industrial basis and did not shy away from dissolving existing occupational
unions to achieve this, the AFL did the exact opposite.

The consequences of this have received substantial attention from labor scholars. As early as 1920, labor economist Robert Hoxie, for example, remarked
that the American labor union movement "is essentially trade conscious, rather
than class conscious. That is to say it expresses the viewpoint and interests of
the workers in the craft or industry rather than those of the working class as
a whole."[5] Nowadays, the realization that there is "little sense of ideological
solidarity in the American worker movement" is commonplace among labor
scholars.[6] The "notoriously weak solidarity of American workers" also has

[2] See, for example, Hockerts, *Sozialpolitische Entscheidungen*, 97; Van Ruysseveldt and Visser,
    Industrial Relations, 227.
[3] This is well described in James A. Cross, *The Reshaping of the National Labor Relations Boards:
    National Labor Policy in Transition 1937–1947* (Albany: State University of New York Press,
    1981), 61–84.
[4] See, for instance, Walter Galenson, *The CIO Challenge to the AFL: A History of the American
    Labor Movement 1935–1941* (Cambridge, MA: Harvard University Press, 1960).
[5] Robert F. Hoxie, *Trade Unionism in the United States* (New York: Appleton, 1920), 45.
[6] Andrew J. Thomson, "The United States of America." In E. Owen Smith, *Trade Unions in the
    Developed Economies* (New York: St. Martin's Press, 1981), 1.

been noted by some welfare scholars.[7] Yet it nevertheless hardly plays a role in writings on the emergence of the "divided" American welfare state. In their attempts to explain the dismally low level of public protection in the United States and the corresponding growth of occupational benefits that mostly cater to higher-paid workers, scholars of the American welfare state have paid much attention to labor's organizational weakness and little to its occupational features. They have certainly given little attention to the possibility that the low level of public protection in the United States may be related to the resistance of occupationally organized unions to redistributive state intervention.[8] As a result, existing explanations for the AFL's long-standing resistance to nearly any form of government intervention in the labor market and its meek support for the development of public welfare programs during the postwar period seem quite insufficient.[9]

In Chapter 2, I briefly referred to the strong voluntarist inclinations of the AFL. These were especially strong in the decades before the war. Until its hesitant – or depending on one's interpretation of events, reluctant – acceptance of the New Deal, the AFL opposed almost any instance of government intervention in the labor market. Such instances included the introduction of a statutory national minimum wage, a public health insurance program, a public unemployment insurance scheme, and a national pension. The AFL also opposed measures such as the introduction of legislation aimed at setting maximum work hours for male workers.[10] In the literature, the voluntarist inclinations of the AFL are generally explained through either its fears that this would undermine its future ability to attract workers or its distrust of government institutions.[11] The latter explanation, which centers around the conservative

[7] Hacker, *The Divided Welfare State*, 134.

[8] One of the few scholars who have paid much attention to the importance of craft unionism for welfare state outcomes in the United States is Jill Quadagno, in her *The Transformation of Old Age Security: Class and Politics in the American Welfare State* (The University of Chicago Press, 1988). Yet, while she emphasizes that the skilled members of craft unions needed state intervention less, she does not mention that they may have opposed overly redistributive measures. Theda Skocpol nevertheless felt that Quadagno had gone too far in her emphasis on the importance of craft unionism. In Skocpol's view, "a comparison of the American Federation of Labor with the British Trades Union Congress suggests that the reason lay to some extent in the characteristics of American unions, but mostly in the experiences those unions had during that period with U.S. policy." Skocpol, *Social Policy in the United States*, 101.

[9] See, for example, Edwin E. Witte, "Organized Labor and Social Security." In Milton Derber and Edwin Young, *Labor and the New Deal* (Madison: University of Wisconsin Press, 1961), 245; Quadagno, *The Transformation*, 61–2.

[10] See Gary M. Fink, "The Rejection of Voluntarism," *Industrial and Labor Relations Review* 26:2 (1973), 815.

[11] On union fear of weakening its organizational base, see Brown, "Bargaining for Social Rights," 663; Nelson Lichtenstein, *State of the Union: A Century of American Labor* (Princeton, NJ: Princeton University Press, 2002), 3; Derthick, *Policymaking*, 119; Witte, "Organized Labor and Social Security," 270; Marie Gottschalk, *The Shadow Welfare State*, 7; Hacker, *The Divided Welfare State*, 96. See also Stephens, *The Transition*, 89; Rimlinger, *Welfare Policy*, 80; Flanders, *The Tradition*, 367.

actions of U.S. courts in that period and the many resulting judicial challenges to unions, does indeed have much merit.[12] Yet there are nevertheless good reasons to believe that it alone cannot explain the strong voluntarist inclinations of the AFL at the time. Because many of these reasons are similar to the ones put forward to disprove existing explanations for the TUC's voluntarist inclinations in Chapter 2, I will discuss them here only briefly.

The most important problem with explaining the voluntarist inclinations of the AFL in the decades before the war through its fear of undermining its future ability to attract workers or through its distrust of government institutions is that these fears were clearly not shared by all unions. The industrially organized Congress of Industrial Organizations (CIO), for example, never developed equally strong voluntarist inclinations.[13] Neither did the many local labor leaders who criticized the voluntaristic assumptions of the AFL on social insurance and other forms of "positive state action."[14] Needless to say, the doctrine of voluntarism was most clearly rejected by "socialist" union leaders.[15] It is for this reason that political scientist Michael Rogin and labor historian Gary M. Fink viewed the voluntarist inclinations of the AFL as "justified in terms of freedom" but "serving other purposes" and therefore being "above all an organizational ideology, serving organizational needs."[16] These needs may very well have required defending the privileged position of AFL members. Measures such as the introduction of a national minimum wage, as we have seen, certainly conflicted with such needs.

As late as 1937, only one year before its eventual introduction, the AFL still voiced its opposition to the introduction of a national minimum wage. There is ample evidence that its hostility was to a large extent motivated by the fear that the introduction of a statutory minimum wage would reduce craft differentials. In a 1933 hearing by the House Labor Committee, AFL representatives, for instance, clearly stated that they opposed the introduction of a minimum wage because it would likely "depress the rates of unionized craftsmen in industries in which these workers enjoyed substantial differentials over unorganized

---

[12] On the consequences of these judicial challenges to the AFL's view of state legislation, see, for example, Hattam, *Labor Visions and State Power*; William E. Forbath, "The Shaping of the American Labor Movement," *Harvard Law Review* 102:6 (1989); and Skocpol, *Social Policy in the United States*, 105–14.

[13] This difference was still noticeable during the 1930s. According to Colin Gordon, the "CIO stepped forward as an advocate of national and universal health programs in 1938." And according to Martha Derthick, the CIO had "a position well to the left of the Social Security Board." According to Edwin Witte, though, the differences were only "minor." See Gordon, *Dead on Arrival*, 277; Derthick, *Policymaking*, 113; Witte, "Organized Labor and Social Security," 267.

[14] See Fink, "The Rejection of Voluntarism," 815; Quadagno, *The Transformation*, 52; Hacker, *The Divided Welfare State*, 90.

[15] See Gary Marks, "Variations," 84.

[16] See Michael Rogin, "Voluntarism: The Political Functions of an Antipolitical Doctrine," *Industrial and Labor Relations Review* 15:4 (1962), 535; Fink, "The Rejection of Voluntarism," 807.

unskilled workmen."[17] This fear would continue to haunt AFL leaders for long after the Fair Labor Standards Act came into operation.[18] Tellingly, industrially organized unions such as the United Mine Workers and the International Ladies' Garment Workers' Union, and later the CIO, did support the introduction of a statutory national minimum wage wholeheartedly.[19]

The AFL displayed no such hostility toward the 1935 Social Security Act. Then again, the Social Security Act could hardly have been seen as a threat to the privileged position of its membership. Its largest program, old-age insurance, for example, had little redistributive value.[20] Moreover, it did not cover many of the nation's poorest workers.[21] The AFL did not press for the inclusion of all workers at the time (although it would do so in later years), did not support any of the more "radical" proposals that were circulating, and did not come forward with alternative, more redistributive proposals of its own.[22] For all this, it received much credit from the act's liberal drafters.[23] The Social Security Act's other major initiative, the introduction of federally funded but state-administered unemployment programs, was equally limited in ambition. The AFL nevertheless lent only grudging approval to these programs.[24]

[17] Irving Bernstein, *Turbulent Years: A History of the American Worker 1933–1941* (Boston: Houghton Mifflin, 1970), 25–6.

[18] See, for instance, George Paulsen, *A Living Wage for the Forgotten Man: The Quest for Fair Labor Standards 1933–1941* (Cranbury, NJ: Susquehanna University Press, 1996), 33.

[19] See, for instance, Flanders, "The Tradition of Voluntarism," 367; Bernstein, *Turbulent Years*, 25–6; David Dubinsky and A. H. Raskan, *A Life with Labor* (New York: Simon & Schuster, 1977), 119–20.

[20] The system of contributions and benefits did treat lower-paid workers somewhat more generously than higher-paid workers, but the effect of this was quite limited. In coming years, there were some changes in the benefit formula to the further benefit of lower-paid workers. Yet these were not nearly enough to grant lower-paid workers a generous, or even a substantial, benefit. The system was at its most generous during the mid-1970s, when "low earnings," with low earnings defined as 50 percent of the average wage, received a replacement rate of roughly 70 percent. This entitled pensioners with low earnings to a pension of roughly 35 percent of the average wage. By 1983, the replacement rate had decreased to 48.7 percent, which was roughly similar to the replacement rate in the decades before the 1970s. See Dan McGill, Kyle N. Brown, John J. Haley, and Sylvester J. Schieber, *Fundamentals of Private Pensions* (Oxford University Press, 2005), 48.

[21] Initially, only wage and salaried workers in the private sector were covered (these were some 60 percent of all workers at the time). By the mid-1950s, most employed persons had become eligible. See McGill et al., *Fundamentals of Private Pensions*, 32; and Rimlinger, *Welfare Policy*, 236.

[22] According to Jennifer Klein, "[T]he AFL did not intend old-age benefits to be applied universally.... [T]he AFL clearly intended pensions to go to particular male wage earnings." Jennifer Klein, *For All These Rights: Business, Labor and the Shaping of America's Public-Private Welfare State* (Princeton, NJ: Princeton University Press, 2003), 69.

[23] According to Edwin Witte, for example, "Organized labor is entitled to much credit for at all times making its influence felt against the impossible proposals labeled as programs for social security." Witte, "Organized Labor and Social Security," 255.

[24] Ibidem, 245.

The AFL, like the CIO, did support a further extension of social security during the postwar period. At the time, AFL union members were actively engaged in private bargaining for extension of occupational benefits. This has led to much scholarly attention to the question of why "the labor movement chose to compromise its postwar agenda by pursuing private social protection at the bargaining table."[25] Most scholars have answered this question by arguing that the unions were forced to do so because conservative opposition made it impossible for them to acquire adequate public provision.[26] Some scholars have even argued that the pursuit of occupational welfare by unions was mainly designed to induce business support for public welfare policies by increasing the costs of fringe benefits.[27] Others have relied on traditional voluntarist arguments.[28] Finally, several scholars have pointed out that the spread of occupational benefits may have undermined the support of unions in which members were well provisioned through a combination of public and private benefits.[29]

One could argue that this scholarly preoccupation with the union drive for private benefits during the postwar period is somewhat misguided. After all, the Dutch example shows that an expansion of private provision does not have to stand in the way of attempts to increase the generosity of public provision. Much more important than the question of why the American unions turned to private bargaining during the postwar period is how committed they were to the expansion of public provision and whether they were willing to support redistributive measures to achieve this. Tellingly, the existing literature on American welfare state development offers little evidence of instances in which American unions offered concrete proposals to improve public programs by increasing the redistribution of income and risk among workers.[30] On the contrary, scholars have often noted the union movement's meek support for liberal

---

[25] Brown, "Bargaining for Social Rights," 648.

[26] For this view, see Brown, "Bargaining for Social Rights," 648; Hacker, *The Divided Welfare State*, 126; Gordon, *Dead on Arrival*, 281; Klein, *For All These Rights*, 215; Beth Stevens, "Blurring the Boundaries: How Federal Social Policy Has Influenced Welfare Benefits in the Private Sector." In Ann Orloff, Margaret Weir, and Theda Skocpol, *The Politics of Social Policy in the United States* (Princeton, NJ: Princeton University Press, 1988), 146; and Quadagno, *The Transformation*, 160.

[27] See Nelson Lichtenstein, "From Corporatism to Collective Bargaining: Organized Labor and the Eclipse of Social Democracy in the Postwar Era." In Steve Fraser and Gary Gerstle, *The Rise and Fall of the New Deal Order, 1930–1980* (Princeton, NJ: Princeton University Press, 1989), 122–52; and Seth Wigderson, "How the CIO Saved Social Security," *Labor History* 44:4 (2003), 483.

[28] See Gottschalk, *The Shadow Welfare State*, 43.

[29] See Hugh Mosley, "Corporate Social Benefits and the Underdevelopment of the American Welfare State," *Contemporary Crises* 5 (1981), 152; Gottschalk, *The Shadow Welfare State*, 1; Gordon, *Dead on Arrival*, 281; Hacker, *The Divided Welfare State*, 134.

[30] One frustrating feature of much of the literature on American welfare state development (and of the literature on welfare state development in most other nations) is also that scholars have simply paid little attention to the actual features of the programs put forward by policy makers.

public welfare initiatives.[31] This makes it quite tempting to present another view of the involvement of the American union movement in the development of the postwar American welfare state. After the war, public and private provision against labor market risks in the United States remained inadequate mainly for the nation's lower-paid, more-risk-prone workers. To improve matters for these workers, there would have to be a substantial degree of risk and income distribution between different categories of workers. Although they were certainly committed to an expansion of public provision in principle, it is quite questionable whether the powerful occupationally organized unions in the United States would have accepted this.

UNION STRUCTURE AND LABOR MARKET DEVELOPMENT

Although this book's main concern has been with explaining postwar welfare state development, it also has paid much attention to the development of labor markets. The close relationship between the domains of "welfare" and "work" made this inevitable. So far this book has only paid attention to labor market developments insofar as they mattered to welfare state outcomes in the Netherlands and the United Kingdom. Yet the findings of this work also have important consequences for our understanding of the process of postwar labor market development in advanced industrial countries. Many of these consequences are important enough to warrant further exploration. I will therefore briefly turn to them in the remainder of this chapter.

In Chapter 2, I pointed out that the emphasis on class divisions and the related tendency to view labor as a homogeneous and disadvantaged group is by no means limited to the literature on welfare state development. Both are equally strong in the broader literature on labor market development. Two resulting tendencies have already received substantial attention in this book. The first is the strong inclination to assume that labor unions always bring an egalitarian agenda to the bargaining table, which includes promoting wage compression among different categories of workers. With this comes the tendency to assume labor union support for the redistributive consequences of government intervention in the labor market. The second is the predilection to resort to "voluntarist" antistate explanations for instances in which labor unions have not supported redistributive government intervention in the labor market.

My criticism of this interpretation of voluntarism, as well as my pointing to its relationship with the resistance of unions representing privileged workers to any attempt to reduce wage differentials among different categories of

---

[31] I have already mentioned that "the existing labor movement had little to do with the creation of Social Security." Wigderson, "How the CIO Saved Social Security," 486. Scholars have also noted its weak support for public health care proposals across time periods – from Truman's proposal to Clinton's. See, for example, Gottschalk, *The Shadow Welfare State*, on this.

workers, need not be examined here. After all, I have already explored this fully in earlier sections of this book. Instead, I will briefly turn to the implications of my findings for the literature on neocorporatism and wage inequality. The internal organizational blueprint of labor union movements has been a crucial and largely neglected factor in the development – or lack thereof – of so-called neocorporatist modes of decision making in many continental European countries. Its great importance for wage and income inequality has similarly received insufficient scholarly attention.

Just as the persistence of "voluntarism" has attracted substantial attention from scholars working on labor market development in what could roughly be described as the "Anglo-Saxon world," so have scholars of labor market development in continental European countries emphasized the extent to which labor and capital there became formally integrated into the state's postwar policy-making arena. This integration has often been described as a move toward "neocorporatist" decision making. Although thoroughly divided on its origins and even its exact definition,[32] scholars generally agree about the consequences of neocorporatism. Most important among these is arguably the relatively harmonious state of affairs between (and in the case of the first, I should add among) unions and employer interest groups in neocorporatist countries.[33] The presence of neocorporatist institutions has been used, among other factors, to explain labor unions' relative willingness to cooperate with wage-moderation policies and to refrain from the use of the strike weapon to achieve their goals in many continental European countries.[34]

Throughout this book I have noted the presence of neocorporatist institutions and their importance for decision making in the Netherlands. I have nevertheless refrained from treating them as a separate explanatory force for the extremely generous and redistributive outcome of welfare state development in the Netherlands. I have done so for two reasons. First, I simply did not encounter enough evidence for this. Of course, the decision to make labor unions and organized employers responsible for the implementation of social security schemes certainly contributed to the increase in the number of benefit recipients – especially with regard to the disability insurance program, as shown in Chapter 5.[35] Yet it is much more difficult to argue that

---

[32] The sociologist Göran Therborn described this by saying that "'Corporatism' has become a bit like God. Many people believe it is an important phenomenon, crucially affecting social life. But nobody really knows what it looks like, so disagreement persists, apparently forever, about what it is and about what it does." Göran Therborn, "Lessons from Corporatist Theorizations." In Jukka Pekkarinen, Matti Pohjola, and Bob Rowthorn, *Social Corporatism: A Superior Economic System?* (Oxford University Press, 1992), 430.

[33] See, for example, Visser and Hemerijck, *A Dutch Miracle*, 67–8; Wilensky, *Rich Democracies*, 82; Crouch, *Industrial Relations*; Wilson, *Business and Politics*.

[34] See Visser and Hemerijck, *A Dutch Miracle*, 68.

[35] It is for this reason that most scholars who have emphasized the "neocorporatist" nature of decision making in the Netherlands for welfare outcomes there have pointed to the number of

neocorporatist decision-making institutions were indispensable for or even facilitated the unions' push for higher pension benefits, an increase in the level and duration of the unemployment benefit, and the introduction of minimum benefit levels into the unemployment, sickness, and disability insurance programs. On the contrary, the preceding chapters have made it abundantly clear that the employer federations were very adept at using platforms such as the Sociaal-Economische Raad (SER, Social-Economic Council) to derail union demands for this during endless discussions over technical matters. In Chapter 4, for example, I noted that it took nearly a decade and a half for the employer representatives to the SER to agree to an extension in the duration and level of the 1949 Werkloosheidswet (WW, Unemployment Act) benefit. In Chapter 3, I analyzed how the employer federations managed to delay union demands for further increases in the public pension benefit during the 1950s and 1960s.

There is another, and arguably more important, reason why I did not treat the presence of neocorporatist institutions as a separate explanatory force for the extremely generous and redistributive outcome of welfare state development in the Netherlands. This reason is that the emergence of such institutions in the Netherlands cannot be treated in isolation from the dominance of industrial unionism there. Just as the dominance of craft or occupational unionism contributed to the persistence of "voluntarism" in the United Kingdom, so can the dominance of industrial unionism in the Netherlands be viewed as a major precondition for the emergence of a neocorporatist mode of decision making there. This point deserves some elaboration because it has not received much attention in the comparative literature on neocorporatism.

Earlier I noted that there are a host of different explanations for the development of neocorporatist decision-making institutions in many continental European countries. Over the years, scholars have attempted to explain this through, among other factors, the presence of either left or confessional parties there, the nations' relatively small sizes, the presence of consensus democracy, the strength of national labor union movements, and the strong and disciplined nature of business representation there.[36] Largely absent among these explanations is the strong dominance of industrial unionism in these countries. Many scholars have noted the presence of "hierarchical and monopolistic peak union

benefit claimants. Most of the arguments put forward by these scholars boil down to the claim that these institutions "later made it impossible to apply the brakes." Visser and Hemerijck, *A Dutch Miracle*, 121. See also Therborn, "Pillarization," 215; Van der Veen, *De ontwikkeling*, 34; Tuelings, Van der Veen, and Trommel, *Dilemma's van sociale zekerheid*, 59.

[36] See, for example, Swank, *Global Capital*, 43; Huber and Stephens, *Development and Crisis*, 10–11; Cox, *The Development of the Dutch Welfare State*, 67; Jaap Woldendorp, "Neo-Corporatism as a Strategy for Conflict Resolution in the Netherlands," *Acta Politica* 30:2 (1995), 129; Katzenstein, *Small States*, 24; Arend Lijphart and Markus Crepaz, "Corporatism and Consensus Democracy in Eighteen Countries: Conceptual and Empirical linkages," *British Journal of Political Science* 21 (1991); and Crouch, *Industrial Relations*, 334.

organizations" in neocorporatist countries.[37] Yet they have generally failed to mention that strong peak union organizations can only emerge when their member unions do not bicker among themselves over the division of labor's share of the national income. For reasons described earlier, the absence of such internal bickering depends on the presence of industrial unionism.

The United Kingdom is ideally suited to illustrate how the emergence of a strong neocorporatist tradition depends on the presence of industrial unionism. As occurred elsewhere in northern Europe, various British governments created many different platforms designed to formally integrate labor and capital into the decision-making arena of the state in pre- and postwar years. These included the bipartite National Joint Advisory Council, the tripartite National Economic Development Council, and several committees meant to facilitate tripartite consultation over social insurance matters.[38] In contrast to the Dutch case, however, these councils and platforms never developed into influential advisory bodies. To understand this, it is crucial to note that the influence of such bodies depends on their ability to produce uniform advice. When the union movement is itself deeply divided over issues related to public welfare development and other instances of government intervention in the labor market, it is hard to see how such uniformity might be achieved. If anything, this book has shown how strongly divided the British labor union movement was on many such issues.[39]

Once we realize the importance of industrial unionism for the development of neocorporatist modes of decision making, we also may review some of its supposed consequences. Earlier I noted the scholarly tendency to argue that neocorporatist modes of decision making lead to a more harmonious state of affairs. One also could argue that both the emergence of neocorporatist institutions and the relatively harmonious nature of industrial relations in most of continental Europe have their origins in, or at least depend on, the dominance of industrial unionism there. Another supposed consequence of neocorporatism can be dismissed immediately. This is the idea that it leads to more generous welfare state outcomes because it increases the political power of the "organized working class."[40] This idea has often been put forward but has

---

[37] Philippe Schmitter deemed this so important that he defined neocorporatism as an interest-group system in which groups are organized into national, specialized, hierarchical, and monopolistic peak organizations. See Schmitter, "Reflections," 259–60.

[38] The National Joint Advisory Council was actually created in 1939, and the National Economic Development Council was created in 1961. The National Insurance Advisory Committee and the Industrial Injuries Advisory Council were important committees on social insurance matters.

[39] It is no wonder, then, that so many scholars have condemned the "possessive individualist" culture of British unions and their inability to "subordinate short-term self-interest to wider long-term interest." David Marquand, *The Unprincipled Society* (London: Fontana, 1988), 158–66. See also Schmitter and Lehmbruch, *Patterns*, 21; and Wyn Grant, *Business and Politics in Britain* (Basingstoke: Macmillan, 1987), 9.

[40] Douglas A. Hibbs, "On the Political Economy of Long-Run Trends in Strike Activity," *British Journal of Political Science* 8 (1978), 165–6. See also Hans Keman, *The Development Toward*

rarely been investigated. Most of the time it simply rests on the observation that the neocorporatist nations of continental Europe have relatively high public spending levels.[41] The findings of this study give little reason to assume that Dutch corporatist institutions increased the political power of the organized working class in the Netherlands. Instead, its findings emphasize the importance of a solidaristic union movement. Likewise, this study found that in the British case, the absence of strong neocorporatist institutions did not decrease the political influence of the organized working class. On the contrary, the ability of Britain's craft unions to block so many of Labour's policy initiatives clearly demonstrates how immensely powerful the British labor union movement was.

The findings of this study also have important implications for our understanding of why unions may support wage compression among different categories of workers. In Chapter 2, I mentioned the popularity of the assumption that labor unions compress wages among different categories of workers, and scholars' resulting use of cross-national differences in union density levels to explain cross-national differences in wage inequality. I have also noted that the assumption of labor union support for wage compression among different categories of workers generally rests on what is often called the "median voter model." This model is based on the idea that in situations in which the mean wage is higher than the median wage (which is typically the case), a majority of union members will benefit from and therefore favor wage compression.[42] The median voter model clearly does not work in nations in which the union movement is largely organized along occupational lines. In such nations, higher-paid workers organize separately and thus cannot be forced to support wage compression by a majority of lower-paid workers. In sum, to fully understand cross-national variation in wage inequality, scholars must start paying attention to union structure.

In Chapter 2, I paid much attention to the strong resistance of craft and occupationally organized white-collar unions in the United Kingdom to any attempt to reduce wage differentials between their members and lower-skilled workers. This makes the United Kingdom an excellent example of how the median voter model does not work in nations characterized by strong occupational divisions. In the same chapter, I suggested several reasons for why the median voter model also may come up short in explaining the redistributive

---

Surplus Welfare: Social-Democratic Politics and Policies in Advanced Capitalist Democracies (1965–1984) (Amsterdam: CT Press, 1988); Alex Hicks, Duane Swank, and Martin Ambuhl, "Welfare Expansion Revisited: Policy Routines and Their Mediation by Party, Class and Crisis, 1957–1982," *European Journal of Political Research* 17 (1989), 401–30.

[41] See, for example, Wilensky, *Rich Democracies*, 257; Lijphart and Crepaz, "Corporatism and Consensus Democracy," 334; Markus Crepaz, "Corporatism in Decline? An Empirical Analysis of the Impact of Corporatism on Macroeconomic Performance and Industrial Disputes in 18 Industrialized Democracies," *Comparative Political Studies* 25:2 (1992), 139–68.

[42] See footnote 91 of Chapter 2 on this.

efforts of the industrially organized Dutch union movement. Among other reasons, many of the redistributive initiatives put forward by the three Dutch union federations simply benefited too few workers for this. In the final section of this chapter I will elaborate the consequences of this for our understanding of union support for redistributive welfare state development.

MAPPING SOCIAL SOLIDARITY

I began this book by noting the strong disparities in the degrees to which postwar Western societies have been able to achieve adequate protection for all their members against the risks of economic misfortune and dependency. I argued that improving our understanding of these disparities requires a fundamental reappraisal of the role of organized labor in welfare state development. As we have seen, the main purpose of the welfare state is not to compensate labor for its disadvantaged position on the labor market. Nor is it to redistribute income and risk from a small minority of affluent workers to a vast majority that suffers in destitution. Instead, one of its main purposes is to assist workers who cannot achieve adequate wages and security against labor market risks without a redistribution of income and risk from other occupational categories. Often these vulnerable workers make up only a small minority of the labor category.

One of the most striking features of the redistributive measures proposed in the Netherlands and the United Kingdom during the period under investigation here is that they often benefited only a small minority group of very low-paid workers. Since these measures were far more successful in the Netherlands, several Dutch examples can be mentioned here. One excellent example is the introduction of a minimum benefit rate into the Dutch unemployment, disability, and sickness insurance programs during the 1960s. As we have seen, this move benefited only 12 percent of all married men aged twenty-three and over, whereas its costs had to be borne by all insured workers. The choice to combine flat-rate benefits with earnings-related contributions in the Netherlands during the early 1950s was clearly also designed to benefit a minority of low-paid workers. Finally, the introduction of a statutory national minimum wage in the late 1960s and its subsequent increase relative to average wages likewise benefited only a small group of workers.

More generally, it should be noted that the Netherlands was no exception to the rule that redistributive welfare measures often do not affect the highest income brackets. Relatively low wage limits and contribution thresholds severely limited the redistributive scope of all social security schemes in the Netherlands, making it doubtful whether the median or average worker necessarily stood to gain from them. The 1949 WW represents an extreme example. Until the mid-1960s, this act maintained a wage limit that severely limited the scope of risk reapportioning by excluding all workers who earned more than

120 percent of the modal wage. This further suggests that the redistributive efforts of the three Dutch union federations cannot be explained through the notion that they believed this to be in the interests of "labor" as a whole or even a majority of workers. Instead, it suggests that they were prompted by the aim to make sure that *all* workers could count on a sufficient level of protection against the risk of unemployment – including the lowest-paid workers. In other words, the three union federations actively put the notion of worker solidarity into effect.

Unfortunately, the elusive concept of solidarity does not sit well with existing approaches to welfare state development. Most of these assume that interest-group policies are an outcome of an aggregated form of individual means-end rationality. Yet labor unions, as already emphasized in Peter Swenson's *Fair Shares*, are more than mere welfare maximizers whose policies are a direct extension of the interests of a majority of their members. Union policies evidently also can be guided by normative orientations that emphasize fairness and broad worker solidarity. How these norms play out crucially depends on their organizational blueprint, though. Once more, the crucial distinction here is between unions whose organizational logic emphasizes class unity and those that organize along occupational lines. In the former case, as we have seen, union policies will reflect broad worker solidarity. In the latter case, as we have seen as well, they likely will not do so.

Bibliography

Aarts, Leo, Richard Burkhauser, and Philip de Jong, "Introduction and Overview." In Leo Aarts, Richard Burkhauser, and Philip de Jong, *Curing the Dutch Disease: An International Perspective on Disability Policy Reform* (Aldershot: Avebury, 1996).

Abel-Smith, Brian, and Peter Townsend, *The Poor and the Poorest* (London: Bell, 1965).

Ackers, Peter, and Adrian Wilkinson, "British Industrial Relations Paradigm: A Critical Outline History and Prognosis," *Journal of Industrial Relations* 47 (2005), 443–56.

Albeda, Wil, *Arbeidsverhoudingen in Nederland* (Alphen aan den Rijn, 1989).

Alber, Jens, *Vom Armenhaus zum Wohlfahrtsstaat* (Frankfurt: Campus, 1982).

Alcock, Peter, *Poverty and State Support. Social Policy in Modern Britain* (Harlow: Longman Group, 1987).

Arnoldus, Doreen, *In goed overleg? Het overleg over de social zekerheid in Nederland vergeleken met België, 1967–1984* (Amsterdam: Aksant, 2007).

Ashford, Douglas, *The Emergence of the Welfare States* (Oxford: Basil Blackwell, 1986).

Atiyah, Patrick, *Accidents, Compensation and the Law* (London: Weidenfeld and Nicolson, 1975).

Bain, George Sayers, "The Growth of White-Collar Unionism in Great Britain," *British Journal of Industrial Relations* 4 (1966), 304–31.

  "The Minimum Wage: Further Reflections," *Employee Relations* 21:1 (1999), 15–28.

Baldwin, Peter, *The Politics of Social Solidarity: Class Bases of the European Welfare State 1875–1975* (Cambridge University Press, 1990).

Bannink, Duco, "Het Nederlandse stelsel van sociale zekerheid. Van achterblijver naar koploper naar vroege hervormer." In Willem Trommel and Romke van der Veen, *De herverdeelde samenleving. De ontwikkeling en herziening van de Nederlandse verzorgingsstaat* (Amsterdam University Press, 1999).

Bartolini, Stefano, *The Political Mobilization of the European Left: The Class Cleavage* (Cambridge University Press, 2000).

Bazen, Stephen, Mary Gregory, and Wiemer Salverda, *Low-Wage Employment in Europe* (Cheltenham: Edward Elgar, 1998).

Beer, Paul de, *Het verdiende inkomen* (Houten/Zeventhem: Bohn Stafleu van Loghum, 1993).

Bell, J. D. M., "Trade Unions." In Allan Flanders and Hugh Clegg, *The Changing System of Industrial Relations in Great Britain: Its History, Law and Institutions* (Oxford: Blackwell, 1954).

Beltzer, Ronald, and Renske Biezeveld, *De pensioenvoorziening als bindmiddel. Sociale cohesie en de organisatie van pensioen in Nederland* (Amsterdam: Aksant, 2004).

Berg, Johannes Th. J. van den, Max G. Rood, and Teun Jaspers, *De SVr 40 jaar: einde van een tijdperk, een nieuw begin?* (Deventer: Kluwer, 1992).

Bernstein, Irving, *Turbulent Years: A History of the American Worker 1933–1941* (Boston: Houghton Mifflin, 1970).

Berthoud, Richard, *Disability Benefits: A Review of the Issues and Options for Reform* (York, PA: York Publishing Services, 1998).

Beveridge, William, *Social Insurance and Allied Services: Report* (London: HMSO, 1942).

Blackburn, Sheila, "The Problem of Riches: From Trade Boards to a National Minimum Wage," *Industrial Relations Journal* 51:2 (1988), 124–38.

Blanpain, Roger, *Collective Bargaining and Wages in Comparative Perspective: Germany, France, The Netherlands, Sweden and the United Kingdom* (The Hague: Kluwer, 2005).

Blundell, Richard, and Paul Johnson, "Pensions and Labor-Market Participation in the United Kingdom," *American Economic Review* 88:2 (1998), 168–72.

Boon, A. de, *Rapport van de commissie van externe adviseurs terzake van vervroegd uittreden van oudere werknemers* (Den Haag: Ministerie van Sociale Zaken, 1975).

Borg, M. B. ter, "Het confessionalisme en de sociale zekerheid," *Sociale Wetenschappen* 29:3 (1986), 191–214.

Bosch, Gerhard, *Low-Wage Work in Germany* (New York: Sage, 2008).

Bowlby, Roger L., "Union Policy Toward Minimum Wage Legislation in Postwar Britain," *Industrial and Labor Relations Review* 11:1 (1957), 72–4.

Bowles, Samuel, "Egalitarian Redistribution in Globally Integrated Economies." In Pranab Bardhan, Samuel Bowles, and Michael Wallerstein, *Globalization and Egalitarian Redistribution* (New York: Sage, 2006).

Bradley, David, Evelyne Huber, Stephanie Moller, Francois Nielsen, and John D. Stephens, "Distribution and Redistribution in Postindustrial Economies," *World Politics* 55:2 (2003), 193–228.

Bridgen, Paul, "The One Nation Idea and State Welfare: The Conservatives and Pensions in the 1950s," *Contemporary British History* 14:3 (2000), 83–104.

"The State, Redundancy Pay, and Economic Policy-Making in the Early 1960s," *Twentieth Century British History* 11:3 (2000), 233–58.

"A Straitjacket with Wriggle Room: The Beveridge Report, the Treasury and the Exchequer's Pension Liability, 1942–1959," *Twentieth Century British History* 17 (2006), 1–25.

Bridgen, Paul, and Rodney Lowe, *Welfare Policy under the Conservatives 1951–1964: A Guide to Documents in the Public Record Office* (London: Public Record Office, 1998).

Brown, Michael K., "Bargaining for Social Rights: Unions and the Re-Emergence of Welfare Capitalism, 1945–1952," *Political Science Quarterly* 112:4 (1997–98), 645–7.

Bruggen, J. van, and B. C. Slotemaker, *Commentaar op de Ziektewet. Handboek voor de practijk* (Deventer: Kluwer, 1935).

Calvert, Harry, *Social Security Law* (London: Sweet and Maxwell, 1987).

Campbell, Alan, Nina Fishman, and John McIlroy, "The Post-War Compromise: Mapping Industrial Politics, 1945–1964." In Alan Campbell, Nina Fishman, and John McIlroy, *British Trade Unions and Industrial Politics*, Vol. I: *The Post-War Compromise, 1945–1964* (Aldershot: Ashgate, 1999).

Card, David, "Falling Union Membership and Rising Wage Inequality: What's the Connection?" *NBER Working Paper Series* 6520 (Cambridge, MA: NBER, 1998).

"The Effect of Unions on Wage Inequality in the U.S. Labor Market," *Industrial and Labor Relations Review*, 54 (2001), 296–315.

Card, David, Thomas Lemieux, and Craig Riddell, "Unions and the Wage Structure." In John T. Addison and C. Schnabel, *International Handbook of Trade Unions* (Cheltenham: Edward Elgard, 2003) 248–92.

Casey, Bernard, and Gert Bruche, *Work or Retirement? Labour Market and Social Policy for Older Workers in France, Great Britain, the Netherlands, Sweden and the United States* (Aldershot: Gower, 1981).

Casey, Bernard, and Stephen Wood, "Great Britain: Firm Policy, State Policy and the Employment of Older Workers." In Frieder Naschold and Bert de Vroom, *Regulating Employment and Welfare: Company and National Policies of Labour Force Participation at the End of Worklife in Industrial Countries* (Berlin: Walter de Gruyter, 1994).

Castle, Barbara, *The Castle Diaries, 1964–1970* (London: Weidenfeld and Nicholson, 1984).

Castles, Francis, "The Impact of Parties on Public Expenditures." In Francis Castles, *The Impact of Parties: Politics and Policies in Democratic Capitalist States* (Beverly Hills, CA: Sage, 1982).

Centraal Bureau voor de Statistiek, *Overzicht van den omvang der vakbeweging op 1 januari 1920. Bijdragen tot de Statistiek van Nederland* (Den Haag: CBS, 1921).

Sociaal-Economische Maandstatistiek (August 1993).

Charles, Rodger S. J., *The Development of Industrial Relations in Britain 1911–1939: Studies in the Evolution of Collective Bargaining at National and Industry Level* (London: Hutchinson, 1973).

Chechi, Daniele, Jelle Visser, and Herman van der Werfhorst, "Inequality and Union Membership: The Impact of Relative Earnings Position and Inequality Attitudes," *British Journal of Industrial Relations* 48:1 (2009), 84–108.

Clegg, Hugh, *The Changing System of Industrial Relations in Britain* (Oxford: Blackwell, 1979).

Cliff, Tony, *The Crisis. Social Contract or Socialism* (London: Pluto Press, 1975).

Confederation of British Industry, *Earnings-Related Social Security* (Newcastle: Hindson Reid Jordison, 1970).

Cox, Robert Henry, *The Development of the Dutch Welfare State: From Workers' Insurance to Universal Entitlement* (University of Pittsburg Press, 1993).

Crepaz, Markus, "Corporatism in Decline? An Empirical Analysis of the Impact of Corporatism on Macroeconomic Performance and Industrial Disputes in 18 Industrialized Democracies," *Comparative Political Studies* 25:2 (1992), 139–68.

Cross, James A., *The Reshaping of the National Labor Relations Boards: National Labor Policy in Transition 1937–1947* (Albany: State University of New York Press, 1981).

Cross, Michael, *Managing Workforce Reduction: an International Survey* (London: Croom Helm, 1985).

Crossman, Richard *The Politics of Pensions* (Liverpool University Press, 1972).

The Backbench Diaries of Richard Crossman (London: Hamilton, (1981).

The Diaries of a Cabinet Minister, Vol. 3: *Secretary of State for Social Services, 1968–1970* (London: Hamilton, 1977).

Crouch, Colin, *Industrial Relations and European State Traditions* (Oxford University Press, 1993).

Cruchten, Jo van, and Rob Kuijpers, "Vakbeweging en organisatiegraad van werknemers," *Sociaaleconomische Trends* (January 2007), 7–17.

Daunton, Martin, *Just Taxes: The Politics of Taxation in Britain, 1914–1979* (Cambridge University Press, 2002).

Department of Employment and Productivity, *A National Minimum Wage: An Inquiry* (London: HMSO, 1969).

Department of Health and Social Security, *Explanatory Memorandum on the National Superannuation and Social Insurance Bill 1969* (London: HMSO, 1969).

Social Insurance Proposals for Earnings-Related Short-Term and Invalidity Benefits (London: HMSO, 1969).

The New Pensions Scheme: Latest Facts and Figures with Examples (London: HMSO, 1969).

Social Security Act 1975: Reform of the Industrial Injuries Scheme (London: HMSO, 1981).

Dercksen, Willem, Pim Fortuyn, and T. Jaspers, *Vijfendertig jaar SER-adviezen, deel I 1950–1964* (Deventer: Kluwer, 1982).

Derthick, Martha, *Policymaking for Social Security* (Washington, DC: Brookings Institution, 1979).

Dinardo, John, Nicole Fortin, and Thomas Lemieux, "Labor Market Institutions and the Distribution of Wages, 1973–1992: A Semi-Parametric Approach," *Econometrica* 64 (1996), 1001–44.

Disability Alliance, *The Case for a Comprehensive Income Scheme for Disabled People* (London: Disability Alliance, 1975).

Dolado, Juan, Francis Kramarz, Stephen Machin, F. Manning, David Margolis, and Coen Toenings, "Minimum Wages in Europe," *Economic Policy* (October 1996).

Doorn, J. A. A. van, and C. J. M. Schuyt, *De stagnerende verzorgingsstaat* (Amsterdam/Meppel: Boom, 1978).

Dorey, Peter, *Wage Politics in Britain: The Rise and Fall of Incomes Policies since 1945* (Brighton: Sussex Academic Press, 2001).

Dubinsky, David, and A. H. Raskan, *A Life with Labor* (New York: Simon & Schuster, 1977).

Duncan, Colin, *Low Pay: Its Causes, and the Post-War Trade Union Response* (Chichester: Research Studies Press, 1981).

Ebbinghaus, Bernhard, "Denmark." In Bernhard Ebbinghaus and Jelle Visser, *The Societies of Europe: Trade Unions in Western Europe since 1945* (London: Macmillan, 2005).

Reforming Early Retirement in Europe, Japan and the USA (Oxford University Press, 2006).

Ebbinghaus, Bernhard, and Philip Manow (eds.), *Comparing Welfare Capitalism: Social Policy and Political Economy in Europe, Japan, and the USA* (London: Routledge, 2001).

Ebbinghaus, Bernhard, and Jeremy Waddington, "United Kingdom/Great Britain." In Bernhard Ebbinghaus and Jelle Visser, *The Societies of Europe: Trade Unions in Western Europe since 1945* (London: Macmillan, 2005).

Edwards, Paul, Mark Hall, Richard Hyman, Paul Marginson, Keith Sisson, Jeremy Waddington, and David Winchester, "Great Britain: From Partial Collectivism to Neo-Liberalism to Where?" In Anthony Ferner and Richard Hyman, *Changing Industrial Relations in Europe* (Oxford: Blackwell, 1998).

Eichengreen, Barry, *The European Economy since 1945: Coordinated Capitalism and Beyond* (Princeton, NJ: Princeton University Press, 2007).

Esping-Andersen, Gøsta, *Politics Against Markets: The Social-Democratic Road to Power* (Princeton, NJ: Princeton University Press, 1985).

The Three Worlds of Welfare Capitalism (Princeton, NJ: Princeton University Press, 1990).

Esping-Andersen, Gøsta, and Roger Friedland, "Class Coalitions in the Making of Western European Economics." In Gøsta Esping-Andersen and Roger Friedland, *Political Power and Social Theory*, Vol. III (Greenwich: Jai Press, 1982).

Esping-Andersen, Gøsta, and Kees Van Kersbergen, "Contemporary Research on Social Democracy," *Annual Review of Sociology* 23 (1992), 187–208.

Esping-Andersen, Gøsta, and Walter Korpi, "Social Policy as Class Politics in Post-War Capitalism: Scandinavia, Austria, and Germany." In John H. Goldthorpe, *Order and Conflict in Contemporary Capitalism* (Oxford: Clarendon Press, 1984).

Eurostat, *Poverty in Figures: Europe in the Early 1980s* (Luxembourg: Eurostat 1990).

Fase, W. J. P. M., *Vijfendertig jaar loonbeleid in Nederland. Terugblik en perspectief* (Alphen aan den Rijn: Samson, 1980).

Fawcett, Helen, "The Beveridge Strait-jacket: Policy Formation and the Problem of Poverty in Old Age," *Contemporary British History* 10 (1996), 20–42.

"Jack Jones, the Social Contract and Social Policy 1970–1974." In Helen Fawcett and Rob Lowe, *Welfare Policy in Britain: The Road from 1945* (London: Macmillan, 1999).

Ferner, Anthony, and Richard Hyman (eds.), *Changing Industrial Relations in Europe* (Oxford: Basil Blackwell, 1998).

Fink, Gary M., "The Rejection of Voluntarism," *Industrial and Labor Relations Review* 26:2 (1973).

Finlayson, Geoffrey, *Citizen, State, and Social Welfare in Britain, 1830–1990* (Oxford: Clarendon Press, 1994).

Flanagan, Robert J., David W. Soskice, and Lloyd Ulman, *Unionism, Economic Stabilization and Income Policies: The European Experience* (Washington, DC: Brookings Institution, 1983).

Flanders, Allan, "The Tradition of Voluntarism," *British Journal of Industrial Relations* 12 (1974), 352–70.

Flora, Peter, *Growth to Limits: The Western European Welfare States since World War II*, Vol. 4: *Appendix (Synopses, Bibliographies, Tables)* (Berlin: Walter de Gruyter, 1987).

Forbath, Willam E., "The Shaping of the American Labor Movement," *Harvard Law Review* 102:6 (1989).

Fraser, W. Hamish, *A History of British Trade Unionism 1700–1998* (Basingstoke: Macmillan, 1999).

Fraser, Derek, *The Evolution of the British Welfare State: A History of Social Policy since the Industrial Revolution* (London: Macmillan, 2003).

Freeman, Richard B., "How Much has De-Unionization Contributed to the Rise in Male Earnings Inequality?" In S. Danziger and P. Gottschalk, *Uneven Tides: Rising Inequality in America* (New York: Sage, 1993).

Friedman, Milton, "Some Comments on the Significance for Labor Unions on Economic Policy." In David Wright, *The Impact of the Union* (New York: Kelley and Millman, 1956).

Fulcher, James, "On the Explanation of Industrial Relations Diversity: Labour Movements, Employers and the State in Britain and Sweden," *British Journal of Industrial Relations* 26:2 (1988), 246–74.

Funk, Lothar, and Hagen Lesch, "Minimum Wage Regulations in Selected European Countries," *Intereconomics* 41:2 (2006), 78–92.

Galenson, Walter, *The CIO Challenge to the AFL: A History of the American Labor Movement 1935–1941* (Cambridge, MA: Harvard University Press, 1960).

Ginneken, Paul van, *VUT: Vervroegde uittreding en ontwikkeling* (Den Haag: Ministerie van Sociale Zaken, 1981).

Glennerster, Howard, *British Social Policy since 1945* (Oxford: Blackwell, 2000).

Glennerster, Howard, and Martin Evans, "Beveridge and His Assumptive Worlds: The Incompatibilities of a Flawed Design." In John Hills, John Ditch, and Howard Glennerster, *Beveridge and Social Security: An International Retrospective* (Oxford University Press, 1994).

Goldthorpe, John, *Order and Conflict in Contemporary Capitalism* (Oxford: Clarendon Press, 1984).

Gordon, Colin, *New Deals: Business, Labor and Politics in America, 1920–1935* (Cambridge University Press, 1994).

Dead on Arrival: The Politics of Health Care in Twentieth-Century America (Princeton, NJ: Princeton University Press, 2003).

Gordon, Margaret S., *Social Security Policies in Industrial Countries: A Comparative Analysis* (Cambridge University Press, 1988), 20–36.

Gospel, Howard, and Gill Palmer, *British Industrial Relations* (London: Routledge 1994).

Gottschalk, Marie, *The Shadow Welfare State: Labor, Business, and the Politics of Health Care in the United States* (Ithaca, NY: Cornell University Press, 2000).

Goudswaard, Kees, and Philip de Jong, "The Distributional Impact of Current Income Transfer Policies in the Netherlands," *Journal of Social Policy* 14:3 (1985), 367–83.

Grant, Wyn, *Business and Politics in Britain* (Basingstoke: Macmillan, 1987).

Griensven, Peter van, "Het sociale beleid van minister Joekes." In P. F. Maas, *Parlementaire Geschiedenis van Nederland na 1945. Het kabinet Drees-Van Schaik (1948–1951): Liberalisatie en sociale ordening* (Nijmegen: SSN, 1992).

"Sociale Zaken: spanning tussen het sociaal wenselijke en het economisch mogelijke." In J. J. M. Ramakers, *Parlementaire geschiedenis van Nederland na 1945. Het kabinet-Drees II (1951–1952): In de schaduw van de Koreacrisis* (Nijmegen: SSN, 1997).

Guillemard, Anne-Marie, and Martin Stein, "Comparative patterns of retirement: recent trends in developed societies," *Annual Review of Sociology* 19 (1993).

Hacker, Jacob S., *The Divided Welfare State: The Battle over Public and Private Social Benefits in the United States* (Cambridge University Press, 2002).

Hacker, Jacob, "Bringing the Welfare State Back In: The Promise (and Perils) of the New Social Welfare History," *Journal of Policy History* 17:1 (2005), 125–54.

Hacker, Jacob, and Paul Pierson, "Business Power and Social Policy: Employers and the Formation of the American Welfare State." *Politics and Society* 30:2 (2002), 277–325.

Hall, Peter A. *Governing the Economy* (Oxford: Polity Press, 1986).

Hall, Peter A., and David Soskice (eds.), *Varieties of Capitalism: The Institutional Foundations of Comparative Advantage* (Oxford University Press, 2001).

Hannah, Leslie, *Inventing Retirement: The Development of Occupational Benefits in Britain* (Cambridge University Press, 1986).

Harmsen, Ger, and Bob Reinalda, *Voor de bevrijding van de arbeid: beknopte geschiedenis van de Nederlandse vakbeweging* (Nijmegen: SUN, 1975).

Harmsen, Ger, Jos Perry, and Floor van Gelder, *Mensenwerk. Industriële vakbonden op weg naar eenheid* (Ambo: Baarn, 1980).

Harris, José, *William Beveridge: A Biography* (Oxford: Clarendon Press, 1997).

Harris, Amelia I., Elizabeth Cox, and Christopher R.W. Smith, *Handicapped and Impaired in Great Britain* (London: HMSO, 1971).

Hassing, Wolter, Jan Van Ours, and Geert Ridder, "Dismissal Through Disability," *De Economist* 145:1 (1997), 29–30.

Hattam, Victoria, *Labor Visions and State Power: The Origins of Business Unionism in the United States* (Princeton, NJ: Princeton University Press, 1993).

Häusermann, Silja, *The Politics of Welfare State Reform in Continental Europe: Modernization in Hard Times* (Cambridge University Press, 2010).

"Solidarity with Whom? Why Organized Labour is Losing Ground in Continental Pension Politics." *European Journal of Political Research* 49:2 (2010), 223–56.

Heclo, Hugh, *Modern Social Politics in Britain and Sweden: From Relief to Income Maintenance* (New Haven, CT: Yale University Press, 1974).

Hertogh, Mirjam, *"Geene wet, maar de Heer." De confessionele ordening van het Nederlandse sociale zekerheidsstelsel, 1870–1975* (Den Haag: VUGA, 1998).

Hibbs, Douglas A., "On the Political Economy of Long-Run Trends in Strike Activity," *British Journal of Political Science* 8 (1978), 153–75.

Hibbs, Douglas A., and Hakan Locking, "Wage Dispersion and Productive Efficiency: Evidence for Sweden," *Journal of Labor Economics* 18:4 (2000), 755–82.

Hicks, Alex, *Social Democracy and Welfare Capitalism* (Ithaca, NY: Cornell University Press, 1999).

Hicks, Alex, and Duane Swank, "The Political Economy of Government Domestic Expenditure in the Affluent Democracies, 1960–1980," *American Journal of Political Science* 32:4 (1988), 1120–49.

Hicks, Alex, Duane Swank, and Martin Ambuhl, "Welfare Expansion Revisited: Policy Routines and Their Mediation by Party, Class and Crisis, 1957–1982," *European Journal of Political Research* 17 (1989), 401–30.

Hill, Michael, *The Welfare State in Britain: A Political History since 1945* (Brookfield: Edward Elgar, 1993).
   Social Policy: A Comparative Analysis (London: Prentice-Hall, 1996).
Hockerts, Hans Günter, *Sozialpolitische Entscheidungen im Nachkriegsdeutschland. Allierte und Deutsche Sozialversicherungspolitik* (Stuttgart: Klett-Cotta, 1980).
Hoogenboom, Marcel, *Standenstrijd en zekerheid. Een geschiedenis van oude orde en sociale zorg in Nederland* (Amsterdam: Boom, 2004).
Howell, Chris, "Trade Unions and the State: A Critique of British Industrial Relations," *Politics and Society* 23 (1995), 149–83.
   Trade Unions and the State: The Construction of Industrial Relations in Britain, 1890–2000 (Princeton, NJ: Princeton University Press, 2005).
Hoxie, Robert F., *Trade Unionism in the United States* (New York: Appleton, 1920).
Huber, Evelyn, and John D. Stephens, *Development and Crisis of the Welfare State. Parties and Policies in Global Markets* (The University of Chicago Press, 2001).
Hueting, Ernest, Frits de Jong, and Rob Neij, *Naar groter eenheid: de geschiedenis van het Nederlands Verbond van Vakverenigingen 1906–1981* (Amsterdam: Van Gennep, 1982).
Hulst, N. van, *De effectiviteit van de geleide loonpolitiek in de praktijk* (Amsterdam: Wolters-Noordhof, 1984).
Iversen, Torben, *Capitalism, Democracy, and Welfare* (Cambridge University Press, 2005).
Iversen, Torben, Jonas Pontusson, and David. W. Soskice, *Unions, Employers, and Central Banks: Macroeconomic Coordination and Institutional Change in Social Market Economies* (Cambridge University Press, 2000).
Iversen, Torben, and David Soskice, "Distribution and Redistribution: The Shadow of the Nineteenth Century," *World Politics* 61:3 (2009), 428–86.
Jacobs, Klaus, and Martin Rein, "Early Retirement: Stability, Reversal, or Redefinition." In Frieder Naschold and Bert de Vroom, *Regulating Employment and Welfare. Company and National Policies of Labour Force Participation at the End of Worklife in Industrial Countries* (Berlin: Walter de Gruyter, 1994).
Jefferys, Kevin, "British Politics and Social Policy during the Second World War," *Historical Journal* 30 (1987), 123–44.
Johnson, George, "Economic Analysis of Trade Unionism," *American Economic Review* 65 (1975), 23–8.
Jong, Philip de, and Pieter Vos, *Het wao-debat: de centrale regelingen en de praktijk bij bedrijven* (Amsterdam: Welboom Bladen, 1994).
Kahn-Freud, Otto, "Labour Law." In Morris Ginsburg, *Law and Opinion in England in the Twentieth Century* (London: Steven and Sons, 1959).
Kahn, Hilda, *Repercussions of Redundancy* (London: Allen and Unwin, 1964).
Katzenstein, Peter, *Small States in World Markets: Industrial Policy in Europe* (Ithaca, NY: Cornell University Press, 1985).
Keevash, Stephen, "Wages Councils: An Examination of Trade Union and Conservative Misconceptions About the Effect of Statutory Wage Fixing," *Industrial Law Journal* 14:1 (1985), 217–32.
Kelly, Michael P., *White-Collar Proletariat: The Industrial Behaviour of British Civil Servants* (London: Routledge and Kegan, 1980).
Keman, Hans, *The Development Toward Surplus Welfare: Social-Democratic Politics and Policies in Advanced Capitalist Democracies (1965–1984)* (Amsterdam: CT Press, 1988).

Kerklaan, Peter, "De lange houdbaarheid van de ongevallenwet in Nederland 1901–1967," *Tijdschrift voor Sociale en Economische Geschiedenis* 3:4 (2006), 64–90.

Kers, W. C., *Afvloeiing of herintreding: WAO-toetreding voor en na de stelselherziening 1987* (Den Haag: VUGA, 1996).

Kersbergen, Kees van, *Social Capitalism: A Study of Christian Democracy and the Welfare State* (London: Routledge, 1995).

Kersbergen, Kees van, and Philip Manow, *Religion, Class Coalitions, and Welfare States* (Cambridge University Press, 2009)

Klein, Jennifer, *For All These Rights: Business, Labor and the Shaping of America's Public-Private Welfare State* (Princeton, NJ: Princeton University Press, 2003).

Klooster, Hugo, Jeroen Sprenger, and Vincent Vrooland, *Het blauwzwarte boekje: van beroepsorganisatie naar bedrijfsorganisatie* (Amsterdam: Vakbondshistorische Vereniging, 1986).

Klosse, Saskia, *Menselijke schade: vergoeden of herstellen? De werking van (re)integratiebepalingen voor gehandicapten in de Bondsrepubliek Duitsland en Nederland* (Antwerpen: Maklu 1989).

Korpi, Walter, *The Working Class in Welfare Capitalism: Work, Unions and Politics in Sweden* (London: Routledge and Kegan Paul, 1978).

The Democratic Class Struggle (London: Routledge and Kegan Paul, 1983).

"Power Resources and Employer-Centered Approaches in Explanations of Welfare States and Varieties of Capitalism," *World Politics* 58:2 (2006), 167–206.

Korpi, Walter, and Joakim Palme, "The Paradox of Redistribution and Strategies of Equality: Welfare State Institutions, Inequality and Poverty in Western Countries," *American Sociological Review* 63:5 (1998), 661–87.

Korvenmaa, Pentti, *Social Welfare Administration in the United Kingdom and in the Netherlands* (The Hague: Ministry for Social Work, 1959).

Kwon, Hyeok Yong, and Jonas Pontusson, "Globalization, Labour Power and Partisan Politics Revisited," *Socio-Economic Review* 8:2 (2010), 251–81.

Laczko, Frank, and Chris Phillipson, "Great Britain: The Contradictions of Early Exit." In Martin Kohli, Herman van Gunsteren, and Anne-Marie Guillemard, *Time for Retirement: Comparative Studies of Early Exit from the Laborforce* (Cambridge University Press, 1991).

Lange, Peter, "Unions, Workers and Wage Regulation: The Rational Bases of Consent." In J. H. Goldthorpe, *Order and Conflict in Contemporary Capitalism* (Oxford: Clarendon Press, 1984).

Lautenbach, Hendrika, and Marc Cuijpers, "Meer ouderen aan het werk," *Sociaal-Economische Trends* (2nd quarter 2005).

Lehmbruch, Gerhard, "Concertation and the Structure of Corporatist Networks." In John H. Goldthorpe, *Order and Conflict in Contemporary Capitalism: Studies in the Political Economy of Western European Nations* (Oxford: Clarendon Press, 1984).

Leibfried, Stephan, "Sozialpolitik und Existenzminimum: Anmerkungen zur Geschichte der englischen Entwicklung," *Zeitschrift für Sozialreform* 29 (1983), 713–34.

Leimgruber, Matthieu, *Solidarity Without the State? Business and the Shaping of the Swiss Welfare State, 1890–2000* (Cambridge University Press, 2008).

Lewis, Richard, "Tort and Social Security: the Importance Attached to the Cause of Disability with Special Reference to the Industrial Injuries Scheme," *Modern Law Review* 43:5 (1980), 514–31.

Lichtenstein, Nelson, "From Corporatism to Collective Bargaining: Organized Labor and the Eclipse of Social Democracy in the Postwar Era." In Steve Fraser and Gary

Gerstle, *The Rise and Fall of the New Deal Order, 1930–1980* (Princeton, NJ: Princeton University Press, 1989).

State of the Union: A Century of American Labor (Princeton, NJ: Princeton University Press, 2002).

Lijphart, Arend, and Markus Crepaz, "Corporatism and Consensus Democracy in Eighteen Countries: Conceptual and Empirical linkages," *British Journal of Political Science* 21 (1991), 235–46.

Loach, Irene, and Ruth Lister, *Second Class Disabled* (London: Disability Alliance, 1978).

Lonsdale, Susan, and Mansel Aylward, "A United Kingdom Perspective on Disability Policy." In Leo Aarts, Richard V. Burkhauser, and Philip R. de Jong, *Curing the Dutch Disease: An International Perspective on Disability Policy Reform* (Aldershot: Avebury, 1996).

Loonbureau, *Bovenwettelijke uitkeringen. Bepalingen inzake toekenning van (aanvullende) uitkeringen bij arbeidsongeschiktheid, overlijden en werkloosheid zoals geregeld in de cao's voor bedrijfstakken met meer dan 5.000 werknemers* (Den Haag: Loonbureau, 1978).

Lowe, Rodney, "A Prophet Dishonoured in His Own Country? The Rejection of Beveridge in 1945–1970." In John Hills, John Ditch, and Howard Glennerster, *Beveridge and Social Security: An International Retrospective* (Oxford University Press, 1994).

"The Replanning of the Welfare State, 1957–1964." In Martin Francis and Ina Zweiniger-Bargielowska, *The Conservatives and British Society, 1880–1990* (Cardiff: University of Wales Press, 1996).

The Welfare State in Britain since 1945 (London: Macmillan, 1999).

Low Pay Commission, *The National Minimum Wage, the Story So Far: Second Report of the Low Pay Commission* (London: cmn 4571, 2000).

Lutjens, Erik, *De wet Bpf: 50 jaar verplichte bedrijfspensioenfondsen* (Deventer: Kluwer, 1999).

Marchington, Mick, John Goodman, and John Berridge, "Employment Relations in Britain." In Greg Bamber, Russell D. Lansbury, and Nick Wailes, *International and Comparative Employment Relations: Globalisation and the Developed Market Economies* (London: Sage, 1998).

Mares, Isabela, "Strategic Alliances and Social Policy Reform: Unemployment Insurance in Comparative Perspective," *Politics and Society* 28:2 (2000), 223–44.

"Enterprise Reorganization and Social Insurance Reform: The Development of Early Retirement in France and Germany," *Governance* 14:3 (2001), 295–317.

The Politics of Social Risk: Business and Welfare State Development (Cambridge University Press, 2003).

Taxation, Wage Bargaining and Unemployment (Cambridge University Press, 2006).

"Distributional Conflict in Mature Welfare States." In Ian Shapiro, Peter Swenson, and Daniela Donno, *Divide and Deal: The Politics of Distribution in Democracies* (New York University Press, 2008), 43–71.

Marks, Gary, "Variations in Union Political Activity in the United States, Britain and Germany from the Nineteenth Century," *Comparative Politics* 22:1 (1989), 84–104.

Marquand, David, *The Unprincipled Society* (London: Fontana, 1988).

Marsh, Arthur, and Victoria Ryan, *History Directory of Trade Unions*, Vol. I: *Non-Manual Unions* (Westmead: Gower, 1980).

Martin, Cathie Jo, *Stuck in Neutral: Business and the Politics of Human Capital Investment Policy* (Princeton, NJ: Princeton University Press, 2000).

Martin, J., H. Meltzer, and D. Elliot, *OPCW Report 1: The Prevalence of Disability Among Adults* (London: HMSO, 1988).

McGill, Dan, Kyle N. Brown, John J. Haley, and Sylvester J. Schieber, *Fundamentals of Private Pensions* (Oxford University Press, 2005).

McIlroy, John, *Trade Unions in Britain Today* (Manchester University Press, 1995).

McIvor, Arthur, and Christopher Wright, "Managing Labour: UK and Australian Employers in Comparative Perspective, 1900–1950," *Labour History* 88 (May 2005), 45–62.

McRae, Kenneth D., "Comment: Federation, Consociation, Corporatism: An Addendum to Arend Lijphart," *Canadian Journal of Political Science* 12 (1979), 517–22.

Meidner, Rudolf, "Collective Asset Formation Through Wage Earner Funds," *International Labour Review* 120:3 (1981), 303–18.

Messing, Frans, *De Nederlandse economie, 1945–1980. Herstel, groei, stagnatie* (Haarlem: Fibula-Van Dishoeck, 1981).

Metcalf, David, "The British National Minimum Wage," *British Journal of Industrial Relations* 37:2 (1999), 172–201.

Metcalf, David, Kirstine Hansen, and Andy Charlwood, "Unions and the Sword of Justice: Unions and Pay Systems, Pay Inequality, Pay Discrimination and Low Pay," *National Institute Economic Review* 176 (2001), 61–75.

Middlemass, Keith, *Power, Competition and the State,* Vol. 2: *Threats to the Post-War Settlement* (London: Macmillan, 1990).

Millward, Neil, John Forth, and Alex Bryson, *Who Calls the Tune at Work? The Impact of Trade Unions on Jobs and Pay* (York, PA: York Publishing Services, 2001).

Minkin, Lewis, *The Contentious Alliance: Trade Unions and the Labour Party* (Edinburgh University Press, 1991).

Minns, Richard, *The Cold War in Welfare. Stock Markets versus Pensions* (London: Verso, 2001).

Mommsen, Wolfgang J., and Hand-Gerhard Husung, *The Development of Trade Unionism in Great Britain and Germany, 1880–1914* (London: Allen and Unwin, 1985).

Mosher, James S., "U.S. Wage Inequality, Technological Change, and Decline in Union Power," *Politics and Society* 35:2 (2007), 225–63.

Mosley, Hugh, "Corporate Social Benefits and the Underdevelopment of the American Welfare State," *Contemporary Crises* 5 (1981), 139–54.

Mulder, T. B. C., *Loonvorming in overleg. Gedragingen van het georganiseerde bedrijfsleven in Nederland na de tweede wereldoorlog* (Assen: Van Gorcum, 1956).

Mukerjee, Santosh, *Through No Fault of Their Own: Systems for Handling Redundancy in Britain, France and Germany* (London: MacDonald, 1973).

National and Local Government Officers Association, *National Superannuation and Social Insurance: A Statement by NALGO on the Government Proposals in the White Paper cmd. 3883* (London: NALGO, 1969).

Nørgaard, Asbørn Sonne, *The Politics of Institutional Control: Corporatism in Danish Occupational Safety and Health Regulation and Unemployment Insurance, 1870–1995* (Aarhus: Politica, 1997)

Ogus, Anthony Ian, and Eric M. Barendt, *The Law of Social Security* (London: Butterworth, 1982).

Olofsson, Gunnar, and Jan Petersson, "Sweden: Policy Dilemmas of the Changing Age Structure in a 'Work Society.'" In Frieder Naschold and Bert de Vroom, *Regulating Employment and Welfare: Company and National Policies of Labour Force Participation at the End of Worklife in Industrial Countries* (Berlin: Walter de Gruyter, 1994).

Organisation for Economic Co-operation and Development, *OECD Economic Surveys: The Netherlands* (Paris: OECD, 1979).

Labour Force Statistics (Paris: OECD, various years).

O'Riordan, M. "Minimum Wages in Europe," *Low Pay Review* (1981), 1–12.

Oude Nijhuis, Dennie, "Revisiting the Role of Labor: Worker Solidarity, Employer Opposition, and the Development of Old-Age Pensions in the Netherlands and the United Kingdom," *World Politics* 61:2 (2009), 296–329.

"Explaining British Voluntarism," *Labor History* 52:4 (2011), 373–89.

Ozaki, Muneto, *Negotiating Flexibility: The Role of the Social Partners and the State* (Geneva: ILO, 1999).

Pardaan, Inge, *Passende arbeid: een beschouwing vanuit de sociale wetgeving rond werkloosheid, ziekte, arbeidsongeschiktheid en bijstand en kijkend naar regulieren, seizoens- en gesubsidieerde arbeid* (Deventer: Kluwer, 1997).

Parker, Stanley, *Effects of the Redundancy Payments Act* (London: HMSO, 1971).

Paulsen, George, *A Living Wage for the Forgotten Man: The Quest for Fair Labor Standards 1933–1941* (Cranbury, NJ: Susquehanna University Press, 1996).

Parry, Richard, "United Kingdom." In Peter Flora, *Growth to Limits: The Western European Welfare States Since World War II*, Vol. 4: *Appendix* (New York: Walter de Gruyter, 1986).

Pelling, Henry, *A History of British Trade Unionism* (London: Macmillan, 1971).

Pemberton, Hugh, "Politics and Pensions in Post-War Britain." In Hugh Pemberton, Pat Thane, and Noel Whiteside, *Britain's Pensions Crisis: History and Policy* (Oxford University Press, 2006).

"Relative Economic Decline and British Economic Policy in the 1960s," *The Historical Journal* 47:4 (2004), 989–1013.

Pen, Jan, and Jan Tinbergen, *Naar een rechtvaardiger inkomensverdeling* (Amsterdam: Elsevier, 1977).

Pennings, Frans, *Benefits of Doubt: A Comparative Study of the Legal Aspects of Employment and Unemployment Schemes in Great Britain, France and the Netherlands* (Deventer: Kluwer, 1990).

Pettengill, John S., *Labor Unions and the Inequality of Earned Income* (Amsterdam: North-Holland, 1980).

Pierson, Paul, *Dismantling the Welfare State? Reagan, Thatcher, and the Politics of Retrenchment* (Cambridge University Press, 1994).

Pond, Chris, "Low Pay – 1980s Style," *Low Pay Review* 4 (1981), 1–10.

Pond, Chris, and Steve Winyard, *The Case for a National Minimum Wage* (London: Low Pay Unit, 1984).

Pontusson, Jonas, *Inequality and Prosperity: Social Europe vs. Liberal America* (Ithaca, NY: Cornell University Press, 2005).

Pontusson, Jonas, and David Rueda, "The Politics of Inequality: Voter Mobilization and Left Parties in Advanced Industrial States," *Comparative Political Studies* 43:6 (2010), 675–705.

Pontusson, Jonas, David Rueda, and Christopher R. Way, "Comparative Political Economy of Wage Distribution: The Role of Partisanship and Labour Market Institutions," *British Journal of Political Science* 32 (2002), 281–308.

Potter, Douglas, *The National Insurance Act, 1946, with General Introduction and Annotations* (London: Butterworth, 1946).

Power, Fred, and Donal Guerin, *Civil Society and Social Policy: Voluntarism in Ireland* (Dublin: A&A Farmar, 1997).

Price, Robert, and George Sayers Bain, "Union Growth Revisited: 1948–1974 in Perspective," *British Journal of Industrial Relations* 4 (1966), 339–55.

Putnam, Robert, *Making Democracy Work: Civic Traditions in Modern Italy* (Princeton, NJ: Princeton University Press, 1993).

Quadagno, Jill, *The Transformation of Old Age Security: Class and Politics in the American Welfare State* (The University of Chicago Press, 1988).

Rees, Albert, *The Economics of Trade Unions* (The University of Chicago Press, 1962).

Reinalda, Bob, *Bedienden georganiseerd. Ontstaan en ontwikkeling van handels- en kantoorbedienden in Nederland van het eerste begin tot in de Tweede Wereldoorlog* (Nijmegen: Socialistiese Uitgeverij Nijmegen, 1981).

De Dienstenbonden. Klein maar strijdbaar (Baarn: AMBO, 1985).

Rhodes, Martin, "Restructuring the British Welfare State: Between Domestic Constraints and Global Imperatives." In Fritz Scharpf and Vivien Schmidt, *Welfare and Work in the Open Economy* (Oxford University Press, 2000).

Rimlinger, Gaston, *Welfare Policy and Industrialization in Europe, America, and Russia* (New York: Wiley, 1971).

Ringe, Astrid, and Neil Rollings, "Responding to Relative Decline: The Creation of the National Economic Development Council," *Economic History Review* 53 (2000), 331–53.

Ritter, Erich, *Die Stellungnahme der Gewerkschaften zu den Problemen der Sozialversicherung in Deutschland* (Frankfurt: Wertheim, 1933).

Robinson, Derek, *Solidaristic Wage Policy in Sweden* (Paris: OECD, 1974).

Rogin, Michael, "Voluntarism: The Political Functions of an Antipolitical Doctrine," *Industrial and Labor Relations Review* 15:4 (1962), 521–35.

Root, Lawrence S., "Britain's Redundancy Payments for Displaced Workers," *Monthly Labor Review* (June 1987), 18–23.

Ross, Martin, *TUC: The Growth of a Pressure Group, 1886–1976* (Oxford: Clarendon Press, 1980).

Rothstein, Bo, *Just Institutions Matter: The Moral and Political Logic of the Universal Welfare State* (Cambridge University Press, 1998).

Routh, Guy, "White-Collar Unions in the United Kingdom." In Adolf Sturmthal, *White-Collar Trade Unions: Contemporary Developments in Industrialized Societies* (Chicago: University of Illinois Press, 1996).

Rubery, Jill, and Paul Edwards, "Low Pay and the National Minimum Wage." In Paul K. Edwards, *Industrial Relations: Theory and Practice* (Oxford: Blackwell, 2003).

Rueda, David, and Jonas Pontusson, "Wage Inequality and Varieties of Capitalism," *World Politics* 52:3 (2000), 350–83.

Ruijters, C. M. J., "Sociale Zaken." In M. D. Bogaarts, *Parlementaire geschiedenis van Nederland na 1945. De periode van het kabinet-Beel (1946–1948)* (Den Haag: SDU, 1989).

Russell, Bob, *Back to Work? Labour, State and Industrial Relations in Canada* (Toronto: Nelson, 1990).

Ruysseveldt, Joris van, and Jelle Visser, *Industrial Relations in Europe: Traditions and Transitions* (London: Sage, 1996).

Sapir, André, "Globalization and the Reform of European Social Models," *Journal of Common Market Studies* 44:2 (2006), 369–90.

Scase, Richard, "Inequality in Two Industrial Societies: Class, Status and Power in Britain and Sweden." In Richard Scase, *Readings in the Swedish Class Structure* (New York: Pergamon, 1976).

Social Democracy in Capitalist Society: Working-Class Politics in Britain and Sweden (London: Croom Helm, 1977).

Schmitter, Philippe, "Reflections on Where the Theory of Neo-Corporatism Has Gone and Where the Praxis of Neo-Corporatism May Be Going." In Philippe Schmitter and Gerard Lehmbruch *Patterns of Corporatist Policy-Making* (London: Sage, 1982).

Schrage, P., and E. Nijhoff, "Een lange sisser en een late knal? De ontwikkeling van de Nederlandse werkloosheidsvoorziening in West-Europees perspectief: een terreinverkenning." In W. P. Blockmans and L. A. van der Valk, *Van particuliere naar openbare zorg en terug? Sociale politiek in Nederland sinds 1880* (Amsterdam: NEHA, 1992).

Scruggs, Lyle, "The Ghent System and Union Membership in Europe, 1970–1996." *Political Research Quarterly* 55:2 (2002), 275–97.

Shalev, Michael, "The Social Democratic Model and Beyond: Two Generations of Comparative Research on the Welfare State," *Comparative Social Research* 6 (1983), 315–51.

Skocpol, Theda, *The Politics of Social Policy in the United States* (Princeton, NJ: Princeton University Press, 1988).

Social Policy in the United States: Future Possibilities in Historical Perspective (Princeton, NJ: Princeton University Press, 1995).

Slomp, Hans, *Arbeidsverhoudingen in België* (Utrecht: Het Spectrum, 1984).

Between Bargaining and Politics: An Introduction to European Labor (Westport, CT: Praeger, 1996).

Sociaal-Economische Raad, *Advies inzake de herziening van de invaliditeitsverzekering* (Den Haag: SER, 1957).

Advies over verlening van de maximumuitkeringsduur werkloosheidsverzekering (Den Haag: SER, 1962).

Advies inzake het voorontwerp van een Wet werkloosheidsvoorziening (Den Haag: SER, 1964).

Advies inzake de invoering van een minimumdagloon in de Werkloosheidswet en de Wet Werkloosheidsvoorziening, 14 juni 1968 (Den Haag: SER, 1968).

Eerste advies over de programmering van de sociale verzekering op de middellange termijn (Den Haag: SER, 1970).

Sociale Verzekeringsraad, "Interimadvies overdracht uitvoering ongevallenverzekeringen aan de bedrijfsverzekeringen van 3 oktober 1958." In Sociale Verzekeringsraad, *Advies inzake een arbeidsongeschiktheidsvereniging* (Den Haag: SVR, 1960).

Stationary Office, *Report of the Committee on the Economic and Financial Problems of the Provision for Old Age* (London: cmd. 9333, 1954).

Stephens, John D., *The Transition from Capitalism to Socialism* (London: Macmillan, 1979).

Stevens, Beth, "Blurring the Boundaries: How Federal Social Policy Has Influenced Welfare Benefits in the Private Sector." In Ann Orloff, Margaret Weir, and Theda Skocpol, *The Politics of Social Policy in the United States* (Princeton, NJ: Princeton University Press, 1988).

Streeck, Wolfgang, "Beneficial Constraints: On the Economic Limits of Rational Voluntarism." In Rogers Hollingsworth and Robert Boyer, *Contemporary Capitalism: The Embeddedness of Institutions* (Cambridge University Press, 1997).

"The Sociology of Labor Markets and Trade Unions." In N. J. Smelser and R. Swedberg, *The Handbook of Economic Sociology* (Princeton, NJ: Princeton University Press, 2005).

Swank, Duane, *Global Capital, Political Institutions and Policy Change in Developed Welfare States* (Cambridge University Press, 2002).

Swenson, Peter, "Bringing Capital Back in, or Social Democracy Reconsidered: Employer Power, Cross-Class Alliances, and Centralization of Industrial Relations in Denmark and Sweden," *World Politics* 43:4 (1991), 513–44.

"Arranged Alliance: Business Interests in the New Deal," *Politics and Society* 25:1 (1997), 66–116

Fair Shares: Unions, Pay, and Politics in Sweden and West Germany (Ithaca, NY: Cornell University Press, 1989).

Capitalists Against Market: The Making of Labor Markets and Welfare States in the United States and Sweden (Oxford University Press, 2002).

Taylor, Robert, *The Fifth Estate: British Unions in the 1970s* (London: Routledge, 1978).

The TUC: From the General Strike to New Unionism (Basingstoke: Palgrave, 2000).

The Trade Union Question in British Politics (London: Blackwell, 1993).

Terry, Michael, *Redefining Public Sector Unionism: UNISON and the Future of Trade Unions* (London: Routledge, 2000).

Teulings, Coen, Romke van der Veen, and Willem Trommel, *Dilemma's van sociale zekerheid: een analyse van 10 jaar herziening van het stelsel van sociale zekerheid* (Amsterdam: VUGA, 1997).

Therborn, Göran, "'Pillarization' and 'Popular Movements.' Two Variants of Welfare Capitalism: The Netherlands and Sweden." In Francis Castles, *Comparative History of Public Policy* (Cambridge: Polity, 1989).

"Lessons from Corporatist Theorizations." In Jukka Pekkarinen, Matti Pohjola, and Bob Rowthorn, *Social Corporatism: A Superior Economic System?* (Oxford University Press, 1992).

Thomson, Andrew J., "The United States of America," In E. Owen Smith, *Trade Unions in the Developed Economies* (New York: St. Martin's Press, 1981).

Tillyard, Frank, and Willam A. Robson, "The Enforcement of the Collective Bargain in the United Kingdom," *The Economic Journal* 48:189 (1938), 15–25.

Titmuss, Richard, "Pensions Systems and Population Change," *Political Quarterly* 16:2 (1955), 152–66.

Tomlinson, Jim, "Why So Austere? The British Welfare State in the 1940s," *Journal of Social Policy* 27 (1998), 63–7.

Toren, Jan-Peter van der, *"Van loonslaaf tot bedrijfsgenoot": 100 jaar christelijk-sociaal denken, medezeggenschap en sociale zekerheid* (Kempen: Kok, 1991).

Townsend, Peter, *Poverty in the United Kingdom* (Harmondsworth: Penguin, 1979).

Trampusch, Christine, "Industrial Relations as a Source of Social Policy: A Typology of the Institutional Conditions for Industrial Agreements on Social Benefits," *Social Policy and Administration* 41:3 (2007), 251–70.

Trommel, Willem, and Bert De Vroom, "The Netherlands: The Loreley Effect of Early Exit." In Frieder Naschold and Bert de Vroom, *Regulating Employment and Welfare: Company and National Policies of Labour Force Participation at the End of Worklife in Industrial Countries* (Berlin: Walter de Gruyter, 1994).

Trommel, Willem, *Korter arbeidsleven: de wording van een rationele mythe. Loopbaan, arbeidsmarkt en verzorgingsstaat in neo-institutioneel perspectief* (Den Haag: SDU, 1995).

Uden, W. van, "Interim-regeling voor invaliditeitsrentetrekkers," *Sociale Zorg* 24 (1962), 405–9.

Veen, Romke van der, *De sociale grenzen van beleid. Een onderzoek naar de uitvoering en effecten van het stelsel van sociale zekerheid* (Leiden: Stenfert Kroese, 1990).

"De ontwikkeling en herziening van de Nederlandse verzorgingsstaat." In Willem Trommel and Romke van der Veen, *De herverdeelde samenleving: de ontwikkeling en herziening van de Nederlandse verzorgingsstaat* (Amsterdam University Press, 1999).

Veldkamp, Gerard, *Individualistische karaktertrekken in de Nederlandse sociale arbeidsverzekering: een critisch onderzoek naar de grondslagen der sociale arbeidsverzekering* (Alphen aan den Rijn: Samsom, 1949).

Velema, Willem, "De kroongetuige. Hoe het WAO-drama voorkomen had kunnen worden." In J. G. Hibbeln and Willem Velema, *Het WAO-debacle. De fatale missers van wettenmakers en uitvoerders* (Amsterdam: Van Arkel, 1993).

Verbond van Nederlandse Ondernemingen, *Boekje over inkomens 1970–1981. Een VNO-monografie over het in Nederland gevoerde inkomensverdelingsbeleid in de jaren 1970–1981* (Den Haag: VNO, 1981).

Verwey, W., "Het minimumloon – een welvaartsvaste natte vinger," *Sociaal Maandblad Arbeid* (1973), 357–62.

Visser, Jelle, *European Trade Unions in Figures* (Deventer: Kluwer, 1989).

"The Netherlands." In Bernhard Ebbinghaus and Jelle Visser, *The Societies of Europe: Trade Unions in Western Europe since 1945* (London: Macmillan, 2005).

"Union Membership Statistics in 24 Countries," *Monthly Labour Review* (January 2006), 38–49.

Visser, Jelle, and Anton Hemerijck, *"A Dutch Miracle": Job Growth, Welfare Reform and Corporatism in the Netherlands* (Amsterdam University Press, 1997).

Voorden, Willam van, "Employers Associations in the Netherlands." In John P. Windmuller and Alan Gladstone, *Employers Associations and Industrial Relations: A Comparative Study* (Oxford: Clarendon Press, 1985).

Vroom, Bert de, and Martin Blomsma, "The Netherlands: an Extreme Case." In Martin Kohli, Herman van Gunsteren, and Anne-Marie Guillemard, *Time for Retirement: Comparative Studies of Early Exit from the Labor Force* (Cambridge University Press, 1991).

Waarden, Frans van, "Dutch Consociationalism and Corporatism: A Case of Institutional Persistence," *Acta Politica* 37 (2002), 44–67.

Walker, Alan, and Lucy Walker, "Disability and Financial Need: The Failure of the Social Security System." In G. Dalley, *Disability and Social Policy* (London: PSI, 1991).

Walker, Alan, and Peter Townsend, *Disability in Britain: A Manifesto of Rights* (Oxford: Martin Robertson, 1981).

Wallerstein, Michael "Wage-Setting Institutions and Pay Inequality in Advanced Industrial Societies," *American Journal of Political Science* 43:3 (1999), 649–80.

Waltman, Jerold L., *Minimum Wage Policy in Great Britain and the United States* (New York: Algora, 2008).

Westergaard, John, Ian Noble, and Alan Walker, *After Redundancy: The Experience of Economic Insecurity* (Cambridge: Polity Press, 1989).

Wetenschappelijke Raad voor Regeringsbeleid, *Een Werkend Perspectief. De arbeidsparticipatie in de jaren '90*. (Den Haag: SDU, 1990).

Whiteside, Noel, "Industrial Relations and Social Welfare, 1945–1979." In C. J. Wrigley, *A History of British Industrial Relations, 1939–1979: Industrial Relations in a Declining Economy* (Cheltenham: Edward Elgar, 1996).

"Historical Perspectives and the Politics of Pension Reform." In Noel Whiteside and Gordon L. Clark, *Pension Security in the 21st Century: Redrawing the Public-Private Debate* (Oxford University Press, 2003).

Whiting, Richard C., "Ideology and Reform in Labour's Tax Strategy, 1964–1970," *Historical Journal* 41 (1998), 1121–40.

Wigderson, Seth, "How the CIO Saved Social Security," *Labor History* 44:4 (2003), 483–507.

Wijngaarden, J. van, "Inkomensverdelingsbeleid in de verzorgingsstaat. Rechtvaardigheidscriteria voor inkomensverschillen uit arbeid," Ph.D. thesis, Utrecht University, 1982.

Wilensky, Harold R., *Rich Democracies: Political Economy, Public Policy, and Performance* (Berkeley: University of California Press, 2002).

Wilson, Graham, *Business and Politics* (Chatham: Chatham House, 1990).

Windmuller, John P., *Labor Relations in the Netherlands* (Ithaca, NY: Cornell University Press, 1969).

Windmuller, John, D., C. de Galan, and A. F. van Zweeden, *Arbeidsverhoudingen in Nederland* (Utrecht: Het Spectrum, 1983).

Witte, Edwin E., "Organized Labor and Social Security." In Milton Derber and Edwin Young, *Labor and the New Deal* (Madison: University of Wisconsin Press, 1961).

Woldendorp, Jaap, "Neo-Corporatism as a Strategy for Conflict Resolution in the Netherlands," *Acta Politica* 30:2 (1995), 121–51.

Zanden, Jan-Luiten van, "Inkomensverdeling en overheidspolitiek, 1938–1950," *Economisch Statistische Berichten* (August 1986), 768–71.

Index